WHITE KING
AND RED QUEEN

Chess symbolism was ubiquitous during the Cold War:
a Tactical Weapons Chessboard from 1971.

WHITE KING
AND
RED QUEEN

HOW THE COLD WAR WAS
FOUGHT ON THE CHESSBOARD

❖ ❖ ❖

DANIEL JOHNSON

HOUGHTON MIFFLIN COMPANY
BOSTON AND NEW YORK
2008

www.hmhbooks.com

Library of Congress Cataloging-in-Publication Data
Johnson, Daniel, date.
White king and red queen : how the Cold War was fought
on the chessboard / Daniel Johnson.
p. cm.
Originally published: London : Atlantic Books, 2007.
ISBN 978-0-547-13337-9
1. Chess—Soviet Union—History—20th century.
2. Chess players—Soviet Union—History—20th
century. 3. Chess—Tournaments—History—
20th century. 4. Chess—Political aspects—Soviet
Union. 5. World politics—1945–1989. I. Title.
GV1330.S65J65 2008
794.10947— dc22   2008029901

Printed in the United States of America

Book design by Victoria Hartman

DOC 10 9 8 7 6 5 4 3 2 1

TO SARAH

deo gratia

CONTENTS

ILLUSTRATIONS

ACKNOWLEDGMENTS

COMPLETION OF ANY BOOK requires the author to be positive, persistent, and prosperous. My Ph.D. thesis, as old friends occasionally remind me, was about German pessimism: a subject which virtually precluded all three. The thesis remains unfinished. Its ghost has been exorcised by this book, which would never have been written without the positively Panglossian optimism of my editor, Toby Mundy. His team at Atlantic, especially Emma Grove and Amy Jordan, have gone to great lengths to make this book as accurate and elegant as possible. My agent, Georgina Capel, has kept faith in me ever since she took me on a decade ago, and I am grateful to her.

I must also thank the many friends, editors, and colleagues who gave me the opportunity to witness, and even participate, in the last stages of the Cold War. Among them are Sir Tom Stoppard, whose nomination of me for a Shakespeare Scholarship made possible a year of study in Berlin nearly thirty years ago; Professor Timothy Garton Ash, who put me up in his apartment in the Uhlandstrasse and a decade later generously blamed me for the fall of the Berlin Wall; and the late Melvin Lasky, who commissioned me to write for *Encounter*, the spirit of which I intend to revive in a magazine adapted to today's very different challenges to the West. My collaborators, including Miriam Gross and Alan Bekhor, have waited patiently for me to concentrate on that project while this book was finished.

This is not the place to speak of intellectual influences, but I cannot forgo mentioning here my circle of American friends, without whom I would not have acquired the moral clarity that I hope informs this book: Irving Kristol, Gertrude Himmelfarb, Norman Podhoretz, Midge Decter, Neal Kozodoy, Charles Krauthammer, George Weigel, Michael Novak, Amity Shlaes, Seth Lipsky, Anne Applebaum, Radek Sikorski, Bob Tyrrell, Roger Kimball, and Bill Kristol. I should also like to thank the dissidents, past and present, whom I have encountered, among them Leszek Kolakowski and his daughter Agnieszka; Natan and Avital Sharansky; and Garry Kasparov, who uniquely combines the two main themes of this book.

I also owe a debt to my friends in the chess fraternity, among them the late Heinrich Fraenkel, who first introduced me to grandmaster chess as a boy, and Raymond Keene, who has shared his hospitality and his experience with me, Malcolm Pein, Bill Hartston, Nigel Short, and many others.

During the two years spent writing this book, I have been sustained by good lunches and sage advice from many loyal friends, especially Graham Paterson and Martin Ivens. My parents, Paul and Marigold Johnson, and parents-in-law, John and Cynthia Thompson, respectively celebrated their golden and diamond wedding anniversaries during the writing of this book. I owe a great deal to all of them, and to my brother Luke, for their moral and material support. But I owe most of all to my sternest critics: Sarah, Tycho, Edith, Leo, and Agatha Johnson.

PREFACE

WHEN THIS BOOK was completed in mid 2007, the story of chess and the Cold War had not quite come to an end. Since then, three events at least have served to draw a symbolic line under that story: the presidential election in Russia, the first Indian world chess champion, and the death of Bobby Fischer.

Today the Cold War is remembered, if at all, with a shudder: as the period when humanity came closest to annihilating itself. But there was more to it than that. The Cold War coincided with an epoch when the fruits of Western civilization — liberty, prosperity, democracy, the rule of law, the dignity of the individual, the sanctity of life — were spread among a greater portion of mankind than ever before. The origins of this civilization in Greco-Roman rationality and Judeo-Christian morality were undisputed. Moral clarity, of a kind that is increasingly rare today, was normal in a bipolar world divided by the Iron Curtain. Of course, anticommunists, whether liberal or conservative, were often reviled as McCarthyites. "Cold warrior" also became a term of abuse. The cold warriors retaliated against the "fellow travelers," "agents of influence," and "useful idiots," who missed no opportunity to trumpet the shortcomings of the West.

One or two reviewers of the British edition of this book have reverted to such stereotypes, accusing the present author of being a cold warrior and implying that there is no point in reminding readers about what communism was really like, let alone examining why it failed. Yet it is impossible to write the history of chess during the Cold War period without contrasting the rival political, economic, and social systems. Only a book that got to the heart of the matter, to what made the evil empire evil, could give the Cold War chess grandmasters their context.

Most of the journalists who reviewed the book understood this. David Edmonds, coauthor with John Eidinow of *Bobby Fischer Goes to War* — by far the best account of the Fischer–Spassky match — was more than generous. Dominic Lawson drew attention to the fact that the author "was the journalist whose intelligent questioning of the East Berlin communist party secretary in 1989 revealed to the world that the Wall which had divided East from West for more than two generations was about to fall." A journalist of a younger generation, Tobias Ruether of the *Frankfurter Allgemeine Zeitung,* felt the book offered the key to Kasparov's role in Putin's Russia. Mary Dejevsky, who had served as Moscow correspondent for the London *Times* throughout the final phase of the Cold War, suggested that a former cold warrior might even be the "ideal author" of this book. Several distinguished historians of the totalitarian twentieth century — Robert Conquest, Michael Burleigh, and Simon Sebag Montefiore — agreed. Martin Amis and Tom Stoppard, both of whom had written about the same things from the point of view of a novelist and a dramatist, also shared their enthusiasm with the author. So too did chess grandmasters, some of whom had participated in the events recounted here, such as R. G. Wade and Raymond Keene. Even before this U.S. edition appeared, the book's readers included a former secretary of state and a former chairman of the Joint Chiefs of Staff.

This, then, is not a book that appeals only to a grizzled rearguard of hard-core anti-communists still refighting old battles. I hope and believe that it has something useful to say to those too young to remember the Cold War, most especially to those younger Americans, many of whose forebears fought and won it. You should be proud of their contribution to the defense of civilization.

White King and Red Queen shows that the political and military rivalry of the Cold War, banished by the destructiveness of nuclear warfare from the battlefield, was instead fought out on the chessboard. The book ends with an echo of that rivalry: the duel between Kasparov and Putin, in which the battle of ideas has been transposed back from the chessboard to the political arena.

This duel, from the point of view of the Kremlin, is entirely one-sided. In fact, the official line is that Kasparov and his Other Russia coalition are too marginal and insignificant to matter. Though Putin points to his stratospheric approval ratings, Kasparov has consistently maintained that Putin's popularity is an illusion that would not survive exposure to the scrutiny of a real democracy or a genuinely free press. Putin's main strategy against the democratic opposition has always been to deny its leaders any opportunity to make their case on state television or even at public meetings. But silencing the opposition was not enough: insuperable obstacles were erected to hinder Kasparov from participating in the March 2008 presidential election.

On November 24, 2007, Other Russia organized a demonstration by about three thousand supporters on the streets of Moscow to deliver a letter to the Kremlin-controlled Central Electoral Commission, protesting about the parliamentary elections on December 2. Though legal, the march was broken up by police. Kasparov was forced to the ground and beaten, though not seriously injured, before being arrested. He was later sentenced to five days' imprisonment for resisting arrest.

Soon after the incident, Putin broke his usual silence on the subject of Kasparov. Interviewed by *Time* magazine, which had perversely chosen him as its Person of the Year, the Russian president jeered at Kasparov for having spoken English to foreign reporters just after his arrest. This was in keeping with the Kremlin strategy of presenting Kasparov as an American agent of influence, financed by the CIA and with no roots or support in Mother Russia. The fact that Kasparov's family was kept out of harm's way in New Jersey was used in a smear campaign claiming that he had secretly become a U.S. citizen. Kasparov responded angrily: "First, I also spoke in Russian, which oddly enough never makes the Kremlin-controlled newscasts. Second, since opposition statements are almost completely banned in the Russian media, the foreign press usually makes up 90 percent of attending media at opposition events. Lastly, I would be delighted to show Mr. Putin which of us speaks and writes better Russian. Perhaps he will accept my challenge to a debate on national television or allow an editorial of mine to appear in a major newspaper."

Not surprisingly, no response was forthcoming from the Kremlin. During the run-up to the presidential election on March 2, Putin's party, United Russia, was able to monopolize the media and manipulate the electoral process. Indeed, United Russia is not a democratic political party in the Western sense at all: like the Communist Party of the Soviet era, United Russia is indistinguishable from the state apparatus. The Kremlin's influence was more than sufficient to make it impossible for Kasparov to register as a presidential candidate. In order to challenge Putin's nominee for the Russian presidency, Gazprom chief Dmitry Medvedev, Kasparov was supposed to gather two million signatures, with no more than 40,000 from any one region of Russia — a process vulnerable to accusations of forgery that was in practice used by the electoral commission to declare two other candidacies invalid. But Kasparov's candidacy did not even get that far. The first requirement was that his application be endorsed by five hundred citizens at a public meeting. Several times Other Russia hired a venue, only to be told that it was no longer available. So the deadline was missed. It seemed that the authorities had put out the word: Kasparov had to be stopped from getting even to first base.

The election campaign in early 2008 was widely dismissed as a travesty of democracy, and the universally respected Organization for Security and Cooperation in Europe withdrew its team of observers in protest. Only three candidates were permitted to oppose Medvedev: the Communist leader, Gennady Zyganov; the anti-Semitic leader of the extreme right-wing Liberal Democrats, Vladimir Zhirinovsky; and the leader of the small Democratic Party, Andrei Bogdanov, whose sole qualification appeared to be his prominence as a freemason—he was the head of Russia's Grand Masonic Lodge. Bogdanov denied that he was secretly backed by the Kremlin to make the election look legitimate, but doubts persisted over whether he was a genuine opponent of Putin. None of these candidates had the international stature, let alone the democratic credentials, of Kasparov.

On the day of the election, March 2, Kasparov delivered yet another petition to the election commission, while also calling on the outside world to deny Medvedev any recognition: "If the leaders of the free world accept Medvedev, they will be approving and giving credibility to this farce." When the results were declared on March 7, however, Medvedev had over 70 percent of the vote. Ignoring Kasparov, leaders from the free world lined up to congratulate the new president-elect, who appeared in a leather jacket alongside Putin at a rock concert in Moscow to proclaim his victory.

Undaunted by an election he had already dismissed as rigged, Kasparov has kept up the pressure. The regime now seems set to evolve into a duumvirate, with Medvedev as the technocratic head of state and Putin as prime minister, still very much at the center of power. Rather than denouncing the political system and demanding its root-and-branch reform, Kasparov is increasingly playing the role of the Kremlin's chief critic, presenting a detailed scrutiny of government policy. For example, he attacked plans to hold the 2014 Winter Olympics at Sochi, warning that the $6 billion budget was inadequate. Perhaps Kasparov hopes that over time he will look less like a Soviet-era dissident and more like an alternative Russian president. But he knows that the Putin–Medvedev double-act is unlikely to unravel quickly; his own prediction is that it will last for another term, until 2012.

Kasparov's critique of the Russian regime has not changed. He still believes that it rests entirely on high oil and gas prices, the need to maintain which in his view explains every aspect of Putin's foreign policy. Kasparov is well aware that Europe's growing dependence on Russian gas and oil supplies has emboldened Putin and weakened Western support for neighboring states trying to free themselves from Russian influence, not to mention dissent inside Russia. He rejects the notion that the "Russian soul" is predisposed to worship strongmen, pointing out that in divided nations such as Korea, China, or Germany, people grasp at freedom when it is offered.

So aggressive has the Putin regime become, however, that a palpable shift in attitude is taking place in the West. At its summit in Bucharest in April 2008, NATO rebuffed two former Soviet republics, Ukraine and Georgia, that had applied to join the alliance. The Bush administration was unable to persuade its allies to ignore threats from the Kremlin to target missiles at NATO countries.

In a seminal book published early in 2008, the highly authoritative *Economist* correspondent Edward Lucas argued that the West was faced with nothing less than *The New Cold War*. Kasparov has hitherto rejected all talk of a new Cold War, arguing instead that the Putin regime has no ideology comparable to Marxism-Leninism and is anyway too dependent on the West to risk a real confrontation. But Lucas is not suggesting that the new Cold War will exactly resemble the old; rather, that the West will need to stand up for its values and interests against the corrupting influence of the plutocrats, technocrats, and authoritarians now running Russia. This is very much in line with Kasparov's thinking, too. He has been scathing about the way that the Bush administration in his view gave democracy in Iraq a higher priority than democracy in Russia, and he points to arms deals between Putin's Kremlin and Ahmadinejad's Iran as the price the West will have to pay for turning a blind eye to the Kremlin's machinations in the Middle East.

In the political evolution of Garry Kasparov, the decisive moment came with the 1990 crisis in his hometown of Baku, when he saw his fellow Armenians driven out by the Azeri majority. Today, such ethnic conflict is again threatening stability on the periphery of Russia—often encouraged by Moscow. The Putin regime is encouraging separatist movements in Georgia, for example, in order to exploit the unwillingness of NATO to risk provoking the Kremlin by embracing Ukraine and Georgia. Kasparov has warned against attempts by Putin to reassert Russian control over its neighbors, but his own background in Azerbaijan places him at a disadvantage in confronting Russian nationalists. His political challenge is to persuade Russians that stirring up conflict in their "near-abroad" is not only wrong in itself, and usually counterproductive, but could well backfire by spreading to Russia, too, which is host to dozens of national, religious, and ethnic minorities. So far, Putin's autocratic "sovereign democracy" (or "Tsarism," to use a phrase of the American commentator Robert Kagan) has swept all before it by appealing to Russian national pride, while deliberately—and dangerously—fomenting a rancorous sense of injustice. Unlike the Kremlin's siege mentality, Kasparov's pro-Western, pluralistic vision cannot feed on fantasies of conspiracy and encirclement.

If there is to be a new Cold War, might it also inaugurate a new golden age of chess? Without the unique status enjoyed by the royal game in the Union of Soviet Socialist Republics, it seems highly unlikely that chess will again stand proxy for war. The new Cold War will in any case be very different from the old one, if only because we now live in a multipolar world rather than a bipolar one. There was a close analogy between a game of chess and the duel of the two superpowers, the United States and the So viet Union. Today's world resembles an entire chess tournament, with competing powers jockeying for position and shifting alliances between democracies and autocrats. Chess may still be a useful strategic metaphor, but now there are many more players, many more games, and no final checkmate. A very different golden age of chess may be presaged by the fact that the fifteenth world chess champion is, for the first time, neither European nor American, but Indian.

This book relates how chess once emerged from the heart of Asia but migrated to Europe, there to be reinvented in the Renaissance. Now, in the twenty-first century, Asia is reclaiming its lost supremacy in chess. On September 29, 2007, the Russian world chess champion Vladimir Kramnik lost his crown to the Indian Viswanathan Anand. Not only did this mark the end of sixty years of Soviet and Russian hegemony (which had hitherto been briefly interrupted only by Bobby Fischer), but it was seen as signifying a long-term shift in the center of gravity of the chess world away from Europe and toward the new Asian powers, India and China. In order to resolve the disputes that had raged about the title ever since 1993, when Garry Kasparov and Nigel Short broke with the World Chess Federation, FIDE, the succession to the title was decided not by a match between champion and challenger, but by a tournament of the leading contenders in Mexico City. Anand finished comfortably ahead of the rest of the field, without losing a single game.

Although there was nothing unexpected about the Indian's victory—he had already challenged Kasparov in 1995 and had won the FIDE title in 2000—the lack of a decisive duel between Anand and Kramnik left doubts about the new champion's ascendancy over his predecessor. Even after relinquishing the title, Kramnik still held a narrow lead in the fifty-odd games he had played against Anand since 1989. A match of twelve games between

Anand and Kramnik is due to take place in Bonn, Germany, in October 2008, which should finally resolve the future of the championship.

Both these champions, now in their thirties, already find a younger generation snapping at their heels. In January 2008, both Anand and Kramnik were overtaken by the Norwegian prodigy Magnus Carlsen at the Wijk aan Zee tournament. Carlsen won the event jointly with the Armenian Levon Aronian and went on to finish just behind Anand at Linares a few weeks later. At seventeen, Carlsen was less than half Anand's age but already achieving comparable results. He is probably stronger than either Fischer or Kasparov at the same age. That Carlsen will become world champion sooner rather than later already seems more than likely, and he has several years in hand in which to surpass Kasparov's record by becoming the youngest-ever champion.

If a Norwegian were to be the next world chess champion, however, might it not indicate that there is nothing inevitable about the gradual shift of hegemony from Europe and America toward China and India? While it is risky to draw conclusions from the microcosm of chess to the macrocosm of intellectual life more generally, other indicators also suggest that the West is not necessarily predestined to forfeit its intellectual predominance. The best universities and research institutes, the most important centers of excellence in the arts, humanities, and sciences are mostly still in the West, even if many of those who work or study there are not from the West. The rise of India and China to rival Russia, Western Europe, and the United States at chess is an implicit acknowledgment of the globalization of Western culture—for chess in its modern form is a characteristically Western phenomenon.

On January 17, 2008, Bobby Fischer died of kidney failure at his home in Reykjavik, Iceland. It was not merely Fischer's age—sixty-four, the number of squares on a chessboard—that was symbolic. Because he had abandoned chess in 1972, at the height of his fame, his memory had been frozen at that point in the public imagination. The death of Bobby Fischer evoked the history of Cold War chess, but also brought about a kind of closure.

True, Fischer had not been out of the public eye throughout the intervening thirty-six years. He had emerged in 1992 to play Spassky again for $5 million, the largest prize ever offered in a chess match, but the provenance of his patronage—Milosević's Serbia— had tarnished him forever. His pursuit by the U.S. authorities for breaking sanctions and tax evasion was stepped up after 11 September 2001, provoked by his virulent attacks on America and the Jews. After his arrest in Japan in 2005, he escaped extradition to face trial in the United States only because Iceland offered him asylum. Yet Fischer's sudden death touched the hearts of millions who recalled the chess epiphany of 1972. A maverick who had hardly been seen for nearly four decades would not normally attract much notice by the crude expedient of a premature demise. But the death of Bobby Fischer was front-page news around the world—a tribute to the heroic eccentric he undoubtedly had been, if not to the fugitive fanatic he later became.

In death, as in life, Fischer was nonconformist to the point of perversity. He died of kidney failure—stubborn to the last, he had refused medical help that might have prolonged his life—and was buried in the dead of night. The Lutheran pastor in whose churchyard the coffin was laid to rest had not been consulted, and a Catholic priest was reported to have officiated, though there is no reason to believe that Fischer had undergone a deathbed conversion. The secrecy that surrounded his illness, death, and funeral was of a piece with the mystique that the boy from Brooklyn had always cultivated. Fischer's uncannily canny eye for what would capture the imagination of his public never deserted him.

To the bitter end, Fischer remained a creature of the Cold War: in his obsessively suspicious and secretive temperament, in his Manichaean division of the world into friend and foe, and in his not-unfounded conviction that his enemies were out to get him. Yet before his demons got the better of him, Fischer had exemplified some of the virtues that the Cold War had also brought forth: his readiness to stand up for principles at the expense of popularity, a sharp eye for lies and deceit masquerading as humanitarian ideals, the refusal to sup with the devil that stemmed from a revulsion against prewar appeasement. The confrontation of the open societies of the liberal West with the closed societies of the communist East was about morality as much as ideology. Thanks to his firsthand experience of the Soviet manipulation of the chess world, Fischer saw through the highfalutin vocabulary of socialism and denounced the amoral cynicism that it disguised. Like Ronald Reagan, he had no qualms about deploying the language of good and evil, unlike the newly fashionable moral relativism that the liberal intellectuals embraced in the late 1960s.

By breaking the cozy monopoly of the Soviet grandmasters, he created what became known as the "Fischer boom" in the West. That was his legacy to chess. But Fischer also played his part on a much larger stage. By proving that the Soviet Union could be defeated by a single individual, he emboldened dissidents everywhere. The Cold War ended because the Soviets realized they could not win—as much on the intellectual as on the political or economic levels. That realization began to set in with Bobby Fischer and "this little thing between me and Spassky."

Let me end this preface for American readers on a personal note, with an anecdote that first appeared in a slightly different form in my weekly "Letter from London" in the New York *Sun*. Shortly after he died, I went searching for Bobby Fischer. That is to say, I went, like Marcel Proust, in search of lost time. I belong to the generation of adolescents who were inspired by the 1972 Fischer–Spassky match in Reykjavik, though I gave up playing the game seriously more than thirty years ago.

I found what I was looking for in Bush Hall, an old music hall near where I live in West London. A chess tournament was taking place, played at lightning ("blitz") speed—so fast that when each round began, the racket of pieces and clocks being banged down sounded like a hailstorm. Not only the sights and sounds, but the smells and feel of a chess tournament were intensely nostalgic. It was just the kind of occasion that, more than half a century ago, first drew the wunderkind from Brooklyn into the labyrinth of the sixty-four squares.

Before the first round, I found myself standing next to an elderly gentleman who was reading Fischer's obituary in an American newspaper at the bar. This proved to be James Sherwin, a U.S. international master who had been a friend of the champion.

Clearly stricken by the death of a contemporary whom he had first come to know in their youth, Sherwin was glad to share his memories. "Bobby was just a nice kid." They would play blitz for hours on end, and occasionally Fischer would concede a game. In their tournament games, Fischer almost always won, but he had included one of their early encounters as the first of *My 60 Memorable Games* — the one and only book he ever wrote, and a classic of chess literature.

Sherwin was evidently proud of this distinction, conferring as it did a kind of immortality even on the loser. I later looked up the game, played at the New Jersey Open of 1957, when Fischer was just fourteen but on the verge of becoming U.S. champion, his first great triumph. One annotation gives a flavor of Fischer's waspish style: "Sherwin slid the Rook here with his pinky, as if to emphasize the cunning of this mysterious move."

When I asked Sherwin about Fischer's later life, after winning the world championship in 1972, his face clouded over. He had not seen Fischer during the last thirty years, he said, and he was not sorry, because the poor guy had obviously gone crazy. He preferred to remember him as a sane person.

The trouble with this view is that Fischer himself rejected it. He insisted that he was entirely sane and refused to plead diminished responsibility when he was imprisoned in Japan and faced extradition to America, where he would probably have spent the rest of his life in jail.

My own view (as I explain at greater length later in this book) is that Fischer had been kept on the rails by two things that gave his life meaning and purpose: chess and the Cold War. In their absence, he was lost.

Precisely why Fischer's lonely, brave, and ultimately successful struggle against the Soviet chess machine proved to be a Pyrrhic victory, at least for him, is a matter of psychiatry as much as politics. But there is evidence of anti-Semitism much earlier in his career. His friend Larry Evans recalled an occasion in the 1960s when Fischer expressed admiration for Hitler. Baffled, Evans asked him why. "Because he imposed his will on the world," Fischer replied. That was the authentic voice of the megalomaniac.

Yet despite this dark, demonic side to his character, Fischer could not have become world champion if he had already been mad. There is no more daunting feat of mental combat than a world chess championship match, but in order to defeat the combined forces of the Soviet Union Fischer required qualities over and above chess genius. Fischer's anti-communism was denounced at the time as paranoid, but this enemy was real: the communists really were determined to deny him the title that for them symbolized intellectual superiority over the West. Those who lost at Reykjavik were lucky not to be banished to the Gulag. Fischer was not mad to see the Soviet Union as an evil empire, and his triumph at the chessboard played a significant part in its downfall.

The Fischer who reemerged decades afterward had lost all touch with reality. For those like me who had admired him in our youth, sorrow over the waste of his talent was compounded by disbelief at the spectacle of this wild-eyed, foul-mouthed fanatic, ranting against his own country, spitting at Jews, and gloating over 9/11.

For the young people playing blitz chess in Bush Hall, Bobby Fischer was ancient history, but for the middle-aged he was an inescapable part of our own past. We stood for a minute's silence in his memory. It was a painful remembrance, but a flawed hero is still a hero.

INTRODUCTION

CHESS IS A GAME of war, but war is not a game of chess. Chess, indeed, is the supreme sublimation of war. "Checkmate" means literally "The king is dead." There is a poignant reminder of the value of chess for royal belligerents in Windsor Castle, where a chessboard is preserved that belonged (presumably along with a set of chessmen, now lost) to King Charles I, with a Latin inscription that remains relevant: "With these, subject and ruler strive without bloodshed." By the time it was made for him in 1642, it was too late for Charles: the English civil war, which would lead to his trial and execution, had begun. Throughout its history, chess has been the passion of intellectuals more than of warriors. Although it was a favorite pastime of Napoleon, he was as helpless at the chessboard as he was formidable on the battlefield.

Like the arts and sciences of which it is usually a poor relation, chess flourishes not in wartime, but in peace. In an open society, chess is not normally a means to a political or military end; rather it is one of many forms of the pursuit of happiness. Only in a society in which war is internalized in the form of class and ethnic conflict — in the name of which the state kills, starves, deports, and incarcerates its own people by the million — and which is insulated from foreign influence by a permanent state of siege, could chess become a preparation for war. Only in the context of a primarily psychological conflict — a conflict in which everything except military force could be used — could chess emerge as a substitute for warfare.

That conflict is still known as the "Cold War," a metaphor that seems to have been first used as early as 1945 in a newspaper article by — appropriately enough — George Orwell. It was in the novel on which Orwell was then hard at work that the deeper meaning of the concept would first become manifest. Yet *Nineteen Eighty-Four*, with its nightmarish vision of a totalitarian world that existed in a state of perpetual war, was published only four years later in 1949.

By then, the notion of a "cold war" had entered into common parlance and was usually attributed to Bernard Baruch, one of President Truman's foreign policy advisers. Baruch declared in a speech to the South Carolina legislature in April 1947: "Let us not be deceived — we are today in the midst of a cold war." A year before, Baruch himself had attempted to forestall this calamity by persuading Truman to propose to hand over the entire American arsenal of nuclear technology to the United Nations, provided that the Soviet Union did the same. Stalin refused, even though the United States had a nuclear monopoly until 1949. The Baruch Plan was the last attempt to prevent a new arms race in which the stakes would, for the first time, be the survival of the human race. Thereafter, the strategic response to the Cold War would be summed up in another metaphor: "deterrence."

The Cold War was thus the first example of what became an entire metaphorical lexicon, the menacing vocabulary with which a fractured world that was neither at war nor at peace sought to describe its terrifying predicament. That this was above all a confrontation of ideologies, of portmanteau philosophies, meant that it incorporated slogans, superlatives, and scraps of half-digested theory: Iron Curtain, containment, roll-back, deterrence, mutually assured destruction, Ostpolitik, détente, evil empire. What the Cold War lacked in action, it made up for in words.

Chess provided a mega-metaphor for this psychological war, one that derived added significance from the game's all-important role in Soviet communist society. The Russians might lag behind in military technology or economic competition, but over the chessboard they reigned supreme. A battlefield that, for the first time in history, was genuinely global could be represented by sixty-four squares. Since the escalation of political antagonism beyond tacitly agreed limits must lead to inevitable annihilation, chess offered a demilitarized, purely abstract equivalent of war. If, like all wars, the Cold War was a continuation of politics by other means, then chess was the most cerebral of those means. By providing the safety valve that kept the lid on the Cold War, chess helped to save civilization from itself.

That chess was able to play this role is all the more extraordinary, given the fact that no American had a chance directly to challenge Soviet supremacy between 1948 and 1972. The cumbersome system of qualifying tournaments and matches run by the World Chess Federation, FIDE, militated against Western grandmasters who lacked the backup provided by the state-sponsored Soviet chess machine. Americans in particular felt frustrated and longed to short-circuit the system. In 1952, at the height of the Cold War, the *New York Times* was already declaring the leading American grandmaster, Samuel Reshevsky, to be the "chess champion of the free world" and it threw down the gauntlet by proposing that a world championship match be held between him and the Soviet world champion, Mikhail Botvinnik. This, the paper announced, was "one type of Soviet–American conflict that all people would welcome."

From the Kremlin, however, there was no response to this or any other suggestion that the official machinery for choosing a challenger should be bypassed. For a quarter of a century, both the champions and the challengers were all Soviet citizens. Once the vast Soviet effort to acquire the world chess championship had triumphed, it suited the Kremlin to keep the contest in the family. It had nothing to gain, and everything to lose, by reverting to the days when anybody could challenge the champion if he could find the backers. Once Bobby Fischer began his seemingly inexorable progress towards the summit in the late 1950s, fair means and foul were employed to stop him even coming close. Chess became a theater of psychological warfare. And once the threat came from Viktor Korchnoi—a dissident and émigré, thus in the eyes of the Kremlin an unmentionable traitor—preserving the world championship in Soviet hands became a matter for secret policemen as much as for grandmasters.

This is the story of how chess came to play this unique role: at once a symbol of the Cold War and of its antithesis—the culture of old Europe that had somehow survived. Chess illuminates the process by which Western civilization ultimately triumphed over the gravest threat it had ever encountered. And the story of chess in the Cold War has lessons for dealing with present or future threats to that civilization. As the White Queen tells Alice in *Through the Looking Glass:* "It's a poor sort of memory that only works backward."

WHITE KING
AND RED QUEEN

1

FROM BAGHDAD
TO ST. PETERSBURG

C HESS MAKES A GOOD ALLEGORY and a bad teacher. Garry Kasparov, perhaps the greatest player who has ever lived, believes that chess teaches us strategies for survival, and he has written a book to prove it: *How Life Imitates Chess*. The chess-playing philosopher Moses Mendelssohn was, perhaps, wiser: "Chess is too serious for a game, but too much of a game to be taken seriously." It has, nonetheless, enjoyed a modest but unique place in our civilization for at least fifteen centuries. Having served as a staple of the sermons and moralities of medieval and Renaissance literature—the most celebrated of which was *The Game and Playe of the Chesse* by Jacobus de Cessolis (*c.* 1300), one of the first books to be printed in English by Caxton—chess has greatly enriched the language ever since. Every time we speak of keeping an enemy in check, of treating someone as a pawn, or of a political stalemate, we draw on the vocabulary of chess. There are less obvious loan-words, too, such as *exchequer* (from the Norman use of a checkered board by the royal counting house), *gambit* (an opening stratagem, from the Italian *gambetta*), or *jeopardy* (from "juperty," a medieval chess problem).

The Russian word for chess, *shakhmaty*, is a simple transliteration of the Persian *shah mat* ("the king is dead"), which is also the origin of the English "checkmate." Chess is thought to have originated among Buddhists on the banks of the Ganges in India, perhaps as a secularized form of a religious ceremony that involved dice as a means of divining the celestial mind. Having reached Persia around AD 625, it was taken up by Arab conquerors. It soon lost all connection with Buddhism and was instead associated with the rapid expansion of Islam. It is likely, therefore, that the Slavic peoples learned chess from Muslim sources quite early in the history of the game, probably from merchants on the trade route from the Caspian Sea via the River Volga to the earliest kingdom of Rus, of which the capital was Kiev.

Islam dominated the history of chess for much longer than Soviet communism. The first appearances in literature of the medieval form of chess (*chaturanga* in Sanskrit, *chatrang* in Persian, or *shatranj* in Arabic) in the early seventh century coincide with the life of Muhammad, and the game's westward dissemination followed in the wake of the Arab conquests. Ali, the prophet's son-in-law and founder of the Shi'ites, is supposed to have been the first Muslim to encounter chess, which was brought to Arabia from Persia. By the eighth century, the historian of chess H. J. R. Murray wrote, "chess had already become a popular game throughout Islam, from Spain to the banks of the Indus." For the first two centuries of Islam, its legal status was unclear. What saved chess from the Koranic prohibitions against games of chance and the use of images was the importance of jihad in Islam. Because chess was a war game, it could be useful to warriors—and thus was permissible.

Hence chess came to be an integral part of high culture at the courts of the Umayyad caliphs and, from the eighth century, the new dynasty of Abbasids, who ruled a vast empire from Baghdad that stretched across much of the Middle East and North Africa. The mightiest of the Abbasid caliphs, Haroun al-Rashid (who reigned 786–807), was surrounded by grandmasters and historians of chess, such as as-Suli, along with the astronomers, chemists, and physicians for whom his court is still renowned. In *A Thousand and One Nights*—which, according to legend, is set in Haroun's reign but which modern scholarship has traced to an older, Persian collection of folk tales, now lost, that was translated into Arabic around 850—we learn that medieval Islam allowed chess to be played by women as well as men. In one story, the caliph is said to have bought a slave girl who defeated him three times in succession. Invited to name her reward, she asked pardon for another, rather than her own freedom. The girl's astronomical price, 10,000 dinars, proves that the caliph considered her even more valuable at the chessboard than in the harem.

Six centuries after Haroun, chess was no less esteemed by another Muslim potentate, Timur Lenk or Tamerlane (Marlowe's Tamburlaine the Great), who even gave the name Shah-Rukh ("king-rook") to his son, news of whose birth was brought while the emperor was playing chess, as well as to a city he built on the banks of the River Jaxartes in modern Kazakhstan. A Greek historian relates that Tamerlane was playing chess with his son when the Turkish sultan, Bayazid, was brought captive to his tent. At his court in Samarkand, Tamerlane's favourite lawyer and scholar, Ala'addin at-Tabrizi, was nicknamed Ali ash-Shatranji ("Ali the chess master"). Contemporary sources tell us that this Aladdin played up to four games simultaneously while blindfold, and that he composed a treatise on chess that records about twenty-one positions from his games. Having traveled extensively and defeated all comers, Aladdin has some claim to be considered the first world champion. Tamerlane liked to tell him: "You have no rival in the kingdom of chess, just as I have none in government; there is no man to be found who can perform such wonders as I and you, my lord Ali, each in his own sphere."

It is unclear how far this real figure merged in legend with the Aladdin of *A Thousand and One Nights.* The historical Aladdin had no genie in a magic lamp; he was, rather, a genius who could work magic on the chessboard. In a sense, the role of Soviet world chess champions in the empire of Lenin, Stalin, and their successors was analogous to that of Aladdin at the court of Tamerlane. There was one difference: the great khans of communism treated their subjects in general just as brutally as Tamerlane, who liked to be known as the Scourge of God, but the thugs who ruled the Soviet empire were incapable of treating mere chess masters so courteously.

The modern rules of chess, which speeded up the game by making pieces such as the queen and bishop more powerful, emerged in Renaissance Italy during the late fifteenth century. In the medieval game, the queen (the vizier or counselor in Muslim countries) was a much weaker piece than the rook or even the king, moving only one square diagonally. The bishop (an elephant in the East) also moved diagonally, leaping over only the adjacent squares. The new form of chess soon spread from the West to Muscovy as trade routes were established during the reign of Grand Duke Ivan III in the early sixteenth century. Chess had long been frowned on by the Orthodox Church, which associated the game with heresy and witchcraft, not to mention dice and other forms of gambling. There were periodic attempts to suppress chess in Russia. The tsars themselves, however, were so addicted to it that no ban could be enforced.

Ivan the Terrible, the first ruler of Russia to assume the title of Tsar, even died at the chessboard. In 1584, while preparing to play chess with his son Feodor's guardian and eventual successor, Boris Godunov, the tsar suffered some kind of seizure. We owe this fact to a contemporary description by the English ambassador, Sir Jerome Horsey. The queen who had sent him, Elizabeth I, would have been interested in such details, for she was herself very accomplished at chess. Medieval and Renaissance etiquette allowed women equal status at chess, which only later became a male preserve. In the diary of his travels to Muscovy, Sir Jerome records the dramatic circumstances of the tsar's demise:

> He setts his men (all savinge the kinge, which by no means he could not stand in his place with the rest upon the plain board): his chief favorett and Boris Fedorowich Goddonove and others about him. The Emperor in his lose gown, shirt and lynen hose, faints and falls backward. Great owtcrie and sturr; one sent for Aqua vita, another to the oppatheke [apothecary] for marigold and rose water, and to call his gostlie father [confessor] and the phizicions. In the mean he was strangled [choked] and stark dead.

Historians still debate whether Ivan was poisoned by Boris or died of natural causes, but there is no dispute about their common devotion to chess. It was only natural that Sergei Eisenstein (himself a keen chess player) included one of the best chess scenes in all cinema in his three-part epic, *Ivan the Terrible* (1944). The tsar was more than Stalin's hero; he was his alter ego. As his paranoia grew, so did the dictator's identification with the tsar—to the point where even Eisenstein's cinematic epic was not hagiographical enough for Stalin. Actors whose features were deemed too Jewish were weeded out of the cast, and the director, too, came under suspicion. The second part of the trilogy was a window into the soul of a tsar tormented by guilt. When Stalin saw Part 2, he was furious, so it was released only after his death in 1958. The incomplete third part—*The Boyars' Plot*—was destroyed on Stalin's orders. Despite its veneer of Marxist ideology and European culture, the Soviet Union was a reversion to Ivan the Terrible's oriental despotism.

One pursuit that oriental and enlightened despots had in common, however, was chess. Russia's great Westernizers, Peter I and Catherine II, both shared Ivan's passion for the game. Their chessmen and boards are displayed in the Hermitage Museum along with a Fabergé set made for Nicholas II. For most of the Romanovs, chess remained what it had been at the courts of the Renaissance:

an esoteric divertissement for the edification of royal, military, or sacerdotal elites. It was due to Napoleon that thousands of Russian officers learned the game from their French counterparts during their occupation of Paris in 1814–15 and brought it back home with them. Thus chess owed its popularity in Russia not to a Russian emperor but to a French one.

The Russians who took up chess in the wake of the Napoleonic wars belonged to a new class, the educated elite that became known as the intelligentsia. Not only in Russia, but elsewhere in Europe and America, the place of chess closely reflected the rise of this group. A good starting point for the story of the love affair between chess and the intelligentsia is an image that records one of the great encounters of modernity: a group portrait, painted in 1856 by Moritz Daniel Oppenheim. It depicts three major figures of eighteenth-century thought: the dramatist Gotthold Ephraim Lessing, the Swiss divine Johann Caspar Lavater, and the Jewish philosopher Moses Mendelssohn. The focus of the picture, around which these luminaries of the Enlightenment are stationed, is a chessboard.

This is not accidental. Lessing and Mendelssohn first met in 1754 after a mutual friend had recommended the latter to the already celebrated Lessing as a chess partner. It was a fateful meeting of two remarkable minds, as well as of two cultures. In *Nathan the Wise*, the play that proved to be not only its author's most enduringly popular work, but one of the high points of European civilization, Lessing depicted an idealized Mendelssohn as the eponymous Nathan: wise, enlightened, and Jewish.

The play ran counter to the Judeophobia of the continental Enlightenment, the leaders of which, from Voltaire onwards, loved to set an example of courageous resistance to prejudice by sneering at a minority that was far more exposed to prejudice than the *philosophes* themselves. The symbolism of Lessing, the Christian, and Mendelssohn, the Jew, meeting over a game of chess is highly significant. The progress of chess from pastime to artistic or scientific maturity was made possible only by Jewish assimilation, which transformed the German-speaking *Bildungsbürgertum,* or educated middle class, of central Europe into agents of the modernist cultural revolution. That German-Jewish symbiosis—always precarious, usually one-sided, and ultimately doomed by anti-Semitism—provided the cultural context in which chess could become something far more than a diversion: the intellectual recreation par excellence, deserving of serious study by serious people.

In *Nathan the Wise,* chess is depicted as the private passion of Saladin, the no less enlightened Muslim sultan, who is checkmated by his intellectual sister Sittah. (The real Saladin is supposed to have taught Richard the Lionheart how to play, while the latter was his prisoner.) For Lessing's cosmopolitan intellectuals, chess was the perfect bridge with which to overcome prejudice, whether religious, racial, national, or sexual.

Yet the status of chess in the Enlightenment was ambiguous. The game fascinated many of its leading lights, from the philosopher and mathematician Gottfried Wilhelm Leibniz (who anticipated the chess computer and thought chess an excellent mental discipline) to the *encylopédiste* Denis Diderot (whose novella *Rameau's Nephew,* written between 1761 and 1774, immortalized the Café de la Régence, where the best masters in Europe congregated during the *ancien régime*). However, chess, which had been a courtly pastime ever since its first flowering twelve centuries earlier at the Caliph Haroun al-Rashid's court in Baghdad, was still generally regarded as the frivolous diversion of a leisured class rather than a serious pursuit, let alone a profession.

In the course of the nineteenth and early twentieth centuries, chess emerged as a popular competitive activity, with international tournaments that attracted public interest. It was no longer solely the preserve of a cultured elite. Thomas Henry Buckle, whose influential *History of Civilisation* (1857–61) marks the zenith of the Victorian religion of progress, was one of the strongest players of his day, but also one of the last genuine amateurs to achieve real mastery of the game. The rise of global capitalism, beginning in the mid-nineteenth century, created enough prosperity to sustain a thriving transatlantic chess community, and for the first time national champions like the Englishman Howard Staunton and the American Paul Morphy aroused patriotic pride. Not only the capitals but also the spas and seaside resorts of the European bourgeoisie treated chess as a tourist attraction. This vast new urban wealth provided the wherewithal for dozens of masters to earn a precarious living by winning cash prizes in tournaments against their peers, taking on numerous amateurs at once in "simultaneous exhibitions," tutoring the children of the wealthy, or writing chess columns for the press. There was, however, still a tension between those masters whose motivation was aesthetic—chess as art for art's sake—and those who made a living from it. Like many other pursuits, from sport to science, chess was caught up in the nineteenth-century debate between gentlemen and players, amateurs and professionals.

Excluding chance and hence discouraging the ruinous vice of gambling, chess was one of the few games worthy of a gentleman. (It continues to be the only game permitted within the Palace of Westminster—cards and other games of chance are strictly prohibited.) For some, this implied that chess was strictly the preserve of the amateur. Even Lewis Carroll's *Through the Looking Glass* (1871) still treats chess primarily as a children's entertainment, comparable to card games—although Carroll was too good a logician to be blind to the game's more profound potential. But Howard Staunton, the greatest chess personality in Victorian England, thought there was nothing juvenile about the game that could compete with Shakespearean scholarship as his lifelong passion—and set out to demonstrate its manly qualities. Chess was not "an excuse for indolence," he wrote. "Chess was intended to be the recreation of men of genius and practical energies; men who are fully alive to the responsibilities of their social existence; men who, even in their amusements, are desirous of bracing and invigorating to the utmost their intellectual powers." However, Staunton also felt strongly that chess "can never be a profession. It may to a great extent strengthen the mind of the professional man, but it must never become the object of his life."

Gentlemen amateurs naturally still enjoyed higher status than professional coffeehouse players. Of the leading masters, a few achieved eminence in other professions (Adolf Anderssen was a schoolmaster, Ignaz Kolisch a banker, Siegbert Tarrasch a doctor, Amos Burn a merchant, Milan Vidmar an engineer, Ossip Bernstein a lawyer), while others valued their academic and literary achievements (Howard Staunton and Emanuel Lasker) or their social status (Paul Morphy and José Raúl Capablanca) more highly than their chess. By 1900, however, chess at the highest level was no longer a game for amateurs, nor did professionals necessarily have to suffer the indignity of playing all comers for a pittance; indeed, "coffeehouse player" became a term of abuse. Instead, chess aspired to the status of an art form or a science. The years before 1914 witnessed a golden age, not least in Russia.

The last tsar was also the first to treat chess as rather more than a courtly entertainment. Nicholas II ensured that, until the revolution, Russian chess revolved around St. Petersburg. The three great international tournaments there in 1895, 1909, and 1914 were all organized under Nicholas's patronage. Although the tsar made no attempt to nationalize the game, let alone use it to exercise power in the totalitarian manner of the Soviets, Russian "chessists" instinctively looked to the Autocrat of all the Russias to exercise an enlightened despotism over what had become as much a pastime of the rising bourgeoisie as of the aristocracy. They hoped that Nicholas II's patronage would develop into a centralized organization for chess with a hierarchical authority. Faint echoes of this patrician view of chess still reverberated after world war, revolution, and civil war had impoverished Russia to the point when, in 1922, the chess players of Moscow clubbed together to buy a fine chess set and board to present to Lenin, who fulfilled the traditional role of the tsar in this, as in so many other ways.

The first St. Petersburg tournament, in 1895–6, was a quadrangular contest, in which four of the greatest masters of the day played short matches of five games against the other four. Emanuel Lasker, the German world champion, emerged a clear first, having won his individual matches against all the others. The most gifted all-rounder ever to play chess at the highest level, Lasker would hold the title for twenty-seven years—a record that is unlikely ever to be broken. His defeated rival Wilhelm Steinitz, despite his age, came second; Harry Pillsbury, the young American, came third; and the Russian champion, Mikhail Tchigorin, fourth. Steinitz's result, remarkable for a man of fifty-nine, encouraged him to challenge Lasker to a return match for the title. That, too, was played in St. Petersburg, but Steinitz lost heavily. He was in fact suffering from undiagnosed heart trouble, a side effect of which was a bout of madness that resulted in his temporary committal to an asylum. Stories about Steinitz imagining himself playing chess with God gratified the *schadenfreude* of his rivals and excited the ridicule of those who thought, then as now, that a man who devoted his life to chess must be mad anyway.

Returning to St. Petersburg thirteen years later in 1909, Lasker experienced real competition for the first time from a younger rival, Akiba Rubinstein. The world champion lost this individual game and was forced to work hard to tie with Rubinstein for first place. Rubinstein was a Polish Jew, from a poor Hassidic family, and since Poland was a province of the Russian empire, he was thus a subject of the tsar. Yet the unpredictability of patronage meant that no world championship match was organized for Rubinstein, whom Lasker then saw as his most likely successor. Rubinstein's sanity, always precarious, gradually left him and he spent his last thirty years in a sanatorium. Instead, it was the seventeen-year-old winner of the minor tournament in 1909—for which the first prize was not even money, but a "magnificent vase of the Imperial porcelain manufacture" donated by Tsar Nicholas II—who was actually destined to become world champion, though not for nearly two decades. The youth's name was Alexander Alekhine. Born to privilege, with an aristocratic father who was also a member of the

tsarist Duma, Alekhine was destined to lose everything in the Bolshevik revolution. Yet nothing could stand in the way of his ambition to dominate the chess world. The Soviets despised his politics
but emulated his professionalism.

The last of the three St. Petersburg international tournaments
took place in 1914. Held in the opulent rooms of the St. Petersburg
Chess Club, this event was the best of them all. The only notable
absentees were the Austro-Hungarian masters, due to political tensions; the assassination at Sarajevo took place only two months
later. It was at this tournament that the term "grandmaster" was
first officially awarded by Tsar Nicholas II to the five finalists. This
was still a purely honorific title that would not be statistically determined until the sixties, but its echoes of the medieval military
orders and, more recently, of freemasonry lent a certain mystery
to the game. Press coverage was considerable: in Britain alone,
some fifteen national newspapers employed correspondents to
write about it. Emanuel Lasker himself reported the event for the
New York Evening Post. It was a sign of the game's rising status
that the world champion's appearance fee of 4,000 rubles was much
bigger than the first prize of 1,200 rubles. Such a fee was unprecedented, yet his old rival Tarrasch commented: "I do not consider
this excessive. He would well deserve an even bigger bonus for the
splendid games he has played." The audience's excitement overcame the normally strict etiquette of silence after the decisive
game between Lasker and the rising star from Cuba, José Raúl Capablanca; cheering and applause erupted and went on for several
minutes. Lasker won this tournament, just as he had won the other
two, but this time only a thrilling late spurt enabled him to overtake Capablanca. The unfortunate Rubinstein was eclipsed. Alekhine, who proved that he was good enough to compete with the
other grandmasters, came third. These three—Lasker, Capablanca,
Alekhine—would remain the most famous names in chess for another generation, until the era of Soviet domination began after the
Second World War.

This splendid gathering of grandmasters on the eve of the First

World War—a conflict that would destroy imperial Russia forever—marked the end of a golden age. Even in post-revolutionary Russia, the memory of the world's chess elite fighting it out in St. Petersburg lived on and inspired the first Soviet international tournament at Moscow in 1925. During the intervening decade, however, St. Petersburg changed its name twice, symbolizing the fact that every aspect of life in Russia—including chess—had changed more in those ten years than in the two centuries since Peter the Great had founded his new capital.

2

THE RECREATION
OF THE REVOLUTION

C HESS, LIKE THE ARTS and sciences, is influenced by events and ideologies. Political and industrial revolution, nationalism and socialism, naturally all left their mark. The revolutionary years of 1789, 1848, and 1917 sent chess players, among countless others, into exile. Indeed, the first master to be universally acknowledged as supreme, the French composer André Danican Philidor, owed much of his fame at chess to the circumstance of exile. Proscribed by the revolutionary Directoire as an émigré in 1793 while enjoying his much publicized "chess season" in London, Philidor lost his main income after his music was banned in France. Thereafter he earned his living by chess. Philidor's feat of playing blindfold chess against several opponents simultaneously made him briefly a celebrity, but he died a poor refugee.

After the failed revolution of 1848, another chess-playing exile pitched up in London: Karl Marx. Like his intellectual ancestor, Jean Jacques Rousseau, Marx adored chess and (much to his wife Jenny's exasperation) would disappear with his fellow émigrés for days at a time on chess binges. Despite having devoted many hours to its pursuit, he never rose above mediocrity. According to Wilhelm Liebknecht, one of his chess friends and the founder of the German Social Democratic Party, Marx played chess with the same barely suppressed aggression that he manifested in politics: "When Marx got into a difficult position he would get angry and losing a game would cause him to fly into a rage." For much of his life, Marx was a typical coffeehouse intellectual whose fantasies of world revolution seemed unlikely to transcend the narrow bounds of the chessboard. Rousseau had been a similar type of grandstanding bohemian; so, later, were Lenin, Trotsky, Lunacharsky, and other Bolsheviks. Chess has always exerted a peculiar magnetism for megalomaniacs, from Napoleon to Castro. Sherlock Holmes saw excellence in chess as suspicious: "One mark, Watson, of a scheming mind."

Marx and Lenin, however, were also linked by another chess lover: Nikolai Chernyshevsky. The son of an Orthodox priest, Chernyshevsky immersed himself in radical ideas and became the voice of the Russian intelligentsia during the mid-nineteenth century, particularly in his 1863 novel, *What Is to Be Done?* The checkered history of its publication indicates just how incompetent the tsarist police state was compared to that of Lenin and Stalin. Written while the author was in prison awaiting trial for subversion, the manuscript was passed by two censors, lost in a cab by the editor who was to publish it, and had to be retrieved with the help of the St. Petersburg police.

Yet this book did more to make the Russian revolution possible than any other, including the works of Marx himself. It was this book that enthused the angry young men who later formed the Bolsheviks. Chernyshevsky was sentenced to ten years in prison and, although this sentence was later commuted to five, he moldered in Siberian exile almost until his death in 1883. Chernyshevsky's status in radical circles as a revolutionary martyr lent a unique aura to this novel, a strange amalgam of Christianity and atheism, of mysticism and scientism, of socialism and individualism, of idealism and nihilism.

It was Chernyshevsky's hero, Rakhmetov, who furnished a role model for all future revolutionaries. Rakhmetov undergoes a quasireligious conversion to revolutionary principles, after which he is reborn as an ascetic and enigmatic figure, known as "the rigorist." His life is totally subordinated to the cause; his time is strictly allotted, either to the tasks of training mind and body or to conspiratorial activity; he has no social life unless it serves the purpose of revolution, which he (like his creator) believes with millenarian fanaticism is to come in the year 1865. His mortification of the flesh is taken to extremes: he lies on a bed of nails to prove to himself that he can stand torture. A woman whose life he saves is overwhelmed by his fiery speeches: "I see him in my dreams surrounded by a halo," she muses. But he renounces her love: "Pity me. For I, too, am not an abstract idea, but a human being, one who longs to live life. Never mind. It will pass."

Censorship obliged Chernyshevsky to resort to euphemisms; he could do no more than hint at the true aims of his "extraordinary people." His heroine Vera Pavlovna did for emancipated women what Rakhmetov did for radical men. Both were foils for conservative critics such as Fyodor Dostoyevsky, whose *Notes from Underground* was a direct response to *What Is to Be Done?*, just as Chernyshevsky himself had reacted against Ivan Turgenev's critique of revolutionary nihilism in *Fathers and Sons*. Dostoyevsky saw Rakhmetov as the prototype of the diabolical enemies of European civilization who haunt his works, especially *The Possessed*. But for Chernyshevsky, the Rakhmetovs were latter-day apostles of revolution, and he did not hesitate to laud them in language heavy with biblical allusion: "They are the flower of the best people, the movers of movers, the salt of the salt of the earth."

Although chess plays no part in *What Is to Be Done?*, it played a large part in Chernyshevsky's life, and a century later Soviet authors devoted entire monographs to his obsession with the game.

The reason was that among his most avid readers was a young, upper-class Russian, Vladimir Ilyich Ulyanov, better known by his later nom de guerre: Lenin. While in exile, Lenin once defended *What Is to Be Done?* against a critic in a Zurich café. Chernyshevsky, he declared, was

> the greatest and most talented representative of socialism before Marx . . . He ploughed me up more profoundly than anyone else . . . After my brother's execution, knowing that Chernyshevsky's novel was one of his favorite books, I really undertook to read it, and I sat over it not for several days but for several weeks. Only then did I understand its depth . . . It's a thing that supplies energy for a whole lifetime.

Lenin evidently hero-worshipped his brother Alexander. According to his biographer Robert Service, it was a family joke that, whenever he was in a quandary, his first question was always: what would Alexander do? According to his wife, Nadya Krupskaya, Lenin's passion for chess also derived from his ill-fated elder brother:

> Both Vladimir Ilyich and his brother Alexander had been enthusiastic chess players ever since they were children. Their father had played chess too. "Father used to beat us at first," Vladimir Ilyich once told me, "but then my brother and I got hold of a chess manual and started beating him. Once I met my father coming out of our room—it was upstairs—with a lighted candle in one hand and the chess manual in the other. He made a study of it too."

The death of their father in 1886 left Alexander as head of the family. However, while studying at St. Petersburg he had become involved in a plot to assassinate Tsar Alexander III. In 1887 he was arrested by the Okhrana, the tsarist secret police, swiftly tried and—despite all attempts to intercede with the authorities—executed. Soon afterward, Lenin went to live and work in Kazan. It was here that he immersed himself in Chernyshevsky and, not coincidentally, joined a chess club. He also played postal chess with a lawyer friend, Andrei Khardin, who was a strong enough player to be taken seriously by the greatest Russian grandmaster of the tsarist era, Mikhail Tchigorin. Nadya Krupskaya recalled: "Vladimir Ilyich played games by correspondence. He would set out the figures and ponder over the board. He got so enthusiastic about it that he once cried out in his sleep: 'If he moves his knight here, I'll put my rook there!'"

Later, during a peripatetic exile that took him from Finland to Berlin, Paris, and Switzerland, Lenin usually found time for chess amid his politicking, writing, and skirt-chasing. While in Paris he played at a café on the corner of the Avenue d'Orléans and the Place Montrouge. But Lenin found chess too addictive, and would often exclaim: "Chess is too absorbing, it interferes with your work." He was brought up with the rigorous work ethic that Chernyshevsky had demanded from true revolutionaries, and sitting around playing chess was incompatible with preparing for revolution. Krupskaya, for whom chess was a closed book, admired the self-discipline with which Lenin kept his obsession under control: "As Vladimir Ilyich was incapable of doing anything by halves, and always gave himself up wholeheartedly to whatever he was doing, it was usually with reluctance that he sat down to a game of chess when relaxing or when he lived abroad as a political emigrant." After his return to Russia in 1917, Lenin gave up chess altogether. He was able to use real people as pawns instead.

As for Lev Davidovich Bronstein, alias Leon Trotsky, a permanent seat at the coffeehouse chess table was a substitute for permanent revolution in Russia. Trotsky seems to have used chess rather as Marx did, as a safety valve to relieve the frustrations of a man impatient to be an actor on the stage of world history rather than a spectator. None of his games has survived, but one of his opponents was Baron Rothschild—an anticipation, in a sense, of the Cold War confrontation of capitalist and communist over the chessboard. The news of Trotsky's triumph in the Bolshevik revolution was greeted by the head waiter at the Café Central in Vienna, where the prophet in exile had spent much of the last few years, with the words: "Ach, that must be our Herr Bronstein from the chess room!"

When in 1917 the Bolshevik émigrés abandoned the café and took over the Kremlin, they brought chess back with them. At first it was merely one of their pastimes, a relic of the Russian or Jewish bourgeoisie from which they mostly came. Yet within a few years, chess had been embraced by the commissars. By the mid-1920s, the Soviet Union had decided to adopt the game and promote it en masse as a form of mental training, a preparation for war and peace. They were also investing large sums of hard currency in organizing tournaments and cultivating grandmasters in a colossal drive to outdo the West in this most rarefied of competitive recreations.

The fact that Lenin played chess, of course, does not begin to explain the massive effort to popularize chess that began only after his death. *Pravda* boasted in 1936 of Botvinnik's victory at the Nottingham tournament that "the whole country, from the most remote corners to the Kremlin towers, was wishing him success and giving him moral support." In fact, Stalin does not seem to have been a chess player; as a young man, he preferred terrorism. Although he did much more than Lenin to establish chess as a key part of Soviet cultural diplomacy, Stalin's interest in chess was political rather than personal, despite the fact that games purporting to be his were published. Nor did the later Soviet leaders, such as Khrushchev and Brezhnev, care for the game. Unlike Lenin and Trotsky, they were shameless philistines. While several dictators of other communist states were strong chess players—including the Yugoslav Josip Broz Tito, the Hungarian Janos Kádár, and the Cuban Fidel Castro—it was Boris Yeltsin, the first post-Soviet president, who was actually the first Russian leader since Lenin to be a bona fide chess enthusiast. The rest—Zhdanov, Molotov, Khrushchev, Brezhnev, Andropov, Chernyenko, and Gorbachev—supported chess for pragmatic reasons of propaganda and prestige.

One of the most important reasons why the Soviet Union

adopted chess was that the game was not only a symbol of utopian aspirations but also of intellectual respectability. The Bolshevik regime began as, and in some respects always remained, a pariah state. The Western democracies at first supported the White counterrevolutionaries in the civil war of 1917–21, and even after their defeat continued to cold-shoulder the Bolshevik government. Soviet Russia was not invited to join the League of Nations. Britain and France were appalled when the German Foreign Minister, Walther Rathenau, signed the Treaty of Rapallo with the Soviet regime in 1922. Further official recognition of the Bolsheviks by the West was a long time in coming. In 1927 a boatload of American journalists and intellectuals arrived to be feted by Trotsky and Stalin, who were desperate for a better press in the United States. They got it. Even so, it was not until 1933, more than fifteen years after the revolution, that Roosevelt, impressed by Stalin's Five Year Plan, recognized the Bolshevik government. Nevertheless, relations with the West remained icebound, not least because the Bolshevik regime continued to support communist parties elsewhere. Despite Stalin's slogan, "Socialism in One Country," the ultimate goal of world revolution was never abandoned.

The exclusion of the USSR from political and economic contact with the West was a serious problem for Lenin and Stalin. The consolidation of communism required military and industrial technology, which necessitated trade and hence foreign currency. Despite its much trumpeted statistics for collectivization and industrialization, the Soviet government was all but bankrupt, crippled by the burden of a centrally planned economy, and a bloated and avaricious bureaucracy, not to mention the largest and least efficient army in the world. The world's first communist experiment needed Western capitalism to supply capital—human, industrial, and financial. Stalin had no trouble wooing nongovernmental organizations, such as trade unions, but governments were harder. After the rise of Hitler, who became German chancellor in 1933, Stalin pursued talks with Britain and France on collective security, but neither power trusted him. Stalin was excluded from the Munich conference, when Chamberlain and Daladier tried to appease Hitler. Stalin sacked his foreign minister, Litvinov, and replaced him with Molotov, before proceeding to negotiate a pact even with his bitterest enemy, Hitler, in order to ensure that the latter turned his forces against the West rather than against Russia. This "Non-Aggression Pact" was signed by the two most aggressive states on earth in August 1939, partitioning Eastern and central Europe between them and temporarily consigning Comintern, the vehicle of world revolution, to the dustbin of history. Yet the Soviet Union remained isolated until Churchill and Roosevelt were forced to treat Stalin as an ally against Hitler.

For the brief period of the wartime "Big Three" alliance, the Soviet Union came in from the cold. At Yalta, Stalin was as happy to partition his neighbors with the Allies as with the Axis, and now extended his power deep into central Europe. The bad faith evident in postwar attempts at communist subversion caused public opinion in Western Europe and America to treat "Uncle Joe" once again with fear and suspicion. In this respect, the Cold War restored the natural order of things, obliging successive Soviet leaders to lavish scarce resources on propaganda, subversion, "fellow travelers," and "front organizations" in order to impress and undermine the West. The fact that the Kremlin (which simply means "fortress" or "castle," of the kind that virtually every medieval European city possessed) became shorthand for the Soviet government was merely one indication of the siege mentality that persisted throughout the three-quarters of a century that Lenin's revolutionary order endured. In a sense, just as there were two world wars, so there were two cold wars: the first from 1918 to 1941, the second from 1946 to 1991. In both cases, proxy wars were fought: before the Second World War in Spain and China; after it in Korea, Vietnam, the Middle East, Africa, Latin America, Europe, and finally Afghanistan. One major difference between the two cold wars was the virtual isolation of the USSR during its first twenty years, whereas after 1945 it was joined by a large bloc of satellites and other socialist or "nonaligned" states. Both before and after the Second World War, however, it was a key part of the Kremlin's strategy to improve relations with the West, in order to facilitate the creation of pro-Soviet parties and factions there.

Chess became an essential part of the long-term Soviet program to overcome this pariah status. What the Russians, in contrast to the amateur game, called "big chess"—the nurturing of masters and grandmasters, and national or international tournaments, all with the ultimate goal of monopolizing the world championship—promised to enhance the legitimacy and prestige of the communist movement. Long before Soviet competitors began to make a major impact in other sports, their excellence in chess drew admiration in the West—so much so, indeed, that chess became an integral part of the stereotypical view of Soviet society, which was, of course, precisely the intention. Chess fitted perfectly the official image of Soviet man as serious-minded, logical, and "scientific" even in his leisure activity. The "rigorist" philosophy of life that first emerged fully into view with Chernyshevsky's fictional character of Rakhmetov is an almost exact model for the work ethic that Soviet chess masters were later expected to follow. As we shall see, the first and most influential world champion, Mikhail Botvinnik, prescribed a lifestyle that went far beyond the training regime that is normal for any sport. He demanded that young men and women give themselves up body and soul to the service of the Soviet school of chess, which in turn served the higher purpose of the revolution. Without this philosophical background, the Soviet state would not have cultivated chess as the recreation of the revolution.

Chess became a training ground for the wider aim of overtaking the West across the board: in cultural excellence, economic growth, political influence, and military prowess. Because chess was the first—and for many years only—field in which the Kremlin could genuinely claim to have surpassed capitalism in direct competition, it was given priority over other, objectively more important activities. Chess was also, compared to other cultural activities of comparable prestige, very cheap. In a country impoverished by war, revolution, and collectivization, even chess sets were luxuries that ordinary workers could not afford, although they were within the means of trade unions or other state organizations. And so began the unprecedented experiment of incorporating chess into the official culture of the communist revolution.

3

TERROR

THE SOVIET UNION EXCELLED at only two things: war and chess. Socialist central planning emerged from the First World War, the first time in history that the entire resources of modern industrialized states had been harnessed for one overriding objective. War socialism was seen as a success, but in peacetime it proved a lamentable failure—although it was not until after 1918 that the Austrian school of economics, led by Ludwig von Mises and Friedrich von Hayek, was able to demonstrate why collectivist central planning not only did not work, but could never work. Before 1914 the Russian economy had been growing faster than that of any other major European country. Under communism, by contrast, famine was never far away and living standards were deliberately depressed to maintain a war economy. War was a catastrophe for the Russian people, yet without it the Soviet experiment would have been unthinkable. During the Great War, Russia—in common with every other combatant nation—underwent a drastic expansion of the power of the state. The Bolshevik putsch intensified and perpetuated that war economy, but it also encouraged a militaristic mentality that extended into every aspect of culture.

Chess was no exception. In 1914 an All Russia Chess Union had been formed, based in St. Petersburg. Due to the war, and perhaps because the authorities were suspicious of independent societies, this national chess organization failed to establish itself. Moribund during the war, the Union reemerged after the revolution, based in the opulent premises of the Vladimir Gambling Club, complete with a liveried doorkeeper. But this tsarist-era organization stood no chance of survival in the totalitarian culture of Soviet Russia. As Grigory Levenfish, one of the strongest Russian masters of the day, put it: "Unfortunately it used the bourgeois German chess union as a model, although it was clear that in the new circumstances new forms were needed." What this meant was that a bottom-up confederation of independent chess clubs had to be replaced by a top-down organization created and controlled by the state. Such a thing had never happened before, but that was never seen as an obstacle by the new masters of the Kremlin.

Over in Moscow, the ideological nerve center of the new state, the chess community had a very different vision of the future—one that was much more in tune with the prevailing ideology. The revolution, and the Red Terror that followed it, had all but destroyed the middle classes and with them the cultural life of what was now the capital. The Muscovites realized that private patrons could no longer subsidize chess, let alone run its organizations. In Soviet Russia, only the state could do that.

The man who officiated at the shotgun wedding of chess and communism was Alexander Ilyin-Genevsky. Born in 1894, young Ilyin was expelled from school in 1911 along with other members of an underground Bolshevik cell, and he went into voluntary exile in Switzerland. Typically for this radical milieu, his brother Fedor adopted the pseudonym Raskolnikov, after the character in Dostoyevsky's *Crime and Punishment*. Raskolnikov would become one of the heroes of the October revolution. A love of chess was

apparently one of the bonds that united these fraternal revolutionaries: having played in the 1910 St. Petersburg championship aged
sixteen, Ilyin was good enough to become champion of Geneva
by 1914, whereupon he added the city's name to his own ("Genevsky"). At the outbreak of war he returned to Russia and, despite his politics, joined the tsarist army. He was wounded and returned to Petrograd (as St. Petersburg had been renamed by the
half-German Nicholas II as a futile anti-German gesture) suffering
from shell shock. Having lost his memory, Ilyin-Genevsky had to
relearn everything, even how to move the chess pieces. But the
Bolshevik revolution saw him catapulted into the key post of ad-
ministrator of Petrograd's military district, probably thanks to his
brother Raskolnikov, a naval officer who had taken over the key
base of Kronstadt and served on the Military Revolutionary Committee (Milrevkom) that actually carried out the Bolshevik coup.
Still in his early twenties, Ilyin-Genevsky was now a figure of
power and influence in a disintegrating world where the only thing
that counted was force.

War and revolution annihilated the old café culture of chess.
The cafés Dominik and Reiter in Peterburg, the Pechkin in Moscow, and the Warsaw in Kiev—all were gone. In Petrograd, chess
—like other manifestations of bourgeois culture—had been totally eclipsed by the sheer brutality of the Red Guards. They occupied the Chess Society's premises, vandalized chess equipment
that at the time was in short supply—according to Alekhine, the
thugs stole all the knights— and were prevented from burning the
irreplaceable library that dated back to Tchigorin's day only by a
plucky secondhand book dealer, Julius Sossnitsky. He, like many
other patrons, died of typhus; others, such as Saburov, the organizer of Tsar Nicholas's last great tournament in 1914, emigrated.
Moscow, which Ilyin-Genevsky visited in December 1918, was
scarcely less depressing: the members of the famous Chess Circle
were mostly dead or dispersed. There he played a match by candle-
light with the leading master, Nikolai Grigoriev, in the basement

apartment of a Jewish chess fan, G. D. Berman. When the candles ran out, they used matches; one game was abandoned after a spectator discerned in the gloom that both kings were in check.

Ilyin-Genevsky made up his mind to reinstate chess as an activity worthy both of Russia and the revolution. In 1920 he had his chance when he was recruited by Nikolai Podvoisky, Raskolnikov's former chief at Milrevkom, who was now head of the General Reservists' Organization, better known by its acronym Vsevobuch. Although its primary function was military training, Vsevobuch also ran sports and other leisure activities. As a commissar of Vsevobuch, Ilyin-Genevsky persuaded Podvoisky and his Moscow commissar to let him use Vsevobuch's resources to support chess, which had "something that sports cannot develop, strategic ability." Since a Soviet sports Olympiad was scheduled for that autumn, Ilyin-Genevsky proposed holding concurrently an "All-Russian Chess Olympiad." He was assigned 100,000 rubles—the first time that the state (as opposed to a monarch acting in his private capacity) had offered financial support to chess.

Ilyin-Genevsky also broke new ground by starting the first chess column, in the Vsevobuch newspaper, *To the New Army*, and opening the first state-run chess club above the Vsevobuch military sports club. It provided a spacious—and, crucially, centrally heated—venue for the Olympiad, which was retrospectively designated the first Soviet championship. Despite the fact that the civil war, still raging in some regions, prevented many of the masters invited from attending, the turnout was sufficiently strong to make this a landmark in the history of Soviet chess. The tournament was won by Alexander Alekhine who, although one of the younger participants, was the only one with real international experience. Conditions were spartan: the only prizes were goods confiscated from pawnshops selling off the estates of émigrés; paper was too scarce for any official record of the event to be published. Nevertheless, the Soviet state had begun the long process of usurping the traditional role of the private patron. And it was Ilyin-

Genevsky who first envisaged the future of the game: "Chess cannot be apolitical as in capitalist countries."

Not that Ilyin-Genevsky could deliver everything that he promised. He was soon dispatched to Latvia and thence to Petrograd, while Vsevobuch was wound up after the civil war. But in August 1924 the representatives of the beleaguered Russian chess community, meeting in Petrograd, received an unexpected letter from one of the most powerful men in Soviet Russia, offering to persuade the government that it should adopt chess as an "instrument of intellectual culture." It was this man who implicated the most civilized of games in one of the worst crimes of the twentieth century.

The Soviet Union's two genuine success stories, war and chess, were connected from the outset in the person of Nikolai Vasilyevich Krylenko (1885–1938). A schoolmaster by profession, he had been a reserve lieutenant in the tsarist army, but (unusually for an officer) was also a reliable Bolshevik. Immediately after the Bolshevik *coup d'état* in 1917, Krylenko—then only thirty-two, with the military rank of ensign—was appointed Commissar of War by Lenin. Such a sudden elevation is partly explained by the paucity of talent at the apex of a prerevolutionary party of only 80,000 members. However, the real reason for Krylenko's promotion was that he had impressed Lenin during the abortive 1905 revolution and had been a loyal comrade ever since. Lenin needed a man whom he could trust to run the army—and he trusted Krylenko. The new commissar's lack of military experience was considered an advantage, because his attitude to the tsarist officer class lacked any residual loyalties. Faced with the refusal of the commander-in-chief, General Dukhonin, to arrange an immediate armistice with the Germans, Lenin issued an order to the army, in which, as Stalin later recalled, they were to "surround the generals and suspend military operations." The troops promptly "surrounded" General Dukhonin and, urged on by Commissar Krylenko, murdered him. Krylenko took over as commander-in-chief and, in effect, surrendered to the Germans. There followed the draconian Treaty of Brest-Litovsk, which stripped Russia of about half of its prewar empire, including Poland, Ukraine, Beloruosia, Transcaucasia, and the Baltic states, leaving vast regions still occupied by the German army. However, the treaty enabled the Bolsheviks to concentrate fully on the civil war into which Russia had descended. Within weeks of taking over the army of the tsars, Krylenko began its transformation into a revolutionary militia.

Thus not only was Krylenko the gravedigger of imperial Russia—more than any other individual, he created the Red Army—but he was also a Bolshevik, not a Russian patriot. Although this new "Worker-Peasant Red Army" was supposed to defend the motherland against the marauding Germans, or the "international bourgeoisie," Krylenko (following Lenin) saw the real function of the Red Army very differently. Speaking in January 1918 to the Soldiers' Section of the Third Congress of Soviets, Krylenko declared that the Red Army's foremost task was to wage "internal war" and ensure "the defence of Soviet authority." In other words, the Red Army that Krylenko had created was to be unleashed against the civilian population of Soviet Russia. And so it was. The Red Terror killed hundreds of thousands, the civil war millions. The human cost of the Bolshevik revolution is estimated by Orlando Figes in his book, *A People's Tragedy,* at 10 million, including the famine of 1921–2 that was directly caused by Lenin's policies. Others put the deaths as high as 14 million, but even these horrific figures do not embrace the full scale of the damage inflicted by the revolution. Two million of the best-educated individuals chose or were forced to emigrate. In her book, *The Philosophy Steamer: Lenin and the Exile of the Intelligentsia,* Lesley Chamberlain tells the story of some seventy mostly Christian intellectuals who were deported with their families in 1922, yet they were only the last of a mass exodus of talent that was lost to Russia forever. As we shall see, the emigration included Russia's leading chess masters. For those who remained, the demographic impact was catastrophic: survivors had a lower life expectancy due to malnutrition and disease; the fall in the birth rate translated into some 1 million fewer children; 5 percent of babies were born with syphilis; the rest suffered from stunted growth. Thousands of orphans became feral marauders; cannibalism was rife.

These terrible events also gave rise to the creation of the modern concentration camp. In *The Russian Revolution, 1899–1919,* Richard Pipes explains why the Soviet camps were utterly different in kind from those set up by the Spanish in Cuba, the Americans in the Philippines, the British in the Boer War, or the Germans in southwest Africa. These new camps were not temporary measures, employed during a colonial insurrection, but permanent instruments of totalitarian rule, directed against the country's own citizens. Conditions were deliberately harsh and the forced labor exacted from the inmates served an essential economic function in the communist system. By 1920 the communist regime had set up eighty-four concentration camps in Soviet Russia; by 1923 the number of camps had grown to 315, housing 70,000 "class enemies." Anne Applebaum, in *Gulag,* her authoritative history of the camps, explains how the communist system transformed its tsarist antecedents in the early 1920s. The Solovetsky monastery complex, sited on a group of islands in the White Sea, had incarcerated political prisoners since the seventeenth century. In the twentieth, it became the archetypal concentration camp, where the secret police exploited slave labor for reeducation and profit. Stalin's Gulag, which swelled to a population of millions during the 1930s, was merely a vast multiplication of the system created by Lenin, Trotsky—and Krylenko.

Such a state within a state was incompatible with the rule of law, so the rule of law had to go. As Richard Pipes observes, "Soviet Russia was the first state in history formally to outlaw law." Lenin abolished the entire legal system, replacing it with Revolutionary Tribunals and "People's Courts." As public prosecutor for the Revolutionary Tribunals, Krylenko was the man who put this system into practice. Although he had some legal training, within weeks of the revolution he was denouncing "bourgeois 'law,' bourgeois 'justice'" because "translated into the simple language of living reality this meant, above all, the preservation of private property." Krylenko argued that the disappearance of private property would abolish the need for law, which did not prevent but actually caused crime. Socialism would "destroy in embryo" the "psychological emotions" that led to crime. Its true result was that the citizen no longer enjoyed any protection from the state. Soviet Russia became a gigantic prison, in which no individual rights were recognized by the authorities and everyone could be conscripted at any time to perform whatever task the state required. Under socialism, wrote Krylenko, there ought to be no difference between the justice meted out by the police and by the courts; hence it was perfectly acceptable for Lenin's new secret police, the Cheka, to execute counterrevolutionaries without even bothering to bring them before the Revolutionary Tribunals. The Cheka's criterion of guilt was stated explicitly by Martin Latsis, one of its commissars, in November 1918: "We are exterminating the bourgeoisie as a class. In your investigations don't look for documents and pieces of evidence about what the defendant has done, whether in deed or in speaking or acting against Soviet authority. The first question you should ask him is what class he comes from, what are his roots, his education, his training, and his occupation."

Krylenko became head of the Commissariat of Justice and public prosecutor for the Revolutionary Tribunals in 1918, soon after the Treaty of Brest-Litovsk. When the Cheka unleashed the Red Terror later that year, Krylenko declared: "We must execute not only the guilty. Execution of the innocent will impress the masses even more." A man with such contempt for the rule of law was evidently perfectly suited to administer the Commissariat of Justice. Krylenko was made Commissar of Justice in 1931 with responsibility for Russia and, in 1937, for the whole USSR. It was entirely in accordance with communist principles that this office combined the roles of chief public prosecutor and president of the Soviet Union's supreme court. Krylenko was judge, jury, and prosecution all in one.

Throughout his bloody career, Krylenko put into practice the Bolshevik idea of replacing the rule of law by the rule of terror and under Stalin he had even more opportunities than under Lenin. He enforced the notorious "five ears law," which imposed the death penalty on any peasant who took more than five ears of wheat during the Ukrainian famine, in which up to 8 million died. He also masterminded many of the show trials of the 1920s and 1930s. With his ghoulish sense of humor, he boasted that he had abolished capital punishment, but when it was pointed out that an admiral had been sentenced to death despite the ban, Krylenko commented: "Admiral Shchastny is not being executed. He is being shot."

Krylenko was one of several old Bolsheviks —including Kalinin, Frunze, and Kuibyshev—who had the sacred privilege of playing chess with Lenin. The commissar's former secretary recalled an occasion when Lenin scolded Krylenko for his lack of sportsmanship. The Bolshevik leader insisted on three conditions before he would play: no taking moves back, no hard feelings on the part of the loser, and no gloating by the winner. Krylenko, who was a strong amateur, had the advantage but eventually lost. When he took it badly, Lenin teased him: "What's the matter with you, Nikolai Vasilyevich? You're breaking the agreement!" As a loyal comrade since the 1905 revolution, Krylenko was allowed such insubordination by Lenin—but the anecdote captures the creepily artificial atmosphere of camaraderie, with unmistakable undertones of menace, that always surrounded Soviet leaders. Lenin's show of sportsmanship was probably also a sham. The writer Maxim Gorky, who was eventually murdered in 1936 (probably on Stalin's orders), complained that Lenin became "peeved and depressed" whenever he lost at chess. Gorky, incidentally, declared that "experiments on human beings are indispensable," using class enemies who were in any case "degenerate not only on the physical but also the moral plane."

Despite his prowess as an amateur, Krylenko had nothing to do with the chess world until 1924. That year, the Muscovite faction and their trade union allies were trying to persuade the third Russian chess *syezhd*, or All-Union Congress, to complete the communist takeover of chess. Krylenko, who was on vacation, wrote to the congress demanding that chess become a political weapon in the proletarian revolution. His letter was read aloud to the delegates and he was unanimously elected to the post of chairman of the new All-Union Chess Section, attached to the Supreme Council for Physical Culture of the Russian federation. The slogans of the new body were: "Take chess to the workers!" "Chess is a powerful weapon of intellectual culture!" and "Chess must become a feature of every club and every peasant reading room!" This meant abolishing the "bourgeois" All-Russia Chess Union, which had been championed by the Petrograd circle. Samuil Vainshtein, who had kept alive the dream of an independent national organization while allowing his apartment to be used as the headquarters of Petrograd chess, saw the writing on the wall and urged his comrades to throw in their lot with the new order. He was rewarded by a key role at all the major chess events in Moscow and, despite his Jewish name, survived until the war, only to die of starvation during the Battle of Moscow. A new chess magazine was founded with the catchy title, *64*. The editor was—naturally—Krylenko, who used the journal as a platform for the socialist vision of chess. The All-Union Chess Section quickly asserted central control over chess clubs across the land and dispatched instructors the length and breadth of the USSR to disseminate to the masses propaganda on behalf of the new, ideologically charged program of chess. When, in 1928, Stalin announced the first of the Five Year Plans, Krylenko followed suit: "We must organize shock brigades of chess players and begin immediately a five year plan for chess." One can see why Krylenko did not last long as commander-in-chief of the Red Army.

It was also Krylenko's doing that the Chess Section turned down an invitation to join the French organization FIDE, the newly formed World Chess Federation. In keeping with the isolationist party line under the slogan "Socialism in one country," he insisted that "Russian chess organizations were not only not neutral politically, but indeed stood quite firmly on the platform of class warfare." Instead, the USSR joined a short-lived socialist group calling itself the Workers' Chess International, thereby excluding itself from international team events until after 1945. Krylenko did not, however, disdain all contact with the West. The 1925 Moscow international tournament was the first time that foreign masters had been invited to Soviet Russia, where hard currency was in perennially short supply. Krylenko justified the expense as part of the drive under Lenin's New Economic Plan to improve the Soviet economy by employing Western experts (such as the former German officers secretly used to train the Red Army), stating: "The Chess Section considers its duty to make use of Western chess masters for the sake of those general aims for which we employ specialists in any other branch of bourgeois culture." The idea of sending Soviet masters abroad was also gaining ground "in order through victories over bourgeois masters to increase among the proletarian masses self-respect and faith in their strength and youthful talent." The truth was that in trade union and workers' clubs, where most chess was actually played, such confidence was lacking. Drinking vodka and playing cards were more popular than chess. In 1928 the Commissar of Culture, Anatoly Lunacharsky, declared that, unlike chess, "card-playing induces a belief in fate and its power over man . . . it is a corrupting pastime which reproduces the disorganized life of bourgeois society."

Once Stalin's genocide began in earnest during the late 1920s and early '30s, with the collectivization and "dekulakization" of agriculture, followed by the Ukrainian famine, chess was mobilized too as part of the increasingly totalitarian direction of society. Krylenko closed down the last independent chess magazine and announced a new slogan: "Saturate chess with a political content!" It seems that this injunction did not cut much ice with many ordinary players. "Comrades," Krylenko told the 1931 Chess Congress,

> it is no secret from anyone, it was reported in the press in my article "Politics and Chess" that these tendencies not only exist, but that they are very much alive and will probably continue to live. These tendencies were graphically expressed in the formula propounded by an anonymous contributor to an enquiry held by the magazine *Shakhmatnyi listok:* "Enough of all these Krylenkos." This formula, suggested by the anonymous author, expressed very well the concealed tendency, the concealed desires and the concealed aims of a certain group in our chess organizations: enough of politics, we do not need politics, let us play chess in peace.

Warming to his theme, Krylenko proceeded to threaten those who echoed his anonymous critic: "Anyone who now states that questions of politics must be separated from questions of general cultural work and from the life of our organizations is consciously taking up a political position in opposition to us and is our class enemy."

At the time Krylenko was powerful enough to have almost anybody arrested and dispatched to the Gulag, or even shot, but this vehement new drive to raise the ideological consciousness of the chess movement (which by 1934 numbered half a million registered players) was double-edged. When Stalin decided to liquidate the older Bolsheviks in the party, it was easy to accuse those in charge of failing to fulfill the goal of politicization. The All-Union Chess Section was now attached to the Sports Committee, which in turn answered to the Council of Ministers. In return for their mushrooming multimillion-ruble budget, chess masters and bureaucrats were exposed to the same risks as the rest of Stalin's apparat. When the time came, they, like millions of others, were caught up in the Great Terror.

In reality, the terror had never stopped. Krylenko himself conducted many of the show trials of "wreckers" during the late 1920s, while in 1930–31 it was the turn of the Mensheviks. Among the collateral victims of this persecution was the chairman of the All-Union Association of Chess Problem and Study Lovers, Lazar Zalkind, a statistician who composed many exquisite endgame studies. Although many problemists, such as the writer Vladimir Nabokov, had joined the emigration, some of the finest composers of chess problems and endgame studies in the world were among the 250-odd members of this harmless association, including Alexey Troitsky, who had been granted official recognition as an "art worker" by the Kremlin. In 1931 Krylenko had Zalkind sentenced to eight years in prison as a "renegade and traitor to the working class," adding insult to injury by forcing his fellow composers to denounce their friend in his journal, 64. Although Zalkind was due to be released in 1938, he was given another five-year sentence in a harsher camp. When he was released in 1943, he was told of his son's death at the front, but was still not allowed to return home. He died two years later.

Meanwhile, the chess problemists' association was closed down —a victim of guilt by association. Chess composers were now marked men. In 1937 Mikhail Platov, who together with his brother Vasily had composed one of Lenin's favorite endgame studies back in 1909, was overheard criticizing Stalin. Sentenced to ten years in one of the harshest camps in the Arctic, Platov never returned. The same fate befell another composer, Arvid Kubbel, whose Baltic-German background might have doomed him even if he had not committed the cardinal sin of publishing his endgame studies in foreign journals. So terrified was his more famous brother, Leonid, that he tried to airbrush Arvid out of history by omitting his name from a book about Soviet study composers. Even his arrest was kept secret, and the fiction was maintained that he, like his brother and the great Troitsky, had starved to death in the siege of Leningrad. Arvid Kubbel had actually died of nephritis in a Siberian camp, but not until the *glasnost* era could this fact be admitted.

It was in 1934, with the assassination (almost certainly ordered by Stalin) of the Leningrad party boss Sergei Kirov, that the Terror began to extend much more widely and deeply into Soviet society. Stalin gave the NKVD, as the secret police were now called, unlimited powers to arrest, try, and execute "enemies of the people." Between 1937 and 1939, torture was also used on a large scale—it continued sporadically throughout the Soviet era—on the orders of Stalin, who considered "physical pressure" to be a "totally correct and humane method" of extracting confessions that would unmask other conspirators. The big show trials of Zinoviev and Kamenev, Stalin's old rivals, took place in August 1936, shortly after the Moscow tournament, which was undoubtedly intended as a distraction from the waves of mass arrests that preceded the trial.

As Commissar of Justice, Krylenko was at the center of the witch-hunt. Occasionally he could be persuaded to intercede with the NKVD. Nevertheless, many chess players were among the hundreds of thousands who vanished without a trace, either dragged before a firing squad or consigned to the Gulag. Although some were posthumously "rehabilitated" in the Khrushchev era, their precise fate remained a mystery until *glasnost* in the late 1980s, when Sergei Grodzensky traced the fate of a few of them in a series of articles for—appropriately enough—Krylenko's chess journal, *64*. They included Konstantin Shukevich-Tretyakov, one of the leading organizers in Belorussia, who was sentenced in 1938 to five years in a camp but died in 1942 before he could be released. The fact that this active communist had named his daughter "Revolution" offered him no protection. Mikhail Barulin, one of the leading problemists of the day, was denounced for cracking an "anti-Soviet" joke in 1941. Two years later the case against him was dropped for lack of evidence, but by then he had succumbed to the harsh conditions in prison. The wheels of Soviet justice could grind exceeding slow, but they speeded up where plots against Stalin by "Trotskyite Fascists" were concerned. The 1936 trial of Pyotr Izmailov, a promising scientist and Soviet championship finalist, lasted just twenty minutes. He was shot immediately afterward and his wife sentenced to eight years in a Siberian camp. The court knew that both were innocent, as their rehabilitation two decades later revealed.

Several of the victims were among world champion Mikhail Botvinnik's rivals. Mikhail Shebarshin, one of his contemporaries in Leningrad, was charged with "attempting to organize a counterrevolutionary mutiny" in 1930. He was never heard of again. Another of the future champion's rivals was Nikolai Salmin, who was arrested and shot in 1936. The best-documented case is that of Fyodor Bohatyrchuk, who lived to tell his tale. Although from an older generation, the Ukrainian Bohatyrchuk was good enough to win the Soviet championship and to beat Botvinnik in the penultimate round of the 1935 Moscow international, thereby depriving him of undivided first place. This game also had consequences for the victor. In 1937 Bohatyrchuk was accused of embezzling money intended to cover expenses for Capablanca and Lasker during their visits to Kiev. Interrogated by the NKVD, he denied the charge convincingly, but the investigator was more interested in the chess master's "poor political record." He demanded to know why Bohatyrchuk had won the game at the 1935 Moscow international even though "you knew the huge significance for the prestige of the USSR that Botvinnik's receipt of sole first prize would have." It must have required considerable presence of mind for Bohatyrchuk to respond as he did, knowing that his life depended on it: "I am first a sportsman and not a politician, and therefore I'm interested in play, not points." His masterstroke was to quote Krylenko, who had written the tournament book on the 1936 Moscow international, in which he praised Soviet sportsmanship and illustrated the point by reference to Bohatyrchuk. The mention of Krylenko worked, and persuaded the interrogator to release him.

This terrifying experience was enough to disillusion Bohatyrchuk once and for all—although the Ukrainian famine had no doubt already opened his eyes to Stalin's despotism. When his native Kiev fell to the Germans in 1941, Bohatyrchuk functioned as a member of the city council during the occupation. According to Boris Spassky, Bohatyrchuk used his influence to save "hundreds" from the Nazis, but he knew that in Soviet eyes he was a collabo- rator. So when the Red Army recaptured Kiev in 1943, Bohatyr- chuk followed the retreating Germans. A doctor, he volunteered for the "Russian Liberation Army" led by General Vlasov, which fought on the German side, and he even played in one of the last chess tournaments organized in occupied Poland by the chess- crazy governor, Hans Frank. Stationed near Prague in the last days of the war, Vlasov's units actually fought the German SS in de- fense of the Czech uprising, but when the Red Army arrived many of the collaborators were shot on sight. Bohatyrchuk escaped to the West, ending his days in Canada, but Vlasov and his senior offi- cers were repatriated, tortured, and executed as traitors. Vlasov, who was eventually strung up with piano wire from a hook driven into the base of his skull, told his interrogators: "In time, the peo- ple will remember us with warmth." This did not, at any rate, in- clude the old Stalinists: Spassky recalled that Botvinnik's reaction to a postcard from his old rival Bohatyrchuk, by this time in Can- ada, was to declare: "I would personally hang this man in the cen- ter of Kiev."

"Diaspora nationalities" were always more likely to fall victim to the Terror; in 1937–8 alone, some 335,000 Soviet citizens with foreign connections were convicted by the NKVD. One of them was Vladimir Petrov. An ethnic Russian citizen of Latvia, he was almost as bright a star in the chess firmament as his rival from the neighboring Baltic state of Estonia, Paul Keres. In a very strong tournament at Kemeri in 1937, Petrov tied for first with Salo Flohr and Samuel Reshevsky, ahead of Alekhine and Keres. But in 1940 Stalin occupied the Baltic states, and Petrov became a Soviet citi- zen. A fine linguist, he was recruited by the Tass news agency when the Germans invaded, but his Latvian background, knowl- edge of foreign languages, and overseas connections made him vul- nerable to accusations of espionage. In the summer of 1942 he dis- appeared. His fate became known only many years later. Arrested by the NKVD and held at their headquarters, the Lubyanka, Petrov was grilled about the chess tournaments that he had attended in Latin America. Told not to hide anything, he replied almost flippantly: "Why should I hide?" He was sentenced to ten years, but died after only one. Not until 1989 did the KGB admit the truth.

Krylenko was not spared either. In the end, it was his devotion to chess that brought down the Commissar of Justice. Like other old Bolsheviks, he had become an obstacle to the rapid advancement of a new, unquestioningly obedient generation. His moment of truth came suddenly in 1937 at a meeting of the Supreme Soviet — Stalin's rubber-stamp parliament — when a deputy denounced him, evidently at Stalin's instigation. The commissar, it was said, was too preoccupied with chess. In fear for his life, Krylenko retreated to his office, where he was seen to be drinking himself into oblivion, "eyes empty and glassy," with "bottles everywhere, playing chess." Although he was relieved to get a friendly call from Stalin himself, the very next day the NKVD came to arrest him. His trial, like those of so many of his victims, was a secret and perfunctory affair lasting only twenty minutes. He died in prison in July 1938, where he was almost certainly shot.

The All-Union Chess Section issued a decree "on cleansing and purging the chess organization of class enemies and corrupt elements and on raising the level of political literacy among highly graded players and increasing their participation in socio-political life." It seemed that Krylenko's slogan, "Saturate chess with a political content," had not gone far enough. His sister, who had emigrated to the United States and married the writer Max Eastman, commented: "I suppose chess-playing is now considered [to be] wrecking the government." This family connection with an American friend of Trotsky and a critic of Stalin would alone have been sufficient to condemn any Soviet citizen. Krylenko was not only "liquidated" but airbrushed out of history. The October 1937 issue of the magazine *Shakhmaty v SSSR* carried an article by Krylenko, alongside pictures of Lenin and Stalin. Halfway through the printing, the edition had to be pulped, and most copies appeared minus any mention of Krylenko. It was as if the man who had been the virtual dictator of Soviet chess for thirteen years had never existed. Only in the Brezhnev era was the old minister rehabilitated. In 1977 an annual Krylenko Memorial junior team tournament commemorated the man who had forced chess into the heart of Soviet life, for better and for worse.

But Krylenko deserved the accolade of a memorial tournament far less than Ilyin-Genevsky. His moment of glory came when he defeated Capablanca in the 1925 Moscow tournament, with a superb queen sacrifice—the first time that a Soviet player won a game against a reigning world champion. Ilyin-Genevsky also wrote several chess books and edited the journal *Shakhmaty v SSSR*. All the official histories agree that he was killed by Nazi shelling while trying to flee from Leningrad across Lake Lagoda in December 1941. However, the authoritative *Modern Encyclopedia of Russian and Soviet History* has a different version: Ilyin-Genevsky, it states, "was arrested by the secret police during the purges and died in prison in 1941."

This uncertainty is emblematic of the whole history of the Soviet Union and, indeed, of post-Soviet Russia too. What one might call the Soviet uncertainty principle has an analogy with Heisenberg's theory of quantum mechanics. The more certain any "fact" about Soviet history seems, the less clear are its causes, consequences, and motivations. We have little reason to doubt the "fact," attested by magazines, histories, and other reference books, that the Nazis killed Ilyin-Genevsky. Yet the more that this account is repeated, the more we notice that he was exactly the kind of party official who was most at risk in the Terror. Stalin was pitiless in his vendetta against his old comrades. It would be an irony entirely in keeping with the indeterminate, perverse logic of Soviet communism if the revolution had indeed devoured, among tens of millions of others, the founder of Soviet chess.

4

THE OPIUM OF
THE INTELLECTUALS

I N THE PERSON OF KRYLENKO, Soviet chess was inextricably linked to the Great Terror. Yet chess was indubitably popular in the Bolshevik state almost from the outset. The mass popularity of the game that was awakened by the first great Soviet tournament, at Moscow in 1925, is recorded in *Chess Fever*, a delightful silent film that gives no hint of the monsters already brought forth by Russia's sleep of reason. José Raúl Capablanca, the Cuban world champion, makes a cameo appearance in this tale of a young man so obsessed by chess that he neglects his girlfriend and every other area of his life.

The hundreds of thousands of young chess pioneers from whose cadres the first generation of Soviet masters emerged were similarly entranced and distracted from the nightmarish reality that would become the Gulag Archipelago. In a state where the Church was brutally suppressed, it was not religion but chess that became the opium of the people. Chess had always been a passion of the Russian intelligentsia. It was seen as more rational and hence progressive than games of chance, which encouraged fatalism.

The model for all Russian writers, Alexander Pushkin, loved cards no less than chess, as his story *The Queen of Spades* testifies. It was, however, chess that he played throughout that cold winter's night in 1837 before his fatal duel with Baron Georges-Charles d'Anthès, the young French exile who had pursued his flirtatious wife, Natalya, while secretly attached to the homosexual Dutch ambassador. Pushkin was as impetuous in chess as in life, but he thanked Natalya for learning chess — "an absolute necessity in any well-organized family."

Pushkin, however, was much less serious about chess than his two great contemporaries, Tolstoy and Turgenev. These two played each other from the age of fifteen, and both were strong players. Tolstoy was the more erratic — in his diary he wrote: "One's main concern should not be to win at all costs, but to go in for interesting combinations" — yet during the siege of Sebastopol he could hold his own against Prince Urusov, who was one of the few players of master strength in mid-nineteenth-century Russia. Even in his eighties, Tolstoy was still formidable. As for Turgenev, he was probably even better. While living in Paris during the early 1860s he came second in a strong tournament at the Café de la Régence and narrowly lost a six-game match against the Polish master, Maczuski. The connection of chess and literature persisted into the twentieth century, in the form of devotion to the game by such luminaries as Maxim Gorky, Vladimir Nabokov, and Boris Pasternak.

The same passion for chess gripped Russian musicians, from Rimsky-Korsakov, Mussorgsky, and Borodin to the two great composers of the communist era, Sergei Prokofiev and Dmitri Shostakovich. The latter claimed to be attracted to the mysterious combination of art and science in chess, although chess was much more central to Prokofiev's intellectual life — indeed, Stravinsky maliciously said of him that "his mind is truly engaged only when playing chess." He was one of the few émigrés who returned from the West, with a good deal of encouragement from the Soviet authorities. In 1934 he went back to Russia to work on his ballet

Romeo and Juliet. It was no accident that he chose the closing ceremony of the 1935 Moscow international tournament for the première of a new piano composition (perhaps the *Pieces for Children*), which he performed himself. The composer was gripped by both the 1935 and 1936 tournaments, exclaiming: "I'm used to performing as an artist but now I'm a spectator." The enthusiasm for chess that swept Moscow at that time may have compensated for the failure of his ballet and influenced his decision to settle permanently in the Soviet Union in 1936. Prokofiev, however, was a very strong player, good enough to beat Lasker ("the Mozart of chess"), Capablanca ("the Bach"), and Akiba Rubinstein in simultaneous exhibitions, although he lost to Alekhine. The Polish grandmaster, Savielly Tartakower, played Prokofiev and found him to be of master strength. Even during the war, Prokofiev came to watch Botvinnik play Vasily Smyslov—a fine baritone who almost became a professional singer—in the 1943 Moscow championship. Only Botvinnik was unimpressed, perhaps because he rightly suspected that Prokofiev was not much of a communist, dismissing the composer as a prerevolutionary chess romantic who loved to play the King's Gambit. Curiously, Prokofiev's music was criticized by Stalin as too modernist.

Nor was chess an addiction only of composers. Many of the best chess-playing musicians—the pianist Arthur Rubinstein, the violinist Mischa Elman, and the cellist Gregor Piatigorsky—emigrated after the revolution. Of those who remained, David Oistrakh, the violinist, was good enough to take a simultaneous game from Emanuel Lasker. In 1940 the virtuoso served as arbiter at the last Soviet championship before the Nazi invasion. Sviatoslav Richter, the greatest Russian pianist who chose to live under communism, was another chess fanatic. Likewise Mark Taimanov, the grandmaster and Soviet champion, pursued a parallel career as a concert pianist.

The popularity of chess among intellectuals in communist Russia may be explained simply: chess was one of very few officially sanctioned areas of intellectual freedom. Unlike art, music, or literature, chess was a creative pursuit that did not have to be conducted according to rules and theories laid down by the authorities, from which any deviation was punishable by a term in a labor camp or worse. The abstract, impractical nature of chess protected its practitioners from the interference suffered by scientists, who were forced to follow charlatans such as Trofim Lysenko, or by musicians such as Shostakovich and Prokofiev, who practiced self-censorship but still fell foul of Stalin. The ubiquitous presence of the secret police and their informers, which pervades novels such as Mikhail Bulgakov's *The Master and Margarita*, left individuals hardly any private space. Under the inescapable eye of Stalin, magnified by an unprecedented apparatus of control and observation, not only deviation from the party line, but mere contact with the bourgeois world—foreign books, foreign money, and especially foreign people—was tantamount to counterrevolutionary conspiracy. Chess, with its lively subculture of clubs and teams, could be a refuge from the omniscient, omnipotent Soviet state. Chess was a partial exception to institutionalized xenophobia: many chess players, amateurs as well as masters, belonged to the "inner emigration."

Among these amateurs was Boris Pasternak, whose love of chess was second only to his devotion to literature. Like Prokofiev, he was an enthusiastic spectator at the great Moscow tournaments of 1935 and 1936. A surviving game played by Pasternak in 1947 shows that he was a strong amateur, with a liking for the defense pioneered by the Russian émigré, Alexander Alekhine. Unlike Nabokov, who preferred composing chess problems to actual play, the author of *Dr. Zhivago* seems to have been a romantic in chess as in life. It was the psychodrama of cerebral struggle that attracted him to chess. The quixotic temperament that characterized both Pasternak's poetry and his chess also emboldened him to take on Stalin himself.

Pasternak was braver than most Soviet writers, who earned Stalin's contempt by writing ingratiating letters to him. Yet even Pasternak was intimidated by Stalin. After the poet Osip Mandelstam had been arrested in May 1934 for writing a poem denouncing Stalin, Pasternak tried to intercede for his friend—a gesture fraught with peril. Two months later, the telephone rang in the communal apartment where the Pasternaks lived. It was Poskrebyshev, Stalin's *chef de cabinet.* He warned the poet, who was surrounded by noisy children, to expect a call from Stalin. When the boss himself came on the line, it was to reassure Pasternak that Mandelstam was "a genius."

"Yes, but that's not the point," ventured Pasternak.

"What is the point, then?" Stalin fired back.

Pasternak was nonplussed. "It would be good if we could meet for a talk," he stuttered.

"What about?" queried Stalin.

"About life and death," replied Pasternak desperately.

Stalin hung up. When Pasternak tried to call back, Stalin refused to take the call. Later he rang Molotov and gloated over the failure of Pasternak to defend his fellow writer more effectively. Although Mandelstam had more powerful friends, such as Nikolai Bukharin, he was first tortured, then exiled, then rearrested, and finally died in a Siberian camp in 1938. However, when the secret police proposed to arrest Pasternak too, Stalin told them: "Leave that cloud-dweller in peace."

After Stalin's death, Pasternak was back in favor and an edition of his collected poetry was prepared. As an introduction to this volume, which never appeared, he wrote his *Essay in Autobiography,* which stops in 1917. A passage from the epilogue eloquently evokes the experience of three generations of Russians—their nameless dread of the legalized terror exercised in their name—encoded in words to which the censor could not object. "To take it further would be immeasurably difficult," he concluded.

> If I went on with it . . . I would have to speak of years and circumstances, of people and of destinies contained within the framework of the revolution. Of a world of aims and aspirations, problems and achievements previously unknown, and of a new restraint, a new severity and new trials which it imposed

on human personality, pride, honor, industry and endurance. This world, unique and not to be compared with any other, has now withdrawn into the distance of memory; it looms on the horizon like mountains seen from a plain, or like a distant city smoking in its night glow. To write of it one should have to write in such a way as to make the hair rise and the heart falter.

Invoking the Russian classics, Pasternak added that it would be "base and shameless" to write of the communist era less overwhelmingly than Gogol and Dostoyevsky. His conclusion—"We are still far from this way of writing"—is almost as true today as it was half a century ago, with the solitary, towering, but reclusive exception of Solzhenitsyn. Despite the lifting at least of official censorship, in the postcommunist era no major writer has yet emerged equal to the task of describing, even in retrospect, the unspeakable ordeal of seven decades of communism. The most fatal form of censorship is self-censorship.

BY FURNISHING THE Soviet dictatorship with a safety valve for the intelligentsia and its longing for freedom, chess, too, could be a tool of totalitarianism. Soviet chess was both a microcosm of life in a collectivist society, and—as a last refuge of the free spirit— its antithesis. In the eyes of Lenin, Stalin, and their successors, chess was seen as a demonstration of dialectical materialism. As C. H. O'D. Alexander, a leading British master, civil servant, and cryptographer at Bletchley Park, later wrote: "Chess [for the Soviets] was a dialectical game illustrating, in its resolution of conflicts, Marxist modes of thought. By encouraging independent thinking, chess could also be seen as anti-religious." However, Alexander added, it was "as safe from 'dangerous thoughts' as any intellectual activity can be." Chess was deemed to be classless, untainted by bourgeois ideology, and hence suitable to teach socialist values to the new proletarian cadres.

From the outset, Soviet scientists paid a lot of attention to the psychology of chess. Three experimental psychologists carried out laboratory tests on the masters assembled for the 1925 Moscow tournament. According to their influential 1926 study, chess was "a powerful method of self-discipline and self-development, which brings benefit not only to those who are capable of becoming masters, but also to those who do not possess such gifts; chess furthers the development of educationally valuable qualities." The qualities that Soviet psychologists attributed to chess masters were also part of the makeup of the idealized Soviet man: strong nerves, self-control, self-confidence, a disciplined will, disciplined emotions, and a highly active intellect.

In 1961 the Defense Minister Marshal Malinovsky described the role of chess in the Red Army, which had held annual championships since Krylenko's day and by then boasted over 2,000 masters and other strong players: "We in the armed forces value chess highly because it disciplines a man, helps to increase strength of will and powers of endurance, develops memory and quick-wittedness and teaches logical thinking." The irony is that these qualities were all essential weapons in the dissident's psychological arsenal, too. In chess there is no place for conformism, blind obedience to authority, or the dissembling and hypocrisy so typical of those who live under despotism.

5

THE ÉMIGRÉS

T HE FATE OF EMANUEL LASKER, who had been world chess champion from 1894 to 1921, illustrates the impact of the European catastrophe on one individual, and the way in which the wider world was reflected in the microcosm of chess.

Emanuel Lasker was born in 1868 as the son of a poor Jewish cantor from the German–Polish borderlands. He rose to become perhaps the most impressive personality in the whole history of chess. More successfully than his revered predecessor, Wilhelm Steinitz, who had died in abject poverty, Lasker achieved financial independence through journalism and lecturing, while his eminence enabled him to force organizers into providing adequate remuneration and playing conditions for international chess players. He campaigned without success for the introduction of copyright on chess games, to force publishers and newspapers to pay masters for reproducing the fruits of their labor.

As world champion, Lasker defended his title in matches against Wilhelm Steinitz, Frank Marshall, Siegbert Tarrasch, David Janowski, and Carl Schlechter. Like Steinitz before him, he treated the title as his personal property. Any master who had won at least one major international tournament was in theory welcome to mount a challenge if he could raise the necessary stake money. There was no qualifying procedure for the simple reason that there was no international organization to oversee it. This meant that the strongest players did not necessarily get a chance to challenge Lasker, while weaker players with rich backers might get a second opportunity to do so. Long periods passed without a title match, during which Lasker virtually gave up chess in favor of mathematics or philosophy. However, he was canny enough to bolster his claim to genuine supremacy by competing in the strongest tournaments that took place during the twenty-seven years of his tenure, and winning most of them: Nuremberg 1896; London 1899; Paris 1900; and the St. Petersburg tournaments of 1896, 1909, and 1914.

When in 1921 Lasker lost the world championship to his younger rival, José Raúl Capablanca, having offered to resign his title beforehand, it was assumed that his career was over. Yet he had his revenge at the 1924 New York tournament where, at the age of fifty-six, he outstripped not only Capablanca but the entire younger generation of "Hypermodern" grandmasters in a long and exhausting contest.

The Hypermodern school of chess was a romantic reaction against the classicism of the prewar generation and it coincided in the 1920s with the high noon of modernism, an aesthetic revolution, which for its acolytes and patrons served as a substitute for the political one. Iconoclasm in art and chess were combined in the person of Marcel Duchamp, who played well enough to represent France alongside the world champion, the émigré Russian Alexander Alekhine, in four Olympiads between 1928 and 1933.

At about the same time that he pioneered the conceptual art that would virtually eliminate all other art forms by the end of the twentieth century, Duchamp became utterly obsessed with chess. His friend Man Ray described how this obsession wrecked

Duchamp's first marriage: "Duchamp spent most of the one week they lived together studying chess problems, and his bride, in desperate retaliation for no one night while he was asleep and glued the chess pieces to the board. They were divorced three months later."

What elevated Lasker above the rest of his contemporaries was not merely his unique success over the board. He was also a mathematician of the highest caliber, whose celebrated paper, "On the Theory of Modules and Ideals," postulated the "primary ideal," one of the basic concepts of modern algebra. It appeared in 1905, the same year as Albert Einstein's theory of relativity, although it was not in Berlin but many years later, in exile in America, that Einstein and Lasker formed a friendship. In his foreword to Hannak's biography of Lasker, Einstein pays tribute to "one of the most interesting people I came to know in my later life." Einstein saw Lasker as a tragic figure:

> What he really yearned for was some scientific understanding and that beauty peculiar to the process of logical creation, a beauty from whose magic spell no one can escape who has ever felt even its slightest influence. Spinoza's material life and economic independence were based on the grinding of lenses; in Lasker's life chess played a similar part. But Spinoza was luckier, for his business was such as to leave his mind free and independent; whereas master chess grips its exponent, shackling the mind and brain, so that the inner freedom and independence of even the strongest character cannot remain unaffected. This I became aware of whenever I talked to Lasker or read one of his philosophical books.

A poet and inventor, Lasker was also a profound, if sometimes utopian, philosophical and social thinker. His first philosophical essay of 1906, *Struggle,* discovered the meaning of life in conflict, which he tried to reduce to a system, calling it "machology." This was followed by *The Comprehension of the Universe* (1913) and *The Philosophy of the Unattainable* (1918). These books are now forgotten, but Lasker's works on the theory of games, above all his *Manual of Chess*, are still classics.

Lasker believed passionately that, while chess was "only a game" and thus intrinsically trivial, it inculcated principles that were of inestimable value: "Chess, from its very inception, has had coherence with Life." In another book, the primer *How to Play Chess*, Lasker explained that the limitation of chess as a paradigm lay in its lack of grading in the final result. "Loss. Draw. Win. This is the scale of success in chess. Life is infinitely more varied. Life goes on, it knows no permanent defeat, nor permanent victory." But chess, properly taught, provided an education in self-reliance, enabling the student "to find a suitable mean between humble acceptance of the dicta of authority and overbearing self-assertion. Chess provides you with such opportunities, because you can prove propositions in chess, if need be by checkmating your opponent, whereas in other fields of endeavor it is difficult for you to obtain a hearing or to prove your case."

In his "Final Reflections on Education in Chess," appended to the *Manual*, Lasker sought to demonstrate that it was perfectly possible to teach chess with the utmost economy of means; he calculated that it would take a young person, ignorant of chess and with no natural talent, only two hundred hours to achieve the level of a strong player. He deplored the incredible waste of energy by millions whose play nonetheless remained mediocre: "Our efforts in chess attain only a hundredth of one per cent of their rightful result." Lasker believed that the inherent uncertainty of the game forced players to rely on judgment rather than memory. "Chess must not be memorized, simply because it is not important enough," declared the champion who had reigned supreme for longer than any other before or since. "Memory is too valuable to be stocked with trifles. Of my fifty-seven years I have applied at least thirty to forgetting most of what I had learned or read, and since I succeeded in this I have acquired a certain ease and cheer which I should never again like to be without." Nothing, he claimed, should be memorized except methods, which are infinitely plastic and which eventually generate rules. For the sake of a "harmonious life," he believed, the theory of Steinitz must be applied.

Lasker's predecessor as world champion, Wilhelm Steinitz, was no philosopher, but Lasker discerned in his method "a wonderful conception, but beyond practical chess." This theory consisted in the notion of a "balanced position," a pale reflection of the "true balance that exists in the infinite domain of Life." Lasker elevated Steinitz's practical maxim—that only when the balance has been disturbed could the player with the advantage mount a successful attack—to a moral imperative. Chess thus became, for Lasker, a school of both ethics and aesthetics: "He only will grow to be an artist who obeys the command." The coherence of chess with life meant, for Lasker, belated recognition of his work beyond the narrow realm of the sixty-four squares: "The theory of struggle, divined by men like Machiavelli, Napoleon, Clausewitz, molded by Steinitz in accurate detail for the chessboard, longingly desired by some philosophers, established by myself in universal validity, therefore philosophically, will some day regulate the life of man." Lasker did not see his own time as a golden age, but hoped that chess stood on the threshold of a new and visionary era: "There are creative masters but the organization of the chess world does not produce competition between them . . . The future therefore belongs to the creative master and the organization which works in unison with him."

It would be hard to imagine a sharper contrast than that between the monomaniacal revolutionary types who burst on to the world stage during this period and the older representatives of the educated bourgeoisie. Yet the nemesis of the mid-twentieth century overtook even Emanuel Lasker, this idealistic savant and seer. A game that seemed to exist on a sublime plane, far removed from politics and ideology, proved not to be immune to either.

From the outset, gaining Lasker's support was important to the Soviet chess pioneers. In 1924, long before chess had been allotted its privileged role, Lasker was persuaded to visit the Soviet Union.

According to the American historian of Soviet chess, Andrew Soltis, "the former world champion's arrival at Petrograd's Moscow Station, greeted by a delegation of prominent players and academicians, was hailed as the breaking of a capitalist boycott." Lasker was among the first of many Western intellectuals to be initially taken in by the façade of revolutionary Russia. He wrote later to *Izvestia* that he had received "the clear impression of something big, gratifying and strong" in the Bolshevik revolution. It is thus hardly surprising that Lasker was later persuaded to play in Soviet tournaments. It seemed almost as if the grand old man of chess was passing on the baton to the society that claimed to share his vision of the game and its potential value for the society of the future. In reality, however, a gulf separated the humane, if naively utopian, individualism of Lasker from the Soviet collectivization of chess as an instrument of the state.

When the Nazis came to power, Lasker (by then in his sixties and long since retired from chess) immediately prepared to emigrate from Germany. He was, in the first place, a Jew, and his eminence served only to attract hostile attention. His philosophical works had made him a friend of Walter Rathenau, the Foreign Minister who was murdered by anti-Semites; his sister-in-law was the celebrated Jewish poet Else Lasker-Schuler, while his wife, Martha, was a distinguished journalist for satirical journals that were quickly proscribed in the Third Reich. The Laskers' country house at Thyrow, where he had built a laboratory, their Berlin flat, and their savings were all confiscated. Like thousands of other German Jews, they were compelled to lead a nomadic existence in exile. Settling at first in England, Lasker was forced to return to professional chess in his mid-sixties, and at major tournaments in Zurich, Moscow, and Nottingham he held his own with the greatest masters of the younger generation.

At the second Moscow international tournament of 1935 he achieved third place, only half a point behind the joint winners Botvinnik and Flohr — an incredible result for a man of sixty-seven. Afterwards Lasker was invited to stay on in the Soviet capital, working on mathematical research and attached to the Academy of Sciences. During the next two years, spent mainly in Moscow but with the freedom to come and go, Lasker was feted by the party apparatus and seems to have been left to pursue his studies. He was still playing chess at the highest level. In the third Moscow international of 1936, Lasker was still in second place after the first half of the double round tournament, equal with Botvinnik and just behind Capablanca. At sixty-eight, though, he could not withstand the punishing seven-hour sessions. In the second half of the tournament he collapsed, ending in sixth place—the first time in half a century that he had not been among the prizewinners. At the even more arduous tournament in Nottingham later that year, however, Lasker bounced back. He was by far the oldest of the five past, present, and future world champions to take part, who competed against the leading grandmasters of the day. Yet Lasker finished only 1.5 points behind the winners, Capablanca and Botvinnik, having defeated the then current world champion, Max Euwe. In the history of chess, only Lasker's predecessor Steinitz had attempted such a feat, but his fate was hardly an auspicious precedent: crushed by the younger generation, he had died insane, babbling about having played a game against God by telephone. In the post-1945 era, only Viktor Korchnoi and perhaps Vasily Smyslov could compare with Lasker by holding their own against the world's best, well into their sixties.

Emanuel Lasker's residence in Moscow proved short-lived. In 1937 he took his wife on a visit to the United States, from which they told the Soviet authorities that they intended to return. However, they never did so, settling instead in New York, where Lasker died four years later. His wife, Martha, explained the change on health grounds, claiming that her doctors had forbidden her to take long journeys, but there were also political reasons for the decision to emigrate yet again. By 1937 Lasker could not have been oblivious to Stalin's Great Terror, which was unfolding around him, and the danger that this might represent for foreigners, especially stateless Jewish exiles from Nazi Germany. Lasker's five-act verse drama, *Of the History of Man*, which was produced in Berlin in 1925, and his late works of social philosophy, *The World View of the Player* and *The Community of the Future* (1940), were as ideologically incompatible with communism as they were with national socialism.

Moreover, Lasker was outspoken—dangerously so. During a tour of Soviet cities after the Moscow tournament in 1935, Lasker went to Kiev, where he was asked for his impressions by the vice-chairman of the Ukrainian council of commissars. "There are many things that I like about the USSR," Lasker replied, "but I do not understand why words appear to have a different meaning here from the rest of the world. For example," he said, "the hot tap in my hotel room produces cold water. And when it says 'chicken' on the menu, what I am served turns out to be pork." Even such apparently mild criticisms of living conditions in Ukraine were political dynamite at a time when the government had successfully concealed one of the worst famines of modern history. Lasker's coded remarks would have been enough to doom an ordinary Soviet citizen—and even foreign academics were not immune from the Terror.

Most of the Lasker family had stayed behind in Germany, where they ultimately perished in the Holocaust. Only his niece, Anita Lasker Wallfisch, now an eminent cellist who survived Auschwitz by playing in the women's orchestra, lived to tell her story. "Life was completely arbitrary," she told a *Guardian* interviewer in 2005. It so happened that when she arrived at Auschwitz, expecting to die, the orchestra had no cellist. "You'll be saved," she was told by a fellow prisoner—and she was, even after she and her sister Renate were moved to Belsen at the end of the war, where they almost starved to death. Liberated by the British army, for which they got jobs as interpreters, both sisters were able to begin their lives again in England.

In the lives and literature of its devotees, chess illustrates rather well the metamorphosis from freedom to totalitarianism. In the West, the significance of what had happened in Russia since

1917 was not lost on those who longed for a similar apocalypse. The turmoil of war and peace, revolution and counterrevolution seemed to many to toll the death knell for the educated bourgeoisie, upon which the avant-garde, however dismissively, was parasitical. There was even an equivalent of this revolutionary art in chess. By 1929 the speculative bubble of European prosperity had burst, causing collateral damage, not only to the arts and sciences, but also to chess. Like most intellectual endeavors, it turned out that chess was vulnerable to economics. The conditions in which high culture can flourish are rare. Western civilization has sustained this environment over many centuries, but the period of world war, from 1914 to 1945, came close to annihilating those conditions in central Europe. The subculture of chess, like countless exotic blooms in that intellectual hothouse, was uprooted, blasted, and blighted by the ensuing blizzard of dictatorship.

The precarious but creative role of chess in the laissez-faire culture of pre-1914 Europe gave way to a less marginal but much more sinister function in the Soviet system. As the recreation of the revolution, chess ceased to be a private activity and instead was taken over by the all-embracing state. This led to a vast aggrandizement in the scale and status of chess, but also to a no less striking transformation of its practitioners. The "rigorist" lifestyle of the revolutionary fanatic was applied to professions that had nothing to do with politics, including chess. Even this most abstract of pursuits was saturated with dialectical materialism, an ideology that claimed to be applicable to absolutely anything. Communism did not only imply state control—it was also a method of self-control. Party discipline was internalized, and chess was a kind of mental exercise for the cadres. Totalitarian systems had not taken much interest in such psychological disciplines before; Fascists and Nazis were more preoccupied with physical prowess. The Nazis also staged chess tournaments during the Second World War, but they never followed the Soviet example by cultivating chess as a method of demonstrating intellectual superiority. In the vast laboratory that was the Soviet Union, chess was among the least sanguinary experiments. It was also unusual in that its human products, the new men, could be compared directly and objectively with their counterparts abroad.

Lasker, by exchanging Hitler's Germany for Stalin's Russia, had by implication opted to take part in this experiment. Yet by abandoning his privileged position in Moscow in favor of all the uncertainties of Roosevelt's America, he had delivered his verdict—if not on the experiment itself, then at least on those who were carrying it out. His verdict was damning. Lasker could no more survive in the suffocating atmosphere of Stalin's Russia than in the poisonous one of Hitler's Germany. There was no place for him in a country where chess was a means to an end—to create good communists and ruthless warriors.

AFTER THE REVOLUTION, the embattled Russian chess fraternity felt keenly the absence of most of the prewar grandmasters; they had either emigrated, such as Ossip Bernstein, or their nations were independent of the Soviet Union, such as the Balt Aron Nimzowitsch and the Pole Akiba Rubinstein. Both the leading Russian grandmasters of the 1920s—Alexander Alekhine and Efim Bogolyubov—had been interned in Germany during the First World War, although Alekhine escaped and found his way back to Russia, while Bogolyubov returned only after the war had ended. Both masters won early Soviet championships, but both later rejected the revolutionary state in favor of the bourgeois West. Both, from a Bolshevik point of view, were traitors.

The first Soviet international tournament at Moscow in 1925 was indeed won by Bogolyubov, ahead of Lasker and Capablanca, after which he promptly joined the ranks of the Russian émigrés in Germany. Alekhine also emigrated and never returned to Russia, spending the rest of his life drifting restlessly around Europe. He defeated Capablanca in 1927 to become world champion and defended the title against Bogolyubov twice, in 1929 and 1934.

Not surprisingly, both Alekhine and Bogolyubov were vilified in the Soviet press, especially after they played at wartime tournaments organized by the Nazis. Nevertheless, it is significant that, after his death, Alekhine was rehabilitated and depicted as a precursor of the Soviet school of chess. In their seminal book, *The Soviet School of Chess,* Alexander Kotov and Mikhail Yudovich claim that "Alekhine . . . gave an attentive ear to every new word on chess that came from the Soviet Union. During the last years of his life he was keenly aware of his separation from his native land. He realized he had made a great mistake in leaving it in 1921."

This is pure propaganda. There is no evidence that Alekhine ever regretted his emigration, although in later years he did attempt to ingratiate himself with the Soviet chess superpower. As a landowner's son and a member of the intelligentsia, he was indelibly stamped as a class enemy. In 1919, during the civil war, he was briefly imprisoned by the Cheka, the Bolshevik secret police, on suspicion of working for the counterrevolutionary Whites. Having narrowly escaped with his life, Alekhine used his legal training to redeem himself by joining the Communist Party, for which he was perfectly content to work as a low-level judge. He was thus briefly a small cog in the vast machine controlled by Nikolai Krylenko. In 1921 Alekhine used his linguistic skills to obtain a job as an interpreter for Comintern, the Communist International, where he met and married—probably bigamously—his second wife, the Swiss delegate Anneliese Rüegg. With her help, he emigrated to France and settled in Paris. Alekhine got out of Russia just in time, saved by his ruthless opportunism. His brother Alexei was executed during the Stalinist terror in the late 1930s.

Having attacked Soviet communism in émigré circles, Alekhine was denounced by the Soviet authorities. His emigration turned into exile, but during the 1930s there was a partial rapprochement, particularly after the emergence of the young Soviet grandmaster, Mikhail Botvinnik, as a potential challenger. Alekhine praised the Soviet state's recognition and support for chess. If he was angling for communist patronage, he was unsuccessful. Nonetheless,

the great prize that the Russians coveted—the world championship—was still his property.

In 1935 Alekhine lost the championship to the young Dutchman, Euwe. During the match he was drinking heavily, although
Euwe denied that it had affected the play. Reports appeared in the
press, some even suggesting that Alekhine had been found dead
drunk in a field. The organizers had to issue the following extraordinary (and unintentionally comical) statement:

> It is generally known that the World Champion has been in the
> habit of taking a considerable amount of alcohol over the last
> few years. Not only does this have no ill effect on Alekhine,
> but chess experts even believe that it actually often helps him
> to achieve his best results. In that state he is at his most danger-
> ous for his opponents, including Euwe . . . We should also take
> account of the special mentality of the genius that is Alekhine,
> who is of Russian extraction, a mentality that is a far cry from
> the generally level-headed Dutchman. There have not been any
> public incidents. . . The Committee takes the view that if, as a
> result of the above-mentioned inclination, Alekhine were to
> act in an unacceptable manner during his presence in the play-
> ing hall before, during or after the game, the strictest possible
> measures would be taken.

Two years later he regained the title, having drunk nothing but
milk in the meantime.

During the Second World War, Alekhine served briefly as an interpreter in the French army, but after the occupation of France
he played in German-sponsored events all over Europe, in effect
making himself a propaganda tool of the Nazis. He collaborated
with Hans Frank, Hitler's satrap in Poland, who organized chess
tournaments in Krakow while presiding over the death camp at
Auschwitz a few miles away. A number of consultation games survive featuring Alekhine, his fellow Russian exile Bogolyubov, and
Governor Hans Frank. By the end of the war Alekhine had com-
promised himself in the eyes of much of the chess world. Worst of

all, anti-Semitic articles appeared under his name in 1940, claiming that Jewish masters, including Lasker, were lacking in creativity. Alekhine had always opposed what he saw as the attempt to turn chess into a science, which he associated with his rivals Capablanca and Euwe (neither of whom was Jewish), insisting that chess was an art, although at Nottingham four years earlier, Alekhine had declared: "The very idea of chess as an art-form would be unthinkable without Emanuel Lasker."

Alekhine later disowned these contemptible writings, claiming that the Nazis had inserted the offending passages, but his excuses were inconsistent. In view of his long record of opportunism and collaboration, few doubted their authenticity. After the war, he hoped to rehabilitate himself by playing a match with Botvinnik in England; to that end he wrote flatteringly about the Soviet Union. But he was boycotted by the Americans and there was pressure on the world chess federation to strip him of his title. By 1946, however, alcoholism and depression had caught up with him and he was found dead in a hotel room in Estoril, near Lisbon. The postmortem gave the cause of death as accidental: he had choked on a piece of meat. Later, the doctor who examined him was said to have attributed his death to a stroke precipitated by alcohol poisoning. Neither suicide nor murder can be entirely ruled out. Alekhine's death will probably never be satisfactorily explained.

The fate of Alekhine and other uprooted chess masters of his type was immortalized by *The Luzhin Defense*, Vladimir Nabokov's first great novel. Written in Russian, at a time when the young novelist was eking out a living among fellow émigrés in Berlin between 1922 and 1940, it was published in 1930 under Nabokov's pseudonym, Sirin. It tells the story of Luzhin, a chess genius on the borderline of sanity, for whom only the abstract world of chess matters, while phenomena like politics, money, and even love barely exist. He plays a match with the world champion, Turati, but it is interrupted in mid-game when he suffers a nervous breakdown, deliberately precipitated by his sinister former guardian and manager, Valentinov. A young woman—we are never told her first name—sets out to save Luzhin from what she sees as his monomania, although he is not sure he wants to be saved. The doctors tell her that Luzhin must be completely protected from any contact with chess. However, he cannot escape the dilemma: love and sanity require the renunciation of chess, but he would rather be mad if that is the price of the one thing that gives his life meaning. In seeking to save him by protecting him from chess, his fiancée and later wife succeeds in depriving him of his only refuge. Luzhin, in turn, knows that while he cannot live without chess, he must renounce it for his beloved's sake. He can resolve this existential crisis only by suicide.

Nowhere else in Russian fiction do such subtle, gossamer-light depictions of the metaphysical and the physical, the timeless and the ephemeral, combine together to create such an inexorable sense of a human being trapped by his destiny, man and boy, yet somehow transcending his own tragedy. Chess is the gift, both divine and infernal, that makes this miracle possible. Never again could Nabokov return to this theme; Luzhin embodied that particular part of his life, exhausting its potential once and for all. In his foreword to the English edition, written thirty-four years later, Nabokov explains—tongue firmly in cheek—how the structure of the novel has been designed to resemble a chess problem. The final chapters show "a regular chess attack demolishing the innermost elements of the poor fellow's sanity." The title gives a clue: the Luzhin Defense is meant to be a chess opening, but here it stands also for the prophylactic mechanism behind which Luzhin shelters, ultimately in vain. Much of the novel consists of flashbacks to Luzhin's childhood—closely modeled on Nabokov's own—and no writer has better depicted "the keen delight of being a chess player, and pride, and relief, and that physiological sensation of harmony which is so well known to artists." Nabokov had written poems about chess as well as composing problems and endgame studies; it was for him the paradigm of art for art's sake.

Luzhin is one of the great characters of Russian fiction. As Nabokov wrote, not without pride, "Luzhin has been found lovable even by those who understand nothing about chess and/or detest all my other books. He is uncouth, unwashed, uncomely—but as my gentle young lady (a dear girl in her own right) so quickly notices, there is something in him that transcends both the coarseness of his gray flesh and the sterility of his recondite genius." In the film version, John Turturro gives a marvelous performance as Luzhin, having studied the mannerisms and eccentricities of living chess grandmasters with great care.

Although the character of Luzhin is not based on any one person, his fate was suggested by an individual tragedy. An habitué of Berlin chess haunts, Nabokov became friendly with the German master, Curt von Bardeleben. By all accounts a perfect gentleman and—despite a disconcertingly protuberant forehead—something of a dandy, although long since disowned by his noble family, Count von Bardeleben had eked out a precarious existence playing in coffeehouses for stakes in between occasional appearances in tournaments. As he had once been a rising star of the German chess fraternity, Bardeleben's fragile ego had never completely recovered from his defeat at the hands of the former world champion, Wilhelm Steinitz. Their game at Hastings in 1895 is still a classic. Up to that point Bardeleben had been among the leaders, but in Steinitz he succumbed to one of the most remarkable combinations ever made. At the climax of his opponent's astonishing sequence of sacrifices, it dawned on Bardeleben that there was no escape from eventual mate. Rather than resign or play on to the bitter end, he fled and was only with difficulty dissuaded from abandoning the tournament. His punishment was to be remembered solely as the loser of that game. Nabokov chose not to endow his romantically innocent hero with Bardeleben's decidedly disreputable method of keeping body and soul together. As his friend Edward Lasker recounted, the count periodically married ladies who coveted his grand name and then allowed them to divorce him in return for cash. War, inflation, and alcoholism took their toll; by then in his early sixties, Bardeleben was in the last stages of destitution. In 1924 he committed suicide by jumping out of a window. It was this incident that later inspired *The Luzhin Defense*.

Nabokov also drew inspiration from Alekhine. Like Alekhine, Luzhin comes from a Russian aristocratic family, but a broken marriage. Like Alekhine, the young Luzhin leads a peripatetic life, playing chess in the spas and resorts of prewar Europe. Like Alekhine, he goes into exile after the revolution. Like Alekhine, he is driven by his monomaniacal obsession with chess. Unlike Luzhin, however, Alekhine was by no means naive; indeed, he was positively devious in his attitudes towards sex, money, and politics. In his simplicity and mental frailty, Luzhin bears a certain resemblance to two other great émigré masters: Aron Nimzowitsch and Akiba Rubinstein. Both were from pious Jewish families, in Lithuania and Poland respectively; both played chess of immense originality, but did not have the equanimity and stamina to become world champions; both were ascetic loners, psychologically fragile, eccentric and egocentric to the point of madness. Nimzowitsch, a brilliant writer and theoretician but utterly self-absorbed, performed vigorous calisthenics during his games. His "Hypermodern" treatise, *My System*, had a lasting impact on chess. Rubinstein became increasingly paranoid; like Luzhin, he would hurl himself out of windows if a stranger entered. After making a move, he would crouch in the corner of the room until his opponent replied. In 1932 he retired to a Belgian asylum, spending his last thirty years in seclusion, which probably saved his life during the Nazi occupation.

Such extremes of individualism had no place in the collectivism of the USSR. Nimzowitsch was criticized by Botvinnik for "straining after 'originality,'" after "tricks," while Rubinstein was castigated for his "fatalism." "This, of course, had nothing in common with the active, optimistic attitude to chess displayed by the Soviet masters," declared the new world champion.

The historical background to the novel is the Russian émigré community in Berlin. Nabokov mercilessly satirizes the way in which an importunate woman visitor who has married a communist pours scorn on the bourgeois West: "I myself feel how we've outstripped Europe. Take our theater. Why, you in Europe don't have a theater, it just doesn't exist. I'm not in the least, you understand, not in the least praising the communists. But you have to admit one thing: they look ahead, they build. Intensive construction." With her vulgar, newfangled jargon, her obsession with fashion, and her rudeness to shop assistants, this woman represents the antithesis of Luzhin's world.

Nabokov depicts to perfection the psychopathology of chess — although Luzhin is an extreme case of its fatal attraction. He also uses the game as a metaphor for the intellectual life, beset with dangers on all sides. The novel is an elegy for the precarious European culture that he saw collapsing about his ears, with the grim prospect of totalitarian "intensive construction" waiting to inherit the earth. Finally, chess represents Russia: enigmatic, dangerous, but infinitely fascinating. In another of his Russian novels, *The Gift* (1935–7), written in Berlin under one dictatorship while exiled from another, Nabokov satirized an émigré like himself who writes a biography of Chernyshevsky. Instead of chess, he used butterflies as a metaphor for the fragile, evanescent beauty of a Russia to which he longed to return, but where men like himself were crushed like insects. Nabokov, the chess-loving lepidopterist, knew that Russia was no longer his homeland, rather a place where not even these studies, no matter how innocent and recondite, were secure from ideological encroachment. Only in 1988, a decade after his death in 1977, did an extract from *The Luzhin Defense* finally appear in the Soviet magazine *Shakhmaty v SSSR*, one of the fruits of *glasnost*.

Lenin at Maxim Gorky's house in Capri, 1908. Lenin loved chess, but he was a dangerous challenger: a year later he had his opponent here, Alexander Bogdanov, kicked out of the Bolshevik faction.

Recreation of the revolution: the utopian socialist Leo Tolstoy playing chess at his estate, Yasnaya Polanya, 1907.

The natural habitat of bourgeois chess: postcard of a Viennese café, 1911.

WIENER CAFE: DIE SCHACHSPIELER.

The philosopher Moses Mendelssohn (left) made friends at the chessboard with the philosemitic German dramatist Lessing (center) and the Swiss writer Lavater.

The young Sergei Prokofiev in the revolutionary year 1905. A strong player, he composed a piece especially for the 1935 Moscow tournament.

Grandmasters at St. Petersburg, 1914. Standing: Marshall, Alekhine, and Nimzowitsch (second, third, and fourth from left); Sitting: Lasker and Tarrasch (third and fourth from left); Janowski, Capablanca, Bernstein, and Rubinstein (first and fourth from right).

Stalin's prosecutor:
Nikolai Krylenko,
founder of the Red Army,
who was responsible
both for the rise of Soviet
chess and for judicial
murder on a vast scale,
before he too fell victim
to the Terror.

The leaders of the revolution at a rally in Red Square during the civil war.
Krylenko stands center in cap and coat, on the raised stand, with Lenin to
his left. Lenin teased Krylenko for being a bad loser at chess.

6

THE PATRIARCH
AND HIS PROGENY

T HE FIRST AND GREATEST CHESS hero of the Soviet
Union was Mikhail Botvinnik. Born in 1911, he belonged
to the first generation to reach maturity under communism. They were Stalin's children: indoctrinated with the "cult of
personality" and later promoted to replace the Bolshevik old guard,
most of whom perished in the purges. Botvinnik came from a Jewish bourgeois background—his patronymic, Moiseyevich, means
"son of Moses." His parents split up and, like Boris Spassky and
Bobby Fischer after him, he was brought up by his mother.

Botvinnik was no child prodigy, but by the time he was thirteen
he was good enough to play Lasker in a simultaneous exhibition in
what was then still called Petrograd. Lasker apparently moved so
slowly that Botvinnik was obliged to abandon the game after fifteen moves "because it was already time for a schoolboy to be
asleep." Like countless other young Russians he was enthused by
the first great Moscow tournament of 1925. That year, aged fourteen, he made his mark by winning a game against Capablanca in a
thirty-board simultaneous exhibition held in what had by then be-

come Leningrad on a rest day during the tournament—one of four games that the great man conceded. According to Botvinnik, despite his reputation as a gentleman, the world champion was "very angry" after his resignation "and threw the pieces off the board."

Botvinnik never allowed chess to take over his life. Like many of his contemporaries, he trained as an electrical engineer, a profession that he never renounced, and whose scientific methodology he purported to apply to chess. He periodically took time off —sometimes up to three years—to concentrate on his scientific work. As we shall see, he was still producing important research into computer programming after he retired from chess in 1970. If he had had his way, he believed, the Soviet Union would never have fallen behind the West in technology. Nevertheless he always remained a man of his generation: a loyal communist, immensely proud of the Soviet achievement, and blind to the price that had been paid.

Botvinnik was also a great teacher; both Anatoly Karpov and Garry Kasparov were among the pupils at the chess school that he set up in the 1960s. However, the principal vehicle of his didacticism was his writing. In his 1951 book, *One Hundred Games of Chess*, Botvinnik described his preparations for a match or tournament. His procedure became standard for Soviet masters, having been institutionalized in countless training courses across the USSR.

The hallmark of the Botvinnik method was mental and physical rigor. First, there should be fifteen to twenty days in a country dacha, with plenty of fresh air. All the games of one's opponent must be studied, his openings subjected to stringent analysis, probing for weaknesses. (Research of this kind was much harder work before the era of databases, but the centralized Soviet system had the advantage of excellent chess libraries in major cities.) Next, one's own opening systems must be prepared—about four each for White and Black—followed by secret training games with a trusted partner. (In practice, this soon became a professional trainer or second.) One of the purposes of these training games was to eliminate time

problems or other bad habits. Botvinnik was troubled by the leading American grandmaster, Reshevsky, who was a chain-smoker,
so he paid an opponent to blow smoke into his face throughout
their games and thereby acquired immunity to tobacco. He recommended publishing as much analysis as possible in order to subject
it to objective criticism. "Finally, five days or so before the contest
all chess activities must be stopped completely. You must take a
rest; otherwise you may lose zest for the battle." This methodical
approach to the game was not entirely new, but combined with the
"scientific" ideology of Marxism-Leninism and applied on a continental scale, it was to prove revolutionary.

Despite his Stakhanovite dedication, Botvinnik's rise was not
without mishaps. He played well in Soviet tournaments and drew
a match with Salo Flohr, but his first appearance abroad, at the annual Hastings tournament in 1933, was a failure. Undaunted, Botvinnik studied and rectified his weaknesses. In 1935 a second Moscow international tournament was organized by Krylenko. The
foreign masters were even stronger than at the first Moscow tournament, ten years earlier, but so too were the Soviets. Botvinnik
came first, equal with Flohr.

When Botvinnik returned to the international arena, at the great
tournament of Nottingham in 1936, he finished first, equal with
Capablanca and ahead of Euwe, Alekhine, and Lasker—all present
or past world champions. No young Soviet citizen had achieved
such celebrity before. Elated, Botvinnik sent a cable to Stalin that
began: "Dear beloved teacher and leader. . ." Only many years later
did Botvinnik admit that it had been dictated by Krylenko.

After his triumph at Nottingham, Botvinnik was treated as a
favored son, though that favor was strictly conditional on his continuing success against Western grandmasters. The minister of
heavy industry, Grigory Ordzhonikadze, rewarded him with a car.
Apart from the vehicles assigned to the *nomenklatura*, Botvinnik's
may well have been the only private car in the Soviet Union. A
year later, Ordzhonikadze vanished into the vortex of the Terror.
Botvinnik was fortunate not to join him; an aunt in America sent

him a postcard congratulating him on his triumph at Nottingham. "I, of course, did not reply. At that time it was terribly dangerous," he recalled. According to the historian Andrew Soltis, among Botvinnik's treasured mementoes was an order signed by Stalin himself soon after the war, granting him 250 liters of petrol—a privilege unthinkable for strictly rationed ordinary citizens.

Botvinnik was proud of his connections and not afraid to exercise his *telefonnoye pravo*, his right to telephone senior officials. In 1937 he challenged but failed to defeat Grigory Levenfish, a much older master whose career had begun in tsarist days. Levenfish had just won his second Soviet championship, and Botvinnik felt the need to prove that he was indeed the Soviet number one. However, he underestimated old Levenfish, and after twelve games Botvinnik led by only 5–4. The thirteenth game went badly for Botvinnik, and it was adjourned in a lost position. He rang the arbiter, former leading master Nikolai Grigoriev, to resign the game. He was startled when Grigoriev—whose duty was of course to be neutral—offered to help him analyze the position. The arbiter was merely reflecting the fact that Krylenko wanted Botvinnik, the young hero of the Soviet Union, to win the match. He lost the game and the match was drawn 5–5, but that did not prevent Botvinnik pulling out all the stops to ensure that he alone represented the Soviet interest at the most important event of 1938, the AVRO tournament in Holland, which it was hoped would determine the next challenger to Alekhine. According to Korchnoi, Botvinnik wrote to the Central Committee to ensure that he and not Levenfish would be invited to the Netherlands. He also rang an acquaintance who was assistant to Nikolai Bulganin, one of Stalin's most powerful cronies, to request that his wife be permitted to accompany him—an almost unheard-of privilege, since by keeping a spouse as hostage the Soviet authorities could deter their representatives in the West from any temptation to defect. Yet Botvinnik's request was granted.

Botvinnik had one even more powerful protector. In 1943, as the struggle with Nazi Germany hung in the balance, the Foreign

Minister, Vyacheslav Molotov, himself intervened to ensure that Botvinnik was given time off work to study chess. Molotov, who valued chess for its propaganda value in the West, ensured that the Foreign Ministry provided precious foreign currency to pay for Botvinnik's participation in tournaments abroad. He even offered to help finance a world championship match with Alekhine in 1946, despite the fact that in Soviet eyes the world champion was both a renegade and a Nazi collaborator.

The Soviet domination of world chess was established by Botvinnik's victory in the 1948 match-tournament at The Hague and Moscow, which included the five leading grandmasters remaining after the deaths of the world champions Alekhine, Lasker, and Capablanca. Botvinnik was the preferred choice of both Stalin and the then second most powerful man in the Soviet hierarchy, Andrei Zhdanov. Chess was part of Zhdanov's empire, which included propaganda and culture, so before the second leg of the tournament began in Moscow, Botvinnik was called into Zhdanov's office. Would Sammy Reshevsky, the American representative, be world champion? Zhdanov asked. "Reshevsky may become world champion," Botvinnik replied, careful not to leave himself without an escape route. "But this would indicate that nowadays there are no strong players left in the world." Zhdanov got the joke. Botvinnik explained that the American champion's chronic time trouble and his lack of positional sense would be insuperable obstacles to overcoming the Soviet school. Botvinnik was sent on his way.

Suspicion has never been entirely dispelled that Paul Keres, a brilliant young Estonian whose results before and during the war were fully equal to Botvinnik's, had come under pressure from the Soviet authorities as a result of his "collaboration" during the Nazi occupation. According to the Russian grandmaster Yuri Averbakh, a Soviet marine officer named Barkan told him that in 1945, when he took part in the capture of Tallinn, he was under orders to arrest Keres. In fact, Keres had been in Sweden and only returned to Russia two weeks before Estonia fell to the Red Army. Although he was not arrested, his house was confiscated and he was banned from high-level chess. In 1946 he wrote to Foreign Minister Molotov, begging to be allowed to play again in tournaments, but a senior KGB officer, Abakumov, objected. Molotov asked: "If Keres had not returned to the USSR, do you think he would have lived better than in our country?" Abakumov had no reply, so Molotov lifted the ban.

Even in 1948, Keres was not fully rehabilitated. He told the British historian Ken Whyld that he had been warned that if Botvinnik did not become the world champion, it had better not be his fault. Keres played well against his other three rivals but collapsed against Botvinnik, losing his first four games and enabling the latter to emerge as the new champion. It was always rumored that he had been pressured to throw these games as the price of his rehabilitation. Botvinnik himself, in an interview nearly half a century later, said that Stalin had given orders that not only Keres but Smyslov too should lose to him. Averbakh rejected this claim as far-fetched, while not ruling out the possibility that officials lower down the hierarchy might have issued such orders in trying to second-guess Stalin. But Keres's results before and after 1948 show that Botvinnik was always a difficult opponent for him. Keres never quite recovered his form after spending the war years playing in mediocre Nazi tournaments. He may have been blackmailed into losing, or merely intimidated, although Botvinnik might have won the world championship anyway.

Keres did not lose only to Botvinnik, however: he was beaten overall by the U.S. champion Samuel Reshevsky, too. During the Moscow leg of the tournament, the Soviet leadership panicked about the threat posed by Reshevsky, who had outplayed Botvinnik in a fine game. Afterwards, the two men shook hands. The next day Botvinnik was summoned before the Sports Committee. The chairman, Lieutenant-General Arkady Apollonov, got straight to the point: "Mikhail Moiseyevich, how can you, a communist, congratulate an American on winning a game with a Soviet player? And at a time when the battle is being conducted against kowtowing to the West?" Botvinnik did not flinch: "You invited me for this, Arkady Nikolayevich? Excuse me, but I have to prepare for my next game." He then walked out.

It was a colossal risk, but Botvinnik was confident that he had enough support at the highest levels of the party to ignore such attempts to browbeat him. Just to make sure, he immediately phoned one of his friends on the Central Committee. If the American, who faded in the second half of the tournament and ended third equal, had won the title, Stalin might have withdrawn support not only from Botvinnik, but from chess itself.

However, Botvinnik's success went to his head. He began to believe that his prowess at chess entitled him to tell the party leadership where it was going wrong. In 1954 he wrote a letter to *Pravda* in which he set out a strategy for world domination without a world war. He was firmly rebuffed by the political secretariat, which according to Averbakh, even threatened to throw him out of the party. Botvinnik backed off. Forty years later, after the dissolution of the Soviet Union, he tried again, this time trying to influence the economic policy of the Yeltsin government. Again he was rebuffed.

Despite the failure of these forays into politics, Botvinnik really did rule the Soviet chess world for many years. He enjoyed great prestige—when he entered a theater, the audience would give him a standing ovation—and generous perks, thanks to his friends in the government. More important, Botvinnik used the power of Soviet chess to consolidate his own position as world champion, by persuading FIDE to give him the right to a return match. Twice he lost the title to Smyslov and Mikhail Tal; twice he regained it. After the rematch was scrapped, he lost again to Tigran Petrosian. This time there was no comeback. Young hopefuls also resented the rule whereby the number of participants in the candidates' tournament was limited to four from any one country. This excluded several Soviet grandmasters, but when they wrote a letter appealing to the Soviet chess association to repeal this rule, Botvinnik crushed them, declaring that, in Averbakh's words, "If any brick is removed from this edifice I have built, the whole system will be destroyed."

Botvinnik did not merely influence the "Soviet school of chess"; he invented it. It was he who set out the theory, and he who put it into practice, not only in his own games but later as a trainer of future world champions up to and including Kasparov. His seminal 1949 article, "The Russian and Soviet School of Chess," first defined the contrast between the social status of chess in the bourgeois West and under Soviet communism. Botvinnik claimed that chess had such a low, amateurish status in the West that even the great Lasker had succumbed to "the patronizing, philanthropic attitude to chess that existed in his bourgeois milieu" and become a businessman: "For the sake of such transactions he, the world champion, gave up chess!" Even in pre-revolutionary Russia, where great Russian masters such as Tchigorin and Alekhine "took an advanced view of chess," conditions did not permit chess to become a mass activity. By comparison, "when we Soviet masters take part in tournaments and study the game we know we are performing a socially valuable, a cultural activity, that we are bringing benefit to the Soviet state."

It was Botvinnik who created the cult of Tchigorin. Just as the stern, bewhiskered features of Karl Marx presided over the Soviet state, so the bearded, patriarchal figure of Mikhail Tchigorin presided over the Soviet school of chess. Tchigorin was made into a precursor of all the approved virtues of Soviet man. In reality, Tchigorin—like Alekhine—was probably an alcoholic. He had a bottle of brandy beside the board during his world championship matches with Steinitz, and he died of diabetes aged only fifty-eight. But in Botvinnik's hands, Tchigorin—who lost two championship matches against Steinitz and had an even worse record against Lasker—was "the first player in the world to treat the game as it deserves."

Unlike Tchigorin, Botvinnik had known and played against Alekhine. His decision to award the émigré a posthumous place in the pantheon of Soviet chess was controversial; many saw him as a war criminal. For Botvinnik, however, Alekhine's "exceptional fighting qualities, his profound psychological insight into the essence of the chess art" were "a reflection of the specific features of the Soviet school of chess."

Gerald Abrahams, one of the few British masters in the 1950s to have beaten a Russian grandmaster, was a keen student of the Soviet school of chess, but his judgment on it was harsh: "There was, for a few years, a belief—or rather a propaganda—that a socialized world was changing the nature of chess. That claim is no longer made. For the Father-Image of Marx, the Russians have substituted (with justification) the ikon of Tchigorin. And that is more consistent with chess experience." By substituting Tchigorin for Marx, Botvinnik was following the party line. Stalin and his successors found that a combination of nationalism and socialism was an even more effective ideology with which to impose totalitarian rule than pure Marxism.

When the dust settled after 1945, it became clear that the Russians had far outstripped all other countries at chess. The United States—in part thanks to Jewish immigration from Europe—had emerged as the strongest chess nation of the 1930s. Nevertheless, Americans were shocked in September 1945 when, in the first important postwar sporting event between the new superpowers, the Soviet Union defeated the American team in a radio match by the crushing margin of 15.5–4.5. The following year the USSR annihilated England 18–6. For the next three decades, the only serious competition for the Soviet Union at chess came from its own satellite states. It was irritating for the Kremlin that the least obedient of these, Yugoslavia, also proved to be the strongest. After the 1948 breach between Stalin and Tito, the Russians boycotted the 1950 chess Olympiad in Belgrade, enabling the Yugoslavs to take the gold medals. However, the fact that only other communist systems, albeit "nonaligned," could compete with the USSR at chess lent credibility to Khrushchev's warning to the capitalist West: "We will bury you."

Communist supremacy in chess, as in other fields, had both an ideological ("theoretical") and a practical basis. The Soviet school of chess was supposed to have raised the theory of the game, in strategy and tactics, to a much higher level than had been possible in the decadent bourgeois culture of the West: "If a culture is declining then chess too will go downhill," Botvinnik wrote. There was a nationalistic strain in this ideology; openings were renamed after Russian masters, and non-Russian masters denigrated or written out of the script. Like other ideologies, that of the Soviet or Russian "school" was largely myth. The Soviet champions were necessarily eclectic; they incorporated the best ideas wherever they were to be found. Unlike the arts, humanities, and sciences, which were forced to interpret everything through the prism of Marxism-Leninism, such eclecticism was permitted in chess. Chess could boast a genuine marketplace of ideas that was virtually unique in Soviet intellectual life. In a society where mind-numbing uniformity was imposed on leisure as well as work; where the press and broadcasting largely consisted of propaganda; where literature and the arts were censored; where alcohol and tobacco were the only luxuries; where life for most people was lived in the interstices between fear and tedium — in such a society, chess was an oasis for millions thirsting for mental stimulation.

But the practical basis of the Soviet school of chess was its colossal infrastructure. From 150,000 registered players in 1929, the numbers grew to half a million in the mid-1930s. By the 1950s they had reached 1 million and would eventually peak at 5 million. Even more spectacular was the increase of experts, masters, and grandmasters. Until 1935, when Botvinnik became the first Soviet grandmaster, the USSR had no grandmasters and only a handful of masters. By 1957 there were 19 Soviet grandmasters and 110 masters, with an average of 20 new masters every year. As the huge Soviet training campaign bore fruit, a vast system of rewards and punishments was built up, with endless in-fighting and denunciations. The lot of a chess professional was an enviable one: stipends were higher than average wages, but the biggest lure was the likelihood of foreign travel and foreign-currency earnings. In a centrally planned economy, from which choice had been banished, such opportunities conferred almost unimaginable privilege.

The rate of increase began to slow, however, in the late 1950s, as the impact of Stalin and Hitler began to be felt on the generation born before, during, and just after the war. Andrew Soltis writes of an "invisible crisis" precipitated by an article by Vasily Panov in *Izvestia*, provocatively headed: "Don't manufacture Wunderkinder." Panov was attacking a new state recruitment program to boost the numbers of children playing chess, which was in turn a response to the first signs of an incipient malaise that would eventually have a profound impact on Soviet society. Between Boris Spassky (born in 1937) and Anatoly Karpov (born in 1951), there was what grandmaster Yuri Averbakh later called the "missing generation"—dead, exiled, physically or psychologically scarred by adversity. It was only in the 1970s, when the generation born just before the war began to age, that the loss of so much talent became painfully apparent. In politics, when this generation might have been expected to lead the country, a gerontocracy born before the revolution clung to power. And in chess, the gerontocracy was led by Botvinnik. Just as the revolution had devoured its children, so the patriarch of chess had outlived many of his progeny.

7

THE JEWISH FACTOR

L IKE MANY OTHER JEWISH COMMUNISTS from his background, Mikhail Moiseyevich ("son of Moses") Botvinnik believed that the new socialist state would do away with the pogroms of tsarist Russia. Indeed, Soviet chess achieved domination after the Holocaust partly because the Nazis had murdered or driven into exile most of the Jews of continental Europe. Despite Stalinism, several Jewish masters were persuaded to settle in the Soviet Union, including the Czech Salo Flohr and the Hungarian Andrea Lilienthal. In the Soviet Union, Jews made up less than 2 percent of the population, but of the Soviet world champions and leading grandmasters, a majority were wholly or partly Jewish. Besides Botvinnik, they included David Bronstein, Mikhail Tal, Yefim Geller, Viktor Korchnoi, and Garry Kasparov. It was only in the course of the 1970s and '80s—when many Soviet Jews emigrated to Israel, America, or Western Europe—that the balance shifted.

The only non-Soviet world champion during the postwar era, Bobby Fischer, was also Jewish, however vehemently he denied the fact. Some Russian champions who were not Jews, such as Vasily Smyslov and Boris Spassky, were popularly supposed to be so. Whether the Soviet authorities liked it or not, they could not hope to dominate world chess without this unique pool of talent. Jewish preeminence in chess was in any case replicated throughout Soviet culture—and, initially at least, in politics.

Yet the relationship between the Soviet state and the Jews was ambiguous, if not suspicious, from the outset. The tsarist state had openly encouraged anti-Semitism, causing many Russian Jews to emigrate. Those who remained often gravitated to the opposition. After the Bolshevik revolution, Jews were in theory treated equally, but the Bolsheviks, too, had a darker, anti-Semitic tradition. Marx, though himself a baptized Jew, wrote a poisonous tract, *On the Jewish Question,* and later denounced Jews in scurrilous terms in his correspondence. At a popular level Bolsheviks, like other socialists, were not above linking Jews and capitalism. Many Jews also had German names or connections, rendering them suspect after war broke out in 1914. Lenin, whose maternal grandfather was Jewish, thought that Jews could be made willing and useful supporters of the revolution, but he was intolerant of Jews who wanted anything less than total assimilation.

In a celebrated essay on "The Role of Jews in the Russian Revolutionary Movement," the British historian Leonard Schapiro argued that despite its internationalist rhetoric, Lenin's party was always destined to evolve into a Russian nationalist movement from which Jewish revolutionaries were first marginalized and then eliminated: "It was against this Bolshevik nationalism that the Jew collided, and by it he was destroyed." In practice Jewish overrepresentation in the Soviet hierarchy—not least in the organs of repression—made them even more unpopular and therefore dependent on the party. Communist ideologists barely acknowledged the existence, let alone the gravity, of anti-Semitism under socialism. Such prejudices were meant to wither away along with the middle class to which they were supposedly confined. Thus the reemergence in the newest society of this oldest hatred passed unremarked, even when the man who emerged as the leader of the party in succession to Lenin was himself consumed by fear and loathing of Jews.

Joseph Djugashvili, known to history by his *nom de guerre* Stalin ("man of steel"), was, in the words of his most recent biographer Simon Sebag Montefiore, "a vicious and obsessional anti-Semite." Although, as Sebag Montefiore demonstrates, Stalin was well-read and even a published poet, he was also pathologically suspicious of intellectuals and especially Jewish intellectuals, tens of thousands of whom were tortured, shot, or worked to death in the Gulag on his orders. Indeed, under Stalin, anti-Semitism was institutionalized. In 1907, long before he took power, Stalin had written: "It would not be a bad idea for us Bolsheviks to organize a pogrom in the party." Once he took power, new purges were often old pogroms writ large.

Schapiro even writes of the "great holocaust of Jewish Bolsheviks which took place in 1937 and 1938," during which Jews were denounced under various euphemistic slogans, above all "cosmopolitan." Stalin's paranoia grew during and after the war. After the full horror of Hitler's genocide was uncovered by advancing Soviet troops, the idea was mooted of a Jewish homeland in the Crimea, whence the Tartars had been expelled. Stalin not only squashed such hopes, but treated its supporters as traitors. At Yalta in 1944 he denounced Jewish "middlemen, profiteers and parasites" to Roosevelt, while encouraging his lieutenants, such as Khrushchev, Zhdanov, and Suslov, to persecute Jews at every level, including even the survivors of the Holocaust. The Cold War fueled Stalin's anti-Semitism by making all Jews in his eyes potential agents of the American enemy. Once the state of Israel had been established in 1948, Zionism became a new target. It was Stalin who bequeathed to the Left "anti-Zionism" as a politically correct form of anti-Semitism. Oblivious of the origins of this Stalinist legacy, the Left is still demonizing Zionism to this day.

In 1949 a new wave of arrests inaugurated the "Jewish Case," incriminating Jews in the highest echelons of the party as Zionist agents. This was the prelude to the last and most overtly anti-Semitic of Stalin's purges, the "Doctors' Plot," which culminated in a diabolical scheme to force leading Jews, such as Deputy Secretary Lazar Kaganovich, to demand the deportation of Soviet Jewry for their own "protection." Two new camps were being built for the intended victims when this plot was cut short by Stalin's sudden death in 1953. Inevitably that, too, was blamed by many Russians on the Jews, although the doctors who treated him as he lay dying of a stroke were specifically chosen because they were not Jewish, and the only person who claimed to have murdered him was his Mingrelian secret police chief, Beria.

In this sulfurous atmosphere, Jewish chess masters were not immune from suspicion, and some eagerly seized any opportunity to prove their loyalty. During the Doctors' Plot, Stalin's henchmen tried to legitimize the investigation by demanding that all prominent Jews, including chess masters, sign an open letter supporting the authorities. Adding insult to injury in this way was typical of Stalin's sadistic streak. Doubtless he was also aware that his persecution had alarmed Jews in the West, and he mistakenly supposed that such an open letter would allay such fears. In 1951 both the world champion, Mikhail Botvinnik, and his first challenger, David Bronstein, were Jews. According to Viktor Korchnoi, Bronstein—like most of his colleagues—reluctantly gave in to this pressure and signed. Only Botvinnik—who remained a Stalinist all his life—felt confident enough of his status as world champion to refuse to sign. It must have been especially galling for Bronstein, who was fiercely independent, to be obliged to endorse Stalin's anti-Semitic conspiracy theory. Indeed, Bronstein's career illustrates the difficulties encountered by even the most successful Soviet grandmasters during the Cold War, especially if they happened to be Jewish.

David Bronstein was born in 1924, the year of Lenin's death, with a triple handicap in Stalin's Russia: he was a Ukrainian Jew and a second cousin of Trotsky. These connections were enough to have his father, a flour mill manager, arrested in 1937 as an "enemy of the people." Although young David had already shown promise at chess from an early age, he was conscripted at the outbreak of war and survived only because his poor eyesight kept him out of the front line. His family fled from Kiev before the Germans arrived; when Bronstein returned there in 1943 the family home was deserted. In 1944, after seven years in the Arctic Gulag, barely alive but undaunted and still ambitious for his son, Bronstein senior returned home to resume work at the flour mill. Caught between Stalin and Hitler, it was remarkable that the Bronstein family survived.

David Bronstein's first major tournament was the 1944 Soviet championship; at just twenty, he beat Botvinnik himself, but finished only fifteenth. Self-critical to a fault, he rapidly improved and by 1948 could demonstrate his grandmaster strength by winning his first international tournament, the Stockholm Interzonal, without losing a single game. This qualified him for the Budapest candidates' tournament in 1950, where he tied for first with another Jewish grandmaster, Isaac Boleslavsky, and later won the playoff. Bronstein thereby became the first official challenger under the new FIDE world championship system. When Bronstein played Botvinnik in 1951, the stakes were high. This was the first title match since 1937 and the first to be held under Soviet auspices. A great deal had been invested in building up Botvinnik's prestige as the leader of the Soviet school of chess, but he had not played for three years; at the age of forty the engineer had finally been forced to concentrate on his doctorate. Bronstein was then twenty-seven and in seven years had achieved one of the most meteoric ascents in the history of chess, fully comparable to that of Botvinnik himself in the mid-1930s, so it was not surprising that initially he made all the running.

Bronstein was a brilliant attacking player and he treated the world champion with scant respect: in the very first game he played the Dutch Defense, Botvinnik's pet opening. In the twenty-second game he appeared to have clinched the match with a queen sacrifice. But when he asked his fiancée, Lydia Bogdanova, whether she wanted him to be world champion, she disappointed him by replying: "I really don't care." Bronstein himself claimed that he had "no real ambition to win." In the twenty-third and penultimate game, Bronstein overpressed, playing too fast in order to exploit Botvinnik's time trouble. Eventually Botvinnik's bishops outplayed Bronstein's knights in a subtle endgame. The outcome was uncertain until the overnight adjournment. When Botvinnik found the winning move "after a sleepless night at eight o'clock in the morning," he later wrote, "my heart started palpitating." When, after thinking for forty minutes, Bronstein resigned, there was consternation. In the twenty-fourth game Bronstein had White and Botvinnik was such a "bundle of nerves" that he tried to have the game played in private. However, Bronstein's heart was not in it, so game and match were drawn. For the first but by no means the last time, Botvinnik clung to his title.

There was speculation at the time, which has not dissipated since, that Bronstein had come under pressure from the Soviet hierarchy to throw the match. Half a century later, in his autobiography, Bronstein's own response was gnomic: "The only thing I am prepared to say about all this is that I was subjected to strong psychological pressure from various sources and it was entirely up to me to yield to that pressure or not. Let's leave it at that." The fact that Bronstein was the son of a political prisoner meant that it would have been easy to exert such pressure on him; Stalin was still alive in 1951 and more dangerous than ever.

Moreover, Bronstein's intrepid father, though banished from Moscow, had succeeded in bribing a police chief with one hundred pounds of flour to give him a "clean" internal passport. Bronstein senior sat in the front row to watch his son. Sitting nearby was the head of the NKVD's notorious Special Department, Viktor Abakumov — one of the most feared men in Russia, responsible for Stalin's anti-Semitic campaign until he was himself implicated by his own deputy and arrested, just two months after the match ended. Abakumov had the power to punish the entire Bronstein family for the recklessness of its head. It is not impossible that Bronstein was reminded that his father's freedom depended on his losing the match to Botvinnik, the party favorite. However, Andrew Soltis points out that Abakumov was actually there as a Bronstein fan. It is hard to see why Bronstein would have made such an effort to win the twenty-first and twenty-second games, only to deliberately lose the twenty-third. And would Botvinnik have consented to such skulduggery? "Mikhail Moiseyevich is a very proud man," commented Viktor Malkin, who knew them both.

Botvinnik explained Bronstein's failure to capitalize on what proved to be his only shot at the title as due to inadequate endgame technique (a fair criticism) and "deficiencies of character: an inclination towards eccentricity and complacency." This looks like coded language, implying that Bronstein was not seen as a reliable communist. It echoes the charge of "complacency and self-conceit" made in 1954 by the influential Moscow *Literary Gazette* after Bronstein "only" tied for first and second places at Hastings with the British master C. H. O'D. Alexander. These were the years when Bronstein was overtaken by Smyslov in the candidates' tournaments of 1953 and 1956; again, there were rumors that he had been "persuaded" to step aside. By "eccentricity" Soviet officials meant habits such as "wasting" time at the board before even starting. "I love to play when the clock is running," he would say. The chairman of the all-powerful Sports Committee was incensed to see Bronstein take so long over his very first move. "So in one month's training Bronstein couldn't prepare one move?" he snorted.

In later years, as suspicions of his political unreliability grew, Bronstein was allowed to travel abroad only rarely. In 1976 he landed himself in serious trouble by refusing to sign an open letter condemning Viktor Korchnoi for his defection. He was banned from foreign travel for the next fifteen years, until the Soviet Union itself ceased to exist. Having survived cancer, he enjoyed showing visitors his pension book, which bore the legend: "Reduced by 10 percent for disloyalty to the Soviet Union."

Even in the post-Stalin era, the 2.5 million Soviet Jews continued to suffer many forms of discrimination. This was hardly surprising, since Stalin's heirs—Khrushchev, Brezhnev, and the rest—had inherited his anti-Semitism. There were few synagogues or Jewish schools, and virtually no public acknowledgment of Jewish culture. Nonetheless, Jewish identity papers bore the word "Jew" and this indelible stigma was used to deprive them of opportunities for education or employment. Between 1961 and 1963 more than a hundred "speculators" were tried and shot; sixty-eight of them were Jewish. Soviet propaganda against Judaism and Zionism was stepped up. Throughout the Brezhnev era of the late 1960s and 1970s, official anti-Semitism grew to "epic proportions," in the words of Yevgenia Albats, the historian of the KGB. As late as 1983, the Central Committee set up an "Anti-Zionist Committee of the Soviet Public," under the direct supervision of the KGB's chief ideologist, Filipp Bobkov, designed to destroy the informal support networks that sustained Jewish identity. Discrimination against Jews in education, employment, and every other sphere of Soviet life was open. Jews were increasingly suspected of dual loyalties, especially once Jewish dissidents began to demand the right to emigrate to Israel from the mid-1950s, forming a movement known as *aliyah* (Hebrew for "ascent"). Most were refused permission to leave and hence acquired the nickname "refuseniks." The Kremlin feared a brain drain, yet did everything possible to stamp out Jewish life.

It was probably coincidence that the most celebrated refusenik, Natan Sharansky, was also a chess prodigy, but there was nothing accidental about the role that chess played in the ordeal that made him the hero, symbol, and spokesman of the refuseniks. Sharansky's rebellion against the Soviet system had its origins in the confluence of two factors, chess and Judaism, both of which played a decisive part in the final phase of the Cold War.

Born Anatoly Shcharansky (he later changed his name from its Russian to its Hebrew form in honor of his grandfather) in 1948, he learned chess at five from his mother. "I loved the way the game gave me power over grownups," he later wrote. Young Anatoly

("Tolya") had his first problem published at twelve. By fourteen he was champion of his home city of Donetsk and later of the Donbass province. "I remember how much time, labor, and love Tolya devoted to his passion," his mother recalled later, after his incarceration. He astounded many with displays of simultaneous blindfold chess as a teenager. This striking mnemonic accomplishment was proof of the youth's remarkable self discipline. A photograph of the teenage Sharansky playing chess betrays an assurance beyond his years. He was already a young man to be reckoned with.

By now a local celebrity, Sharansky seriously considered turning professional:

> I quickly reached the rank of candidate master and for years my dream was to become a great chess player. But I was always ambivalent about this goal, because the more time I spent on chess, the more I suffered from doubts: Did it really make sense to spend so much time playing games? And yet whenever I neglected chess, I missed those moments of free play and fantasy, those challenging opportunities to test my intellectual powers, and the special delight I took in defeating my opponents.

However, chess had to take a back seat as Sharansky concentrated first on science and then on politics.

Sharansky proved to be a brilliant mathematician and physicist, enabling him to become a graduate student at the Moscow Institute of Physics and Technology (MIPT). This was no small achievement, because Jews were very rarely accepted in this prestigious institution, created under Stalin to train the Soviet scientific elite; the administrators complained that they did not wish to preside over a "synagogue" and from the mid-1960s to the 1980s no Jews at all were admitted. His field was cybernetics, for he had already identified computers as the decisive technology of the future. In Moscow he also took another step towards independence: he learned English, which enabled him to become the interpreter and spokesman for the entire refusenik movement—one of its chief links with visiting Western politicians and journalists. Teaching

English and physics also enabled Sharansky to earn a living after he had been excluded from the academic world, thereby avoiding the criminal charge of "parasitism" used against dissidents with no visible means of support.

Nonetheless, Sharansky had not completely turned his back on chess. In 1972 he worked on a thesis entitled "Simulating the Decision-Making Process in Conflict Situations Based on the Chess Endgame"—an obscure-sounding subject, yet poignant in the light of his subsequent fate. For it was while he studied at MIPT that Sharansky rediscovered his Jewish identity. The Six Day War had already made a profound impact on his and many other Soviet Jewish families. "In addition to fighting for her life, Israel was defending our dignity," Sharansky later wrote.

> On the eve of the war, when Israel's destruction seemed almost inevitable, Soviet anti-Semites were jubilant. But a few days later even anti-Jewish jokes started to change, and throughout the country, in spite of pro-Arab propaganda, you could now see a grudging respect for Israel and for Jews. A basic, eternal truth was returning to the Jews of Russia—that personal freedom wasn't something you could achieve through assimilation. It was available only by reclaiming your historical roots.

The victory of the Jewish state inspired many to apply for exit visas, even though this usually led to instant dismissal and there was no guarantee that the request would ever be granted. In 1972 some 31,000 Soviet Jews emigrated to Israel. According to his biographer, Martin Gilbert, in January 1973 Sharansky began attending a private seminar on Jewish life and letters organized by a prominent refusenik, Professor Vitaly Rubin. The very idea of such a seminar was a direct challenge to the authorities and attendance was perilous.

The first topic was a talk about Gershom Scholem's celebrated rediscovery of Kabbalah, the mystical tradition of medieval Judaism. Scholem was also a leading Zionist, who had given up an academic career in Weimar Germany to help found the Hebrew

University in Jerusalem—an inspirational figure for the young Sharansky. Of course, mysticism of any kind was anathema to Marxist ideology, and Jewish mysticism doubly so. Moreover, as Gilbert points out, Scholem had spoken at a protest meeting of the Scientists' Committee of the Israel Public Council for Soviet Jewry in Israel in August 1972, at which he denounced the dismissal of Jewish scientists in the Soviet Union and the denial of their right to emigrate to Israel. Scholem sought to shame the world, which was appeasing the Kremlin in the name of détente while ignoring the persecution of Soviet Jews. "What has not yet transpired between us and the world of nations? What poisoned cup have we not already drunk?" That autumn, Scholem's committee began publishing a *News Bulletin,* which became the West's main source of information about Soviet refuseniks. It was this growing external interest in their fate that gave Soviet Jews the courage to persist.

Working simultaneously on the cognitive processes that underpin chess endgames while learning about the Jewish heritage that he sought to reclaim as his own had a cathartic effect on Sharansky. The examination commission at the Institute of Physics and Technology "had paid me a flattering but definitely exaggerated compliment, concluding that I had designed, in their words, 'the first chess program in the world capable of playing the endgame,'" Sharansky later wrote in his memoirs. In an endgame, time and space are reduced to their bare elements, and one move may well decide the outcome. Chess is an unforgiving game, in which failure to seize the initiative is severely punished. Within a few weeks of his first attendance at Rubin's seminar, Sharansky himself came to a very personal decision: one that inaugurated his own endgame—and, in a sense, that of communism. In April 1973 he applied for an exit visa for Israel.

Once Sharansky had taken this step, he was seen as little better than a traitor. If he was going to be a refusenik, he might as well be a notorious one, so—not content to await the verdict of the authorities—he organized demonstrations on behalf of imprisoned refuseniks. The Yom Kippur War in October 1973 prompted new protests in support of Israel, at one of which he met his future wife, Avital Shtiglits. United by their common predicament and endeavor, they learned Hebrew together and fell in love—forming a bond that would overcome every obstacle, including enforced separation for more than a decade.

Sharansky's application was refused on the grounds that he had "access to classified materials." In reality, the material he was working on was one of the few things not classified in the Soviet Union: the game of chess. So why was he refused? Having recently lost the world championship to the Americans, the Soviet Union had become ultrasensitive about chess. In particular, the study of endgames in cybernetics had possible military applications. However, the underlying reason for turning down Sharansky, and thereby turning him into a refusenik, was surely anti Semitism.

Over the next few years Sharansky became a leading dissident. In May 1974 he was arrested during a demonstration outside the Lebanese embassy in Moscow, protesting about an Arab terrorist attack that had killed twenty children in Israel. On that occasion, Sharansky had taken charge and led the protesters, among whom was the academician Andrei Sakharov. A month later, Sharansky was arrested again and held in custody throughout a visit by President Nixon.

Meanwhile, Avital's exit visa had been granted, on condition that she leave for Israel within ten days of receiving confirmation. This faced her with a terrible dilemma. Sharansky was in prison, and it was unclear both when he would be released and whether he would also be allowed to emigrate. She and Sharansky wanted to get married in Moscow's only synagogue, because they had been refused a civil wedding. Under Jewish law, the last day that the wedding could take place before August was July 5, the same day that Avital's visa expired. Hoping against hope, she arranged with the rabbi—who did not know that her fiancé was a refusenik—that the wedding would take place on July 4. That morning, Sharansky was still in prison and, like his captors, he had no idea that it was his wedding day. At 10 A.M., he was told that he was free, but with his habitual stubbornness he refused to leave for another two hours, insisting: "I haven't finished my book." He returned home just in time to shower and shave before the ceremony. A few Jewish friends, invited at short notice, were present; so, lurking outside the synagogue, was the KGB. Early the following morning, Avital left Moscow for Vienna, where Soviet Jews were processed before emigration to Israel. They would not see each other again for twelve years.

During these years of precarious freedom, Sharansky became close to the unofficial leader of the dissident movement, Andrei Sakharov. His main aim was to warn the West against a policy of détente before the Soviet Union had moved toward democracy and human rights. When Sakharov was awarded the Nobel peace prize in 1975, KGB boss Yuri Andropov bullied seventy-two other academicians into signing a denunciation and decided to banish Russia's "Public Enemy No. 1" to internal exile in Gorky. The great academician's earlier life as the father of the Soviet hydrogen bomb gave him an additional motive to resist the KGB's efforts to break his will, although they did so by increasingly brutal means, culminating in the use of psychiatric drugs. Sakharov was not Jewish, but his wife Elena Bonner was, and the couple took an active part in the refuseniks' campaign. Denounced as a Jew because he defended Israel, Sakharov had the life of his newborn grandchild threatened by KGB men of Arab appearance. Sharansky acted as Sakharov's English translator and did much to make him the voice of Russia's conscience. He learned from Sakharov the impotence of the apparently omnipotent Soviet system when faced by determined dissidents. He also grasped that insisting on the right to emigrate for Jews would eventually prize open the prison door for all those living under communism.

On November 18, 1974, Sharansky and other refuseniks sent a letter to President Ford, just before the latter met the Soviet leader Leonid Brezhnev in Vladivostok at a summit. The plight of Soviet Jewry caused a sensation back in America and ensured the unanimous passage of the Jackson Amendment in the Senate, which made trade with the Soviet Union dependent on the right to emigrate. It was an astonishing coup for the refuseniks, who despite their obscurity had persuaded the most powerful nation on earth to impose sanctions on their oppressors.

Even more important for them was the 1975 Helsinki Final Act, which provided for human rights to be monitored in all its signatories. The fact that the Soviet Union had signed up to this accord gave Sharansky and the Zionists their chance to unite with other Soviet dissidents in order to put pressure on the authorities. They set up Helsinki Watch, a group that reported on abuses such as the incarceration of political prisoners in psychiatric hospitals.

But it was when Sharansky was arrested in 1977 and charged with treason—a charge that carried the death penalty—that chess, his first love, came to his rescue. Without the comfort of Avital's presence, Sharansky felt desperate at the prospect of many years as a *zek* (political prisoner), or even the firing squad. In his prison memoir, *Fear No Evil*, Sharansky recalls the moment in Lefortovo prison when he overcame his panic at the prospect of being put on trial for his life. He had noticed that under the rules, he was entitled to a chess set even in solitary confinement. Despite initial refusal, he insisted. "A guard brought me a chess set and I arranged the pieces on the board. I immediately began to feel better, for I have always used chess to escape from pressure and anxiety."

Once seated at the board in his cell, Sharansky was immediately transported into the virtual world of chess. He began analyzing his favorite opening, the French Defense, which was a kind of metaphor for his own situation: "If he can withstand White's initial assault, Black's prospects are excellent." Sharansky became so exhilarated that he "started whipping the pieces around as if I were playing both sides in a blitz match. When I reached the endgame I caught myself and returned to the opening position that had intrigued me in the first place. But then it happened all over again: unable to restrain myself, I raced ahead."

After about half an hour of this, Sharansky calmed down. He

was interrupted by a guard bearing a document. It was signed by Yuri Andropov himself. For a moment, the fear returned, but it turned out that Andropov had merely ordered Sharansky's case to be transferred from the Moscow office to the national one, so that he could supervise it personally. In practice, this meant that Sharansky would have a different interrogator, which he took to be a small triumph. "The chess, together with the document signed by Andropov, had a sobering effect, and now that I was less agitated it was time to sit down and think things over." Sharansky concluded that his activities had been too public for the charge of treason, which implied secret contacts with Western spies, to have any plausibility. Yet he was unable to banish the fear. He was worried that he could be surprised by an unexpected accusation—perhaps the contents of a package, detailing the refuseniks' protest activities, that he prepared regularly for Michael Shelbourne, a British schoolteacher, to be passed on to interested parties in London. He had always been open about his protest activities, but it was easy for the KGB to depict any meeting with a Western contact as espionage. "As I sat there, weighing these various possibilities and fearing that at any moment they would summon me to an interrogation for which I wasn't prepared, I looked at the chess set on the table."

What Sharansky did next gives us a fascinating insight into the crucial importance of chess during the Cold War. Drawing on the insights gained while writing his dissertation on "Simulating the Decision-Making Process in Conflict Situations Based on the Chess Endgame," he recalled a central part of his thesis: a "tree" of goals and conditions for attaining them. "And now, as I stared at the chessboard in my cell, it occurred to me that I could take a similar approach in the game I was about to play against the KGB."

On prison lavatory paper, Sharansky wrote down his goals: first, to obstruct the investigation; second, to study the KGB's approach; finally, to expose them, by contact with the West or an open trial. He then decided that all he could do to obstruct the KGB was to refuse cooperation. The enemy's main aims were to present the refuseniks' activities as secret and to use information obtained from him to prepare cases against other refuseniks. Gradually, he built up a diagram, or "tree," of ends and means, similar to those he had formulated in his thesis. "As I look back on it now, my tree seems like pseudoscience, a pathetic attempt to impose order on my racing and chaotic mind. But at the time it was tremendously important, as the familiar terminology from my scientific training helped me to adjust to my new reality." When the guard came, Sharansky flushed the precious paper down the lavatory, but over the next few days he drew the tree repeatedly until he had committed it to memory. Now that he had his endgame plan, Sharansky felt that he had evened up the enormous odds stacked against him.

Sharansky conducted his defense exactly like a game of chess, using logic to glean information from his interrogators or to mislead them about what he knew and how he knew it. His account of this battle of wits often employs chess as a metaphor. When his interrogator Solonchenko takes him unawares, he feels "like a chess player who has planned a beautiful combination and suddenly gets hit with an infantile checkmate. But while Solonchenko had called check, it wasn't yet mate." Later, he turns the tables "and from an especially dangerous state criminal I changed back into a seven-year-old boy who used to sit near the grownups playing chess in the park until somebody left and I'd have a partner, whom I would quickly and proudly defeat." In *Fear No Evil*, he describes several KGB interrogators and other officials whose careers were ruined by their failure to grasp his strategy, let alone to break him.

Sharansky's experience in prison is uncannily reminiscent of one of the finest stories ever written about chess: *The Royal Game* (or *Schachnovelle*), written by the Austrian-Jewish writer Stefan Zweig just before he died in 1942. The tale begins with an encounter between the world chess champion, Czentovic, and the mysterious Dr. B on board a cruise liner. Czentovic is, in the words of the grandmaster and psychoanalyst Reuben Fine, "depicted as a kind of *idiot savant*," not unlike the almost illiterate Indian master,

Sultan Khan. Although an amateur, Dr. B turns out to be a strong enough player to defeat the champion, but it emerges that he had achieved this skill while a prisoner of the Gestapo, kept in solitary confinement. His only distraction was a chess book, stolen during one of his interrogations. Despite not having played a game since his schooldays, he learns how to play without sight of the board against the only available opponent: himself. His games with himself develop into a hallucinatory obsession, and eventually he collapses. Since his release from captivity, he has banished all thought of chess from his mind. When Dr. B plays Czentovic for a second time, the mania returns to devastating effect.

Zweig's terrifying evocation of chess as "thought that leads nowhere, mathematics that adds up to nothing, art without an end product, architecture without substance" is brilliant. Zweig was only a *patzer*—or duffer—at chess, but he knew the Viennese cafés haunted by émigrés, communist and anticommunist, where chess provided consolation for the homesick. His story seems to have been based on the experience of friends who found themselves arrested by the Gestapo immediately after the *Anschluss*. His hero, Dr. B, is said to have been close to the Habsburg family, who for Hitler were indeed objects of particular hostility. There are also aspects of the hero's nervous breakdown that are clearly—and poignantly—autobiographical: Zweig himself was prey to depression and, after emigrating from Europe to Brazil, he and his wife committed suicide. But Zweig's story bears universal testimony to the power of chess as a metaphor for politics. Dr. B's plight, the methods used to break him, his use of a mental discipline (in this case chess) in self-defense, and the trauma that returns long afterwards are all recognizable in the predicament of Sharansky and many other prisoners of conscience.

Sharansky was able to escape the madness of Dr. B, perhaps thanks to his sunny temperament. He never allowed the habit of what one might call "autochess"—playing oneself—to become a compulsive psychological disorder. Nonetheless Sharansky would

surely subscribe to Dr. B's description of the effect that his chess
sessions with himself had on his ability to resist his tormentors:

> It was noticeable at the interrogations that I was thinking more
> clearly and to the point. Without realizing it the chessboard
> had improved my defense against false threats and concealed
> tricks. From that time on I gave them no openings through con-
> tradictory statements and even fancied that the Gestapo was
> beginning gradually to view me with a certain respect. Perhaps
> when they saw everyone else breaking down they asked them-
> selves privately what the secret source of strength was that en-
> abled me alone to put up such unshakeable resistance.

In the Gulag, one of Sharansky's cellmates, Leonid Kolosar, was
also a chess player. They would play long matches in which Sharansky evened the odds by playing without a rook, after which the
loser had to clean up the cell. Kolosar's work at the highest levels
of the Soviet administration had given him an insight into the way
that anti-Semitism worked in the bureaucracy. Of course, there
were many Jews who had made their accommodation with the system, such as the woman advocate whom the KGB provided for
Sharansky's defense, and whose services he refused.

The fact that he received an open trial for treason in 1978 was
the greatest triumph of Sharansky's chess-based methodology. During the trial it stood him in good stead and would certainly have
secured an acquittal if the judge had not been thoroughly biased.
The key witnesses were all informers, but they were no match for
Sharansky's forensic intelligence. A crucial accusation was that in
1975 Sharansky and other refuseniks had met Professor Richard
Pipes, the Harvard historian of Russia, at the apartment of Professor Vitaly Rubin. Among the company was an architect, Vitaly Riabsky, who turned out to be a KGB informer. Pipes was alleged by
Riabsky to have been an American agent "with specific instructions to act as a Zionist emissary." It was true that in 1976, a year
later, Pipes had advised the CIA on Soviet affairs and would later

join the National Security Council during the Reagan administration, but he was never a CIA agent. As for being a "Zionist emissary"—this simply meant that Pipes was Jewish. In *Vixi: Memoirs of a Non-Belonger*, Pipes recalled that "the talk that afternoon [with Sharansky] was of no particular significance." It was, though, of huge significance for Sharansky, for the mere fact of his meeting Pipes proved to be the gravamen of the treason trial. The charge was that the idea of using the Helsinki Final Act to unite the refuseniks and other dissidents of the Helsinki Watch group had come from Pipes, and that the Helsinki Watch group was therefore a kind of CIA front organization. Riabsky claimed that the text of the Final Act was "lying right there on the table." Sharansky was able to show that the meeting had taken place more than a month before the Helsinki conference. Riabsky then claimed that the meeting had occurred a year later, but by then Pipes was not in Moscow and Rubin was in Israel. So the whole story was a lie.

This discrepancy enabled Sharansky to checkmate Riabsky, but it was all to no avail. After the procurator ranted about how international Zionism and imperialist secret services were in league with Soviet Jewry, it was Sharansky's turn to defend himself in open court, with his brother Lenya present. He was able to show that all the evidence against him had been concocted by the KGB. He was accused of slandering the Soviet regime by alleging that a film shown on state television, *Traders in Souls*, was anti-Semitic. The KGB had collected vox pop responses to the film, and Sharansky was able to quote one of these statements, thanking the producers of the film for proving that "the Jews are doing the only thing that their nation is capable of—living at the expense of other people." Sharansky turned toward the Soviet journalists in court and asked: "Isn't this anti-Semitism in the purest form? These are the kind of feelings that the producers of so-called anti-Zionist material want to arouse in the people."

Before the verdict was announced, Sharansky had his moment to address the court. Demonstratively ignoring the judge, he delivered his speech to his brother, who was able to repeat it later to the outside world despite the fact that his notebook, in which he had recorded the entire proceedings, was confiscated by the KGB.

In his speech, Sharansky explained how the KGB had offered him a short sentence and the chance to join his wife in Israel in return for cooperation. He had refused, knowing what the consequence would be. Recalling the time since he had first applied for an exit visa, he declared: "These five years were the best of my life. I am happy that I have been able to live them honestly and at peace with my conscience. I have said only what I believed, and I have not violated my conscience even when my life was in danger."

Sharansky then turned to his fellow dissidents, among whom he named Sakharov, Yuri Orlov, and Alexander Ginzburg, "who are carrying on the best traditions of the Russian intelligentsia." He felt, he said, "part of a marvelous historical process—the process of the national revival of Soviet Jewry and its return to the homeland, to Israel." He would, he said, gladly have exchanged his status as a celebrity refusenik for a visa to Israel. With the rest of the diaspora, he repeated the words Lesbanu haba'a b'Yerushalayim ("Next year in Jerusalem!") every year at Passover. "And today, when I am further than ever from my dream, from my people, and from my Avital, and when many difficult years of prisons and camps lie ahead of me, I say to my wife and to my people, Lesbana haba'a b'Yerushalayim." Then, turning to the judge, he concluded: "And to the court, which has only to read a sentence that was prepared long ago—to you I have nothing to say."

The judge ruled that Sharansky had met "confidentially" with Pipes, from whom he had received "concrete recommendations" about "stirring up" anti-Soviet activity including "rousing national hatred," which "influential circles in the USA see as a powerful catalyst, furthering the erosion of Soviet society." This, perhaps the most famous of all the trials of dissidents during the last years of the Soviet Union, ended with the sentence: thirteen years' hard labor. Just before Sharansky was led away, his brother Lenya—hitherto a loyal Soviet citizen—called to him: "Tolya! The whole world is with you!"

As the Soviet autocracy degenerated into gerontocracy, it was still capable of vicious repression. By 1978, according to Anne Applebaum's history of the Gulag, the Soviet Union no longer sent political prisoners to the worst Siberian labor camps, such as Mordovia and Perm, but preferred special high-security prisons such as Vladimir. Apart from physical privations, the greatest danger for Sharansky was psychological. Dissidents like him were subject to constant pressure to collaborate, which took the form of temptation rather than threat. He later described the experience:

> They will invite you for a talk. You think nothing depends on you? On the contrary: they will explain that everything depends on you. Do you like tea, coffee, meat? Would you like to go with me to a restaurant? Why not? We'll dress you in civilian clothes and we'll go. If we see that you're on the road to rehabilitation, that you're prepared to help us—what, you don't want to squeal on your friends? But what does it mean to squeal? This Russian (or Jew, or Ukrainian, depending on the situation) who's serving time with you, don't you realize what kind of nationalist he is? Don't you know how much he hates you Ukrainians (or Russians, or Jews)?

This was a complex game of psychological warfare—once again, a form of chess—in which the prisoner hoped to remain sound in mind and body while smuggling out news via samizdat networks, while the interrogators aimed to break the prisoner and persuade him to recant. By this time, the prize that both sides were playing for was Western public opinion. By holding out and refusing to be intimidated or bought off, the dissidents hoped to convince the United States and its allies that their policy of détente was a delusion—that only robust opposition to the Soviet bloc would achieve security for the West and freedom for the oppressed peoples of the East.

Sharansky's main opponent was Yuri Andropov, the head of the KGB from 1967 to 1982, who briefly became party leader until his death in 1984. Andropov is sometimes depicted as a reformer and Mikhail Gorbachev was his protégé. In fact, Andropov was directly involved in several of the worst cases of late Soviet aggression—the crushing of the Hungarian uprising and the Prague Spring, the invasion of Afghanistan and the shooting down of a Korean airliner. Andropov was responsible for the creation in 1968 of the KGB's Fifth Directorate, which carried out "ideological counterintelligence" against dissidents. In 1969 he set up a network of psychiatric "hospitals" *(psikushkas)* where political prisoners were subjected to appalling abuses.

To the day he died, Andropov was convinced that Sharansky had indeed spied for the CIA. The East German spymaster Markus Wolf has thrown light on Andropov's thinking about Sharansky in his memoirs, *Man Without a Face*. Wolf claimed that he had repeatedly tried to persuade Andropov to exchange Sharansky for a high-profile Eastern bloc prisoner such as Günter Guillaume, the spy who had precipitated the fall of Willy Brandt. Wolf argued that Andropov had solved the problem of Solzhenitsyn by putting him on a plane to West Germany, while Andrei Sakharov had merely been dispatched to internal exile in Gorky; why not be rid of Sharansky too? According to Wolf, Andropov replied: "Comrade Wolf, don't you know what will happen if we give this signal? The man is a spy, but more important, he is a Jew, and it is the Jews he speaks for. Too many groups have suffered under the repression in our country. If we give this sort of ground to the Jews, who will be next? The Volga Germans? The Crimean Tartars? Or maybe the Kalmuks or the Chechens?" Andropov reportedly feared that Sharansky would be even more dangerous to Soviet interests once he regained his freedom in the West: "[Sharansky] will carry a flag for all the Jews. Stalin's anti-Semitic excesses have left these people with a big grievance against the Soviet state and they have powerful friends abroad. We cannot allow that at the moment." Wolf claims that Andropov "was equally frank about the Soviet Union's decline, the start of which . . . he pinpointed as the 1968 invasion of Czechoslovakia"—an invasion for which Andropov had been in large part responsible. The fact that Andropov was apparently "allergic to [Sharansky's] very name" suggests that by the time of his death he knew that he was losing the endgame.

Sharansky's skill at chess was the best possible training for this deadly psychological duel, but chess was also of more direct use to him. As he later recalled, it was chess that saved him in 1981 when he was placed in solitary confinement during his battle to have the tiny psalm book that Avital had given him returned. In his punishment cell Sharansky recalled a game he had lost many years before to a chess master who had surprised him with a new variation in the Spanish Opening.

> Until now I had never had the time or the desire to think about it seriously. But as I paced in a half-stupor around the punishment cell, trying to sit on the tiny cement stump or lying on the floor, my thoughts often returned to this particular variation. When I thought I had finally found a refutation, the following day I found a way to reinforce White's position. Again and again I played one variation or another, analyzing it for ten, twenty, thirty, even forty moves. I don't know how many games I played, but I did finally find a refutation. Of course, this wasn't the important gain; what chess did was help preserve my sanity.

By playing countless games in his head, Sharansky was able to preserve a private space, ward off despair, and keep a grip on reality. "And guess what?" he later told an interviewer. "I always won."

Having proved that they could not break him, Sharansky was released from solitary confinement and found solace in the company of other political prisoners. His friendship with Sakharov made him a hero to his fellow *zeks*. To obtain the right to send letters to his wife in Israel and his family in Moscow, he endured several hunger strikes and force-feeding, one of them lasting 110 days, which left him with a permanently weakened heart. His resistance earned the respect even of his jailers, who were forced to grant him his legal rights. He refused the offer of a pardon from the Soviet Presidium, even when his mother appealed to him. He never made the slightest concession to the KGB or acknowledged the legitimacy of the Soviet authorities. He gradually realized that he was playing chess by proxy with Andropov himself, the General Secretary and former head of the KGB. Andropov was "determined to prove that [Sharansky] had genuinely started on the road to 're-habilitation,' no matter how [he] actually behaved."

When Andropov died in February 1984, Sharansky's regular punishments, which had ceased for some months, resumed. His wife Avital had been campaigning tirelessly in the meantime for his release, meeting Reagan, Thatcher, Mitterrand, and countless other influential figures in the West. Sharansky knew little of this, except what he could glean from anti-Semitic Soviet propaganda. One of his guards brought him a book about "subversive" Jewish activities, which claimed that world Zionism and U.S. imperialism were collaborating against the Soviet Union. It quoted a letter of support that President Reagan had written to Avital in 1983, two years before Sharansky saw it: "I felt as if the President himself had written to me in the prison of Perm 35. It was hard to say which I enjoyed more—that Reagan had written me this letter or that the prison authorities had unknowingly delivered it." In 1986, after Sharansky had spent nine years inside the Gulag, the Gorbachev regime finally let him go and flew him to East Berlin. There he was released on the notorious Glienicke Bridge, where spies were regularly exchanged. Reunited with Avital, he was at last able to emigrate to Israel.

Sharansky later founded a party to provide a platform for the Russian Jews in Israel and subsequently became a prominent minister in several Likud-led coalition governments. In 2005 he resigned from Ariel Sharon's cabinet over the issue of withdrawal from Gaza. In October 2006—still only fifty-eight—he announced his retirement from active politics, although he is still a member of the Knesset. Sharansky found a niche as a Distinguished Scholar at the Shalem Center in Jerusalem, a think tank devoted to the history and security of the Jewish people. After his retirement, there was speculation that he might replace the scandal ridden Moshe Katsav as president of Israel. From refusenik to head of the Jewish state would have been a fitting denouement to a unique career, but the post went to the more statesmanlike Shimon Peres. On a visit to Washington to receive the Presidential Medal of Freedom, Sharansky insisted that he had had enough of politics. When asked whether he was looking forward to speaking his mind, now that he was freed from the burden of office, he replied: "I always did speak my mind—that's why I am a hopeless politician!" His proudest boast is that when perhaps the greatest of all the Russian world champions, Garry Kasparov, visited Israel and gave a simultaneous display, Sharansky was still strong enough to defeat him. They became close friends, united by chess and the cause of freedom. Even now, Sharansky's devotion to chess is quasireligious. When Avital and their daughters go to synagogue, he stays at home to play chess. However, his most treasured possession is the little book of psalms that she gave him and that he kept throughout his ordeal in the Gulag. He goes nowhere without it.

Sharansky's significance transcends even the emigration of Soviet Jewry, which transformed the state of Israel and helped to bring about the collapse of communism, for Sharansky has become a symbol of resistance in the war on terror, too. In his political career in Israel and in his remarkable book, *The Case for Democracy*, he has invested the moral capital that he accumulated as a dissident in an attempt to persuade the West that its core values do truly have the power to overcome the global jihad currently being mounted by radical Islam. He is now working on a sequel, *The Case for Identity*. This will argue that freedom and democracy are empty without identity; men need to know what they need freedom and democracy for before they will make sacrifices for them. The loss of identity is threatening Europe, particularly when it is faced by aggressors who know exactly who they are and what they stand for. Without his Jewish identity, Sharansky would not have passed the endurance test of the Gulag—indeed, he might have avoided politics altogether and spent his life contentedly creating chess-playing computer programs.

Instead, Sharansky sacrificed his own liberty for that of others. To give the best years of your life for something so intangible, you must see liberty as far more than an abstraction. Yet it is precisely the ability to abstract—to move from the particular to the general and back again—to which chess is so conducive. No other hero of the Cold War embodies so well the victory of mind over matter, of the free spirit over the idolatry of the state—and of the contribution made by chess to that victory.

Sharansky was unique only in the example that he set, not just to Jews but to dissidents everywhere. The fact that he was a Jew and a chess prodigy was entirely typical. From the mid-nineteenth century onwards, an extraordinarily high proportion of chess masters, including most of the great world champions, have been Jews. In this respect, chess may well be a special case of a more general intellectual phenomenon. At the same time and in the same places that Jews became prominent, and in some fields even dominant, in European culture, the anti-Semitic stereotype of the Jew as clever but morally dubious also emerged. The history of this phenomenon in Vienna around 1900 is the subject of Sandor L. Gilman's *Smart Jews: The Construction of the Image of Jewish Superior Intelligence*. Gilman's study was a critical response to the controversy generated in 1994 by *The Bell Curve: Intelligence and Class Structure in American Life*, in which Richard J. Herrnstein and Charles Murray provided statistical evidence to show that "Ashkenazi Jews of European origin" have a higher IQ than any other ethnic group or subgroup. While this part of Herrnstein and Murray's thesis is widely accepted, its causation and the conclusions they draw from it are still hotly contested. In particular, the notion that there is a direct connection between intelligence and morality remains problematic. Both the virtues and vices attributed to Jews on account of their superior intelligence have, to say the least, been exaggerated.

In his more recent work, *Human Accomplishment: The Pursuit of Excellence in the Arts and Sciences, 800 BC to 1950*, Charles Murray briefly discusses chess as an example of a highly competitive field of endeavor in which the most gifted individuals far outstrip the rest. Murray finds that excellence in chess is hyperbolically distributed, shown in graphic form by the Lotka curve. To win games of chess at world championship level is one of the most difficult of all human accomplishments, and the capacity to do it repeatedly is given to only a handful of geniuses. "The measures that produce Lotka curves not only discriminate the excellent from the mediocre, but the unparalleled from the merely excellent."

When, in an article on "Jewish Genius" for *Commentary* in April 2007, Murray returned to the fraught question of why Jews are such high achievers, he did not consider the case of chess. But he did calculate the number of "significant figures" in a number of other comparable fields in Europe and North America during the period after Jewish emancipation: "From 1870 to 1950, Jewish representation in literature was four times the number one would expect. In music, five times. In the visual arts, five times. In biology, eight times. In chemistry, six times. In physics, nine times. In mathematics, twelve times. In philosophy, fourteen times." Even more striking are the numbers of Nobel prizes awarded to Jews. A people that constitutes 0.02 percent of the world's population included 14 percent of Nobel laureates in the first half of the twentieth century, 29 percent in the second half, and 32 percent so far in the twenty-first century.

Murray argues that only a unique gene pool can explain such disproportionate results and suggests a number of hypotheses to account for this genetic selection for high intelligence, particularly in verbal reasoning. The most widely accepted quantitative theory is that offered by the physicist Gregory Cochran and the anthropologists Jason Hardy and Henry Harpending. In their 2006 article on the "Natural History of Ashkenazi Intelligence" for the *Journal of Biosocial Science*, Cochran, Hardy, and Harpending argue that during the Middle Ages, Ashkenazi Jews in Europe north of the Pyrenees were restricted to finance and trade, and that this occupational selection favored those with a high IQ in verbal and mathematical skills. Murray, by contrast, suggests that Jewish genius antedates the medieval period and even the diaspora of the Roman era. Highly significant in this selective process was the universal male literacy that Jews achieved within a century of the destruction of the Temple in the first century, thanks to an ordinance of the leading scholar, Joshua ben Gamla, in AD 64, which established the tradition that all boys must read the Scriptures aloud before the assembled congregation. Murray cites another article (in the *Journal of Economic History*, 2005) by Maristella Botticini and Zvi Eckstein entitled "Jewish Occupational Selection: Education, Restrictions, or Minorities?" which suggests that those Jews who worked on the land saw no benefit in literacy. Over time their Judaism lapsed and they were absorbed by the Christian or Muslim population, leaving only the most intelligent to carry on as a persecuted Jewish minority. But Murray thinks this intellectualization of Judaism worked in the opposite direction, too: the requirement to read and understand complex works such as the Torah and the Talmud ensured that only the most articulate could keep the faith: "Judaism evolved in such a way that to be a good Jew meant that a man had to be smart." Moreover, the literacy that became such a distinctive characteristic of Jewish spirituality was in fact foreshadowed much earlier in antiquity, in the composition over many centuries of the Hebrew Bible. The ultimate origins of Jewish intellectualism defy scientific explanation: "They are God's chosen people."

The proportion of Jews among world chess champions exceeds that in most other fields of intellectual accomplishment and the proportion is even higher if other leading players are included. Since the title was officially created in 1886, six out of fourteen champions have been wholly or partly Jewish; on average their reigns lasted longer than those of their gentile counterparts, and more than half of their rivals and challengers were also Jewish. It is not clear whether Jews had some genetic disposition to excel at chess, or were attracted to it because this intellectually demanding, highly competitive "sedentary sport" (as the chess historian Richard Eales calls it) fitted the prevailing Jewish stereotype in nineteenth-century Europe. What Gerald Abrahams identified as "the chess mind"—a combination of memory, logic, and imagination—has much in common with skills that were, and still are, characteristic of Jewish intellectual life. Above all, the study of sacred texts is conducive to a game on which more books have been written than on all other games put together. The game of the book had a special appeal to the first people of the book.

8

THE AMERICAN
WAY OF CHESS

T HE RUMBUSTIOUS INDIVIDUALISM of the American
way of life found its expression in chess, too. Yet the very
first star to blaze across the Atlantic was so fastidious
that he preferred to renounce the game rather than demean himself to the level of the European professionals who made their living from what he called "our kingly pastime." The first American
Chess Congress, which took place in New York in 1857, witnessed
the spectacular triumph of twenty-year-old Paul Morphy, from an
upper-class Creole family in New Orleans. Morphy's talent first
manifested itself at the age of eight. By the time he was thirteen,
he had beaten everybody in New Orleans. Having received his law
degree while still too young to practice at the Bar in Louisiana, he
went to New York, intending to play chess only until the age of
twenty-one. He told the assembled enthusiasts: "For the first time
in the annals of American Chess, a Congress is being held which
bids fair to mark an era in the history of our noble game. Chess,
hitherto viewed by our countrymen in the light of a mere amuse-
ment, assumes at last its appropriate place among the sciences

which at once adorn and exalt the intellect." Deeply conscious of his social and intellectual status, Morphy never intended to give his life to chess, but he decided to pay one extended visit to Europe.

In a public chess career that lasted only three years, Morphy came, saw, and conquered the greatest masters of Europe. However, there was one man whom Morphy was determined to defeat but who eluded him: the English chess panjandrum Howard Staunton. Although Staunton had retired from competitive chess to finish working on his edition of Shakespeare, he was tempted to make a comeback against the new American star. Morphy's British manager and later biographer, the journalist Frederick Edge, deliberately manufactured a dispute between them, which became acrimonious. The aging Staunton ended by accusing Morphy of being a professional while somewhat pretentiously insisting on his own amateur status. Unlike Staunton, who encouraged the rumor that he was the natural son of the Earl of Carlisle, Morphy was a genuine amateur, having inherited a fortune. By contrast, Staunton was a typical Victorian entrepreneur. He not only conceived and organized the first chess tournament to coincide with the Great Exhibition in London in 1851, but earned a precarious living from his chess books and columns. He also pioneered the sponsorship deal by lending his name to the Staunton pattern sets manufactured by Jaques, which have standardized the design of chess pieces ever since. Yet Staunton, a failed actor, preferred to be remembered as a Shakespearean scholar.

Morphy and Edge then moved to Paris, where further chess duels were fought. Although there was no official world champion, the German Adolf Anderssen, who had won the London tournament, was generally acknowledged to be the best active player in Europe. Morphy crushed him by seven games to two. In 1859, however, Morphy's brother-in-law arrived from New Orleans to take him home. Edge later wrote a tendentious biography that turned Morphy into a legend at the expense of Staunton, whose reputation has only recently been restored by the efforts of Raymond Keene and the Staunton Society.

On his return, the American public acclaimed Morphy as a hero, none more highly than the judge Oliver Wendell Holmes. At a banquet in the Revere House, Boston, the autocrat of the breakfast table toasted him as "the world's chess champion." Morphy was still just twenty-two: "His peaceful battles have helped to achieve a new revolution; his youthful triumphs have added a new clause to the Declaration of American Independence," declared Holmes. No American had been world champion of anything before, and the press made the most of it. Nevertheless, Morphy carried out his pledge to renounce chess. He offered to play anybody in the world at the odds of "pawn and move" (i.e., playing Black and minus a pawn). This was the equivalent of a Wimbledon champion offering to let his rivals serve and start fifteen love up in each game. The offer was a feint, a perversely ingenious way of showing that he was in a different class from his fellow players. In effect, he was asserting that he had no rival. Morphy knew that none of the European masters would play on such demeaning terms. His social pretensions forced him to repress his unique talent.

Having given up chess, however, Morphy found he could do nothing much else. He retreated into morose seclusion, cared for by his mother and sister, occasionally playing an informal game with his friend Maurian in which flashes of his old genius could still be glimpsed. By the time he was found dead of a stroke in his bath in 1884, at the age of forty-seven, his precocity had degenerated into clinical depression and paranoia. The local paper, the *Daily Picayune*, noted that "he never did but scratch the surface of his marvelous ability." Eighty years later, Bobby Fischer noted: "[Morphy] was disillusioned with chess players rather than with chess."

Morphy established a meteoric pattern that has repeated itself down the years: young genius emerges, beats everyone in the New World, crosses the Atlantic to astonish the Old World, then abruptly vanishes from the scene. In 1895, Harry Nelson Pillsbury from Boston burst on to the scene. He had been the hidden operator inside the chess automaton Ajeeb, but otherwise had little experience. Pillsbury came to England for the first Hastings tournament, at which all the leading masters of the day were present. Some regard this as the greatest tournament of all time. Indeed, since 1922 the Hastings chess tournament has become an annual event, making the seaside resort almost as synonymous with chess as with the Norman Conquest. Aged only twenty-two, Pillsbury took first prize, outstripping the new world champion, Emanuel Lasker, the old champion, Wilhelm Steinitz, and the two most successful tournament players of the day, Siegbert Tarrasch and Mikhail Tchigorin. Handsome, charming, and youthful, Pillsbury was proclaimed the new Morphy.

Nemesis followed. The very next year, at the first of three great St. Petersburg tournaments before the First World War, Pillsbury won his matches against Lasker and Tchigorin, but was so thoroughly trounced by Steinitz that he finished only third. Only much later did the cause of this setback emerge: during the tournament he had contracted syphilis. Although he went on to win other tournaments, he was never able to raise the stake money to mount a challenge to Lasker.

To supplement his meager income, Pillsbury made himself supreme in blindfold chess, giving simultaneous displays without sight of the board all over Europe, including one in Hanover against twenty-one players of master strength. His speciality was to play twelve games of chess, six of draughts, and one of duplicate whist (a forerunner of bridge) all at once—and all blindfold. "He could break off a séance for an intermission and upon resumption readily call up the positions on every board at will, and, when requested, would announce the moves made in any particular game from the beginning." At the time, the efforts required by these unprecedented feats of memory were blamed for his later mental collapse. Lasker himself, in an appreciation for the *New York Times*, stated as a fact that Pillsbury "died from an illness contracted through overexertion of his memory cells." Dr. Tarrasch, an eminent physician as well as a grandmaster, rightly rejected such a condition as unknown to medical science. Having examined Pillsbury, he had diagnosed "progressive paralysis"—the contemporary euphemism for syphilis—as he explained in a brilliant postmortem, "The Case of Pillsbury," in his book *Die Moderne Schachpartie*. Yet the myth that blindfold chess was connected to mental illness persisted. No medical basis for this claim has ever been found, yet blindfold displays were banned in the Soviet Union. Perhaps they were associated in the puritanical communist mind with the idea of chess as entertainment, rather than an activity of scientific, educational, or artistic value. Certainly the Soviet chess bureaucracy resisted anything that tended to make chess masters financially independent of the state.

By 1904, when Pillsbury played his last tournament at Cambridge Springs, Pennsylvania, before a home crowd, his syphilis had reached the tertiary stage and was affecting his mind as well as his body. Although he could still beat Lasker in a celebrated game with a new opening (immediately dubbed the "Cambridge Springs Defense") that is still played today, the great hope of the New World was only a shadow of his former self. For the first time he failed to be among the prizewinners. In 1906 he died, aged only thirty-three and living on the charity of his admirers.

The youthful victor at Cambridge Springs, Frank Marshall, became Pillsbury's successor as U.S. champion. Unlike Morphy and Pillsbury, however, his career was not meteoric; he held the title for over a quarter of a century, and died at a ripe old age. Facially, Marshall resembled another contemporary, the great Shakespearean actor Henry Irving, and he dressed flamboyantly in the style made fashionable by Oscar Wilde. A fine tournament player, he played swashbuckling chess and could swindle the best. His most celebrated queen sacrifice was greeted by a shower of gold pieces from the audience. In long matches, however, he was crushed by Tarrasch, Lasker, and Capablanca. Like Morphy and Pillsbury, Marshall created a legend, perpetuated by the Marshall Chess Club in New York that was named after him—the scene in later years of some of Bobby Fischer's most famous exploits.

It was not long before the pattern of New World ambushing Old World repeated itself. This time the young genius who crossed the Atlantic was a Cuban, José Raúl Capablanca. A child prodigy, he learned the moves aged four by watching his father, then promptly took him on and beat him. At twelve he defeated the Cuban champion Juan Corzo, a recognized master. Capablanca was educated in the United States, where he dropped out of Columbia University after playing too much chess—including many friendly games with Lasker—and was fortunate that Marshall accepted his challenge to a match in 1909. To general astonishment, Capablanca (who had never played in a tournament) won 8–1. Having defeated Marshall, Capablanca arrived in Europe aged twenty-three for the tournament of San Sebastian. Many felt that the unknown and inexperienced Cuban had no place in such elite company, for every grandmaster except Lasker was playing. Capablanca won first prize. Apart from Pillsbury, no unknown had emerged from obscurity to win such a great international tournament at the first attempt before—and nobody has done it since. Capablanca immediately challenged Lasker to a world championship match, but wrangles about conditions, followed by the outbreak of war, postponed the match for a decade. Between 1914 and 1924, Capablanca lost only one game. In 1920 Lasker bowed to the inevitable and resigned his title in favor of Capablanca, who, however, insisted on a match. This finally took place a year later in Havana, a climate that did Lasker no favors. Out of practice, ill, and demoralized, Lasker lost four games, drew ten, and won none before he resigned the match, allowing Capablanca finally to become world champion. The Cuban held the title for only six years, but remained one of the strongest players in the world until his premature death in 1942. No other master in history lost so few games, and at least four of his peers—Lasker, Alekhine, Botvinnik, and Karpov—have paid tribute to him as the greatest genius of all.

The era between the world wars was a golden age for American chess. Two great tournaments in New York in 1924 and 1927, won by Lasker and Capablanca respectively, helped to enthuse the public. A new generation, led by Reuben Fine, Samuel Reshevsky, and Isaac Kashdan, quickly established themselves among the world's leading grandmasters. But capitalism and chess were intimately connected, and the Wall Street crash had a devastating effect on the finances of chess in the United States. There were no more major tournaments there until after 1945. Yet the situation was even worse in Europe, and so it was during the hungry 1930s that the United States became the strongest chess-playing nation in the world, winning four chess Olympiads.

American culture in general, and chess in particular, benefited from the influx of talent from Nazi-dominated Europe. Nevertheless, it was a precarious profession for the handful of masters who devoted their lives to the game. In 1939 war broke out during the Buenos Aires Olympiad and several of the European masters chose to settle in Argentina; ominously for the future of American chess, none moved to the United States. Although the American economy revived in the 1940s, American chess went into a period of temporary decline. After a brief period in the early 1930s when he won several tournaments, Kashdan interrupted his chess career to become an insurance salesman. But the greatest blow was the early retirement of Reuben Fine.

Despite never having won the U.S. championship, Fine was the only American who won more games than he lost against the world champions Lasker, Alekhine, and—most significantly —Botvinnik. His short international career lasted less than five years, during which he won eight tournaments. At Nottingham 1936, Fine finished just behind the past and future champions Capablanca and Botvinnik, third equal with his American rival Reshevsky and the reigning Euwe, but ahead of Alekhine and Lasker. After Alekhine regained the title, Fine won the right to challenge him by taking joint first place with Keres at the Avro tournament in 1938, ahead of Botvinnik, among others. Fine's playing was thwarted by the war, during which he worked for the government in Washington. His idea of relaxation was to produce *Basic Chess Endings,* the best book ever written about the most demanding part of chess. Meanwhile he was also studying for a doctorate in psychology. After Alekhine died in 1946, Fine argued that he and Keres, as the officially designated crown princes of chess, should be declared joint champions until a successor was found. Nobody else agreed—not even Keres. As an Estonian who had played in Nazi tournaments, he was grateful to avoid being sent to the Gulag as a collaborator. He was certainly not about to make common cause with an American against the Soviet Union.

Fine, however, was invited by FIDE to the 1948 match tournament to find a new world champion, but after much agonizing he chose not to participate, for several reasons. These were partly political: the Cold War was already freezing U.S.–Soviet relations. With hindsight, Fine told friends that "he didn't want to waste three months of his life watching Russians throw games to each other." There was also the awkward fact that the U.S. Chess Federation, with which he was on bad terms, refused to support his candidature for the world championship, suggesting instead Isaac Kashdan or the current U.S. champion Arnold Denker, although neither had a record comparable to Fine's. Crucially, this unusually long tournament, which required the participants to move from The Hague to Moscow at the halfway stage, would have clashed with Fine's final university examinations. In the end, he decided to forsake chess for a new profession as a psychoanalyst. In 1950s Manhattan, to be a psychoanalyst was both prestigious and lucrative; to be a chess master was neither. In Fine's hands, the wedding of the two eventually gave birth to another classic, *The Psychology of the Chess Player.* However, with his departure the Americans had lost their best hope of a world champion for a generation.

Fine's abdication left the United States with only one world-class grandmaster, Samuel Reshevsky. He began life as the most notorious chess prodigy of them all. Born in 1911, the same year as Botvinnik, as the sixth child of a poor Orthodox Jewish family, he gave simultaneous displays from the age of six, first in Poland and later throughout Europe. He arrived in the United States aged nine and enjoyed two years of freakish celebrity before the American courts intervened and his parents were charged with "improper guardianship." As a result, he retired from chess at the tender age of twelve, having already defeated Grandmaster Janowski in a tournament game—a record that has yet to be broken. Reshevsky went to school and to college, but returned to chess in adult life. In the mid-1930s he made extended tours of Europe. By winning his first major tournament at Margate 1935, ahead of Capablanca, Reshevsky proved that he had matured into a true grandmaster.

With his diminutive stature, chain-smoking habit, and premature baldness (unsuccessfully obscured by a wig), Reshevsky's style was as unprepossessing as his gnomish appearance. His chess had something in common with the American military doctrine of his day, which relied on technical superiority rather than complex tactics: he would build up an impregnable position, often using up to an hour on one move, before the inevitable time scramble, during which he hardly ever blundered. Most of his games were decided in the endgame. Yet his results over the four years from 1935 to 1939 confirmed that he was the equal of his leading contemporaries Fine, Keres, and Botvinnik. Like theirs, however, his career was interrupted by war. He won four consecutive U.S. championships and proved especially formidable in long matches.

In 1944 Reshevsky was tantalizingly close to achieving his goal of becoming world champion when—like his namesake, the prophet Samuel—he heard a voice calling him. God told him that he had committed a grave sin by playing chess on the Sabbath, for which his father's death was a punishment. Thereafter, he would play solely on condition that he was excused from sunset on Friday to sunset on Saturday. Indeed, Reshevsky decided that chess was looming too large in his life, compared to his family and his faith. Having none of the support enjoyed by his Soviet rivals, he resolved to concentrate on a more lucrative career as an accountant and thereafter played chess only intermittently.

Indeed, he hardly played at all during the two years preceding the 1948 match tournament for the world championship at The Hague and Moscow. Botvinnik emerged triumphant, with Smyslov second, while Reshevsky had to be content to share third place with Keres. In 1950 Reshevsky was eager to play in the Budapest candidates' tournament, where he would have stood an excellent chance of qualifying to challenge Botvinnik. However, the State Department decreed that American citizens should not travel to Hungary, where the Soviet satrap Mátyás Rákosi demonstrated his loyalty by being more Stalinist than Stalin himself. This decision, which destroyed what might have been Reshevsky's best chance of becoming world champion, may seem bizarre. There was, however, no comparison between Soviet and U.S. officials in the significance that they attributed to chess; a game that for the Kremlin involved *raison d'état* was for the U.S. government a purely private matter.

Just how strong Reshevsky was in match play around this time was demonstrated by his decisive defeats in 1952–3 of his two most formidable non-Soviet rivals, the Yugoslav Svetozar Gligoric and the Polish-Argentinian Miguel Najdorf. The *New York Times* then proposed an unofficial match with Botvinnik. Many experts believe that Reshevsky would have won; the Soviets evidently thought that it was not a risk worth taking, because they prudently ignored the challenge.

By the time FIDE gave Reshevsky another chance to seize Botvinnik's throne, at Zurich in 1953, he was forty-two and already had younger rivals to reckon with. Nonetheless, Reshevsky made one last supreme effort which almost succeeded. Smyslov was just beginning the sustained ascent that would eventually carry him to the summit in 1957. David Bronstein and Yuri Averbakh, two of the Soviet grandmasters playing at Zurich, described the tensions within the Soviet delegation. It was led by Dmitri Postnikov, an official from the Sports Committee, the trainer Igor Bondarevsky, and a KGB officer by the name of Moshintsev. Their task, according to Bronstein, was to stop Reshevsky from winning the tournament and thereby gaining the right to challenge Botvinnik. Averbakh differs in his recollection: he was not punished for losing to Reshevsky. In the end Smyslov edged ahead and Reshevsky had to content himself with second place, jointly with Keres—yet again. It was still a magnificent achievement for this Lone Ranger of the chessboard. In the eighteen years since 1935, he had won half of the fourteen major tournaments in which he had played, and in the rest only once came lower than third: a better record even than Botvinnik's during the same period. Thereafter, Reshevsky's hopes of the world title receded. He was still the best match player in the New World; he won a match against the strong Hungarian émigré Pal Benkö in 1960. By then Bobby Fischer had eclipsed him, but the younger man could only tie their match. Reshevsky was still playing chess at a high level in the 1980s, more than seventy years after his career began. Other grandmasters, such as Smyslov and Korchnoi, have carried on playing at the top in old age, too, but because Reshevsky began so early his record may never be beaten.

Other chess masters became impresarios and writers, including Kashdan, the amazingly prolific Fred Reinfeld, and Al Horowitz, who gave up active play to found and edit *Chess Review.* The next generation of masters who emerged in the mid-1950s— among them Larry Evans, Bill Lombardy, Robert and Donald Byrne—were certainly talented, but none showed as much promise as Reshevsky and Fine had done. Nor, in the early years of the Cold War, were there many refugees from the Soviet bloc. Apart from the Hungarian grandmaster Pal Benkö, who arrived in 1955 and twice qualified as a candidate for the world championship, and the Czech Lubomir Kavalek, the United States was left largely to its own human resources. Not until the 1980s, when Soviet émigrés such as Boris Gulko, Lev Alburt, and Gata Kamsky emerged on the scene, was there a major new influx of chess talent to compare with Reshevsky. In 1955, as the Cold War entered its second decade, the chess world had forgotten that the United States had once been its leading nation, and there seemed no prospect of anybody from the West mounting a serious challenge to Soviet domination. Chess, moreover, had a negative image in the West that bore no comparison with its status in the communist bloc. Unlike sport, which was increasingly professionalized after 1945, chess was if anything taken less seriously than before, despite the valuable war work done by many chess masters in Britain and the United States. (Reuben Fine, for example, had the task of using his chess skills to plot the whereabouts of U-boats.)

Then, in the mid-1950s, there burst on to the lively but provincial New York chess scene perhaps the most extraordinary genius in the history of the game. Bobby Fischer came from nowhere and would eventually disappear back into a twilight world of madness and myth. For fifteen years, however, he illuminated the chess firmament with games of sublime beauty and irresistible force. He also changed irrevocably both the economics and the politics of chess, propelling it into the public arena by the sheer force of his personality. Bobby Fischer did not merely put chess on the map—he *was* the map.

9

BOBBY'S ODYSSEY

BOBBY FISCHER WAS BORN in Chicago, Illinois, in 1943. He was brought up with his elder sister, Joan, by their mother, Regina. It might be more correct to say that Joan brought up Bobby while Regina was saving the world. Her own passion was politics—the kind of politics that put her on a collision course with her country. Like her Polish-American brother, her German husband, and her Hungarian lover, Regina was a communist. Like them, too, she was Jewish. Regina's family, the Wenders, had emigrated from Poland before the First World War, first to Switzerland (where she was born) and later to the United States. In 1932, having already studied at three American universities, Regina returned to Europe to study in Berlin while supporting herself as a governess.

She was nineteen when she met the biophysicist Gerhardt Fischer. It was he, presumably, who recruited her to the Communist Party. After the Nazis came to power in January 1933, Fischer persuaded Regina not to return to America, but to follow him to the Soviet Union, where they married that November. As Jews, the couple had every reason to leave Germany, but their flight from the Third Reich was not solely motivated by self-preservation; Fischer was probably already a Comintern agent. With her husband, Regina spent the years 1933 to 1938 in Moscow—a peculiarly insecure place to be at the height of Stalin's Great Terror. She studied at the First Moscow Medical Institute, he was working at the Brain Institute. They were privileged foreigners, living in an apartment reserved for party apparatchiks.

In 1938, before Regina had taken her degree and for obscure reasons, doubtless connected to Fischer's secret activities for Comintern, the couple separated. Gerhardt Fischer went to join the International Brigades on the Republican side in the Spanish civil war, where he acquired a Spanish passport. Regina informed the U.S. embassy that her husband had left her, and moved to Paris with her young daughter, Joan. There the couple were reunited, but when Regina and Joan returned to the United States in January 1939, Gerhardt was refused entry. The family never saw him again. The following year he fetched up in Chile, where he lived under a new identity ("Don Gerardo Fischer Liebscher"). For a time he stayed in correspondence with his wife, but during the war they seem to have lost touch. In 1945 she obtained a divorce.

Now a single mother, Regina was determined to continue her autodidactic existence as a perpetual student. Although she obtained a science degree, she was forced to scrape a living as an elementary school teacher, a stenographer, a shipyard welder, and an instructor at a U.S. Air Force radio training school. The Fischers' peripatetic, hand-to-mouth existence took them to Denver, Colorado, Washington, D.C., Chicago, Idaho, Oregon, St. Louis, and Arizona, before they eventually settled in Brooklyn, where Regina became a nurse.

In the course of this itinerant career, Regina had her second child, Bobby, after she had been befriended by Dr. Paul Felix Nemenyi. A Hungarian scientist who had arrived in the United States from Imperial College, London, in 1939, Nemenyi took a post as an assistant professor of mathematics in Colorado. It was there that he met Regina. Later he worked at the Naval Research Laboratory in Washington, D.C., where he found the Fischers an apartment. Fischer's biographers Edmonds and Eidinow, who have examined the evidence thoroughly, conclude that Nemenyi was Bobby's father. Until he died in 1952, he took a close interest in Bobby's progress and helped Regina financially. However, Bobby's biological father seems to have been no less ideological in his outlook than the legal father whose name he inherited. Nemenyi was suspected by the FBI of communist sympathies, a concern increased by the fact that his work for the U.S. Navy was militarily sensitive, although the evidence against him was too inconclusive for any action to be taken.

Regina's relationship with Nemenyi raises the question of whether Regina was herself a spy. In 1945 she tried using her knowledge of Russian to get a job as a translator for the Soviet embassy, but nothing came of it. She certainly joined the Communist Political Association while working in Oregon, and later the Communist Party. Whether or not she would have been willing to undertake intelligence work, however, she does not seem to have been judged suitable espionage material. Instead, she became a militant pacifist. In 1961, when Bobby was eighteen, Regina became an activist for the Committee for Non-Violent Action and took part in the Walk for Peace, the longest in history, from San Francisco to Moscow. It was this event that occasioned the final break between mother and son; Regina moved out of the Brooklyn apartment, went to California, and never came back. On the march she had struck up a friendship with an English pacifist, Cyril Pustan, and later married him. They moved to Europe, where she spent the rest of her life as a peace activist. By the time she died in 1997, she had not spoken to her son for more than thirty years. Feisty, even ferocious in pursuit of her ideals, Regina tried to enlist her son in what she saw as the cause of peace but never began to understand the passion for chess that drove him. Still less did she understand his politics.

As the son of Jewish communists in Cold War America, Bobby

Fischer grew up in an atmosphere of secretiveness and paranoia, but he was on the opposite side of the fence. While still a teenager, he became an ardent anticommunist. In a sense, he was a typical rebel of the 1960s—only, in his case, the rebellion took a right-wing rather than a left-wing form. Fear of communist subversion obsessed Bobby Fischer—yet his own mother was a fellow traveler. Fear of McCarthyism obsessed Regina Fischer—but her only son became a McCarthyite. His endless battles with authority were part of the same syndrome. As he saw it, the bureaucrats and mediocrities who governed the world of chess, whether at a national or an international level, were obstacles to his progress as well as to the elevation of chess to a status worthy of its intrinsic importance.

Fischer never had been "normal." When he was a schoolboy in Brooklyn, his IQ was assessed at 180–190—among the highest ever recorded—but he was entirely indifferent to academic work. Aged six, he had learned chess with his elder sister, Joan, after they bought a cheap set and figured out the rules together. Within a year, Bobby was hooked and Regina Fischer was at her wits' end. "For four years I tried everything to discourage him, but it was hopeless," she said. On the advice of Hermann Helms, the grand old man of American chess, she took her seven-year-old son along to the Brooklyn Public Library, where he played in a simultaneous exhibition against a master, Max Pavey. Although Bobby lasted only fifteen minutes, his destiny was fixed forevermore.

By the time he was eleven, he was playing, reading, or thinking about chess every waking hour, staying out till midnight and testing his skills against the best players in New York. In 1956, having won all the junior tournaments there were to win, the thirteen-year-old Bobby Fischer was invited to compete in his first master tournament at the Manhattan Chess Club, the Lessing J. Rosenwald Trophy (the name was characteristic of the role of capitalism in American chess). His game against Donald Byrne, one of the best young players in the country, won a brilliancy prize and was hailed as "The Game of the Century." In 1957, the centenary of the first

American Chess Congress, Fischer emulated Morphy. Aged fourteen, he won the U.S. championship, ahead of Reshevsky, without
losing a game. Thereafter, he took first prize in every tournament
on American soil in which he competed—with the sole exception
of the Piatigorsky Gold Cup at Santa Monica in 1966, when the
world's elite played and Fischer came second to Spassky. Only the
Russians could now offer Fischer serious competition.

They, too, were eager to meet the prodigy. Regina Fischer, in
a characteristic gesture, had written to Nikita Khrushchev, asking for her son to be invited to a youth festival in Moscow. Her
son went along with his fellow-traveling mother's fantasy that he
might be converted to her ideals by actually visiting the Soviet
Union—but the truth was that he just wanted a crack at the world
champion. By the time Bobby arrived at Moscow in 1958 aged
just fifteen, accompanied by his sister, Joan, he was already reigning U.S. champion. He immediately demanded to play Botvinnik
and other grandmasters. Petrosian was deputed to play some blitz
games with the lad, but this did not satisfy Fischer. After being received by the senior chess bureaucrat, Lev Abramov, head of the
Chess Section of the Sports Committee, Fischer asked him: "What
payment will I receive for these games?"

Abramov replied: "None. You are our guest, and we don't pay
fees to guests."

He claims that Fischer's interpreter reported that the boy said:
"I'm fed up with these Russian pigs." This could have been a
mistranslation, but the authorities were irritated and the Fischers
were sent home.

He met the Russians seriously over the board for the first time
later that year at Portoroz in Yugoslavia, the Interzonal tournament
for which he had qualified by winning the U.S. title. The Soviet
phalanx was formidable: Bronstein had drawn a world championship match with Botvinnik; Averbakh had been Soviet champion;
and Petrosian was clearly destined to be a future world champion.
The youngest Soviet player was also one of the most brilliant in
the whole history of chess: just twenty, Mikhail Tal was only five

years older than Fischer and already beginning the unstoppable run of victories that would propel him to dethrone Botvinnik two years later.

Still a gawky teenager in jeans and pullover, Fischer had neither the experience nor the emotional maturity to overcome these paladins. Untypically, he offered a draw to Averbakh, later commenting: "He was afraid to lose to a child and I was afraid to lose to a grandmaster!" Yet he finished in fifth place, good enough to give him the grandmaster title. Still fifteen, he was the youngest ever at the time. Next year Fischer returned to Europe to play at a very strong tournament in Zurich, tying for third with Paul Keres, just behind Tal and Gligoric. The boy from Brooklyn won his game against Keres, who had been one of the best in the world for two decades, and came within an ace of overtaking Tal, the brightest of the new generation of postwar Soviet grandmasters.

At this, the Soviet elite scented danger. The contrast between Fischer's uncompromising will to power and the caution of the Russians impressed Tal: "Fischer disliked easy draws and fought on until the material on the board was completely exhausted." The 1959 candidates' tournament—which, thanks to the devotion to chess of Marshal Tito, was again held in the Yugoslav cities of Bled, Zagreb, and Belgrade—pitted the eight best players in the world, apart from Botvinnik, against each other over four rounds—a grueling schedule of twenty-eight games. The Soviet grandmasters, all in their prime, took the first four places: Tal, Keres, Petrosian, and Smyslov. Fischer was disappointed to come fifth again, but in reality this was another huge step forward. He now had a claim to be the strongest non-Soviet player in the world—and he was still just sixteen. That, however, was not good enough for Fischer. He was by now convinced of his own destiny: to be the greatest, not only of his own time but of all time. Only the Russians stood in his way, and he was confident of beating them in the next world championship cycle.

It did not happen.

There were several reasons why Fischer was unable to seize the

throne in the early 1960s. First, the Russians were no less confident than he was. Tal, who beat Fischer soundly in the 1959 candidates' tournament, winning all three of their games, took to signing both their names for autograph hunters. Asked why he did this,
Tal replied: "Well, you see, I've already beaten the lad three times,
and I consider that this fully entitles me to scribble his name." On
another occasion, Tal waved to him, saying: "Bobby, coo-coo!" Fischer later burst into tears, thinking that Tal was mocking him by
suggesting that he was "cuckoo." At Leipzig a year later, Fischer
tried to get his revenge on Tal by telling his fortune: "But I see
that in the near future you will lose the title of world champion
to a young American grandmaster." Tal turned to the watching
William Lombardy and shook his hand: "Bravo, Billy! So it is you
who are destined to succeed me at my post!" When Fischer finally
beat Tal, at Bled 1961, the former world champion declared: "It is
very hard to play against Einstein's theory"—but then proceeded
to win the tournament.

A second reason was the incredible strength in depth of the Soviet chess machine in the 1950s and '60s, when Fischer first encountered it. Just before his rise, the Soviet team had beaten the
Americans 20–12 in a four-round match in Manhattan in June 1954.
They crushed the British 18.5–1.5 on the same tour. The following
year the Soviet victory over the United States was even more decisive: 25–7. According to the *New Statesman*'s correspondent, Assiac, by 1960 there were 3 million registered players in the USSR,
rising to 5 million by 1970, organized in a vast network of clubs,
trade unions, schools, and colleges. Perhaps ten times as many
people followed the game without seriously playing it, and world
champions such as Botvinnik were among the most celebrated individuals on the national stage. In 1958 Chernigov, a single region
of Ukraine, had over 10,000 active players—more than the entire
United States. Even in the central Asian republics, such as Uzbeki-
stan (with 45,000 players around 1960), competitive chess enjoyed
a popularity that dwarfed its status in the West. Under Petrosian's
editorship during the 1960s and '70s, the chess journal *64* had a

circulation of more than 100,000. Many chess books sold out as soon as they were published. The East European satellites also had larger numbers of registered players than their Western counterparts: in 1968 the *Deutsche Schachblätter* reported that Hungary had 36,000, Czechoslovakia 25,000, East Germany over 30,000. Only West Germany, with 40,000 players and a club team championship that attracted professionals from all over Europe, could match these figures. Britain, by contrast, had only 5,500 club players before the Fischer boom of the 1970s.

Aware of this formidable machine, Fischer was at first respectful towards the Russians. When he first met Spassky and Bronstein in Argentina in 1960, he spent time with them on a long railway journey, speaking a mixture of English and Russian. He told them that *Shakhmaty Bulletin*—the most recondite of the Russian chess journals—was "the best chess magazine in the world." Asked how he had drawn a difficult endgame with Taimanov at Buenos Aires 1960, Fischer replied that he had seen it analyzed seven years earlier by Averbakh in another Soviet magazine. He thought he knew what he was up against, but he was still underestimating the Russians.

This attitude changed dramatically after the Curaçao candidates' tournament of 1962. Fischer's conviction that the Soviets had, as he put it, "fixed world chess," which grew to become an obsession as his career progressed, was based on what is now an established fact. There really was a conspiracy against him, although it was not quite as extensive as he supposed. At Curaçao, the first occasion on which Fischer might have won the right to play Botvinnik for the world championship, he came fourth behind three Soviet players: Petrosian, Geller, and Keres. The winner, Petrosian, went on to defeat Botvinnik in their world championship match in 1963.

Fourth place in such exalted company would not have been a bad result for anybody else, but Fischer was interested only in coming first. His disappointment quickly turned to anger. In August 1962, soon after the tournament, he wrote an article for the mass-circulation American magazine, *Sports Illustrated*, under the headline: "The Russians Have Fixed World Chess." Fischer alleged that the three Soviet prizewinners agreed to draw their games with each other in order to concentrate on beating him, pointing out that none of their games lasted more than twenty-two moves. He also alleged that a fourth Russian, Viktor Korchnoi, deliberately lost three crucial games to his Soviet colleagues during the second half of this grueling twenty-eight-round tournament, played in stifling equatorial heat.

> In the first half of the tournament, [Korchnoi] also drew with the other Russians. Halfway through the tournament there was a rest period of six days, when all participants went to the island of St. Martin. The four Russians had roughly the same number of points and there was talk that one of them would be bound to lose against one of the others. Whatever happened during the Russians' discussions in St. Martin, Korchnoi's game suddenly collapsed after them.

Fischer acknowledged that the fifth Soviet participant, Mikhail Tal, the ex-world champion and pre-tournament favorite, was not part of the "combine." Indeed, Tal was the only Soviet master (apart, much later, from Spassky) for whom Fischer had much respect. But Tal's lifestyle—he was a heavy smoker and drinker—had begun taking its toll: he was already afflicted with the kidney disease that eventually killed him at the age of fifty-six. He had lost his return match for the world championship against Botvinnik the previous year and at Curaçao he was forced to withdraw halfway through the tournament.

Fischer's allegation against Korchnoi—that he had been chosen "as a sacrifice" by Sergey Gorshkov, the sinister KGB colonel who acted as head of the Soviet delegation—was plausibly denied by the indignant Korchnoi. "Surely he wasn't being serious," Korchnoi wrote in his autobiography. "I am incapable, by character, of being made a sacrifice, the more so since, if I had won those three games, it wouldn't have been Petrosian who would have won the tournament!" Korchnoi denies that he was involved, although one of his games against Petrosian was so feeble that many believed he had lost it deliberately. He admits that his wife was under the thumb of her fellow Armenian, Petrosian's formidable wife, Rona, who was determined that her husband would win, yet it is not clear why this should have affected Korchnoi's game. Korchnoi's denial is all the more believable because his poor form at Curaçao, which he attributed to fatigue and the tropical climate, prompted Gorshkov, his KGB minder, to write a critical report about him. That report began the long process of official disapproval that would lead eventually to Korchnoi's disgrace and his decision to emigrate.

The Dutch grandmaster Jan Timman, who has studied all the evidence, concludes that Petrosian, Geller, and Keres did indeed agree to form a "combine" during the halfway break. There is, however, no proof that any of them was following orders from the KGB minder or anybody else. Their motives were various. Keres, a generation older than the other two, was trying to conserve his strength, realizing that he would tire toward the end of the twenty-eight rounds. He seems to have been dropped from the combine in the final rounds of the tournament, because Petrosian and Geller both needed to beat him as well as Fischer in order to win the tournament. The devious Petrosian, who benefited most from the arrangement, always denied it, but one of his games against Keres was agreed drawn in a position that (as Fischer pointed out at the time) should have been won by Petrosian. By then, Petrosian needed only to draw his games. If he had won this game, it would merely have increased his margin of victory, rather than helped Fischer. But for the most crucial part of the tournament, the combine did enable its three co-conspirators to take things easy against each other. This allowed them to concentrate on preventing Fischer from recovering from his bad start, once he hit his best form.

What is not clear is whether Fischer could have won the tournament without the combine. In all likelihood, he was not quite strong enough at the age of nineteen to beat the entire Soviet elite.

It was true that by 1962 he had already shown himself their equal. After the 1961 tournament at Bled, where Fischer defeated three of the four Soviet grandmasters taking part (Tal, Geller, and Petrosian), he won the Stockholm Interzonal by a spectacular margin, far outstripping the Russians who had hitherto dominated these qualifying tournaments for the world championship. In his games against Soviet grandmasters during the year before the Curaçao candidates' tournament, Fischer was leading 6–2. By this time he had convinced himself that Botvinnik's crown was his by right. That was certainly a mistake: the Russians knew that they merely had to finish in the top six at Stockholm to earn a place in the candidates' tournament, so they had not exerted themselves to the utmost. Anticipating a possible challenge from the American upstart, Botvinnik—who had yet to play Fischer at all—contented himself with the condescending remark: "For the moment, Fischer is not as terrifying as he paints himself." The Hungarian émigré, Pal Benkö, who had more reason than Fischer to hate the communists, having been tortured and imprisoned by them, dismissed Fischer's complaint with the laconic putdown: "He simply wasn't the best player."

Although Fischer had broken the Soviet monopoly over the chess elite, he had yet to prove himself in a long match against more experienced opponents. The previous year, 1961, he had been unable to defeat his American rival Samuel Reshevsky in a sixteen-game match. Reshevsky was clearly past his best, but he had never lost a match and had won individual games from every world champion of the century up to that time. The match was still tied when it was abandoned amid recrimination and litigation after Fischer refused to reschedule a game from Saturday to Sunday to accommodate Reshevsky, an Orthodox Jew. A sober assessment of his own strengths and weaknesses would have given the nineteen-year-old American no better than even chances against the formidable Soviet phalanx.

However, at the height of the Cold War, in the feverish atmosphere of the Cuban Missile Crisis, with American–Soviet rivalry at its most intense, a sober assessment was never likely to happen. Fischer was not the only American who believed in what the *New York Times* had called "possibly collusion between Soviet players to help one win a tourney, as against a non-Soviet opponent." Fischer's bitterness at the "Russian cheats" seems to have damaged his chances of achieving the title that he felt was rightfully his. He began to suspect not only a Soviet conspiracy to deprive him of a match for the world championship—for which there was a good deal of evidence (documented in the volume *Russians versus Fischer* by Dmitry Plisetsky and Sergey Voronkov)—but also a deliberate refusal by America and the West to back up his ambitions. Fischer made it clear that he would no longer participate in the world championship organized by FIDE, which he accused of being "fixed" in favor of the Russians. "The system set up the Fédération Internationale des Échecs. . . insures [sic] that there will always be a Russian world champion," he wrote in his notorious *Sports Illustrated* piece.

This claim was denied at the time, but the world chess federation took the allegations seriously enough to change the rules for the next three-year world championship cycle, replacing the candidates' tournament by a series of elimination matches, which would be harder to fix. The preponderance of Soviet grandmasters made any system open to abuse, but Fischer's principled refusal to stand for such tricks as "buying" or "throwing" games shamed many other players into a less cynical attitude. On the other hand, when FIDE imposed a rule banning draws in under thirty moves at the 1962 Olympiad, Fischer was the first to break it. Warned by the Soviet referee, Grandmaster Salo Flohr, to stick to the rules, Fischer replied: "Those rules are for the Communist cheaters, not for me."

The author of *The Soviet School of Chess*, Grandmaster Alexander Kotov, pointed out that he had beaten Botvinnik and Smyslov at critical moments when they were fighting for first prize at the crucial tournaments of Groningen 1946 and Zurich 1953. This bombastic propagandist went over the top, however, by claiming:

"No Soviet player has ever thrown a game to a Soviet competitor in an international tournament." Botvinnik, on the other hand, went to the opposite extreme: he was convinced that Spassky threw his world championship match against Fischer in 1972 for $100,000. Both old Stalinists were in denial; Kotov refused to hear a word against his compatriots, while Botvinnik could not believe that Spassky had simply met his match. The culture of lies was so all pervasive that in the end the Russians did not believe the truth, even when it was staring them in the face.

In the mid-1960s, no theater of the Cold War was more important than Cuba, and no Soviet satellite gave chess a higher priority. Although Capablanca had no interest in politics and was almost as much American as Cuban—he spent his formative years in the United States, frequently resided and died there—his memory was appropriated by the coalition of Cuban and foreign revolutionaries who overthrew Batista in 1959. By an accident of history, the two charismatic leaders of the Cuban revolution happened to be addicted to chess: Fidel Castro, the jovial megalomaniac who presented himself as the savior of his people because he had replaced their pro-American authoritarian regime with an anti-American totalitarian one; and "Che" Guevara, his photogenic but pitiless Argentinian henchman. Guevara took part in tournaments when only twelve years old, and Castro himself has played chess with many of the grandmasters who have visited Cuba during the half-century of his dictatorship. No opportunity to exploit the cult of "Capa" for propaganda purposes has been missed by the Castro regime. In 1962, the year of the Cuban Missile Crisis, Castro staged the first Capablanca Memorial tournament. This event has been held almost annually ever since, a major financial commitment for a country whose economy declined from first-world to third-world status under Castro. The star guests were always the Soviet grandmasters, and articles about these tournaments on "the island of freedom" featured prominently in Soviet journals.

By far the most celebrated of these Capablanca Memorial tournaments was that of 1965. That year Castro invited Bobby Fischer to take part. Scenting a propaganda stunt, the State Department refused to give him permission to travel to Havana, despite editorial protests in the *New York Times* and *Wall Street Journal*. Nothing daunted, Fischer offered to play the match by teletype while sitting in the Marshall Chess Club in New York. This involved an elaborate ritual to prevent any suspicion of cheating. Fischer sat in a small room with only the chessboard and a referee. He wrote his moves down on a slip of paper, which the referee gave to a courier, who took it to another room for it to be keyed into the teletype machine. When the reply came back from Havana, the process was reversed. All this took many more hours than a normal game and imposed a huge extra strain on both players, particularly Fischer, who had to endure it over twenty-one rounds. When Fischer defeated the former world champion Vasily Smyslov, a voice was heard on the telephone line that the Cubans kept permanently open: "Ha-lo? Bo-bie?" It was the Russian grandmaster, graciously congratulating Fischer on his beautiful endgame. Smyslov could afford to be magnanimous; despite this reverse he ultimately won the tournament, just ahead of Fischer, who had dropped a few points against lesser lights.

This laborious, long-distance method of playing chess, necessitated by Cold War politics, was by no means Fischer's only problem, however. Before the event began, Castro announced that Fischer's participation was "a great propaganda victory for Cuba." Fischer fired off a telegram to Castro, stating that he would only take part if Castro promised that "neither you, nor your government, will attempt to make political capital out of my participation." Castro retorted with brazen chutzpah: "Our land has no need of 'propaganda victories'. . . If you are frightened and repent your previous decision, then it would be better to find another excuse or to have the courage to remain honest."

The media went wild at this exchange, which took place only three years after the Cuban Missile Crisis, when relations were still tense. But feelings ran even higher a year later, when the 1966 Olympiad was held in Havana. No expense was spared, and for the weeks of the tournament the entire island went chess mad. Capablanca's victory over Lasker at Moscow 1936 was reenacted as a living chess ballet before 15,000 spectators—a "Cecil B. DeMille extravaganza come to life," commented Fischer's biographer Frank Brady. This time the Americans were allowed by their own government to field a team, led by Fischer. However, the Russians refused to postpone the game between Fischer and Petrosian, the Soviet world champion, for two hours to respect Fischer's Saturday Sabbath, even though this had been agreed with the Cuban organizers in advance. The row quickly developed into a full-scale international incident, especially after the arbiter (a Czech communist) forfeited the U.S. team for nonappearance. An ad hoc appeals council was assembled to adjudicate; the Russians were told to "reconsider," the match was rescheduled, and the Cuban press hailed the Soviet climb-down as a "noble gesture."

The Olympiad culminated in a "World Day of Chess" on Capablanca's birthday, with a floodlit monster simultaneous display given by 380 masters on 6,840 boards in the Plaza de la Revolución—the largest such exhibition in history. A photograph appeared in the American press of the cigar-chomping Castro playing Fischer. Even more bizarrely, it was reported that an uncharacteristically tactful—not to say obsequious—Fischer had deliberately "lost" to the dictator. However, this account appears to have been false. Other photographs show the Soviet world champion Petrosian apparently advising Castro. A Mexican master, Filiberto Terrazas, wrote that he and Fischer had actually played a consultation game against Petrosian and Castro, which the latter had won fair and square. It is quite implausible that Fischer would have voluntarily thrown even a casual game against a team consisting of Tigran Petrosian, then his bitterest Soviet rival, and the most notorious figure in the communist bloc outside the Soviet Union, Fidel Castro.

That this anything but friendly game was played at all was remarkable enough, but its symbolic significance is only fully grasped when one realizes how the pictures were distorted by a false interpretation almost certainly planted by Cuban propagandists, who could still control the visual images that reached the outside world. Once technology made it a simple matter to send pictures to the West, the state's monopoly could no longer be sustained. Two decades after Castro and Fischer met over the chessboard, Mikhail Gorbachev signaled a more liberal policy towards press freedom. His slogan of *glasnost* was, however, less about embracing openness than an admission that in an information age the time-worn methods were not always sufficient to keep control of hearts and minds. As Vladimir Putin showed, however, the old KGB tactics still work if the West is craven enough to accept what it sees at face value.

Fischer's unexpected and traumatic setback at Curaçao may have triggered a gradual retreat from reality and the onset of a pathological suspicion of friends and foes alike. Over the next eight years he began to exhibit the symptoms of his later paranoia. After the fiasco at Curaçao, Fischer began listening to broadcasts by the radio evangelists Herbert W. Armstrong and his son Garner Ted Armstrong. Soon afterwards he joined their Worldwide Church of God: a fundamentalist Christian sect that combines Baptist ideas of total bodily immersion with strict adherence to the Hebrew Scriptures, including Judaic sabbatarian and dietary laws. In practice this meant that he henceforth refused to play chess from sundown on Fridays till sundown on Saturdays, thereby presenting tournament organizers with yet another condition to be fulfilled— and the Soviets with another opportunity to obstruct his progress to the summit.

The most tragicomic example of this was the debacle at the 1967 Interzonal held at Sousse in Tunisia. Like the Soviet–American stand-off at the Olympiad in Havana the year before, the Sousse affair began with a dispute about playing on the Sabbath. Both Fischer and Reshevsky refused to begin their games on Saturdays before sunset—i.e., starting at 7 P.M. rather than 4 P.M. The tournament organizers at first tried to make the other players follow suit, but the later start meant that by the time most games finished, around midnight, all the restaurants would be closed. Grandmasters would then miss dinner, which was particularly tough on those who had to finish adjourned games early in the morning on the following day. There was a protest and the Tunisian organizers gave in.

Fischer at first accepted this change to the schedule and began the tournament by streaking ahead of the rest of the field. Later, however, the dispute flared up again. Not only were his other demands concerning lighting, noise, and photography ignored, but Fischer was expected to play six games without a break. The inevitable row then occurred; he abruptly announced his withdrawal. He failed to appear for his game against the Latvian grandmaster Aivars Gipslis and was forfeited. Then Fischer left Sousse for Tunis. There was a last-ditch bid by the Americans to persuade him to return, with the promise that the Gipslis game would be ruled on by FIDE.

Back in Sousse, everyone assumed that he was gone for good—and those who had lost to him, including the Soviet champion Leonid Stein, were doubtless looking forward to Fischer's games being annulled. He was due to play Reshevsky, then aged fifty-six, and his clock was started. As the minutes ticked by, everyone—including Reshevsky—assumed that Fischer would not show up. Suddenly, just before he was due to be defaulted, Fischer returned from Tunis. For his veteran rival, who was in shock, Fischer might as well have been a revenant back from the dead. So confident was Fischer that, when told he had only ten minutes left, he waited another five minutes before entering the playing hall, echoing Sir Francis Drake awaiting the Armada: "I still have enough time for Reshevsky!"

And, indeed, Fischer won the game effortlessly. The furious Reshevsky organized a petition to the arbiters, who presented a memo to Fischer, inviting him to apologize for his behavior and abide by the rules. Fischer tore it up without reading it. But the forfeit against Gipslis was upheld by the Sousse committee, after the Soviet contingent threatened to leave en masse. Fischer refused to appear for his next game against the Czech Vlastimil Hort, which was also forfeited. Although he had not lost a single one of the games that he had actually played, and might even have won the tournament despite these forfeits, Fischer decided to withdraw. When reminded by an American diplomat that he was a representative of the United States, Fischer tellingly retorted: "I represent no one here but myself!" It was a foretaste of his total alienation from his native land in later life.

After Sousse, apart from a couple of minor tournaments in 1968, Fischer effectively retired from chess. For the next two years it looked increasingly unlikely that he would ever return to the board. Hopes rose when he turned up to play for the U.S. team at the Olympiad in Lugano, Italy, only to be dashed when his demand that he be allowed to play in a private room, away from spectators, was turned down. Fischer immediately left town, leaving his teammates to manage as best they could. In an interview, Fischer blamed the chess authorities for denying him the chance to challenge the Soviet hegemony. "This all means the destruction of FIDE," he declared. "I must have my self-respect." Most Americans agreed with him: they blamed the FIDE president, Folke Rogard, for failing to intervene at Sousse to ensure that the best man won through to have a chance of playing Petrosian. When in 1970 a new FIDE president was elected, the former world champion Max Euwe, he immediately adopted a more activist role. Air travel had ushered in the age of shuttle diplomacy. In his own low-key, Dutch way, Euwe made it his business to mediate between the Soviet and American camps. He grasped, as his predecessors had not, that Russian bluffs could be called, because the Soviet Union had too much at stake in chess.

Having moved from New York to Los Angeles, Fischer found himself forced for the first time to confront the fact that without chess, his life was a void. The nearest thing he had to a friend, his second Larry Evans, recalled Fischer's state of mind during his self-imposed exile: "He was feeling depressed about the world and thought there was an excellent chance that there would be a nuclear holocaust soon. He felt he should enjoy whatever money he could get before it was too late." For want of anything better to do, Fischer wrote a book. It was about the only two subjects that interested him: chess and himself. The result was *My 60 Memorable Games.* The title said it all: in the eyes of its author, the sole memorable thing about his life was chess. Yet despite the fact that the book contained no politics, no autobiographical information, nothing at all to leaven Fischer's austere though brilliant annotations, it instantly achieved classic status in the literature of chess. It was not an expression of megalomania; unlike most grandmasters, Fischer included nine draws and three losses among his sixty games, while excluding his most famous victory, the "Game of the Century" against Donald Byrne, which had announced the arrival of the prodigy in 1956. Needless to say, there were endless wrangles with the publisher, not least because Fischer was wary of revealing too much in his notes that would help his Soviet rivals. Nevertheless, the book was a bestseller and has never been out of print since. A new generation of fans taught themselves how to play chess seriously with Fischer's help.

Fischer played only one game in public during 1969, a New York club match against grandmaster Anthony Saidy, but it was a masterpiece—tantalizing for those who wanted him to take on the newly crowned world champion, Boris Spassky. Instead, he continued his war against the Soviets by other means. Reviewing a Russian book, he touched a raw nerve: "There is a bias running through Soviet chess literature in general; they dislike giving credit for opening innovations to foreigners," he wrote in *Chess Digest,* adding: "Examples of this glaring lack of integrity are manifold." There was anger in Moscow, as well as satisfaction that Fischer was devoting his energy to propaganda rather than playing chess. Soviet grandmasters relaxed as the threat that Fischer had posed to their hegemony receded.

In the West, however, chess fans looked on aghast as hopes of an American world champion dwindled. It seemed as if the tragedy of Paul Morphy was repeating itself. For the first time, serious doubts about Fischer's sanity began to surface. His biographer, Frank Brady, claims that after the debacle at Sousse, Fischer wrote "a long, involved, and painful letter stating that he would never play another game of chess." If it ever existed, this document (which Brady extravagantly compared to Beethoven's "Heiligenstadt Testament") has never surfaced. Nonetheless, Fischer's withdrawal from active participation in the chess world left a vacuum which he filled with fantasies about communists and Jews.

Fischer's anti-Semitism was nothing new. The Dutch grandmaster Jan Hein Donner recalled conversations with Fischer at Bled in 1961 that suggest that "Fischer's view on the world had taken on morbid forms; he thought that all the evil in the world stemmed from Jews, communists, and homosexuals. . . At that time he was enraptured with Hitler and he read everything that he could find on this topic. His anti-Semitic comments were normally greeted with embarrassed laughter, but no one did anything." Donner took Fischer to a concentration camp museum, which made "a big impression on him, since in the depths of his soul Fischer was not a bad person, and he significantly toned down his behavior, at least when he was talking with me."

As time went on, Fischer did not "grow out" of his anti-Semitism; indeed, his outbursts got worse, their peaks coinciding with his periods of self-imposed exile from chess: 1962–5, 1968–70, and 1972–92. His sometime friend and second, Grandmaster Larry Evans, recalled an occasion in the 1960s: "Fischer and I saw a documentary about Hitler at the old Amsterdam Theater on 42nd Street [in New York]. As we left the theater, he said that he admired Hitler. Baffled, I asked him why. 'Because he imposed his will on the world,' he replied." While spending two months in 1967 staying with his friend Lina Grumette, Fischer told her, too, of his admiration for Adolf Hitler. Even his surname was too Jewish for his taste, and so he preferred to sign himself "Robert James." The depths to which this self-loathing caused him to sink remained hidden from public view until much later. In 1984 he wrote an open letter of complaint to the editor of the *Encyclopedia Judaica*, demanding that his name be removed from this standard reference book. Not only was he not Jewish, he protested, he had not even undergone its primary ritual: "Knowing what I do about *Judaism*, I was naturally distressed to see that you have erroneously featured me as a Jew . . . I am not today, nor have I ever been a Jew, and as a matter of fact, I am uncircumcised."

One of the many paradoxes of Bobby Fischer was that, although he abhorred communism, in his exalted estimation of chess he was closer to his Soviet rivals than he was to his countrymen. Throughout his life, he was prey to persecution mania. Yet his one-man war with the "Commie cheats" during his rise to the top differed from his later, increasingly irrational, and ultimately certifiable ranting against Jews and the United States. By wresting the world championship away from the mighty Soviet array, Fischer succeeded where nobody else had done so, before or since. This was not the achievement of a madman, because it required qualities over and above genius at chess. The same could not be said of the wild-eyed, foul-mouthed Fischer who reemerged in later years as a fugitive not only from justice, but from reality itself. From the moment that he renounced chess after becoming world champion, he fell prey to his demons. It is too easy to say that because Fischer became both mad and bad, his condition should be retrospectively diagnosed, to the detriment of his earlier career. It was not chess that made Fischer what he eventually became—it was the abandonment of chess. Without the sociability and routine that came from competition, his mind turned in upon itself. No less disastrous for Fischer was the end of the Cold War. If it was chess that had preserved his sanity, it was the Cold War that had given his genius the stage it required on which to perform and had channeled his destructiveness. In the absence of both chess and the Cold War, Fischer nursed a terrible rage against the world that would consume his reason, his reputation, and ultimately his liberty.

10

AN ACHILLES WITHOUT
AN ACHILLES' HEEL

F OR ONE GLORIOUS SUMMER, chess surpassed all other games in popularity and significance. Remote as Reykjavik is, the reverberations were felt all over the world. More than a generation afterwards, the events that took place there in July and August 1972 still resonate. Fischer–Spassky was far more than a chess match. It took on something of the grandeur of an epic—perhaps the only epic of the Cold War.

An epic, by Dr. Johnson's definition, "is supposed to be heroic, or to contain one great action achieved by a hero." The events that form the basis of the *Iliad* are no more representative of the Trojan War than Fischer–Spassky was of the Cold War. Even the decade-long siege of an ancient city-state was far too vast and sprawling a subject to serve the narrative purposes of an epic. Instead, Homer invites us to dwell on one supremely heroic and symbolic episode: the anger of Achilles and its consequences, culminating in his duel with Hector.

The Cold War took place on an incomparably larger scale than the Trojan War, yet it is already receding from our consciousness.

It left no epic—indeed, very little mark on literature at all, other than the thriller. Unlike the real or fictional spies who populate this genre, however, Fischer and Spassky at least approached a more authentic heroism. The Cold War was the first war caused and dominated by intellectuals, and it was best symbolized by the game of the intellectuals. In the age of genocide, when war was no longer the arena in which deeds of sublime heroism might be accomplished, chess was the sublimation of the sublime. The grandmasters embodied an abstract antagonism on an abstract battleground using abstract weapons, yet their struggle embraced all human life. Even if they were both too flawed to be heroes, they were revered as such; their struggle was more heroic than they were. "They always suggest that the world leaders should fight it out hand to hand," Fischer told the BBC science correspondent James Burke. "And this is the kind of thing that we are doing—not with bombs but battling it out over the board."

It is perhaps no coincidence that, reeling from the shock of annihilating defeat, the most literary of Fischer's vanquished opponents, Mark Taimanov, resorted to Homer for a comparison: "He is an Achilles without an Achilles' heel." Fischer had a good deal in common with Achilles, proudest and most impetuous of the Greeks. Without him and his Myrmidons, the other Greeks were helpless against Hector and the Trojans. Likewise, Fischer was the West's only hope of challenging the Soviet hegemony over chess. The action of the *Iliad* turns on the moment when Achilles, stricken with remorse after the death of his beloved Patroclus at the hands of Hector, resolves to return to the fray to seek revenge, despite the warning of his mother Thetis that he, too, is destined to die.

Achilles' war cry alone is enough to strike terror into Trojan hearts. Such was the reaction of the Russians to the news in March 1970 that, after two years of sulking in his tent, Bobby Fischer was back. The circumstances of his return were dramatic. For the first time, a match had been organized in Belgrade, under the aegis of the chess-mad Marshal Tito, which pitted the USSR against the

Rest of the World: ten players a side, four games each. Without Fischer, this "Match of the Century" would have been hopelessly one-sided; even as it was, most experts predicted a crushing victory for the Soviets. It was this factor that, according to Fischer, persuaded him that it was time to make his comeback.

The Yugoslav arbiter Bozidar Kazic told him: "If you don't take part in the 'Match of the Century,' it will simply be the greatest chess absurdity of the century!"

"It was hard for me to say anything in reply," Fischer recalled. He also wanted revenge: on FIDE, on his critics, above all on the Soviets. He told an interviewer: "I wanted to come back and put all those people in their place."

Most doubted whether Fischer would actually play. There had been several attempts to woo him back to the international arena. Most recently, negotiations had come close to fruition for an eighteen-game exhibition match in the Dutch city of Leiden with the ex-world champion Botvinnik. The patriarch had been indulged by the Soviet Sports Committee; his career had begun with a match against a Western player, Salo Flohr, and he hoped to end it by giving another Westerner, Fischer, a run for quite a lot of Dutch money. Just how seriously Botvinnik took his own chances is apparent in the fact that the world champion, Spassky, spent three weeks training with him in September 1969. The match was wrecked at the last minute when Fischer suddenly demanded that the rules be changed to a match of unlimited duration, the winner to be the first to win six games, draws not to count. Neither Botvinnik, then fifty-nine, who saw this as his swansong, nor the organizers wanted to risk an open-ended match. Fischer was less than half his opponent's age and even Botvinnik assumed that he would lose, but as they had played only once—a famous draw at the 1962 Varna Olympiad—a rare chance was lost to see two of the greatest players in history do battle.

So Fischer's arrival in Belgrade electrified the atmosphere. Both the USSR and the Rest of the World teams included plenty of other monstrous egos, all jostling to play on a higher board. The Soviet team had trained thoroughly at a country resort near Moscow, each member having received a bulky file on his expected opponent. For the first time, Professor Arpad Elo's rating system was rigorously adhered to, with the result that older players, such as Botvinnik and Keres, found themselves demoted to lower boards. "Half of our players did not say hello to one another," recalled Spassky, the world champion. "The atmosphere was terrible. It was repulsive for me to play. If I could have avoided playing, I would have done so."

There was even less camaraderie on the Rest of the World side. Other grandmasters were paid a mere $500; they resented Fischer's special appearance fee, which was five times as much, and the twenty-three conditions that he had insisted on, even though most of these (such as good lighting) benefited everybody. Bent Larsen, the Danish grandmaster who was then at the height of his powers, insisted that his recent results had been superior to Fischer's. He threatened not to play except on board one, even though his Elo grade was lower than Fischer's. It was taken for granted that Fischer would refuse to play on board two, and that the Rest of the World team would have to do without one or other of its two best players. Max Euwe, the team captain, sought out Fischer in his hotel room to explain. To his astonishment Fischer unhesitatingly replied: "I don't object." Why did he agree to play second fiddle? "Larsen has a point," he said. "Besides, to create a better image doesn't require that I do anything dishonorable." Although he later had second thoughts about his decision, it did indeed improve his image. It was also quite cunning, for it meant that Fischer would play, not Boris Spassky, the world champion, but the man Spassky had recently dethroned: Tigran Petrosian. "I thought that it would be easier playing Petrosian," Fischer said afterward.

Yet for Fischer this was a grudge match. To another American grandmaster, Walter Browne, Fischer revealed that he had never forgiven Petrosian for having qualified to play Botvinnik for the world championship at Curaçao in 1962 "by fraud." He accused Petrosian of having been "the Russians' tool for slandering my name, for denigrating my character and chess ability, for down-grading my results, ridiculing and lying his head off about me generally." In Fischer's eyes, Petrosian was an impostor, who had abused his prestige as world champion and his patronage as editor of the leading Soviet chess journal. This seething resentment, to-gether with the knowledge that after his two-year absence his rep-utation was at stake, left Fischer uncharacteristically nervous. The Russian grandmaster Mark Taimanov observed that Fischer was "half an hour late, white as a sheet, and for a long time could not bring himself to make his first move." Even Fischer admitted that "I wasn't too sure of myself—I was actually an unknown quantity even to myself. But somehow just looking at Petrosian's face was reassuring. He looked scared! And I know why. This was the mo-ment of truth for Petrosian."

It was a moment of truth for Fischer, too. Of the leading players of his day, Petrosian was considered the hardest to beat. He rarely exerted himself to win, but he had a devilish ability to draw even the most unpromising positions. When they sat down to play in Belgrade, Fischer had a negative score against the former cham-pion, having lost three games and defeated him only once. If, hav-ing waited so long to represent the West against the evil empire, Fischer had lost to the wily Armenian, it is conceivable that he would have renounced chess there and then.

Instead, something remarkable happened. Within fifteen moves, Petrosian—the master of defense—had blundered. Struggle as he might, there was no escape, and he was crushed. The second game also went badly for Petrosian; this time he played passively and drifted into a lost endgame. Fischer, having evened up their life-time score, boasted that if he conceded even one draw he would give Petrosian the Soviet Moskvich car that was the prize for the winner on board two. On board one, Larsen's sensational nineteen-move defeat at Spassky's hands in the second round made Fischer's triumph resound even more.

The last two rounds proved to be tougher for the American. Petrosian pulled himself together and it was Fischer's turn to defend. Restless as usual, he had changed his hotel room three times, ending up in the room next to his opponent's—by accident rather than design. After the fourth game was adjourned in a favorable position for Petrosian, Fischer "heard the telephone ring every few minutes, and a team of Soviet chess analysts were discovering ever new ways of winning the game." As Tal put it, "Fischer drew the last two games by the sweat of his brow."

It was enough. Fischer had won the mini-match with Petrosian 3–1, giving him the best score in the Rest of the World team. Overall, the match ended with the narrowest of victories for the USSR; they won by just a single point, 20.5–19.5. In the last round, the Hungarian Lajos Portisch offered Viktor Korchnoi a draw in a position in which he was ahead both on material and on the clock. If he had won, the Rest of the World would have tied the overall score. Fischer was furious that the free world had missed its chance and suspected foul play. "I'm really mad! It's disgraceful. Korchnoi's position was hopeless." Rumors that Portisch had come under political pressure were hotly denied by him but never entirely dispelled. True, the Hungarian grandmaster was a loyal communist, yet he had trounced Korchnoi in the previous round. Even if Portisch did allow politics to influence his chess, in general the East Europeans—who made up the majority of the Rest of the World side—did well against their Soviet comrades.

Despite having beaten the Rest of the World overall, the USSR had been worsted on the top boards—an ominous portent, especially as the Soviet players had an average age of forty-three, four years older than their opponents. The result dismayed the Soviet authorities. "It's a catastrophe," an unnamed Soviet player was reported to have admitted. "At home they don't understand. They think it means there's something wrong with our culture." Spassky's miniature game against Larsen proved to be the only victory achieved by the Soviet side on the top four boards, out of sixteen games. Fischer's convincing triumph overshadowed the patchy performance of Spassky, who ended with honors even against Larsen. So elated were the Americans that at the closing banquet they proposed a nontitle match between Fischer and Spassky, to be played in Moscow, New York, Chicago, and Los Angeles. Both men were interested — the winner's prize of $15,000 in gold, put up by the American Chess Foundation's president Rosser Reeves, then seemed a fabulous sum to Russians accustomed to modest purses in rubles — but Spassky knew that the Soviet authorities would never permit him to risk his prestige in such a match. He politely declined, explaining that it would be unfair on his countrymen.

In the American hemisphere, capitalism dominated chess. Tournaments were organized, usually in New York, by private patrons, paid for by subscription or by self-made tycoons. Just as there had never been an imperial court, so there was no state or party apparatus to replace it as the fount of largesse. Soviet grandmasters, accustomed to the subsidized life of a civil servant, disdained the naked commercialism of American chess, although they had no objection to hard currency. At the Fried Chicken tournament, held at San Antonio, Texas, in 1972, first prize was shared between the Russian Anatoly Karpov, the Armenian Tigran Petrosian, and the Hungarian Lajos Portisch. Each took home $2,333 — a vast sum compared to the paltry prizes in communist countries. Yet Karpov's ghosted autohagiography, *Chess Is My Life*, sneers at this tournament merely because the sponsor happened to be a Texan fried chicken magnate. American capitalism was not merely the antithesis of Soviet communism — it was vulgar, too.

Spassky flew home to prepare, but Fischer wanted new challenges. For his next trick, the magician from Brooklyn competed against about half the members of both teams in an unofficial "World Blitz Championship" at the Yugoslav resort of Herceg Novi. With only five minutes each for all their moves, the games were uneven in quality, but the result was unequivocal: Fischer finished 4.5 points ahead of Tal, his nearest rival, having won seventeen and lost only one game (to Korchnoi) out of twenty-one. His overall score against the Soviet elite — an awesome 8.5 to 1.5 — was dismissed in Moscow because these were only speed games, not "serious" ones.

However, one or two Russians were privately longing for him to challenge the Soviet establishment. David Bronstein, who knew and liked Fischer, listened to a long explanation from him about why he hated FIDE and would not play in the next world championship cycle, which was about to begin. "Suddenly Bobby stopped and muttered in confusion: 'Do you think I should play?' 'Yes' was all I said. He became thoughtful and didn't return to this topic." (One other significant remark, this time to Petrosian, was reported by the Yugoslav journalist Dimitrije Bjelica: "[Fischer] said he believed in chess computers, which one day would even defeat world champions. When would this be? It all depended on how many scientists would work with the machines." Given the skepticism about chess computers that still prevailed among professional masters, Fischer was prescient. He may have calculated that 1972 would be his last chance to achieve his life's ambition before he was challenged not only by a younger generation, but also by the brute force of the computer. It would actually take until 1997 for computers to defeat a reigning world champion in a formal match; Fischer anticipated it by a quarter of a century.)

Still in Yugoslavia, Fischer won another victory over the Russians and other communists at the strong "Tournament of Peace" in Rovinj and Zagreb. He drew with the four Soviet grandmasters but crushed the lesser lights to finish well ahead of the field. Afterwards Korchnoi revealed to Moscow that Fischer was confident that he could beat Spassky. "Of the foreign players no one, apart from him, is a threat to the crown," he wrote. "Larsen is much weaker." Tal pointed out that, unlike Fischer, "our leading players are simply not accustomed to fighting for first place."

After his long sabbatical, Fischer had spent nearly three months in Yugoslavia, playing chess almost continuously. He evidently enjoyed the adulation, too—so much so that he seriously contemplated buying a house on the Adriatic and settling there. But his next appearance, in Buenos Aires, was even more sensational. There he won thirteen games, conceding four draws and no losses, earning rapturous applause from the equally chess-obsessed Argentinians. The up-and-coming Russian Vladimir Tukmakov, who came a distant second, admitted that the "Fischer cult" had affected him. "Fischer is fanatically devoted to chess," he reported back to Moscow in tones of awe. "Even when his first prize was secure, he continued to play the remaining games as if his fate in the tournament depended on them." He played on against former world champion Smyslov until only two kings were left on the board. Faced with such aggression, even Russians were intimidated.

Fischer was by now surrounded by an aura of invincibility and began to believe in his own myth. When he arrived at the nineteenth Olympiad at Siegen in West Germany in September 1970, he had not lost a serious game of chess to a Soviet opponent for well over three years. Now, however, he knew that when the USSR played the USA he would inevitably come up against one Russian he had never beaten: Boris Spassky.

Of all the Soviet world champions, Spassky was the most cultivated, the most charming, the most good-looking, and the most popular. From the Kremlin's point of view, there was only one problem with Spassky, but it was a big one: he was not a communist. Born in 1937, he was the last of the prewar vintage that included giants such as Korchnoi, Petrosian, and Tal; after him came the deluge, and there were no more geniuses until Anatoly Karpov (born in 1951) emerged in the 1970s. He was a scion of the Orthodox clergy, who continued an underground existence even during the darkest days of Stalinist persecution. His paternal grandfather had been the last of a long line of Orthodox priests, personally invested with a golden cross by the last tsar, Nicholas II. His mother, too, was deeply religious and revered the saintly monk, Seraphim of Viriza, who blessed the family of the young Boris. His father, a structural engineer, survived the war but played little part in his son's life. Boris was four when the siege of Leningrad began in August 1941. The Spasskys were among the 636,000 who were evacuated before the Nazi ring closed; the ten-year-old Viktor Korchnoi was among the half a million women and children who were left behind. The evacuees were taken to Moscow and Boris was initially billeted with another family, where he learned to play chess. His parents promptly divorced, which left him fatherless: "When I was six or seven years old I was the chief in my family."

Like Fischer, Spassky grew up in a mainly female household. Unlike his American rival, he became a ladies' man. His mother, a teacher and Komsomol (communist youth organization) leader, combined Christianity and communism with a stoical survival instinct. To feed her children, she did backbreaking manual labor until she injured herself. Returning to Leningrad after the war, the preadolescent Boris rediscovered chess at the sports pavilion on an island in the Central Park. "I fell in love with the white queen. I dreamed of caressing her in my pocket, but I did not dare to steal her. Chess is pure for me." He spent the whole day there if possible until 11 P.M., but "it was a tragedy for me when it closed down in September. It was like death with no chess."

Boris soon found a better chess club at the Palace of Young Pioneers. The Spasskys were so poor that in winter he had to wear his mother's military boots, which were much too big for him. He was discovered by the brilliant teacher, Vladimir Zak, and improved rapidly: by the age of ten he was the youngest first-category player in Russia. Grigory Levenfish also became his patron and Boris began receiving a monthly stipend of 120 rubles. Chess had become his livelihood and thereafter he was the family breadwinner. At thirteen, he was the youngest candidate master; at fifteen, the world's youngest international master; at eighteen, world junior champion and youngest grandmaster. Not to be outdone, his sister later became Soviet draughts champion. A photograph of Boris aged eleven shows an unusually mature face. Like Fischer, he learned the hard way not to let himself be exploited. Playing fifteen Red Army officers simultaneously, he permitted one opponent to take back a move, lost—and burst into tears. However, his fee paid for his first winter coat—a matter of life and death. Life under Stalin made Boris the *wunderkind* wise beyond his years.

Spassky had been the greatest prodigy of Soviet chess, but he grew up to be its prodigal son. At first, everything seemed to come effortlessly to him; he was handsome, clever, and charming. Even his laziness, for which he was legendary, did him no harm; he resembled the much-loved national stereotype Oblomov—a far cry from the Stakhanovite ideal personified in chess by Botvinnik. "It's in my nature to be like a Russian bear," he joked to his biographer Bernard Cafferty, "who even finds it an effort to find the time to stand up." Nor did he hide his preference for the old tsarist Russia. As between the two old rivals who had dominated chess in Leningrad for decades, Levenfish and Botvinnik, it was the former—"a man of Russian culture and intelligence"—rather than the world champion—"a Thirties man of Soviet culture"—with whom Spassky identified, as he admitted many years later after moving to France.

By 1956 and still aged only nineteen, Spassky established his place among the elite by finishing third in the candidates' tournament at Amsterdam, just behind Smyslov, who went on to defeat Botvinnik for the world title, although he lost the rematch. Just as Spassky seemed destined in due course to end the monopoly of Botvinnik and Smyslov, his career hit the rocks. First, he was overtaken by Mikhail Tal, who burst on the chess scene in 1957, winning the Soviet championship. The following year the event was held in Tal's home town of Riga. In the last round Tal played Spassky, with not only the Soviet title but a place in the world championship cycle at stake. After missing a forced win and refusing a draw, Spassky spent the night analyzing the adjourned position, searching for the elusive clincher. Arriving at the board exhausted, Spassky let not only the win but the draw slip away. Much, much later he felt able to describe the traumatic scene: "When I resigned, there was a thunder of applause but I was in a daze and hardly understood what was happening. . . I felt there was something terribly wrong. After this game I went on the street and cried like a child." Blindly wandering home, Spassky met his friend David Ginzburg, a Gulag survivor: "Borya, why are you crying? I'll tell you what will happen. Misha [Tal] will go and win the Interzonal. Then he'll win the Candidates' tournament. After that he'll have a match with Botvinnik. He'll win from Botvinnik. Then there'll be a return match. He'll lose to Botvinnik. But you will still play and play and achieve everything you want."

Sure enough, Tal went on to become the youngest ever world champion—but his reign lasted only a year. Tal never regained the title; a decade later it was Spassky's turn to inherit the crown. For the moment, however, Spassky's life fell apart. He quarreled with his trainer, Tolush, who had shielded him from the KGB and they parted on bad terms. He had married young and the couple had a daughter, but by 1961 he and his wife had become "bishops of opposite colors" and they divorced. Spassky's one consolation was his victory over the new American star, Bobby Fischer, in their first game at Mar del Plata in 1960—with a dashing King's Gambit, an opening that had gone out of fashion a century before.

After his divorce, Spassky's career had resumed its progress to the summit. His new trainer, Igor Bondarevsky, was a Cossack whose dashing style and paternal advice restored Spassky's self-esteem. In 1965 he won matches against Keres and Geller. Finally he took his revenge on Tal and qualified to play Petrosian for the world championship in 1966. The match took place as usual in Moscow's Hall of Columns before a capacity audience, with thousands more queuing outside. Although Spassky felt himself to be unstoppable, things did not go according to plan. He was outwitted by the subtle strategist Petrosian, even in his own strong suit, tactics. When the world champion won the tenth game brilliantly, Armenians in the audience mobbed him. Spassky rallied, but in the end lost by one point. It was the first time in over thirty years that a defending champion had actually won a match.

Nothing daunted, Spassky continued to improve. Happier in his private life—he remarried in 1966—he was the most successful player of the late 1960s. Fischer had responded to his first defeat at

Spassky's hands in 1960 with characteristic overkill. In a classic article for *American Chess Quarterly* in 1961, he had declared that he had "refuted" the gambit once and for all time. When they met again at Santa Monica in 1966—a double-round event reserved for world title contenders, sponsored by the Russian émigré and virtuoso cellist Piatigorsky—the opening was different but the result was the same: Spassky won an elegant attacking game and, despite Fischer's astonishing recovery, went on to win the tournament.

His prize—$5,000 in hard currency—dwarfed anything he had earned before, while the liberal atmosphere and luxurious surroundings in California gave him a taste for life in the West. Chess grandmasters were among the few Soviet citizens to own significant private property, in a country where 99.6 percent of the economy belonged to the state. As the possibility of making serious money in the West beckoned—not least thanks to Fischer's charisma—the eyes of some Russians were opened to the grotesque aspects of Soviet life. It was a system that tried to use a pathological form of carrot and stick—privilege and fear—as a substitute for the financial incentives of the market. It perverted noble ideals, such as justice, honor, patriotism, and excellence, by turning them into propaganda. It was a system that Spassky grew to loathe.

In 1968 Spassky resumed the ever more arduous qualification process for the world championship, beating Geller, Larsen, and Korchnoi en route to a rematch against Petrosian. This time, Spassky was ready for the Armenian and could beat him at his own game. Prophylaxis, maneuvers, and siege warfare did not make for exciting chess, but by proving that Petrosian's defensive strategy was not impregnable, Spassky paved the way for the revolution in chess theory of the 1970s—and nobody studied his methods more carefully than Fischer. Spassky's victory, by 6–4 with thirteen draws, was popular both at home—ethnic Russians liked the fact that he was neither Armenian nor Jewish—and abroad, as the most glamorous world champion since Capablanca.

In the Kremlin, however, the new champion was seen not as part of the solution to the drying up of chess talent, but as part of the problem. By the late 1960s, Spassky had already acquired a reputation for the independence of his character and opinions. Unlike even the unruly Korchnoi, he refused to join the party. Proud of his heritage as the scion of a sacerdotal dynasty and a citizen of the tsarist capital of St. Petersburg, Spassky showed by discreet but unmistakable signals that he held the official ideology in contempt. When Czechoslovak grandmasters wore black armbands at the Lugano Olympiad soon after the Soviet invasion in 1968, Spassky was the only Russian to shake each one by the hand—a gesture of solidarity that risked severe censure, or worse, from his own side. Spassky always played the game by his own rules, trusting to his results to protect himself. "Others would never have been permitted to go abroad if they had acted in the same way as Spassky," recalled Mikhail Beilin, head of the chess department of the Soviet Sports Committee.

Spassky saw himself as an intellectual, but not as a member of the Soviet intelligentsia. Although he switched from mathematics to journalism at university (due to sheer "laziness"), he had no desire to join the ranks of propagandists and even refused to write about the politics of chess. It is not hard to pinpoint one source of Spassky's intellectual self-confidence: the literary tradition of Russian Orthodoxy and nationalism. Edmonds and Eidinow elicited from him the fact that his favorite Dostoyevsky novel is *The Brothers Karamazov*—a work that was officially blacklisted yet unofficially ubiquitous. Even Stalin loved it. Dostoyevsky may have been a bitter enemy of socialism in his day, but by his 150th anniversary in 1971 the great prophet of authoritarian nationalism was ready for rehabilitation, and a new edition of his works was sanctioned.

Spassky's affinity for Dostoyevsky probably owed more to his own depressive temperament than to what Lesley Chamberlain calls the "existentialism in disguise" that was institutionalized under communism. "The Soviet world gave existentialism a totalitarian framework," she writes in *Motherland: A Philosophical History of Russia*. Having distanced itself from the most extreme

forms of Stalinist repression during the 1950s, the Soviet system
was attempting to internalize the pre-revolutionary high culture
that had somehow preserved itself intact. Spassky was a product of
the same discontents that, a generation after Stalin, produced the
dissident movement, but he was also influenced by the *Zeitgeist.*
Hence he took refuge in reserve, in ambiguity, in a private space
where he could preserve his self-respect and integrity. Even if he
was not the perfect representative of the Soviet state, he was nevertheless proud to represent the Russian people.

When Spassky faced Fischer at Siegen in September 1970, therefore, their game was invested with considerable symbolism. Both
men knew what was at stake: not only victory in the Olympiad,
but a foretaste of the championship match for which the chess
world had waited so long. The game was a thrilling one. Although
Fischer had several chances to draw, he overplayed his hand—and
lost to a rook sacrifice that won his queen. When the American
resigned, the Soviet ambassador to West Germany, Semyon Tsarap-
kin, rushed to give Spassky a bear-hug. Despite this official embrace, it was an even sweeter victory for Spassky than the world
championship; for Fischer it was the worst blow to his ego since
Curaçao in 1962. His score sheet told its own story: in recording
his moves, his handwriting gradually became more manic and ultimately illegible. Spassky's estimate of the game's quality was
modest, even though he saw its significance in their war of nerves:
"He failed to find a good plan and play accurately." More magnani-
mously he conceded that "Fischer himself may have contributed
to my high spirits. It has always been a pleasure to play against
him. . . I respect him as a man who loves chess passionately and for
whom the game is everything in life." Fischer's response was brief
and to the point: "Wait till next time. Spassky was lucky."

Thanks to this defeat, the American team failed to mount a serious challenge to the Soviets and had their worst ever result with
Fischer in the team. Nevertheless, this failure only fueled Fischer's
desire for another crack at the Russians—and especially Spassky.
Attention now shifted to the question of whether Fischer, who had

not qualified for the Interzonal stage of the world championship cycle, could somehow be substituted for one of the three Americans who had. The choice fell on Pal Benkö, who accepted $2,500 in return for ceding his place to Fischer. The Russians grudgingly acceded to this deal and two months later—to the amazement of those who had given up hope of ever seeing him play again for the world title—he was in Palma with the rest of the world's elite.

From the outset it was clear that Fischer was on better form than ever. He knocked down his opponents with ease, and even his one defeat—against Larsen—seemed to have no effect. He bounced back and beat the Russians resoundingly: Smyslov, Taimanov, and his old bête noir Geller. That game began with Geller offering a draw after only seven moves—a calculated insult to the famously combative American, who refused "grandmaster draws" on principle. He made an inaudible reply and Geller's face was seen to turn red. The game went badly for Geller, despite attempts by other Soviet officials to distract Fischer by whispering and laughing, which resulted in their expulsion from the room. Finally, just as he was within sight of a draw, Geller blundered. Of the Russians, only Lev Polugayevsky avoided defeat. Fischer's result—18.5 out of twenty-three—left him 3.5 points clear of the field. The Soviets comforted themselves that Fischer had also dominated the Stockholm Interzonal in 1962, but had flopped at the candidates' stage in Curaçao. This time, however, Fischer could not be stopped by a cartel: he would face successive opponents in individual elimination matches. The quarter- and semifinals would be the best of ten games, the final best of twelve. The first of Fischer's opponents was a Russian: Mark Taimanov.

At this point the Soviet chess establishment began to experience what became known as "Fischer fear." Botvinnik, while remaining skeptical of all talk of "genius," was nevertheless clear that "Fischer has become a real threat to Soviet chess . . . We have been deceived and lulled by our successes. Therefore, after losing our vigilance, we have not prepared a new generation." The patriarch argued that "Spassky has no reason to fear Fischer" and

Spassky insisted that "I fear only myself." But Fischer fear certainly stalked the committee rooms of the bureaucrats who controlled chess in the USSR. One manifestation of this was a smear campaign during the months preceding Fischer's match against Taimanov. In 64 (whose editor was Petrosian) an article by Alexander Golubev claimed that Fischer was "morbidly mistrustful," "by no means respectful to his opponent," and "does not know how to lose." The article considered that Fischer's play at Palma was "substantially inferior to his usual performance" and speculated that it might be due to "the beginning of a retrogression." Having cast doubt on his chess, Golubev poured scorn on his character: "Unintellectual, lopsidedly developed, and uncommunicative, Fischer unwittingly promotes that 'intellectual hippiness' that, like a malignant growth, is spreading in the chess world."

The Russian who actually found himself as the first line of defense against Fischer was under no such illusions about his opponent. Like Spassky, Taimanov was a nonconformist from Leningrad. However, he was even more creative: not only had he invented the eponymous Taimanov Variation of the Sicilian Defense, but he had enjoyed a successful parallel career as a concert pianist. Although he had never quite fulfilled his potential in the fiercely competitive field of Soviet chess, Taimanov was proof that Russian culture could survive even in the suffocating atmosphere of Brezhnev's state. Moreover, Taimanov liked and admired Fischer. His preparation was supervised by Botvinnik himself, who had prepared a dossier on Fischer for his own abortive match. Taimanov obeyed the patriarch's strictures, but he later regretted not taking Tal as his second. Botvinnik bluntly told him: "Both of you are given to bohemianism and the atmosphere may be insufficiently ascetic for such a test" (although what "bohemian" activities the puritanical Botvinnik thought that Taimanov, at the age of forty-five, might get up to on a Canadian campus was not spelled out). Frustrated in his own hopes of a crack at Fischer, the former world champion saw Taimanov as his proxy.

While Fischer started as the hot favorite, Taimanov began confidently. He was privately glad that the match was held in the West. Vancouver had a similar climate to Leningrad, and the winner's prize—$2,000—was still larger than Spassky had received for the world title two years before, and even the loser's fee of $1,000 was princely compared to the 170 rubles for which the candidates' match winners had to be grateful in the Soviet Union. The financial factor is rarely mentioned in Soviet documents, but the gap between East and West was widening all the time.

The first game was a tactical mêlée of the kind the Russian relished, and though he was outplayed he was not discouraged. In the second game he got to play his trademark defense, but Fischer gained a small edge in a long and complex endgame that was adjourned twice. This meant that it was actually finished after the third game, which proved to be decisive. The whole match turned on one move: the twentieth. Taimanov had the chance for a strong but risky attack, and he agonized for seventy-two minutes—the longest think of his entire career—before his nerve failed him. "Psychologically I simply collapsed," he wrote. Fischer later said that Taimanov missed a win, although this is uncertain. What is certain is that he went down to a crushing defeat, after which he lost the adjourned second game, which should have been drawn. After that, Taimanov was rushed to the hospital with high blood pressure. When he returned, he lost again. Eager to avoid a rout, Taimanov took risks in the last two games. He lost both, one of them to a simple blunder. "I'm sorry," said the normally pitiless Fischer as he won the Russian's rook.

Fischer had won the match 6–0, an unheard-of result at world championship level. According to the chess psychologist Nikolai Krogius, Taimanov was reduced to a gibbering wreck: "He kept repeating 'Fischer knows everything.'" High blood pressure and a nervous breakdown were the least of Taimanov's worries, however. On his return to Sheremetyevo airport, his luggage was searched—grandmasters were usually waved through—and a copy of Solzhenitsyn's banned novel, *The First Circle*, was found. He was also carrying undeclared currency: 1,100 Dutch guilders that

Max Euwe had asked him to pass on to Salo Flohr as a fee. Everybody knew that these technical offenses were a pretext and that Taimanov was really being punished for his humiliating defeat. The customs officer who arrested him admitted as much: "If your score against Fischer had been better, Mark Evgenevich, I would have been prepared to carry the complete works of Solzhenitsyn to the taxi for you." Taimanov was summoned before the Sports Committee, which subjected him to a "civic execution." He suffered "devastating criticism from all quarters: from the Communist Party's Central Committee to my own party cell." A secret letter to the Central Committee from the chairman of the Sports Committee, Panov, accused him of "incorrect behavior and gross violation of customs rules," and reported that he had been stripped of his title, "merited Master of Sports," as well as kicked out of the national team. Taimanov was also banned from publishing, foreign travel, or even public performance at the piano. Botvinnik, who shared his protégé's humiliation, now accused Taimanov of deliberately throwing the final games because he had bet money against himself. What saved Taimanov from even worse consequences was the fact that others, too, were similarly crushed by Fischer. Mstislav Rostropovich, the greatest Russian cellist, used to tell a typical Soviet-era joke about two of his friends: Solzhenitsyn, who was then disgraced and living in his dacha, and Taimanov. "Have you heard that Solzhenitsyn is in trouble? They have found Taimanov's book *The Nimzowitsch Defense* among his belongings!"

Shortly after the match, Taimanov was summoned to a postmortem at the USSR Chess Federation Trainers' Council, including most of the Soviet chess elite. He was told that this was "the biggest setback in the entire history of Soviet chess" and was asked for an explanation. "I normally play in a relaxed manner," he replied, "but here I was aware of a sense of mission. This was probably the main mistake." He pleaded: "I now know Fischer better than anyone and I am ready to help those who have to play him." Nobody took up this offer, although the discussion exposed almost incredible ignorance about Fischer's personal details. Anticipating

Taimanov's disgrace, Spassky asked: "When we all lose to Fischer, will all of us be carpeted?" Petrosian replied: "Yes, but not here" — implying that much worse could be in store. Without apparent irony, Colonel Baturinsky, the former KGB interrogator, reassured the grandmasters: "This is not a trial." He proceeded to criticize every aspect of the match preparation, adding: "Perhaps it would have been more useful to send a doctor." Spassky attempted to make a joke: "A sexologist." Baturinsky responded with the humorlessness common to all secret policemen: "I see, Boris Vasilievich, that you are in a jovial mood." He admonished that "it pays, even in psychological terms, to take a tougher stand" with Fischer. He then warned the Trainers' Council that the result was "totally unsatisfactory."

In July, Fischer played Bent Larsen in the semifinal at Denver, Colorado. This match was expected to be quite close, as Larsen's tournament results had been outstanding and his record against Fischer was much better than Taimanov's. Larsen himself expected not only to beat Fischer, but to be the next world champion. The great Dane bore himself like an aristocrat, the nobility of his features reflecting an exquisite sensibility and a powerful intellect. Unfortunately for him, Fischer treated him with no more respect than he had Taimanov. The first game foreshadowed the rest. Fischer gave up his queen for several pieces and an overwhelming attack, leaving Larsen unsure quite where he had gone wrong. More than once Larsen could have drawn, but he played desperately for a win and lost. He, too, had fallen under Fischer's spell.

When Larsen resigned the last game to make it 6–0 again, not only chess fans but the world sat up and took notice. In the Soviet Union, television broadcasts were interrupted by the announcement. The news from Denver escalated "Fischer fear" into a full-scale panic. There had never been anything like it in the history of chess. For the first time in the Cold War, a president of the United States grasped the full significance of the Fischer phenomenon. Although Richard Nixon knew little and cared less about chess, he was quick to react to a story that was now making the front pages and which showed an American beating the Soviets at their own game. The president wrote Fischer a fulsome letter:

> I wanted to add my personal congratulations to the many you have already received. Your string of nineteen consecutive victories in world-class competition [including Fischer's last seven games at Palma] is unprecedented, and you have every reason to take great satisfaction in your superb achievement. As you prepare to meet the winner of the Petrosian–Korchnoi matches [sic] you may be certain that your fellow citizens will be cheering you on. Good luck!

For the following year, chess would temporarily take on something of the ideological importance for the USA that it had always enjoyed in the USSR. Nixon kept himself informed of Fischer's progress, and his chess-playing National Security Adviser, Henry Kissinger, made it his business to do what could be done to help Fischer deprive the Russians of the world championship.

At Spassky's training camp outside Moscow, planning had already begun for a probable Spassky–Fischer match, for which the Soviet chess hierarchy now ordered the presence of all Soviet grandmasters. Before Larsen had been wiped off the board, four grandmasters had met to produce a twenty-six-page analysis of Fischer's play to assist Spassky. The champion's trainers, Krogius and Bondarevsky, were left none the wiser as to how to stop the juggernaut. All eyes now turned to Petrosian, the last major obstacle between Fischer and his goal of a challenge to Spassky.

A long bidding war had ended with the match being held in Buenos Aires. Petrosian grumbled that the Argentinians favored Fischer, but this was not true and the Armenian could not complain about the prize fund — $7,500 for the winner, $4,500 for the loser — nor about the arbiter, Lothar Schmid, who was friendly with them both. Even the two main negotiators, Edmondson for Fischer and Baturinsky for Petrosian, got on well, perhaps because both were retired colonels. There was nothing amicable about the chess, however, which began on September 30, 1971. Fischer still detested Petrosian, whom he accused of using his editorship of the magazine 64 to add insults to the injury of fraudulently depriving Fischer of the world championship in 1962. As for Petrosian, he wanted revenge for his humiliation in Belgrade the previous year. The two could not even bear to stay in the same hotel.

The first game was interrupted by a mysterious power cut, during which the players sat in darkness while engineers restored the electricity. It was Fischer's move, and Petrosian complained that his opponent was continuing to analyze. Fischer gamely allowed his clock to be restarted and pondered his move in the dark. Petrosian's seconds had prepared a trap for Fischer, but it backfired. Petrosian got into time trouble, missed drawing chances, and resigned on the fortieth move. In the second game five days later, however, Petrosian turned the tables with a brilliant attack that ended Fischer's winning streak, which had now extended to twenty games. The ecstatic crowd sensed that Fischer—who was visibly in shock—would not have a walkover this time. They chanted: *"Tigran un tigre!"* Urged on by his team, Petrosian sought to step up the pressure while Fischer was still struggling. Just as he seemed close to a second win, however, Petrosian allowed Fischer to claim a draw by repetition of moves. The fourth game, too, was drawn; so was the fifth, although Spassky wrote that "Petrosian outplayed Fischer in a battle of quiet maneuvering" while unable to "reap the fruits of his strategy." Thus far the match was finely balanced, but the sixth game proved to be decisive—indeed, one of the most important in the careers of both men. Fischer was his old, confident self again and gradually wore down his tenacious opponent. Petrosian blamed his seconds for failing to find a draw during the overnight adjournment, but the game was lost. Scenting blood, Fischer "felt Petrosian's ego crumbling after the sixth game" and pressed his advantage in the seventh—a flawless masterpiece. Now it was the American who had the Armenian tiger by the tail. "The last three games were no longer chess," Petrosian confessed. Fischer won all three to take the match by the crushing score of 6.5–2.5. The wunderkind from Brooklyn had come of age, and he stood on the threshold of his life's goal.

Back in the USSR, Armenia went into mourning and the Soviet hierarchy went into denial. Botvinnik praised Petrosian's "great achievement" in showing that "it is possible to play against Fischer." He sneered at Fischer, insisting that Spassky—who had beaten Petrosian only at the second attempt and by a much narrower margin—was superior to the American boor. To have visited such merciless destruction on a world champion—and a Soviet world champion, too—must be the work of the devil. Back in Moscow, Bondarevsky, Spassky's trainer, remarked to the Russian grandmaster, Alexander Kotov, that Fischer was merely adept at "counting variations." Kotov replied that he was good at counting points, too: "At least he has become highly expert at counting up to six!" Suddenly, nobody wanted the normally desirable post of chairman of the Soviet Chess Federation. Averbakh reluctantly accepted, knowing that it meant taking responsibility for losing the world title: "There were not many candidates for this dangerous position," he later recalled. The mood among the Soviet elite in the aftermath of Buenos Aires resembled that of Wagner's gods in Valhalla, awaiting their *Götterdämmerung.*

Meanwhile, Fischer returned to the United States to find that he had become a public figure. President Nixon was the first to hail the conquering hero: "I want you to know that together with thousands of chess players across America, I will be rooting for you when you meet Boris Spassky next year." Along with the boom in chess activities of all kinds, the symbiosis of patriotic enthusiasm, celebrity cult, and unprecedented media coverage held out the tantalizing hope that chess might follow other minority pursuits in catching the national imagination. Like Richard Feynman with particle physics, Muhammad Ali with boxing, or Milton Friedman with economics, Fischer had the chance to bring chess to a wider public. He was the first grandmaster with real star quality—the first but, in America at least, also the last.

Alekhine and Capablanca in 1914. They dominated chess between the wars. Alekhine died in 1946, leaving the world championship seat vacant.

Botvinnik and Lasker in 1935: the future and the past. Botvinnik's victory at Moscow in 1935 put Soviet chess on the map.

Chess scene from *Ivan the Terrible,* Eisenstein's wartime epic. The real Ivan probably died at the chessboard.

Moscow's Hall of Columns, during the 1948 match-tournament. Euwe (left) is playing Botvinnik in the game that clinched the world championship for the Soviet school of chess. To the right is Smyslov.

A propaganda poster showing Botvinnik, Smyslov, and Keres at Moscow, 1948.
The Estonian, Keres, lost four games to the Russian, Botvinnik, in suspicious
circumstances.

Soviet naval officers play chess at sea early on in the Cold War, ca.1950.

Chess training for children at the Young Pioneer Palace, Leningrad, 1959. The former capital produced many great masters, including Botvinnik, Korchnoi, and Spassky.

In 1955, aged thirteen, Bobby Fischer was already giving simultaneous exhibitions against adults, such as this one in Jersey City. A year later, he was U.S. champion.

The early 1970s were years of détente. This new orthodoxy was a refinement of the postwar doctrine of containment. Instead of containing communist aggression, the West settled for containment of its consequences—the periodic crises that sent seismic waves through the global economy from about 1947 to about 1970. After the two most frightening decades in history, both sides sought the comfort zone of a system of diplomacy. The new settlement was intended to make the crises and confrontation of the postwar era a thing of the past. Détente was supposed to create a framework of rules, agreements, and understandings that, without ending the Cold War, would at least make it predictable. The point about the strategic doctrine that preceded détente, mutually assured destruction (MAD), was not that it was destructive but that it was mutual and assured. Détente took the logic of MAD several steps further. The status quo that détente perpetuated was inhumane, certainly, but it was not unpredictable. The trouble with the doctrine and its apostle, Henry Kissinger, was that they elevated stability above liberty, so depriving the West of its strongest weapon. The compromises that were intended to be the means to preserve peace soon became ends in themselves. Sooner than anybody suspected, the subversive power of truth would shatter the institutional carapace of détente, while in the meantime its high priests engaged in elaborate rituals of self-congratulation. *Realpolitik* was the watchword of the day, but it concealed the true significance of détente, which was to mask the consolidation of Soviet imperial expansion.

In the Brezhnev era, the Soviet empire, surrounded by satellites, embarked on the colonization of Asia, Africa, and Latin America. The illusory power of this vast oriental despotism had reached its utmost extent. Soviet imperial overstretch was fueled—often literally so—by primitive oil plants that could not begin to compensate for the metastasis of Soviet bureaucracy and the obsolescence of Soviet heavy industry. At this turning point, Solzhenitsyn published *The Gulag Archipelago,* the judgment in literary form that laid bare the lie at the heart of communism and lit the fuse that would ultimately detonate the entire structure. In his *Letter to the*

Soviet Leaders of 1973, he warned: "The aims of a great empire and the moral health of the people are incompatible." Yet, as he later acknowledged in *The Russian Question,* his postmortem on the Soviet Union, the Machiavellianism of Soviet diplomacy was modeled on grandmaster chess:

> The Communist leaders knew exactly what they wanted, and every action was directed exclusively towards the realization of this useful objective—never a single magnanimous or disinterested move; and every step was calculated precisely, with all possible cynicism, ruthlessness and sagacity in assessing the adversary. . . it always surpassed and defeated the West. . . Soviet diplomacy was furnished with such ideologically attractive plumage that it won the rapturous sympathy of progressive society in the West.

If the Cold War was the best thing that ever happened to chess, chess furnished the best metaphor for the Cold War. The Fischer–Spassky duel came at exactly the right moment, when the threat of nuclear war had receded just sufficiently for the accumulated animosities and fears of a schizoid epoch to be projected on to something as intrinsically harmless as a chess match. There were, of course, other metaphors: artistic, sporting, scientific. The space race, which reached its climax at about the same time, was a peaceful by-product of the arms race, but it also provided an arena where prestige and patriotism could be let off the leash. Chess, however, was a perfect match for the peculiarities of Cold War culture: abstract purism, incipient paranoia, sublimated homicide. Preserving a delicate balance between objective logic and subjective fantasy, chess resembled a parallel universe, alien to the inexpert in theory yet all too human in practice, where a radical dualism transfigured all life into a zero-sum game. Like no other single event, the great match refined and concentrated the complexities of a global conflict within the narrow confines of a checkered board on a remote island, thereby creating the iconographical consummation of an epoch.

Fischer–Spassky was the Cold War's supreme work of art—a manifestation of the *Zeitgeist* more pregnant with meaning than any "happening" staged by a decadent avant-garde. This was an event that was not haphazard; rather, it foreshadowed the course of the cosmic conflict with all the elegant economy of an end-game.

11

THE DEATH OF HECTOR

THE SECOND SECTION OF T. S. Eliot's poem, *The Waste Land*, entitled "A Game of Chess," is interrupted by a loud and ever more insistent voice repeating the line: "HURRY UP PLEASE ITS TIME" [sic]. Leaving aside Eliot's complex web of allusions to Thomas Middleton's 1624 play, *A Game at Chess*, this line summed up the sentiments of the chess world in early 1972. At last the showdown that the world had waited for was on—yet the complexity and acrimony of the negotiations seemed more like a Cold War stand-off than a chess match. The Soviets, who had most to lose, launched a preemptive strike against, of all people, Max Euwe, accusing the FIDE president of favoring Fischer. It was true that Euwe, the Dutch mathematician who had been the only genuine amateur to become world champion in the 1930s, liked Fischer and openly predicted that he would win. However, his sole concern was to make sure that the match actually took place.

Fischer, meanwhile, was represented by Colonel Ed Edmondson, the executive director of the U.S. Chess Federation. A plain-spoken veteran of Cold War confrontations, he was determined to accomplish his mission to install an American on the throne of chess. After a long bidding contest between cities from several continents, accompanied by bad-tempered commentary from the Soviet press, Edmondson flew to Moscow in February to conduct final negotiations. The decision was made to divide the match between Reykjavik, which had made only the third-highest bid but had been Spassky's first preference, and Belgrade, which had offered more money and was therefore Fischer's favorite. Although neither side was satisfied, after a whole month of wrangling two agreements were signed, one covering match rules, and the other covering the business arrangements between FIDE and the organizers in Iceland and Yugoslavia. The purse would be $138,000, splitting the difference between Belgrade's offer of $150,000 and Reykjavik's of $125,000. A generation later these sums, even allowing for inflation, seem laughably small. At the time they were dwarfed by the purse in the "fight of the century" between Muhammad Ali and Joe Frazier, who earned $2.5 million each in 1971. However, the stakes in Fischer–Spassky were of a different order of magnitude than anything seen before in chess.

Hopes rose at the news that a deal had been done. By this time Euwe had left on a tour of the Far East, so there was nobody to mediate when a cable arrived from Fischer, addressed to the Icelandic and Yugoslav chess federations, which threw the entire match into doubt again. After hearing from Edmondson the details of the agreement, Fischer had exploded. His telegram was as unambiguous as it was ungrammatical, and concluded: "I will not play your match in Iceland." To FIDE he addressed another tirade, repudiating Edmondson and the U.S. Chess Federation, and declaring: "I personally will handle all future negotiations and agreements in regard to the Spassky match."

This was a blow to at least three individuals: Euwe, whose reputation depended on the possibility of mediating across the Iron Curtain; Edmondson, who had in effect been fired after years of devotion to Fischer's cause; and Gudmundur Thorarinsson, president of the Icelandic Chess Federation, who was responsible for the biggest sensation that his country had witnessed since the Vikings colonized Iceland in AD 847. It was Thorarinsson who responded first: "Any changes are . . . unacceptable." Fischer replied instantly: he would not play in Iceland at all. Unlike Thorarinsson, who ignored Fischer, the Belgrade organizers panicked. They suspended all preparations, demanding a deposit from the U.S. Chess Federation that the Americans were unable and unwilling to give. Alarmed by the spectacle of the match unraveling, Euwe sent Fischer an ultimatum: either he agreed to play on the existing terms by April 4, or he forfeited his rights.

This was a critical moment in the story. Having achieved the desired effect of reminding all the bureaucrats who was the real star of the show, Fischer now did what any other celebrity would do—he handed over the whole thing to his lawyers. Paul Marshall, a Hollywood attorney who also represented David Frost, sent an emollient cable stating that Fischer was "ready, willing and expects to play." But this was not what Euwe had demanded, and when the deadline passed the Soviets called on him to carry out his threat. The Icelander remained cooler than his Yugoslav rivals. Thorarinsson now exploited their hesitation by offering to host the whole match. It was now mid-April, less than three months before play was due to start. For Euwe, this was the last chance to rescue the match and he seized it. Curtly informing both players that the entire match would now take place in Reykjavik, he warned that if Fischer refused, Spassky would play Petrosian again instead. The prospect of a third round between the two Soviets was so appalling to everyone except Petrosian that Fischer finally relented. "Under protest," he agreed to play in Iceland but refused to sign anything. Without Belgrade, the prize fund would be $125,000—so Fischer's antics had actually served to reduce the purse.

Back in Moscow, the Soviet hierarchy was increasingly concerned, not only about Fischer but about Spassky, too. The world champion had friends in the Kremlin—specifically, Piotr Demichev, a member of the Politburo and secretary of the Central Committee responsible for ideology. Following Marxist doctrine, chess had always been treated in common with the rest of culture as an aspect of ideology. Suddenly it had assumed unprecedented significance across the communist world. At Spassky's request, Demichev ordered Sports Minister Sergei Pavlov to keep him informed about the preparations for the match, especially Spassky's training regime. Although Pavlov was an old crony of Brezhnev's, he was obliged to obey the higher-ranking Demichev—but he made sure that the party leadership received a detailed catalogue of Spassky's shortcomings. The series of secret memoranda that Pavlov wrote to the Central Committee forms the single most important source to have emerged from the Kremlin archives on the match.

The first, in July 1971, warned about the danger posed by Fischer to Soviet prestige and accused Euwe of "pandering to Fischer's interests." Pavlov tried to reassure the party leadership while reprimanding Spassky, saying that he was "uncritical of his [own] behavior, makes immature statements, violates the competitive regime, and is not sufficiently industrious." More damagingly, Pavlov insinuated that "certain people at home and abroad are trying to exacerbate these shortcomings by fostering in Spassky an attitude of megalomania, emphasising his 'exceptional role' as world champion [and] fanning his already unhealthy mercenary spirit." If either player was guilty of megalomania, it certainly was not Spassky. Nevertheless, the absurdity of the accusation is a reminder of how the dead hand of collectivism weighed heavily on even the most talented individuals in the USSR. It was certainly true, though, that Spassky's choices of match venue were all in the capitalist world, and he openly admired Fischer's "mercenary spirit." Even after losing his title he would tell journalists that Fischer "is the best trade union boss we ever had. He's upped our wages!"

The one fair accusation, however, was the charge of laziness. In his last tournament before going into rematch purdah, the Moscow Alekhine Memorial in December 1971, Spassky performed badly, coming only sixth. The youthful winner, Anatoly Karpov,

was assigned to play a training match with Spassky. Minister Pavlov reassured the Kremlin that the Academy of Medical Sciences
and the All-Union Scientific Research Institute (which boasted a
"chess laboratory") were on Spassky's case. Pavlov's deputy, Viktor Ivonin, and Baturinsky reported that Spassky's long-standing
wish for a new apartment for his family in Moscow, commensu-
rate with his status, had been granted. From March to May 1972,
the world champion and his retinue stayed at a variety of resorts.
A month was spent at a luxurious house at Arkhyz in the Cauca-
sus Mountains. It is an indication of the importance that the Kremlin attached to Spassky that this dacha belonged to the Council of
Ministers and was a favorite of Prime Minister Kosygin.

Then the caravanserai moved on to a sanatorium near Sochi, on
the Black Sea. Spassky's entourage was able to deceive Colonel
Baturinsky about the lack of preparation when he went there in
May, but the beady-eyed Karpov, who was too junior to be worth
the charade, later described the relaxed regime that he found: "I
was amazed to observe that Spassky was doing nothing . . . He
could find time for anything, as long as it wasn't chess . . . I also
consider myself to be lazy, but the scale of Spassky's laziness stag-
gered me." Allowance must be made for exaggeration—Karpov
was just emerging as the young pretender to Spassky's throne and
as a model communist he must have been repelled by the champion's cynical attitude to Soviet pieties.

Yet Karpov was not the only visitor to Camp Boris to report back
a disturbing lack of any sense of urgency. Krogius, his psychologist
and minder, later recalled that "Boris thought the [chess] sessions
were too long, whereas he was ready to play tennis from morning
till night." Most seriously, Spassky's chief trainer and father-figure
for more than a decade, Igor Bondarevsky, suddenly resigned. Kasparov quotes Baturinsky thus: "Igor Zaharovich openly explained
his decision to me: Spassky was not preparing seriously for the
match, and he, Bondarevsky, did not want to bear responsibility for
the outcome." At the insistence of the Sports Committee, Bondarevsky was replaced by Yefim Geller—a stronger player and,

more importantly, a fanatical Communist Party loyalist. Then Spassky quarreled with his chief minder, Baturinsky, who was dropped from the privileged team that would accompany him to Reykjavik. Apart from making a powerful enemy, this left Spassky without his toughest negotiator. The champion also fell out with his most influential predecessor, Botvinnik. The chess *nomenklatura* had begun to lose faith in Spassky—even if he still had faith in himself.

Of the grandmasters whose comments on Fischer were solicited by the Soviet Chess Federation, only Korchnoi told Spassky anything he did not know. He warned the champion to expect surprises from Fischer, and even anticipated the appearance of openings that the American had never played before. However, Korchnoi also wrote that "Spassky is experiencing a crisis . . . Nihilism . . . is a chronic illness . . . Spassky overestimates his mastery of defense." Privately, Korchnoi was even more scathing—he thought Spassky had been "backsliding" ever since becoming champion and had not studied chess at all—but he kept these views to himself until after the match. Even mild criticism, however, caused Spassky to ignore Korchnoi's valuable advice, particularly this admonition: "With Fischer you have to be prepared to play every game from beginning to end, without relaxing." Spassky, on the contrary, thought that nothing was more important than to be relaxed, to preserve a "clear mind." According to Karpov, the champion steeped himself in Greek mythology during the weeks before the match; perhaps he already saw himself in the role of a tragic hero.

While Spassky was preparing with a regime of fresh air, fine food, and as little chess as possible, Fischer went to the opposite extreme. Immured in Grossinger's, a hotel resort in upstate New York, he emerged from his room only to eat and work out in the gym. The kosher diet at Grossinger's, where the Jewish Sabbath was observed, appealed to Fischer, whose Christian fundamentalist sect adhered strictly to Mosaic law. Wherever he went, he took the fat dossier of Spassky's games known as the "Big Red Book" (Fischer loved anti-communist jokes) compiled for him by R. G. Wade, a master from New Zealand who had gone through the same exercise before each of the previous three matches. It was a thankless task—in the pre-Internet age, chess games had to be located in obscure bulletins and journals—for which Wade received no thanks. Fischer worked alone, with unremitting concentration, probing for chinks in Spassky's armor. This was normal for a man who, as Euwe put it, existed "in a world entirely his own." The nomadic life of a chess master, with no home but hotel rooms, suited Fischer just fine; apart from a pathological aversion to noise, he was indifferent to his surroundings. His only break in routine came when David Frost flew him to Bermuda for a celebrity lunch, at which Fischer chatted with the economist John Kenneth Galbraith. It is hard to imagine what the Brooklyn boy had in common with the waspish (and WASP) Keynesian guru. As the match approached, Fischer paid a quick visit to San Diego, to receive the blessing of his Church, then repaired to the unaccustomed elegance of the Yale Club in New York, where he was a guest of his lawyer.

Apart from his legal representatives and a reporter from *Life* magazine, Fischer was accompanied to the match by only a handful of companions. The hard-bitten Fred Cramer acted as his spokesman, declaring: "I am authorized only to complain." The only man Fischer trusted sufficiently with his chess secrets to be his second was William Lombardy, perhaps because he was both a childhood friend and at the time a Catholic priest. (He has since resigned from the priesthood.) His choice may also have served to remind Spassky of his defeat twelve years earlier at Lombardy's hands on the top board in the world students' team championship in Leningrad. There was unintended symbolism in the portly priest's conspicuous presence at Fischer's side: the Christian West versus communist atheism. Father Lombardy was not merely decorative but also efficient, as a strong grandmaster who had been world junior champion.

With the opening ceremony of the World Chess Championship fixed for July 1, 1972, the world's media descended on Reykjavik.

A brash New York entrepreneur, Chester Fox, had bought the exclusive TV rights, while the more highbrow magazines sent literary grandees who dabbled in chess, such as Arthur Koestler and George Steiner. Suddenly Iceland, a largely uninhabited volcanic isle with a population of only 210,000, came under microscopic scrutiny. Although Reykjavik was firmly in the Western camp and home to a major U.S. military base, it was geographically midway between the superpowers, and its Cold War symbolism would later be enhanced by the summit held in Reykjavik in 1986 between Reagan and Gorbachev. The "white nights" of Reykjavik, during which the sun never sets, appealed to Spassky, whose native Leningrad was on a similar latitude, and they lent the events of summer 1972 a surreal quality. The one thing that everybody agreed on was how nice the inhabitants were—and how besotted with chess. Or almost everybody: the discreet charm of this very bourgeois nation was lost on Fischer, who upset his Icelandic fans by telling the press: "It's an awful choice. It's a hardship place where they give GIs extra pay to serve there." On a cold, wet day in early August, he joked: "Iceland is a nice place. I must come back here in the summertime." The locals had the last laugh, however. Some thirty-three years later in 2005, the only country on earth ready to grant asylum to Fischer, by then a fugitive from justice, was Iceland.

The match was almost over before it began. Spassky and his entourage arrived on June 25, to be installed in the Saga, the best hotel in town. Fischer was due the following day, but failed to show up. The same thing happened the next day, and the next. At one point Fischer got as far as JFK airport, where he was spotted in a restaurant and mobbed; he turned tail and fled. What had gone wrong? A new dispute had blown up behind the scenes. As usual, it was about money—but for Fischer, money was always merely a weapon. He had, he claimed, never signed the financial deal, and he now demanded a 30 percent share of the gate receipts as part of the purse, plus a share of the sale of TV rights to Chester Fox. Both he and the Icelanders knew that the match could only be financed by the two income streams from spectators and television, yet Fischer was prepared to risk sabotaging both.

Having retreated from the public eye to the New York suburb of Queens, where his old friend Anthony Saidy put him up, Fischer was denounced by all sides. The *New York Times* and the Soviet news agency Tass were equally critical, although from contrasting ideological standpoints: the Soviets sneered at his greed, while the Americans thought he was just naive: "His prospective earnings would make the amount he is arguing about now seem trivial." Others thought Fischer devilishly cunning to wear Spassky down by keeping him guessing. (Fischer's response to this theory was: "I don't believe in psychology. I believe in strong moves.") His biographer, Frank Brady, argues that Fischer's brinkmanship was directed not at Spassky but at Thorarinsson, the Icelander who was by now in charge of the match. Some thought Fischer mad: Robert Byrne, the second-strongest American grandmaster, wondered: "Perhaps Bobby has lost touch with reality." Later, after phoning Fischer, Byrne retracted: "Bobby sounded calm and reasonable. His demands are entirely financial."

It was easy for those involved to lose sight of the bigger picture—the Cold War—but it was ultimately politics that would decide whether the match took place. The trouble, said Arthur Koestler, who was reporting the match for the *Sunday Times*, was simple: "Bobby is a genius, but as a propagandist for the free world he is rather counterproductive." On July 1, the opening ceremony took place without Fischer: an Icelandic *Hamlet* without the prince. If it was all great theater, it was also a nightmare for those in charge. Fischer's lawyer had just told Thorarinsson: "There'll be no match." In his speech, Euwe admitted that "Mr Fischer is not an easy man. But we should remember that he has lifted the level of chess for all players." He was still hopeful: "Even though he is not here, I am personally convinced that he will come tomorrow and the match will begin." Spassky, on the other hand, was already looking forward to a holiday, followed by a match with Petrosian. The next day, Euwe told Spassky that he was considering a postponement. The Russian delegation was against it, while the champion vacillated, probably because he really wanted the match to go ahead. If Spassky had refused to agree to a delay, Euwe would have had no choice but to disqualify Fischer. Instead, he used Spassky as an excuse to give the challenger two days' grace: he had until noon on July 4, Independence Day.

Meanwhile, Thorarinsson—facing the financial ruin of Icelandic chess—also spoke to Spassky, pleading with him to phone Fischer himself. The champion rejected this idea, certain it would be vetoed by his delegation. Then Spassky made a cryptic remark: "This can only be solved at a higher level." He meant that he was under pressure to return to Moscow, and that intervention from the Kremlin alone could prevent his superiors aborting the match. Thorarinsson, interpreting Spassky's remark to mean intervention in Washington, contacted the prime minister of Iceland, who persuaded Theodore Tremblay, the U.S. chargé d'affaires, to send a telegram to the State Department. This dispatch set out the damage that would be done to the image of the United States in this strategically vital base if Fischer did not show. Although Tremblay wrote it as a favor to his hosts, privately he dreaded the match and hoped the "damned thing" would never happen. He wanted nothing to do with it: "Indeed, I had been instructed by the State Department not to spend one cent of American taxpayers' money on Bobby Fischer since he had been so disrespectful of everything. So that was the way it was."

Tremblay's telegram, however, came to the attention of Dr. Henry Kissinger. The president's national security adviser was under no pressure to intervene in the world chess championship; he had bigger headaches, from terrorism (this was the summer of the Munich Olympics) to nuclear conflict (the Strategic Arms Limitation Talks in Geneva). He told Edmonds and Eidinow: "It was not a big political thing." Nevertheless, Kissinger took a more capacious view of diplomacy than the penny-pinching bureaucrats at State. He knew exactly what he was doing when he took the time to track down Fischer in his hideout. Not to have done so would not merely have left an ally in the lurch; it would have left the field to the enemy. Kissinger knew that the West's greatest vulnerability was at the level of culture, ideology, and public diplomacy He knew better than most the truth of Marshall McLuhan's adage: "The Vietnam War was lost in the living rooms of America." It was the cultural ascendancy of the Left that made possible the inexorable advance of Soviet influence in Africa and Southeast Asia, in Latin America, and even in Europe. Détente had made nuclear war more remote, but by relieving the tension it risked conceding the initiative to the Russians, who merely shifted the conflict on to a different plane. The West must not blink, even if all that was at stake was a chess match.

Kissinger instinctively sensed that losing this talisman of Soviet intellectual pride would not only be uncongenial to the Kremlin, but profoundly unsettling for the peoples living under its tutelage. So he rang Fischer and introduced himself with the carefully scripted words: "This is the worst player in the world calling the best player in the world." When Fischer heard Kissinger's already famous *basso profundo* wish him well on behalf of the U.S. government, something happened. Although there is no transcript of the conversation, the lawyers Andrew Davis and Paul Marshall gathered that what Fischer had heard was: "America wants you to go over there and beat the Russians." Kissinger later informed Nixon of his intervention; the president approved. Fischer practically stood to attention during the call. Later he told the world: "I have decided that the interests of my nation are greater than my own."

Kissinger's call had answered a deep need for recognition. Fischer, whose whole life had been defined by the Cold War, was at last acknowledged as a Cold Warrior. It must have been gratifying, for Fischer was already aware that his anti-communist views were no longer fashionable in the era of détente. The liberal intellectuals who were now taking an interest in Fischer held their noses at what George Steiner, writing in the *New Yorker*, ridiculed as "the simplistic rawness of Fischer's politics" and the "sycophantic Red-baiting in his entourage." At least there was someone in the Nixon White House—not yet submerged by the Watergate scandal—who understood and valued him.

Yet the call to arms from the commander-in-chief was still not enough to winkle Fischer out of his foxhole. Was it that he needed to feel adequately rewarded by his own side? If he was to represent the West against communism, the capitalists would have to pay him properly. Or was Fischer really just afraid to sit down and play—in case he might shatter his self-image by losing? After all, he had never beaten Spassky. This theory was put to the test in a manner that thrilled and delighted the world. On Monday, July 3, a day before the new and final deadline, a swashbuckling British tycoon, Jim Slater, heard that hopes were fading. On the way to his office, he resolved to donate £50,000 in order to double the prize money to $250,000. "I want to remove the problem of money from Fischer and see if he has any other problem," said Slater. "If he isn't afraid of Spassky, then I have removed the element of money." The London press taunted Fischer: "Come out and play, chicken!" While Fischer was suspicious of the offer, the suggestion of cowardice nevertheless stung. Marshall, his attorney, says that Fischer was privately resigned to defaulting the match until Slater's offer came through. He never thanked his benefactor, who later wrote: "Fischer is known to be rude, graceless, possibly insane. I didn't do it to be thanked. I did it because it would be good for chess."

The combination of Kissinger and Slater finally persuaded Fischer to board a plane to Reykjavik, arriving early on July 4, just in time for the deadline. To his fury, he was mobbed at the airport by the assembled press, so he ignored the Icelandic dignitaries waiting to greet him and dived into a waiting car. He was taken to a villa outside the capital where he promptly slept for twelve hours. Meanwhile, the deadline passed for the drawing of lots. Spassky duly appeared, but Fischer was represented only by a figure in full clericals: his second, Father Lombardy. Now it was Spassky's turn to take umbrage. He issued a statement demanding that Fischer be punished by a "just penalty"—meaning that he should be forfeited the first game. "Only then can I return to the question whether it is possible to conduct the match." What had happened?

The Kremlin had taken a hand. Alexander Yakovlev, the Central Committee member responsible for ideology and propaganda, had reproved Viktor Ivonin of the Sports Committee for letting Spassky be "humiliated." "Yakovlev accused me personally of not creating a situation where Spassky could come home," recalled Ivonin. "He said that . . . I was helping the Americans." Soviet citizens were sent to psychiatric prisons or the Gulag for less than this. Ivonin offered to fly to Reykjavik and bring Spassky back to Russia. This was countermanded by Yakovlev's more senior colleague Demichev, who argued that too much Soviet prestige was now at stake: "Spassky must not be the first to leave." Ironically, under Mikhail Gorbachev, the hardliner Yakovlev would later become the "godfather of glasnost."

Spassky's protest was a compromise. It elicited a unique apology from Fischer, who had now decided to play, which he personally delivered to Spassky's hotel room. What became known as the "Dear Boris" letter was cleverly worded to sound suitably contrite—only to make it clear that Fischer would not agree to give Spassky the odds of the first game—especially as the world champion already had the advantage of retaining his title if the match were drawn after twenty-four games. Fischer argued that if he were forfeited, he would need to win three games to make up the deficit. Cunningly, it concluded with an appeal to the chivalry that made Spassky so popular: "I know you to be a sportsman and a gentleman . . ." From then on, Spassky was praised by everyone as a gentleman, and he may have felt that he had to live up to his image. That suited Fischer fine. Korchnoi put it more brutally: "Spassky was a gentleman. Gentlemen may win the ladies, but gentlemen lose at chess."

Fischer's apology disarmed the Soviet side and frantic phone calls to Moscow followed. Soviet accounts differ about what happened next. Most agree that Sports Minister Pavlov spoke to

Spassky. Did the champion refuse to be recalled? No transcript of the call was kept. Instead, Spassky persuaded Lothar Schmid, the urbane arbiter of the match, to postpone the first game until July 11, to give Spassky time to recover his composure. This was agreed. When Fischer and Spassky finally met face to face to draw lots, Geller read a statement that incensed Fischer, whose Russian was good enough to detect its condescending tone: "The challenger apologized in writing and the President of FIDE has declared that the match rules of FIDE will be strictly observed in the future. Taking into consideration the efforts made by the Icelandic organizers of the match, and the desire of millions of chess admirers all over the world to see the match, the World Champion has decided to play with Robert Fischer." If the American apology had been belated, the Soviet acceptance was graceless. Nevertheless, the ceremony passed off without incident, and the players had several days to cool off. The match was back on again. There would be a maximum of twenty-four games; a tied match meant that the champion retained his title.

But Spassky might not have accepted the apology at all. He could have gone home before the match, keeping his title at least pro tem. One later champion, Garry Kasparov, is in no doubt about the psychological forces that drove Spassky to his doom: "The main thing was that Spassky did not regard himself as the strongest player in the world! It was for this reason that he considered himself obliged to play Fischer, to establish definitively which of them was the stronger. But by making concessions he gave his opponent a psychological advantage." Kasparov argues that Fischer needed this advantage to overcome the fact that he had never beaten the Russian. Once the match began, he complained only when he was not winning and needed to increase the pressure on his opponent. "And whereas Spassky was very susceptible to this," Kasparov argues, "I am sure that such tricks would not have worked with Karpov, who would have been little concerned with all these problems, feeling no piety towards Fischer." When, three years later, Fischer chose not to defend his title against Karpov, he may have sensed that the younger Russian was made of sterner stuff.

Aware that he had regained the initiative, Fischer now imposed his will on the organizers. By the time the first game began, Fischer had already forced them to change his chair, the chessboard, the lighting, the table, and many other things. He also turned up late, sauntering on to the stage six minutes after Spassky (who played White) had made the first move. The game proceeded without incident until an equal endgame was reached, with only bishops and pawns on each side. In this drawn position, Fischer took a pawn with his bishop, which was instantly trapped and he soon lost. The move caused a sensation. Although it looked like a beginner's blunder, it has been debated ever since. *Izvestia* interpreted the bishop capture ideologically, as a symptom of capitalist greed. Karpov saw it as a power play: Fischer sacrificed the bishop "without rhyme or reason" to prove that Spassky could not force him to accept a draw. Others felt that Fischer was just impetuous, thinking he could create winning chances by muddying the waters. "Basically that's right," Fischer himself confirmed decades later, but at the time he complained that he had been distracted by noise.

The game was adjourned in a hopeless position for Fischer, who resigned the next day. Before they parted, Fischer said in Russian (in which he was fluent): "Till tomorrow." Subsequent computer-aided analysis has shown that the result was by no means a foregone conclusion. The British grandmaster Jon Speelman tried to prove that Fischer should still have drawn the game with best play. That Fischer missed a chance is confirmed by Kasparov: "It was very hard for Fischer to get into his stride."

Then came a second catastrophe, which almost aborted the match. Fischer blamed his loss of the first game on the TV cameras and refused to play unless they were removed. Chester Fox, who had paid good money for the rights, threatened to sue. The organizers sought a compromise in vain. Even after the cameras were hidden, Fischer failed to show up for the second game at 5 P.M. on July 13. Then the cameras were removed altogether. Still Fischer would not appear unless his clock was restarted—which Spassky would not allow, so Lothar Schmid was forced to declare that Fischer had lost by default. However, he knew better than anyone what mattered most: "We had to save the match." He was up till midnight, trying to persuade the American to appeal against his own decision within the permitted six hours. But although the match committee found that the appeal had been made properly, it also ruled that the default must stand. All bets were now on Fischer flying home in high dudgeon.

What stopped him? In part, it was the fact that his two-point deficit—an almost insuperable handicap in a championship match—was at some level a psychological gambit. Having resisted Spassky's demand that he forfeit the first game, Fischer in effect told him: have the point anyway—and a second too for good measure! He could afford it. His unnecessary loss, followed by an even more unnecessary forfeit, implied a kind of cavalier condescension towards the man he had lost to thrice and had yet to beat once. Fischer had said more than once: "Anyone who knows anything about chess knows that I've been champion of the world, in every way but name, for the past ten years." His seemingly self-defeating behavior during the first phase of the match encouraged Spassky to develop an inferiority complex. The champion's inhibitions about the political role in which he found himself reinforced his self-doubt about his chess.

At this decisive moment, Fischer heard the voice of America again. Henry Kissinger called from California, where he was having informal talks with the Soviet ambassador, Anatoly Dobrynin. One of Chester Fox's cameramen claimed to have overheard Henry Kissinger tell Fischer: "You're our man up against the commies." Given Fischer's attitude to Fox and his cameras, this is implausible, but Kissinger certainly galvanized his protégé to return to the fray. Perhaps Fischer was flattered to be invited to talk grand strategy with the world champion of *realpolitik*. At all events, the horse did not bolt. While the *New York Times* editorialized about "Bobby Fischer's Tragedy," to most it looked more like a farce. Like some deus ex machina, Kissinger resolved the complexities of the drama. Fischer promptly told the BBC: "It is really the free world against the lying, cheating, hypocritical Russians . . . This little thing between me and Spassky. It's a microcosm of the whole world political situation." Only now did the contest begin in earnest. Fischer was ready to fight the Cold War; Spassky was not.

It was high time. The world in general, and the microcosm of it gathered in Reykjavik, had turned against Fischer. When he failed to appear for the second game and was defaulted, Spassky was given a standing ovation. "He is the Soviet government's strongest piece on the chessboard of the Cold War," the match bulletin raved. The mood was ugly: not only anti-Fischer but anti-American, too. Fischer was receiving "thousands" of cables and letters, most begging him to play, but many bitterly hostile. Kissinger's intervention had not put an end to Fischer's psychological war of attrition. He was still booking himself on flights to America every day; still refusing to give an inch on the cameras, even though no equipment could detect any audible sounds; still making new demands, such as that traffic lights should be switched to green for him, or that the next game be played in a small back room, away from spectators. The latter demand was a bitter pill for the Icelanders, who had sold tickets in advance, but Schmid saw it as the only hope of getting Bobby Fischer back to the board. He put the idea to the champion. Without consulting his team, Spassky unexpectedly agreed: "That's fine by me . . . but just for this one game."

It was the last, seemingly least significant of many concessions —yet it was fatal. "Spassky should have refused. If he had dug his heels in—that would have been it!" wrote Kasparov. "It was not so much that Fischer changed the match conditions, but rather that he simply broke Spassky. He began dictating the conditions off the chessboard, and then also on it!" The champion had forgotten the warnings of Larsen and Petrosian not to yield to Fischer's demands. Karpov, unusually, agrees with Kasparov on this point:

Spassky "the philosopher" was checkmated off the board by Fischer's forfeiture, a "stroke of genius" from which Spassky took ten games to recover. Schmid, who was there, sees it differently: "Of course, Spassky was in the lead. For him, it was worth agreeing to move the game to get Bobby back." According to Spassky himself, he spoke for half an hour by phone to Sports Minister Pavlov, who wanted him to issue an ultimatum that they both knew would be unacceptable. Pavlov wanted the match aborted; Spassky was equally determined to go ahead. "The whole conversation consisted of an unending exchange of two phrases: "Boris Vasileyvich, you must issue the ultimatum!" "Sergei Pavlovich, I'm going to play the match!" After this conversation I lay in bed for three hours, shaken . . . I saved Fischer by playing the third game. In essence I signed the capitulation of the whole match."

Fischer's state of mind was no less disturbed, although his demons were inside his head rather than in the Kremlin. According to his friend Frank Brady, "He must have experienced an overwhelmingly phobic dread, almost a stark terror . . . In that he confronted and conquered this existential uncertainty, Fischer emerges as his own hero, true to himself and his destiny." In the claustrophobic loneliness of the little back room, Fischer had Spassky where he wanted him, but he had also cornered himself. On the day when he was due to play, Fischer drove to the airport, having booked himself on a flight home. Pursued there by his delegation, he then switched the flight to Greenland. More Americans arrived to reason with him. Suddenly he decided to play after all.

Just after play began in the third game, the tension erupted into a full-scale row between the players. Fischer started manically looking for cameras, flicking switches, and shouting. Told politely to be quiet, he yelled at Schmid to shut up, whereupon Spassky threatened to leave. Schmid had to break the rules, stopping Spassky's clock while he calmed both men and coaxed them back into their seats. It crossed Spassky's mind that he could just walk out and forfeit the game. That would have turned the tables on Fischer and left him "in a terrible psychological position," he said twenty-five years later. In that case, he was sure, he would have won the match. However, this was mere *esprit d'escalier.* Both men cooled down, the game resumed, and on the eleventh move it burst into life with an aggressive flank attack by Fischer's knight. The move had been played before, but Fischer was gambling that Spassky would not know what to do. Krogius later revealed that although the Russians had prepared a plan, even after thirty minutes' thought Spassky could not recall the analysis. Gradually Fischer built up an advantage on both sides of the board, yet the position was still unclear when Spassky blundered just before the time control. When play resumed next day, Spassky needed only to see that Fischer had sealed the winning move. He resigned after five minutes' thought, before Fischer had even arrived. Spassky insisted that future games be played in the auditorium. But it was too late. The spell of invincibility was broken. After the match he admitted that "I idealized Fischer as a person and tried to meet him halfway. My idealism was smashed in the third game and Fischer began to get on my nerves." He had not only been outplayed, he had been outwitted—and he knew it.

The knowledge that he had let Fischer draw blood for the first time rankled and demoralized the champion, whose Olympian calm had suddenly deserted him. Those who watched breathlessly as the moves of the third game were relayed live to a television studio in London—an unprecedented response to an unprecedented demand—were aware of something more, however. Just as Zeus weighs Achilles against Hector, so the scales now tipped against Spassky. Struggle as he might, from the third game onwards, nothing went right for him. As for Fischer, his boasts of supremacy could be dismissed as vainglory no more; he now had proof.

It was vital for Spassky to strike back immediately. Counting the default, the score was still in his favor. Only by winning a convincing victory could he restore the natural order of things. Only by beating the usurper at his own game could the champion staunch the loss of self-confidence that was oozing from his damaged ego. By luck the opportunity presented itself in the very next game, the fourth, which took place in front of the audience again, although without cameras. Playing Black, Spassky essayed the Sicilian Defense, inviting Fischer to follow his usual plan of attack. The American decided to run the gauntlet. On the thirteenth move, Spassky ambushed him with a new move, gambiting a pawn to seize the initiative. Fischer rashly accepted the sacrifice. The play followed the Russian analysis, which should have given Black good winning chances, although Fischer played rapidly and confidently. On move twenty-one Spassky sank into thought for forty-five minutes. When he finally moved, it was to diverge from the agreed continuation. He thought he had found a stronger move, and at the back of his mind was the paranoid Soviet fear that his secret analysis might have leaked. Whilst Spassky preserved a strong attack, Fischer defended tenaciously. "I was presented with an opportunity to win," recalled Spassky. "But here I cracked." The game fizzled out into a draw.

According to Krogius, Geller turned on Spassky afterwards, reproaching him for his "inexcusable" lapse of memory in the third game as well as for his deliberate decision in the fourth, which "signified a mistrust of us, of our entire preparation." It was true: Spassky did not trust Geller, or Krogius for that matter—both men whose loyalty was to the party, not to him. Spassky could trust nobody in his team, not even his tennis partner, Ivo Nei. This gregarious man felt lonelier than he had ever done. He missed his family, for he knew how much was at stake for them too. The Sports Committee had refused to let him bring his wife, Larisa, and he now renewed his request for her to be allowed to join him.

Although Fischer always played for a win, especially with White, this time he was well satisfied with the draw. He had fallen into a trap prepared by the combined might of the Soviet school of chess—and survived! True, he would have to find a new way to counter the Sicilian Defense, but he had a trick up his sleeve that would obviate the need to do so. When the fifth game began, Spassky was still ahead. By the time it ended, his early triumph seemed a distant memory. Fischer tried a line of the Nimzo-Indian

Defense that he had never played before. Spassky played uncertainly: "I stopped working too early." Fischer fixed his opponent's weak pawns, blockaded his bishops, and prepared for a long siege. However, Spassky saved him the trouble: on move twenty-seven he played one of the worst mistakes of his career and was promptly vanquished. The crowd chanted: "Bobby! Bobby!" Despite the fact that Fischer had meanwhile told his long-suffering bag carrier Cramer to issue a new list of fourteen demands, most of them embarrassingly petty (more pocket money and magazines, a better car, etc.), he no longer looked like the spoiled brat from Brooklyn, but a champion in waiting. By now, the magnitude of the reversal of fortunes was dawning on the world. *Time* and *Newsweek* fell over themselves to praise Fischer, whose "crushing and triumphal win in the fifth game possibly signifies that Spassky's sentence has already been signed." These exultant reports, relayed back to Moscow, provoked not only alarm and despondency, but indignation. Sports Minister Pavlov summoned the Soviet chess elite, including three former world champions, to his office to brief him. While the experts all had views about where Spassky had gone wrong, nobody could say why.

Worse was to come for the Soviet side. The sixth game was the first in which Fischer showed his true strength—the awe-inspiring form that had broken the spirit of Taimanov, Larsen, and Petrosian. It was a sensation from the very first move. The commentators on television were astonished when Fischer broke the habit of a lifetime and switched to a Queen's Gambit. Spassky, who had dismissed Krogius's contingency plan for such a surprise with the words "Fischer will never play that," must have cursed his own complacency. After missing the right continuation on move twenty, Spassky failed to grasp a chance to fight back two moves later. The Russian's forces were outmaneuvered, step by step, until the American was ready for his final assault. Then, with a precisely calculated sacrifice, Fischer broke through. With his position in ruins, and checkmate only a matter of time, Spassky resigned. Pandemonium broke loose. The Soviet delegation—now joined by the vice-chairman of the Sports Committee Viktor Ivonin, a more senior apparatchik—watched aghast as the champion showed his magnanimity by joining in the applause for his opponent.

With this victory, Fischer moved into the lead—and never relinquished it. For Kasparov, this game demonstrates that, although there was only a six-year age gap between them, Fischer and Spassky "were already in different chess eras." "The older generation, who were defeated by the American, were not accustomed to such uncompromising play!" After this second successive defeat, Spassky was under pressure from his team and from Moscow to take a time-out, as was permitted under the rules. Spassky, intuiting that the Americans had been waiting for this, as a first sign that he was cracking under pressure, just as Fischer's previous victims had done, refused to take a break. "He wanted revenge," said Krogius. For the seventh game, Spassky turned up late, to pay Fischer back for his own persistent tardiness. Even so, the opening did not go well for him; Fischer repelled his attack and won several pawns. Spassky's position was objectively lost. However, the champion launched a raid against the Black king and forced Fischer to be content with a draw: "For the first time I displayed my fighting spirit," Spassky concluded.

It was a false dawn. The eighth game was no masterpiece, like the sixth, but again Spassky was already all at sea in the opening, wasting more than an hour. After drifting into a bad position, he gave up the exchange (rook for bishop). This was not a blunder, as some assumed, but a standard tactic to generate counterplay. However, almost immediately Spassky committed a genuine oversight, allowing Fischer to swap queens and regain a pawn, leaving an easily won endgame. This demoralizing loss, leaving the score 5–3, forced Spassky to take time off, officially to recover from a cold. Fischer was confident that he had Spassky on the run and told friends the match would be over in a fortnight. He was content to concede a dull draw in the ninth game. A pattern was developing: Fischer was drawing with Black and winning with White. Spassky knew he had to stop the rot before it was too late. His desperation, and Fischer's determination, brought the match to its climax over the following weeks.

The tenth game was one of the finest ever played in this or any other world championship match. Fischer, playing White, reverted to the oldest and most celebrated of all openings: the Ruy Lopez, also known as the "Spanish Torture." Its name derives from a sixteenth-century priest at the court of King Philip II, who was Machiavellian enough to advise his contemporaries to position the board so that the light was in their opponent's eyes. Spassky knew that he was taking a risk by permitting an opening of which Fischer was the supreme living exponent, but he felt sure of his preparations and was spoiling for a fight. Spassky offered a promising gambit; having accepted the pawn, Fischer then retaliated with a sudden and unexpected counterattack, using the notorious "Spanish" bishop. "The subsequent events of this game were etched for a long time in the memories of many generations of players," commented Kasparov, whose analysis shows, however, that Spassky might still have drawn the game with computerlike accuracy. With an elegant combination, Fischer simplified into an advantageous endgame, which he won in fifty-five moves. Although Spassky had played his best chess of the match so far, Fischer had risen to the occasion and played superlatively.

The match score was now 6.5–3.5 to Fischer, who was halfway towards his goal of 12.5 points. As Kasparov notes, if it had been the best of twelve games, like the shorter candidates' match against Petrosian, Fischer would have won by now. Apart from his default, Fischer had not lost since the first game and he had also leveled his lifetime score against Spassky, but in a twenty-four-game match this could still be turned around.

The next game, the eleventh, demonstrated that the match was far from over. Like Hector, who ran three times round Troy pursued by Achilles, Spassky had been on the run from Fischer for weeks. Like Hector, Spassky now summoned up his courage and resolved to make his last stand. Fischer showed his sense of invulnerability in this game by repeating an earlier opening variation for the first time in the match, thereby inviting his opponent to spring a trap. This high-risk strategy was compounded by the choice of opening: the notorious "Poisoned Pawn" variation of the Sicilian Najdorf. This exotic name disguises a deceptively simple idea: a bold sortie by the Black queen, aimed at grabbing a pawn deep inside the White camp and hanging on for dear life until, if all goes well, an endgame is reached in which the extra pawn will be decisive. The pawn is "poisoned" because unless Black is careful, the queen may not get out alive. Now, Fischer was the world's greatest authority on this variation—the chess equivalent of a daring commando raid behind enemy lines—and he loved its complexity. Moreover, he was inclined to be dogmatic about its soundness; it was an article of faith for him that any initiative that White might obtain while Black wasted time extricating his queen was outweighed by the pawn plus. The Russians, of course, knew this and saw it as a weakness, just as Fischer's hardheaded insistence on his market value was often caricatured in Soviet propaganda as typical of the extortionate greed of capitalism.

The first thirteen moves of the eleventh game followed familiar paths. Then Spassky uncorked what some watching grandmasters saw as the most remarkable move of the whole match. It was a move so counterintuitive as to be virtually unforeseeable. The White knight retreated to its original square! It was a kind of aggressive retreat—a case of *reculer pour mieux sauter*. Fischer and just about everybody else assumed that this novelty was the product of midnight oil by the Soviet team, but Spassky has always averred that he came up with the idea alone at the board. Whatever its genesis, the knight maneuver had the desired effect: Fischer became suspicious, lost the thread, and made a couple of inaccurate moves. In such a sharp opening, such vacillations are fatal. This time Spassky did not miss a trick. His pieces swarmed around the Black queen, as onlookers whispered. After only twenty-four moves, she was surrounded. The excitement boiled over and the arbiter, Lothar Schmid, had to demand silence. Nobody could remember anything like this happening to Fischer. He could have resigned then and there, but he was so shocked that he carried on by inertia until move thirty-one. Spassky, irritated at this breach of etiquette, had by then left the stage to pace the corridors. Before he could return, Fischer had resigned and fled. The crowd had waited a long time for this, and they cheered "Boris" until he begged them to stop. Afterwards, he celebrated with typical understatement: "The rest of the match will be more interesting for me." His reward was the news that Larisa, his wife, was flying out to join him. The eleventh game was not the greatest victory in the quarter-century that had elapsed since Boris began supporting his family as a boy, but it was perhaps the sweetest. He would never forget it.

Fischer, meanwhile, having just suffered the bitterest humiliation of his life, was beset by dark thoughts akin to those of Achilles who, having cornered Hector, hurled his spear—and missed. "So, godlike Achilles," Hector taunts him, "Zeus gave you the wrong date for my death after all! You thought you knew everything." The scale of the defeat had sown the seeds of doubt. Could it be that his title, the sole purpose for which he had been put on earth, was yet again to elude him? This was Fischer's worst moment—worse even than after his default, which, after all, had been his own choice. There was nothing voluntary about the rout of the eleventh game. For the first time, he really needed his second, Lombardy, whose calm counsel steadied him. The twelfth game broke the long run of Fischer's victories with the White pieces, but he was not seriously trying to win—a draw was enough to stem the tide.

They had reached the halfway point of the twenty-four-game series with the score still 7–5 in Fischer's favor. However, the concentration required for world championship chess—an art form in which composition and performance occur simultaneously—is so great that a sudden collapse can occur suddenly. That was just what had befallen Petrosian after losing the sixth game in Buenos Aires. Psychologically, what mattered to Fischer was to exorcise the specter of his lost queen. And that could only be done by beating Spassky with the Black pieces. If he failed, there was no knowing what this obsessive perfectionist, for whom nothing else existed, might do. Koestler wrote that Fischer, asked what chess really meant to him, replied: "Everything."

As for Spassky, after the match he recalled that, beginning with this thirteenth game, "I felt that Fischer was like a large fish in my hands. But a fish is slippery and hard to hold onto, and at certain moments I let him slip. And then again the psychological torment would begin. Everything had to be begun again from the start."

Thus both men knew that the thirteenth game was Spassky's last real chance to turn the match around and both put everything into it. For this reason alone, it deserves the accolades that have been heaped on it. Kasparov does not exaggerate when he describes the latter stages of this marathon as "the most colorful and gripping in the history of chess." Bronstein said of this game: "Like a mysterious sphinx, it still teases my imagination."

Once again, Fischer had a surprise on the first move: he played Alekhine's Defense, a staple of the "Hypermodern" school in the 1920s, but a rarity at this level. The idea was to use a lone Black knight to entice the White pawns forward, in order to undermine the rickety structure by long-range bombardment. As the game unfolded, however, it became clear that Fischer's strategy was succeeding. Having encouraged Spassky to start "flying solo," without the aid of prepared analysis, much earlier than usual, Fischer won a pawn, after which he built a formidable barricade. Not for nothing was the American a disciple of Steinitz, the Victorian apostle of defense, as Smyslov observed. As White threw not only his cavalry but the foot soldiers in front of his king into the battle, the Black bishops began to menace his position. Then Fischer faltered, leaving Spassky with a chance to launch a blitzkrieg that might have thrown the game into chaos. Perhaps lacking a sense of danger, the Russian missed it and the window of opportunity closed. Fischer now forced an exchange of the queens, leading to an endgame with only two rooks and a bishop apiece, in which the win for Black should now have been a matter of technique. Yet Spassky fought for dear life, conjuring up an attack out of nothing, even as

Black's pawns raced toward promotion. By the time the game was adjourned for the night, the position was no longer clearly lost for Spassky. Today, adjournments are obsolete because of computers, but in 1972 computer chess was still in its infancy. While the players and their seconds analyzed for much of the night, they could only scratch the surface of this inexhaustible endgame.

When they resumed next day, the struggle intensified still further. Exploiting the presence of bishops of opposite colors to conduct a brave rearguard action, Spassky obliged Fischer to sacrifice his bishop. In return, however, Fischer obtained an army of pawns. Although both players had foreseen thus far in their overnight analysis, now the battle moved into unknown territory. Spassky, too, had a dangerous passed pawn ready to queen. Fischer found the only reply—but what a reply! He stalemated his own rook in order to block the White pawn and bishop. Then the five advancing Black pawns fought it out against the White rook. Fischer's king marched down the board to lead his pawns home, but Spassky's monarch defended magnificently. With one final flourish, Fischer sacrificed one of his pawns to lure the rook away and enable his king to penetrate into the heart of the White camp. This was high-risk stuff—Black could even lose—but Fischer had always known when to raise the stakes. "Bobby poured more into that endgame than he ever did in his life," wrote Lombardy. Fischer said afterward: "I also sensed that Spassky underestimated the danger of his position, when five of my pawns were fighting against the rook." Both players were exhausted by the strain of finding the right path in this labyrinth.

On the sixty-ninth move, after more than eight hours' play, Spassky finally erred: he moved the right piece, his rook, but gave the wrong check. After Fischer's reply, it gradually dawned on everyone that the Myrmidons could no longer be resisted. As Spassky realized his mistake, his face told its own tragic story—one that Fischer could read like a book. Time seemed to stand still as the two antagonists contemplated one another. Although the drama had still to be played out to the bitter end—there were eight more games left—this was the moment of truth. Spassky, like Hector, grasped that the gods had abandoned him. Fischer, as pitiless as Achilles, had murder in his heart and victory in his grasp. In Spassky's submission to his fate and Fischer's fierce, exultant triumph, the Cold War's denouement was already foreshadowed.

By this time, a month into the match, it was not only the political background or even the "human interest" that was exciting a global audience. Millions had got hooked on the chess. For countless youths playing over the moves thousands of miles from Reykjavik, most of whom knew little about the Cold War background to the match, this climactic thirteenth game was a miraculous revelation of the infinite potential of the intellect. Here was something that transcended the mundane, including its co-creators. Chess like this seemed to possess a divine spark, evoking an ecstatic gratitude for the blessed fact of its existence. This was what Spinoza must have meant by the intellectual love of God. The enthusiasm, however, was not restricted to callow adolescents; indeed, it was contagious and ubiquitous. In many London pubs, it was reported to the *New Statesman*'s correspondent Heinrich Fraenkel, the chessboard had temporarily replaced the dartboard as the main focus of attention. In eighteen out of twenty-one bars in Manhattan, according to Edmonds and Eidinow, the TV was tuned, not to the New York Mets baseball game, but to Channel 13's show, broadcasting Fischer–Spassky live from Reykjavik. This show gained the largest ratings ever recorded for public television. By popular demand, reports of the Democratic Presidential Convention were postponed in favor of the chess. In the Eastern bloc such a phenomenon was commonplace, but nothing quite like this has ever happened in the West, before or since.

Both players were now exhausted. Spassky, who was granted a couple of days' respite on health grounds, seemed almost spent. This was the point at which all Fischer's previous opponents had collapsed. Over the next fortnight, however, Spassky showed that he was a true champion. He summoned up hidden reserves of strength and fought like a wounded lion. He was also motivated by anxiety about the fate that would befall him if he were not seen to have exerted himself. He was able to stop Fischer from winning again—much to the American's disgust—but he was unable to win himself. "[Spassky] played very well in the second half," Fischer said afterwards. "For about six or seven games in a row I was under pressure in every game, it was terrible." In the fourteenth game Spassky won a pawn and had a very promising endgame, but towards the time control he let his advantage slip. It was much the same in the fifteenth game. In Korchnoi's words, although Spassky played "confidently and strongly," again Fischer escaped with a draw. The sixteenth game, like the tenth, was a Ruy Lopez. This time Fischer played his trademark Exchange Variation, which he had often used to grind out a win in the endgame. However, Spassky equalized and even counterattacked so that it was Fischer who had to work hard for a draw.

At this point the real battle again shifted away from the board. It was plain to all that only a miracle could stop Fischer now. Being good communists, the Soviet team did not believe in miracles; they believed in conspiracies instead. The fear of what might await them back in Moscow fueled the atmosphere of paranoia that had pervaded the Spassky camp ever since Baturinsky had warned back in October 1971 that "there has been some conjecture about the influence on these results of nonchess factors (hypnosis, telepathy, tampering with food, listening in on domestic analysis, etc.)."

The team had been forced to sign a contract not to disclose official secrets. The presence of the American military base at Keflavik worried Botvinnik (an engineer by training and a Stalinist by inclination) so much that he warned the authorities not to agree to a match in Iceland. According to Krogius, between eighty and a hundred kilos of fan mail was received by the Spassky camp during the match, some of it written in the Russian equivalent of green ink. One crackpot from Holland wrote to "Super-arbiter of the World Championship Chest" [sic] Lothar Schmid, wanting to know whether Fischer's chair, specially shipped at exorbitant cost, had been inspected for bugs that might be transmitting instructions from a computer. If it sounded like science fiction, that was because it *was* science fiction; the writer had got the idea from a film. In 1972, of course, Fischer was incomparably better at chess than any computer. Perhaps the depiction of the intelligent computer HAL in *2001: A Space Odyssey* persuaded the Russians that there was something in it. The Dutchman told Schmid: "I sent a letter to Mr. Yefim Geller in his function as assistant of Spasski [sic] and hope that my idea is pure nonsense. But i felt me [sic] forced to write this letter."

The amazing thing is that Geller did take such accusations seriously, partly due to Soviet hysteria about CIA dirty tricks. The Russian defector Gennady Sosonko recalled that Geller believed every Soviet propaganda story about "the Colorado beetle scattered by the Americans on fields of collective farms, and intrigues by imperialists of every color, demanding high vigilance and a stern rebuff. He guarded the interests of the empire, of which he was simultaneously the servant and the pride." Geller was convinced that American spies were going through notes in his suitcase. He attributed to the Americans vast resources that existed only in his fantasy: "They had a technical team. What did they need that for? They had a psychological team, a security service, an information service."

Larisa Spassky, too, believed that her husband's energy was being drained by mysterious forces, perhaps psychotropic drugs. He had lost weight and he was unnaturally drowsy, she claimed, until the couple moved out of the Hotel Saga to the Soviet embassy and thence to a country house. He felt better after he could enjoy her home cooking and freshly squeezed orange juice—as one might expect. At the time Spassky himself was reluctant to believe that his losses might be due to "nonchess factors," such as radiation. But in 2003 he said: "I now think that such radiation could have been employed."

Back in Moscow, the Sports Committee wanted to know why Spassky was losing, and sent its own experts to investigate the possibility of hypnosis or telepathy. According to Krogius, two

Soviet psychiatrists, Vartanian and Zharikov, "happened to be visiting Reykjavik." Although they were widely assumed to be KGB agents, declassified documents reveal that, as Plisetsky and Voronkov put it, "they were specially sent when the situation in the match became altogether ominous." Their conclusion was startling: "Fischer is a strong personality of psychopathic mentality, and his behavior affects Spassky." However, they added, "hypnosis and telepathy should be ruled out." It seems that the outburst of hysteria in the Spassky camp originated, not in Moscow, but in the febrile imagination of Spassky's second, Yefim Geller.

On August 22, after the sixteenth game, Geller issued a long, rambling statement that must rank among the most bizarre records of Cold War paranoia. After a litany of complaints about Fischer's behavior, he came to the point:

> We have received letters saying that some electronic devices and chemical substance which can be in the playing hall are being used to influence Mr. B. Spassky. The letters mention, in particular, Mr. R. Fischer's chair and the influence of special lighting over the stage installed on the demand of the U.S. side. All this may seem fantastic, but objective factors in this connection make us think of such seemingly fantastic suppositions.

These "objective factors" included Fischer's protests against the TV cameras ("he is anxious to get rid of the constant objective control"), the supposed presence of "the Americans" in the hall "even at night," and the insistence on Fischer's having a special chair. Geller concluded by demanding that "the playing hall and the things in it should be examined with the assistance of competent experts."

According to Cramer, when Fischer read this letter he "split his sides laughing." Whilst the Icelandic authorities were not amused, nevertheless they brought in an electronics engineer and a chemist to investigate. X-rays of the chair revealed an unidentified object, which an American IBM engineer, Don Schultz, thought just might have been a listening device. His theory was that a rogue KGB agent had planted it in a botched attempt to incriminate the Americans. However, the mysterious object failed to show up in a second examination. Inside the lamp, they found two flies. Harold Schonberg of the *New York Times* called for a postmortem on the insects: "Did they die naturally? Or was the cause of their death an American death ray? Or perhaps they passed away after licking the poisoned pawn in the Sicilian Defense?" The possibility that the CIA really was involved can be ruled out. Although a dossier published in 2007 about the agency's campaigns from 1950 to 1970 showed that it did use dirty tricks, the world chess championship simply was not a high enough priority. The whole affair of the dead flies served only to make the Soviets in general, and Geller in particular, look ridiculous. Yet was this cock-up part of a much larger conspiracy? Not a real CIA conspiracy, but a KGB one designed to look like it?

After the poisoning in London in 2006 of Alexander Litvinenko, we are less inclined to make light of such plots, and certainly we do not trust the assurance of Colonel Baturinsky that fear of the KGB in Reykjavik was mere "spy mania." What, though, was really going on in Reykjavik? The stories about the chair and the lighting, including the letters from the Dutch crackpot, were almost certainly all part of a KGB disinformation campaign. It is now clear that the KGB took an intensive interest in the match, that an unknown number of their operatives were present throughout, and that there were numerous meetings at the highest level between the Sports Committee and KGB deputy chairman Viktor Chebrikov, who would succeed Yuri Andropov as chief when the latter became party leader a decade later. Another senior KGB officer, Major-General Valentin Nikashin, was assigned to the case. Edmonds and Eidinow speculate that he was behind not only the dispatch of the two psychiatrists and the hysteria about "nonchess factors," but also the rumors that began to circulate during the match that Spassky was about to defect. It is hard to see how these rumors, which were fueled by the tedium felt by numerous journalists cooped up on a remote island, could have served the KGB's purposes, but Nikashin wanted an informant whom Spassky trusted as a friend to go to Reykjavik to keep an eye on him. Pavlov disagreed, fearing that Spassky would realize he was being spied on.

Toward the end of the match, Spassky bought a Volvo—a great luxury for a Russian—and arranged to have it shipped back to Leningrad. Even such a trivial detail was reported all the way up to Yakovlev, the propaganda chief, because it implied that Spassky would not defect. In 2001, the memoirs of KGB colonel Georgy Sannikov appeared on the Internet, claiming (among other things) that Spassky's villa was bugged by the CIA and that the Americans, "knowing the tastes of the bachelor Fischer, hired an expensive prostitute" and kept this "attractive, shapely blonde" at the Keflavik base "in order in case of necessity to take her to Fischer. It did not prove necessary." Such uncorroborated stories have little credibility.

We may never know precisely what the spies were up to in Reykjavik, but we know enough to say that the KGB's influence on the outcome of the match was negligible. Like so many of the secret operations that consumed the scarce resources of the Soviet bloc throughout the Cold War, the KGB failed to save Spassky's crown.

Overshadowed by events offstage, the last few games were little more than the twitches of a dying hero. In the nineteenth game, with the score at 10.5–7.5, Spassky offered most of his pieces in a desperate attempt to lure Fischer's king into the open. However, the American neatly returned the sacrificed material and the game fizzled out. As August turned to September, the long run of eight draws finally ended when Spassky overreached himself in the twenty-first game. Although he might still have saved the complex endgame, after eight weeks his heart was no longer in it. The game was adjourned overnight, but Spassky's analysis convinced him to give up the struggle. He phoned Schmid to resign the game and the match. "There's a new champion," Spassky told a photographer, who promptly rang Fischer with the news. "Are you sure it's official?" he replied suspiciously.

It could not be said that Fischer was magnanimous in victory. To the mortal injury that he had inflicted on the prestige of Soviet chess, he added the insult of dragging the corpse behind his chariot. "The Russians are wiped out," he told the BBC. "They probably now feel sorry they ever started playing chess. They had it all for the last twenty years. They talked of their military might and their intellectual might. Now the intellectual thing . . . It's given me great pleasure . . . as a free person . . . to have smashed this thing." At the closing ceremony, Fischer ostentatiously ignored the proceedings. When Spassky joined him, they discussed a rematch in Las Vegas, outside the normal FIDE championship cycle. Such talk alarmed listening Russians. The game that had for so long been a showcase for Soviet culture was spinning out of control.

Chess had indeed become an embarrassment for the Kremlin. Its prominence in the Soviet press had gradually diminished as Spassky's defeat approached. *Izvestia* buried a brief Tass report of Fischer's victory at the bottom of a sports page. Even *Shakhmaty v SSSR*, the leading chess journal, ran only an unsigned piece about the match, which managed not to mention the result until the last of nineteen paragraphs. Fischer told his fellow New Yorkers: "I did not think that there would come a day when chess would become headline news in our country [America] and produce only a small comment in *Pravda*. And that is undoubtedly my fault: it all depends on who wins!" Fortunately for the Soviet media, at the Munich Olympics a Russian runner beat the Americans in the 100-meter sprint, shortly before Soviet-backed Palestinian terrorists took the Israeli team hostage and murdered eleven of them. The KGB suppressed a demonstration by Russian Jews and dissidents, including Sakharov and Sharansky. Meanwhile, they were busy closing down the Soviet Union's most important samizdat publication, *The Chronicle of Current Events*. The period of détente also witnessed the most severe crackdown on dissidents since Stalin. While it lasted, the match in Reykjavik had been a breath of fresh air in the suffocating atmosphere of Brezhnev's state.

For the losers, there was a price to pay. Even before the match ended, one of Spassky's seconds, the Estonian Ivo Nei, had already been sent home in disgrace. He had been secretly recruited by Fischer's lawyer, Marshall, to write a book about the match jointly with the American grandmaster, Robert Byrne. Tipped off by the KGB, Geller and Krogius interrogated Nei, with Spassky present. There was a row and Nei was ordered home, to be banned from foreign travel for two years. Baturinsky was not the only official to accuse Nei of spying, but nothing could be proved.

Back in Moscow, Spassky had to face a postmortem at the Sports Committee. Those present were united in condemning Spassky and his team, particularly for making concessions to Fischer. One member of the committee, Rodionov, summed up the meeting: "Spassky forgot that he is a sportsman—but in a red T-shirt! As a result of Spassky's unsatisfactory performance, the prestige of our state has suffered." Ivonin, who chaired the meeting, shared the blame more widely: "We have been derelict in our duties." Nevertheless, Baturinsky got his revenge for Spassky's refusal to include him in the team. He reported that on a visit to Spassky's dacha during the run-up to the match, he and Ivonin were greeted with the question: "Have you brought any liquor?" Baturinsky went on: "Then he invited us to look at the pictures in a copy of *Playboy* which was on the table." Spassky's punishment was mild: his stipend, which had been raised by 200 rubles, was cut again, and he was banned from foreign tournaments for nine months. He fell into a deep and prolonged depression, which ended only when he divorced and remarried for a third time. Even his share of the Reykjavik purse ($93,750) did not comfort him much: deserted by friends, he quickly frittered away what was by Soviet standards a large fortune. If Spassky had indeed thrown the match, as Botvinnik told everyone, it was soon apparent that he did not know what to do with his winnings. By winning the very next Soviet championship ahead of Karpov and Korchnoi, however, he reminded the

authorities that they still needed his talents. Spassky could not recover from his defeat, but he managed to rebuild his life. To stop
him defecting, he was allowed to live in France while remaining a
Soviet citizen.

Soviet chess was never quite the same again. Many agreed with
Fischer's critique: "They have killed chess with their boring methods of play, with their boring matches in their boring country."
Reykjavik did produce a new crop of young players, notably Garry
Kasparov, but they were enthused by Fischer's example rather than
by the bureaucratic shake-up that followed the defeat. The young
man who recaptured the title and emerged as the new Soviet stan-
dard-bearer in the Cold War was much more boring (in Fischer's
sense) than Spassky: Anatoly Karpov. The 1970s was a period of
harsh repression from which even chess was not immune. Baturinsky recalled that in 1974, during the Karpov–Korchnoi match to
decide who would challenge Fischer, he received an unexpected
visitor at the Hall of Columns in Moscow where the event was
taking place. It was the Interior Minister, Nikolai Shchelokov, who
asked him: "How come you yielded the crown to an American? If I
had my way, everyone who was in Reykjavik with Spassky would
have been arrested."

What of Fischer? New York welcomed its hero, who responded
by scotching "a rumor that undoubtedly originated in Moscow: it's
not true that Henry Kissinger phoned me and suggested moves in
my games!" Perhaps prompted by Kissinger, President Nixon was
said to have invited "the absolute champion of the most difficult
game in the world" to a reception at the White House. Nobody re-
fuses an invitation from the most powerful man in the world—
except Bobby Fischer. "I declined, because I found out that they
wouldn't pay me anything for this visit. Besides, it would have
been a serious distraction." (Thirty years later, Fischer denied this
story.)

A distraction from what, though? Not chess. The new world
champion promised to play far more often than his predecessors,
but he actually played less than any of them. The brittle perfection

of his achievement inhibited risk. He was richer than ever before, but without the spur provided by the political imperative of defeating the Soviets at their favorite game, Fischer lost his motivation. Instead of becoming a great champion, even a hero of the West, he lapsed into apathy and seclusion. Las Vegas offered $1 million for a rematch; in 1975 Manila offered $5 million to stage the world championship match with Karpov. Fischer could have earned a further $5 million more from sponsorship deals. Instead, he did none of this. He demanded new rules for world title matches, similar to those invented by the first official champion, Wilhelm Steinitz. When FIDE agreed to all but two of his conditions, Fischer told them they had decided to exclude him: "I therefore resign my FIDE world championship title." Kasparov thinks Fischer was trying to revert to the prewar period, when the title belonged to the champion rather than the world federation. When, under huge Soviet pressure, FIDE refused to budge, he declared: "I will punish the chess world. It will not see any more of my games. I will not play anymore!" Fischer meant what he said. He disappeared from view to join the ranks of J. D. Salinger, Howard Hughes, Greta Garbo, and other great recluses. There were sightings in various countries, a brief incarceration in a Pasadena jailhouse, a self-justifying pamphlet that suggested serious mental disturbance. Then—silence.

When, Rip van Winkle–like, Fischer emerged in 1992 to play a rematch at the Adriatic resort of Sveti Stefan with a much diminished Spassky under the auspices of the Serbian president Slobodan Milosević, he was still claiming to be world champion. Fischer won 10–5, with fifteen draws, but the match was even more of a Pyrrhic victory for Fischer than Reykjavik. By breaking sanctions against the Milosević regime, he incurred the lasting enmity of the U.S. government, which issued a warrant for his arrest. His public appearances destroyed the legend of Bobby Fischer. His play was a shadow of its former brilliance, as he perhaps realized; there were to be no more comebacks. And his comments showed that anti-Semitism had now taken over his mind. Zionism and communism had merged with anti-Americanism to become a persecution complex. Obliged to lead a nomadic existence to escape the law, he resurfaced after 9/11 to exult in the downfall of America and the Jews—especially, it seemed, American Jews like himself. Finally, in 2005, he was arrested in Japan on charges including tax evasion and sanction-breaking. Facing extradition to the United States, where he could expect a life sentence, Fischer was offered asylum by the country he had underestimated—Iceland.

Ultimately Fischer's victory over Spassky was a misfortune, both for him and perhaps also for chess. After the Cold War ended, he gravitated back to the scene of his former triumphs, Yugoslavia, and one of the last Cold War dictators, Milosević—an attraction that proved fatal. And when the West found itself threatened by Islamist terror, Fischer sided with the enemy. Chess had preserved his sanity while he played it. Once he gave up chess, his belligerence on and off the chessboard degenerated into a morbid misanthropy. He did have an Achilles' heel: the Cold War. It dominated the life of Bobby Fischer. While helping to make his name, it also did much to unhinge him. And in its absence, he simply fell apart.

12

THE MACHINE AGE

H UMAN BEINGS HAVE ALWAYS dreamed of creating a being like themselves, only more obedient—from the golems of the Talmud to the robots of Karel Capek's 1920 play *R.U.R.* Artificial intelligence raises profound philosophical questions—questions that became more acute in the era of totalitarian politics. In his eagerness to create a new political and social order, the revolutionary intellectual dispensed with the notion of the human being as unique, of human life as sacred, of humanity as the only creature endowed not only with consciousness but also with conscience. In such a society, where human beings were mere raw material, the concept of artificial intelligence took on a new and sinister significance. Capek's play, which coined the term "robot," imagines a world in which leaders of the radical intelligentsia manufacture a race of synthetic slaves ("Rossum's Universal Robots") to do the work of mankind. By presuming to "end the slavery of work," men usurp the role of God, but in doing so they abase themselves to the level of the robots. Those who warn against the spiritual catastrophe that this leisured utopia will engender are ignored by the utopians—who, however, reap a terrible harvest when the robots rise up in rebellion against their exploiters. A society that tries to transform the old Adam into a "new man" may end by treating humans like robots.

Chess plays a peripheral but important part in the rise of thinking machines. In fact, the symbiosis of chess and the computer is almost as old as the idea of artificial intelligence. Chess has always been the intellectual's recreation of choice and is therefore associated with high intelligence—although by no means identical with it. Hence, there is a natural affinity between the study of simulated intelligent behavior and a game that permits direct comparisons to be drawn between the capabilities of humans and androids. The European public was fascinated by the notion of a chess-playing machine as early as the mid-eighteenth century, and interest shows no sign of abating even today, when there are literally billions of chess-playing computers in existence.

The first and most famous chess automaton was Wolfgang von Kempelen's invention, the Turk; it was unveiled at the court of the Empress Maria Theresa in 1769 and incinerated in Philadelphia in 1854. The early chess automatons had nothing to do with computing, of course. By the ingenious use of mirrors, they merely concealed a man behind an array of cogs and pulleys. Exhibited as Maelzel's Chess Automaton by the inventor of the metronome, the Turk was the subject of a celebrated article by Edgar Allan Poe published in 1834, in which the inventor of the horror story claimed to have used purely deductive logic to work out how the trick was done. He argued rightly that the Turk must be operated by a human, but for the wrong reasons. Among other mistakes, Poe thought that the fact that the automaton did not always win was a giveaway. In fact, of course, a real automaton would be fallible too: to err is not exclusively a human failing. Ironically, although Poe did not fully grasp the mechanical problems that Kempelen had solved with such ingenuity some seventy years previously, he has been generally credited with dispelling the mystery of the Turk ever since. The last of the human chess automatons was Ajeeb, which was operated by the American grandmaster Harry Pillsbury from 1898 to 1904 and lasted until 1926. More sophisticated was Mephisto, which was first shown in London by Charles Gümpel, an Alsatian-born inventor, in 1878. Mephisto, an android resembling the eponymous devil, was not large enough to conceal a man inside. Instead, it was operated from another room by electromechanical means, usually by Grandmaster Isidor Gunoberg.

Although automatons like these played little part in the history of computer chess, the suspicion lingered on that computers could win only with human assistance. That suspicion still played a part in Garry Kasparov's sensational defeat by the IBM computer Deep Blue in 1997, when the then world champion was convinced that the computer had been "helped" by its operators (one of whom was a grandmaster). Today, however, the suspicion has also been reversed, namely that human players use computers secretly to assist them. A suspicion of this kind—although wholly unjustified—lay behind an undignified dispute that nearly aborted the 2006 World Championship match. The Bulgarian Veselin Topalov accused the Russian Vladimir Kramnik of taking frequent breaks to go to the lavatory so that he could consult a computer. Though he could produce no evidence, Topalov's allegation paid off indirectly. In deference to his complaint, the FIDE arbitration committee altered the playing conditions by requiring the players to share a bathroom, provoking a protest from Kramnik at a clear breach of the match contract. Kramnik's protest led to a second dispute, which resulted in his being forfeited a game. This decision, widely condemned in the chess world, in turn enabled Topalov, who had been trailing badly, to tie the match. Nevertheless, Kramnik won the speed-chess tie break and kept his title.

The pioneers of true chess-playing computers were not illusionists, but they did need to be visionaries. Several were also among the fathers of computer science. The great German mathematician and philosopher Gottfried Leibniz had already "solved" the game of solitaire in 1710, using the branch of mathematics known as combinatorics; he also designed an arithmetical calculating machine, the "Leibniz wheel," and conceived the grandiose idea of a universal system of knowledge. His equally brilliant compatriot, Leonhard Euler, first realized the mathematical significance of the ancient problem of the "knight's tour," in which the knight visits every square on the board only once. The man often credited with creating the first computer, Charles Babbage, devoted much thought to adapting his Analytical Machine to play chess, but gave it up as too daunting a computational task—as indeed it was in his pre-electronic or even pre-electrical age. The crucial issues, however, concerned not engineering but mathematics. In 1914 the Spanish inventor Leonardo Torres y Quevedo unveiled his chess automaton, El Ajedrecista ("the Chess Player"), based on his research into analog calculators. This was a genuine automaton, although it could handle only three pieces. Using king and rook against king, it could reliably checkmate a human opponent, moving the pieces by electromagnetism.

The decisive step was taken by the Englishman Alan Turing, who is best remembered today as one of the leading codebreakers of the Second World War: it was he who cracked the German "Enigma" naval cipher machine and served as the head of the celebrated Hut 8 at Bletchley Park. His posthumous cult status rests partly on his suicide in 1954 at the age of forty-one, after being arrested for alleged indecency. The insupportable predicament in which he found himself, as a very private man who dreaded public humiliation as a homosexual, led to the tragic waste of a genius. Turing's scientific stature rests on just three celebrated papers. The first of these papers, written when Turing was in his early twenties and published in 1936, was "On Computable Numbers, with an Application to the *Entscheidungsproblem*." It first described the mathematics of computing machines, by means of a brilliantly original application of the work of the Austrian logician Kurt Gödel. Turing was the first to define "computability" as a specific property of numbers whose decimals could be recorded by a machine. He had already realized that using a formal procedure of computational operations known as an algorithm, such "universal computing machines" were capable of almost infinite development. Even today, learning to program a "Turing machine" remains an essential element in the training of any computer scientist.

As part of the Allied war effort, two electronic calculating machines were built: one in the United States, called Eniac; the other at Bletchley Park, called Colossus. It is a matter for dispute among historians of science whether either of these machines was a computer in the modern sense, because neither could store programs. In Turing's fertile mind, however, the experience that he had gained during the war had shown him how to use the new science of electronic engineering to build his universal machine. He became convinced that a Turing machine could, in principle, simulate anything of which the human brain was capable. This opened up the question of how to construct a computer that could simulate many or even all the functions of the mind.

In 1950 Turing published his second great paper, "Computing Machinery and Intelligence," in the leading philosophical journal *Mind*. Its opening sentence—"I propose to consider the question, 'Can machines think?'"—has become famous. The "Turing Test" arose from a thought experiment, an "imitation game" in which an interrogator would question both a human being and a computer without knowing which was which. Turing's argument was that if the interrogator could not distinguish between the two sets of answers, then the computer would necessarily be, by any reasonable definition, intelligent. This broad definition raised a practical question, however: what kind of operation would enable the scientist to compare human and artificial intelligence? One answer, he decided, was chess.

Although Turing himself was a *patzer* with only a basic grasp of chess, during the war he had worked at Bletchley Park alongside several of the leading chess masters in Britain, including Stuart Milner-Barry, C. H. O'D. (Hugh) Alexander, and Harry Golombek. In conversations with a fellow cryptographer, Jack Good, and a student, Donald Michie, Turing became fascinated by the problem of creating a computer that could play chess, using decision "trees" to find the best move. In early 1946, Turing wrote a report on "The Proposed Electronic Calculator" and, later that year, gave lectures on "The Automatic Computing Engine" at the Ministry of Supply. In these papers, using the concept of "machine intelligence," he discussed chess playing as a paradigm for human thought. Then in 1948 he challenged Michie to see which of them could first devise a chess-playing algorithm. At Edinburgh in the 1960s, Michie, who lived on until 2007, became the first computer scientist in Britain after Turing to develop the field of machine intelligence.

Turing continued to work on chess programs, even though he never tried to use the only computer to which he had access, at the University of Manchester. In 1951 he simulated a chess-playing computer program "by hand," which meant that he had to make thousands of calculations merely in order to "see" two moves deep. It took at least half an hour for Turing to calculate each of the computer's moves. According to his evaluation function, chess positions could be broken down into quantifiable factors: material and mobility; king safety; check and mate threats or pawn advances. His program played a game against Alick Glennie, a friend of Turing's, aged twenty-six, and "a weak player who did not know the system" that he was using. As the historian of computer chess Monty Newborn comments, even on the fourth move of this very first game between a human being and a computer, the distinctive (and seemingly eccentric) style of play shows that "computers have a mind of their own." As early as the sixteenth move, it is apparent that the computer's limited "horizon" leads it to delay the loss of a pawn for as long as possible. By the twenty-ninth move this inability to look more deeply causes the computer to lose its queen and the game.

Turing published the results of this research on chess as a chapter, "Digital Computers Applied to Games," in the volume *Faster than Thought* (edited by B. V. Bowden, London, 1953). This is the third of Turing's important papers, and its perspective extends far beyond chess. The paper is mainly devoted to the question of whether a computer could play "a reasonably good game of chess" and it includes a description of his own efforts to create such an algorithm or program. But he also argues that a chess-playing computer would be able to improve its play, profiting from experience. Turing suggests that "it would be quite possible to program the machine to try out variations in its method of play (e.g., variations in piece value) and adopt the one giving the most satisfactory results. This could certainly be described as 'learning,' though it is not quite representative of learning as we know it. It might also be possible to program the machine to search for new types of combination in chess." What Turing meant was that the computer could learn by trial and error to calculate the value of, say, a bishop under specific circumstances, rather than treating it as always worth the same. Thus the computer could move beyond the level of a beginner and gradually approach—maybe even transcend—that of a grandmaster.

Fundamentally, Turing was interested in what constitutes artificial intelligence and where its limits might lie: "If this product produced results which were quite new, and also interesting to the programmer, who should have the credit?" It is also evident that Turing already intuited that a human player who understood the computer's system would soon learn how to exploit its weaknesses—as indeed happened for the next half a century, until most of those weaknesses had been eliminated. Turing was already looking beyond that initial stage to envisage a computer that could calculate at infinite speed and with unlimited storage capacity; it "would give a result that in a sense could not be improved upon." Such an unbeatable program could in principle be devised quite easily for a simple game such as tic-tac-toe, Turing remarks, and his friend Donald Michie would indeed later create a machine ("Menace") that did precisely that. In chess, Turing admits, the sheer number of possible moves (larger than the number of atoms in the known universe) means that an attempt to calculate exhaustively, even for such an ideal computer, "is of merely academic interest." In the early 1950s, the future number-crunching abilities of computers were only just beginning to be foreseen, but even then Turing had realized that this power opened up the possibility of a machine that could imitate—and ultimately surpass—the processes of thought that enable humans to play chess. By focusing research on this goal, the Holy Grail of artificial intelligence, Turing had laid the foundations for a machine that, at least according to his test, really could think.

In 1945, while Alan Turing was carrying out his largely private research, in the United States the Hungarian-born mathematician John von Neumann had already published a description of an electronic digital computer, using a single storage structure to hold both program and data. Although "Neumann architecture" became the basis of all future computers, the basic concept was derived from the Turing machine. In 1945 he persuaded the Institute of Advanced Study at Princeton to allocate $100,000—a large sum even by American standards—to build a "von Neumann machine." It was appropriately known by its acronym "Maniac" (mathematical analyzer, numeral integrator, and computer). Later funding came from the Pentagon; the U.S. military recognized the strategic value of computer science long before most civilians understood its commercial potential.

Von Neumann's research, like Turing's, was closely connected to military projects, but unlike Turing, who was inclined to pacifism, von Neumann was a staunch anti-communist and an enthusiastic Cold Warrior. Having worked on the Manhattan Project, von Neumann became, with Edward Teller, one of the fathers of the hydrogen bomb. During the early years of the Cold War, Maniac and its descendants enabled the Americans to keep ahead of their Soviet rivals, who included Andrei Sakharov in his predissident days as a nuclear physicist. Until his death in 1957, von Neumann wielded considerable political influence, which he used to encourage the United States to believe that it could ultimately win the Cold War. He maintained that this would not be due to nuclear attack—indeed, he helped to develop the scenario of "mutually assured destruction" (MAD)—but by means of the superior technology made possible by capitalism. From 1946 onwards, scientists at the Rand Corporation, a think tank set up by the U.S. government, worked on many new fields of inquiry, such as systems analysis, to create the war games and "scenarios" that informed political and military decision making throughout the Cold War.

What, however, did all this have to do with chess? Von Neumann was also one of the founders of game theory, together with Oskar Morgenstern. In 1944 he published *Theory of Games and Economic Behavior*, which has created a prodigiously fertile new field of inquiry, extending far beyond economics. Game theory introduced terms such as "zero-sum game" into the language. Von Neumann's analysis focused on "games with perfect information" and chess was the key paradigm (although his own favorite game was *kriegspiel*, a nineteenth-century German version of chess in which neither player can see the other's pieces). Von Neumann's game theory used a formalized mathematical description of games of strategy to elucidate many fields, from the functioning of the market to nuclear war. But he was too busy putting to work the vast range of his scientific interests in order to win the Cold War to pursue the project of computer chess for its own sake.

It was another American scientist who in 1950—even before Alan Turing had published his experimental game—showed how a computer chess program should look. Claude Shannon (1916–2001) was the third pioneer of the generation that created computer science. Like Turing and von Neumann, Shannon was a brilliant mathematician, but unlike them he was also an engineer who wanted to improve the primitive analog computers of his day. As a telephone engineer, he understood how complex electrical switching systems worked. In 1936 he showed how Boolean algebra could be combined with binary arithmetic to improve the relay systems used by telephone companies to connect their customers to one another. What he did not then know was that this procedure could be reversed. What we would now call digital relay systems could help to solve algebraic problems. The telephone network had acquired the characteristics of a computer. Without realizing it, Shannon had hit on the basic principle that underlies the circuitry of all digital computers.

After applying his theory to genetics at MIT, Shannon was employed by the National Defense Research Committee during the Second World War to design fire control systems, which he treated as a special case of the general problem of data processing. He also worked on cryptography, and although he enjoyed less success than Turing at codebreaking, this work aroused his interest in the problem of how to encode information. After the war Shannon was employed by the Bell Telephone Laboratories. It was in the Bell company journal that he first published "A Mathematical Theory of Communication" in 1948—two articles that demonstrated how binary-coded messages could be sent, using more such codes to detect and correct errors in transmission. This paper created the vast field that soon became known as information theory, with countless applications from satellites in space to the manufacture of software. The Internet is only one of many communications systems that would have been inconceivable without Shannon's theory. Later, Shannon transformed two more fields of inquiry—sampling theory and cryptography—while conducting one of the first and most famous experiments on artificial intelligence: he tried to "teach" Theseus, a robot mouse, how to find its way out of a labyrinth.

Not surprisingly, given this unique combination of interests, it was Shannon who published the classic paper that inspired the computer chess revolution. "Programming a Computer for Playing Chess" appeared in the *Philosophical Magazine* in 1950. Shannon's thesis is stated in wholly modern terms: "Modern general purpose computers can be used to play a tolerably good game of chess by the use of a suitable computing routine or 'program.'" Shannon was working along parallel lines to Turing, and he too saw chess as a key test of artificial intelligence. "Chess is generally considered to require 'thinking' for skilful play," he wrote. "A solution of this problem will force us either to admit the possibility of a mechanized thinking or to further restrict our concept of 'thinking.'"

Shannon first analyzed random play, calculating that there was an infinitesimally small probability ($10-75$) that such random play could defeat the then world champion, Botvinnik. Shannon further proposed two methods of searching for the best move, which he called Type A and Type B. This approach proved to be hugely influential and is still the basis of all chess programs—not to mention many others. Type A strategies are "fixed-depth," i.e., the computer has a horizon of a fixed number of moves and explores all the possible lines within that limit, assigning a score to the position at the end of each one. The strength of a Type A strategy depends on the complexity of its evaluative functions. This is roughly the method also attempted at about the same time by Turing. Shannon, however, grasped that such a program could not "learn" or improve its play.

It is notable that Shannon took account of what chess experts themselves had written about their mental processes. The leading American grandmaster, Reuben Fine, for example, had pointed out that the popular idea that grandmasters would routinely foresee positions ten or twenty moves ahead was "pure fantasy," except in the case of "forced" variations, where only one line of play was possible. Shannon therefore proposed a second, Type B strategy. This would be "variable-depth"—searching some lines more deeply than others, eliminating "obviously bad" moves by a process of "forward pruning." In practice, this strategy proved to be difficult to implement, but Shannon rightly grasped that the computer's strength would be its speed and accuracy. "Hence it should make more use of brutal calculation than humans, but with possible variations increasing by a factor of 103 every move, a little selection goes a long way towards improving blind trial and error." Shannon also incorporated a description of the "minimax" algorithm, the mathematical basis of all future chess programs.

Chess masters with mathematical aptitude were recruited in

the early days of computer science, among them the Dutch former world champion, Max Euwe. In 1956 Euwe was recruited by the American firm Remington to work on cybernetic theory in Minneapolis. According to his biographer, Alexander Münninghoff, Euwe became impatient with the primitive approach, then still widespread, that saw computers as mere calculators: "Its inventors ought to dig much more deeply and make a far better analysis of its potential." He later returned to his native Netherlands, where he carried on his research, holding chairs at Rotterdam and Tilburg Economic High Schools, but Euwe never created a chess program of his own.

The first proper chess computer was built in 1958: the IBM 704, which could evaluate two hundred positions a second—then considered an astounding number. By the end of the 1950s, electronic computers in both the United States and the Soviet Union had been programmed to play chess. In both cases, there was military interest in and funding for the research. Interestingly, the Americans—led by Alan Kotok at MIT and John McCarthy at Stanford —concentrated on Shannon's Type B strategy, while the Russians focused on Shannon's Type A approach. The Soviet team was based at the Institute of Theoretical and Experimental Physics (ITEP) in Moscow, led by Vladimir Arlazarov, with George Adelson-Velsky as its most creative thinker and Alexander Bitman as its chess expert. In November 1966 the two teams confronted one another in a friendly match by telegraph. Even with games adjudicated as drawn after forty moves, it took nine months for the match to be completed using the primitive computers of the day. To the surprise and alarm of the Americans, the ITEP program easily won the match with a 3–1 score: two wins and two draws. Even the two drawn games would have been won by the Soviet side if they had been played to completion. Mikhail Botvinnik, who analyzed the games with the eye of a scientist as well as that of a former world champion, declared that the forward pruning system used by the Americans was inadequate and too often rejected good moves as well as bad. This match proved that Shannon's Type A strategy was superior to Type B, and also that the deeper the search, the stronger the program. The Russians were outplaying the Americans because their program could search more deeply.

The next generation of Soviet chess computer was called Kaissa (after Caissa, the goddess of chess). Programmed by Mikhail Donskoy, Kaissa could still evaluate only two hundred positions a second—the same number as the first IBM computer a decade earlier. In 1972, the same year as the Fischer–Spassky match at Reykjavik, Kaissa played a two-game match against the readers of *Komsomolskaya Pravda*, the newspaper of the communist youth wing. The previous year, the same readers had drawn a game with the world champion, Boris Spassky. In the first game, the computer took forty minutes over its second move, examining 540,000 positions before playing a routine line in the Sicilian Defense. Programmers had yet to learn how to install the huge databases of opening and endgame theory that would later make computers such formidable opponents. What is more astonishing, however, is that Kaissa was nevertheless already good enough to draw the game with the *Komsomolskaya* readers. The fact that the Kaissa team had to use a Western computer, made by the British firm ICL, on which to run their program did not bode well for the future of Soviet information technology.

Two years later, in 1974, Kaissa could still outplay the Americans; it won the first world computer chess championship in Stockholm. While all the participants were still mainframe computers, a new American computer developed at Northwestern University, Chess 4.0, took part using software that would become the basis of all future chess programs. The Northwestern team, led by David Slate, discovered a new technique—"iteratively-deepening search"—that enabled their computer to carry out a sequence of progressively deeper searches to find the best move. The format of the 1974 event meant that Kaissa won the championship without playing Chess 4.0, but by the next championship at Toronto in 1977, the application of their new search technique had given the Northwestern team a head start. It became clear that the Americans had far outstripped the Soviets in computer science and technology. Kaissa lost in the first round to the American Duchess and ended up in sixth place, while the much improved Chess 4.6 won the tournament.

This event marked another milestone in the rivalry between game-playing humans and machines, thanks to the presence of Mikhail Botvinnik himself. The turning point came at move thirty-four in the Kaissa–Duchess game, when Kaissa appeared to blunder by giving away a rook. In fact, it had foreseen a queen sacrifice that would lead to a beautiful mate and giving up the rook was not simply the best but the only move to prolong the game. "Even Botvinnik, who was sitting in the audience, was surprised by this move, the first time a world champion missed what was happening in a game played by computers," commented Monty Newborn. It was an unprecedented spectacle: a computer had seen further ahead than—had even out-thought—one of the grandest of all human grandmasters.

What Botvinnik had witnessed was not merely one more piece of evidence that the computer age had arrived, but also the impending defeat of Soviet science and technology. Early in the Cold War, Botvinnik had realized that arsenals of intercontinental ballistic missiles would not be enough to preserve the Soviet system from infiltration by Western ideas. In the 1960s he had written *Computers, Chess, and Long Range Planning,* explaining the victory of the Soviet chess computer over the American one as a manifestation of the superiority of socialist planning, and hence of the Soviet system. He had devoted many of the best years of his life, and most of his retirement, to a large-scale project that—with characteristic fidelity to the vocabulary of his Stalinist youth—he called the Pioneer Project. Botvinnik hoped to create a chess program that would come much closer to reproducing the actual processes of the human brain—including the intuitive "feel" for a position that enables grandmasters to grasp its key strategic features.

According to Anatoly Karpov, in the mid-1960s Botvinnik told the young players in his chess school, which he supervised alongside his scientific work, that "in several years this program would beat not just masters but even grandmasters, and eventually even the world champion wouldn't stand a chance against it . . . We understood one thing: The champion had left the arena, but in his place he was preparing an avenger, a soulless chess murderer to defeat everyone in the name of its creator." Karpov recalls that he and his fellow students were "shocked" by Botvinnik's vision, and far from reassured by his promises. "'Don't worry, kids,' said Botvinnik. 'You'll find work. After all, my machine will need strong chess player-programmers. You will be the first.'"

Yet Pioneer never got off the drawing board. Botvinnik's ideas were too complex and ambitious to be translated into the language of programming. According to his fellow grandmaster, Yuri Averbakh, who was also an engineer, Botvinnik tried to imitate the way that the brain works "but he did not know how our brain works." Averbakh failed to persuade Botvinnik to leave such things to the younger generation, "people who know much more mathematics than Botvinnik and I. But because Botvinnik believed he could do anything, he agreed to do these things." The most powerful figure in the Soviet computer science establishment had failed to create a chess computer that could make so much as a single move. Far from outdoing Kaissa with his visionary project, he had not even come close to matching the existing program. Now he had come to North America for the first time, only to see his hopes dashed by the triumph of American, not Soviet, technology.

There was worse to come for the Soviet old guard. The emergence of the "microchip," or microprocessor, in 1971 had drastically accelerated the evolution of the microcomputer. In 1977, the same year as the defeat of Kaissa, the first commercial chess computers went on sale in the West. They played badly, and average club players could usually best them, but the point was that anyone could buy one. At the "big chess" end of the market, AT&T developed a new computer, Belle, which was already playing at master level by 1980. Three years later the Cray Blitz computer had one chip per square of the board. Once microcomputers began to privatize the hitherto rarefied world of computer chess around 1980, the unequal struggle between American and Soviet researchers using publicly owned mainframe computers soon became completely one-sided. By 1982 there were four hundred times more computers per capita in the United States than in the Soviet Union, a gap that would continue to widen until the collapse of communism. Nor was it possible to conceal this technological disparity with the West from the peoples of the Soviet bloc.

Centrally controlled, publicly funded Soviet science simply could not keep pace with the democratic capitalism of the United States. A society in which the spontaneous order of the market could allocate capital almost instantaneously in response to consumer choices had an advantage even in the hitherto low-tech game of chess. The advent of affordable personal computers in the West rapidly transformed the way that chess was played, by both amateurs and professionals. In what would prove to be the decisive battleground of computer science, the Russians had already lost the Cold War in the 1970s. It was not won at the macroscopic level but at the microscopic one. Ronald Reagan's Star Wars program, which finally convinced the Kremlin that the Cold War could not be won, was made possible by microcomputers. It was not the technologies of mass destruction that proved decisive in the end, but technologies of filigree miniaturization—above all, the microchip and its close relation, the microcomputer. Botvinnik's world of big chess and big computers would be swept away by this microrevolution.

The cyber-gap between East and West was not only about computers—it was also about every kind of information technology. Raymond Keene recalls an incident as late as 1986, when he reported for the *Times* on the Karpov–Kasparov world championship match from Leningrad. In order to send the moves of each game back to London, he and hundreds of other journalists were forced to wait while copies of the score sheets kept by both players were transcribed by a secretary at the Leningrad Chess Club and carbon copies brought back to the press room to be distributed. Fax and photocopier machines were almost unheard of, and the methods by which information was disseminated struck visitors from the West as unbearably slow. Suddenly it dawned on Keene that the Soviet failure to keep up with a new postindustrial capitalism driven by information technology must inevitably prove fatal to the whole communist system. The decline of Soviet domination of world chess was only a symptom of what Friedrich von Hayek called the "fatal conceit" of socialist central planning.

Fischer's triumph was a harbinger of even more momentous things to come. Although chess computers were originally developed in part to assist the military to plan battle scenarios during the Cold War, what had always baffled the boffins—and not only them—was the question of *how* a computer could defeat a human being. Even in 1964, the philosopher Herbert Dreyfus, a leading critic of artificial intelligence, claimed that no computer would ever beat even a ten-year-old boy who was competent at chess. Some twenty-five years after the Soviet chess machine was defeated by a solitary Western genius, a Western chess machine defeated a solitary ex-Soviet genius. Garry Kasparov's chess record outshines all others, but if he is remembered for one event it will be his defeat by the IBM computer Deep Blue in 1997.

Many assumed that chess as a game was now "solved," even though grandmasters continued to defeat even the best computers. While the symbolism of the man versus machine confrontation had a unique resonance, which generated a wave of chess fever on the Internet, the chess played by computers alone somehow lacks the aesthetic attraction of the human game. The drama comes from the contest between flesh and blood, with its inevitable lapses in concentration, and silicon—a contest that is inherently unequal. It is hard to imagine a game between two machines, however highly rated, living on in the folk memory of the chess world, as have Adolf Anderssen's "Immortal" and "Evergreen" games for more than 150 years. As the *Guardian*'s chess correspondent, Leonard Barden, commented after the world champion, Vladimir Kramnik, lost to a computer program, "Nobody wants to buy the collected games of Deep Fritz." This attitude may one day seem old-fashioned, but so far the public's appetite for matches between computers—as opposed to man versus machine encounters—has been limited to those with considerable technical expertise.

Nevertheless, the assumption that underlies the perennial interest in computer chess is that the game represents the perfect arena for human and artificial intelligence to compete. But is the assumption true? Does chess have anything to do with what most people understand by intelligence? And does the computer's defeat of human beings at chess indicate its intellectual ascendancy over man? What happens when intelligence is divorced from humanity—and hence from morality?

"To play chess requires no intelligence at all," declared no less an authority than Capablanca, whose natural talent and intuitive feel for position caused him to be nicknamed the "chess machine." The Cuban genius was deprecating about his accomplishments—and even more so about those of his peers. In his view, skill at chess may be compatible with mediocre intellectual capacity in everything else. In stark contrast is the view of Gerald Abrahams, the British philosopher, political theorist, and barrister, who was one of the most brilliant men ever to play and write about chess. In the second (1960) edition of his remarkable treatise *The Chess Mind*, Abrahams rejected Freudian as well as Marxist "determinism" in chess. To the argument of Freud's friend and biographer, Ernest Jones—that the case of the nineteenth-century American genius Paul Morphy shows how a neurotic obsession with his father was canalized into chess—Abrahams insists that such "phantasmal processes" or "ulterior messages" cannot have caused the objective mastery shown by Morphy. Chess is far too demanding a game to follow any logic other than its own. "If operations of pure intelligence ever take place," Abrahams asserts, "chess is among them." He points out, however, that even when chess masters succumb to paranoid forms of insanity, such as Morphy, Steinitz, Rubinstein, and Torre—to which we must now add the name of Fischer—their ability to play chess is scarcely, if at

all, impaired. Chess, even if proof of intellectual ability, is a function of the human mind that is largely independent of sanity. It is
also compatible with an amoral, even criminal, propensity. Stalin's
hangman Nikolai Krylenko and the Nazi ruler of occupied Poland,
Hans Frank—both mass killers—were keen chess players.

The ability of computers to play superlative chess does not tell
us anything about whether the attitude of an artificial intelligence
toward its human masters would be benign or malign. This uncertainty has exercised American scientists, philosophers, and practitioners of science fiction, such as Isaac Asimov. His Three Laws of
Robotics (1940) ought, he argued, to be built into any future artificial intelligence. They are summed up in the idea that a robot may
not harm humanity or, by inaction, allow humanity to come to
harm. These laws were designed to prevent a robot turning, like
Frankenstein's monster, against its creator. More recently, the focus among moral philosophers has switched to the "rights" of robots against "exploitation" by humans. In 2006 Sir David King, the
British government's chief scientific adviser, praised a report he
had commissioned that predicted that robots would demand housing, health care, and other rights or benefits before the end of the
twenty-first century.

It was Asimov's rival as a pioneer of modern science fiction,
the Englishman Arthur C. Clarke, whose writing formed the basis
for the first and still most celebrated example of a film in which
the villain turns out not to be an alien, but a chess-playing computer: Stanley Kubrick's *2001: A Space Odyssey*. The computer
HAL 9000 is depicted not merely as intelligent—"the brain and
central nervous system of the ship"—but also as unexpectedly
evil. When HAL (whose name is an acronym: *H*euristically programmed *AL*gorithmic computer) defeats the astronaut Dave Bowman at chess—still a novel idea in 1967—this is intended as proof
of the computer's cognitive superiority over humans.

Subsequent events, however, demonstrate that ratiocination is
not the same as rationality. HAL has been programmed to believe
that only humans can err. When the computer proves not to be

infallible, the two active crew members decide to disconnect it. Once HAL discerns their intention, its artificial intelligence turns out to be governed by a ruthlessly utilitarian code. HAL subordinates the lives of the crew, most of whom are in a state of suspended animation, to the success of the mission, which it equates with its own self-preservation. When HAL invents a fault in order to trick the two active crew members into leaving the ship, its motive is to kill them. HAL succeeds in killing the hibernating humans and sending Frank Poole hurtling into outer space, but Dave Bowman succeeds in reentering the ship and proceeds to crawl inside HAL to shut it down. As he does so, the computer gradually reverts to more and more primitive levels of intelligence, rather like a victim of brain damage or Alzheimer's. (Curiously—and this is pure sentimentality—HAL's last words after "My mind is going" are: "I'm afraid" and "I can feel it.")

Just as chess is associated with the infallibility of artificial intelligence, so fear and sentience, two primary human characteristics, are identified with a primitive, prerational stage of evolution. The computer then briefly reverts to its "childhood," singing the song ("Daisy, Daisy") that it was taught by its programmer. In the end, all that is left of HAL is a pre-recorded message, revealing the true purpose of the mission to Jupiter: to investigate alien life on the giant planet, evidence of which has been discovered in the crater Tycho on the moon.

Interestingly, the film works on the assumption that the Cold War has ended well before the dawn of the twenty-first century. Russian and American astronauts cooperate as a matter of course: the "space race" has become a team event. *2001* is nonetheless as much a Cold War movie as Kubrick's other masterpiece, *Dr. Strangelove*, despite what in 1967 must have seemed a utopian scenario of Soviet–American cooperation. The film is dominated by two mysterious nonhuman forms of intelligence. Benign extraterrestrial intelligence is contrasted with malign artificial intelligence. The naive and fallible but resourceful human being, Dave, defeats the supposedly omniscient and infallible but treacherous, amoral, and murderous computer. The outcome of his encounter with the unknown being—variously depicted as a stone monolith and a fetuslike "star child"—is open-ended, however. The subtext is that the freedom and humanity of the American ideal will always triumph over the determinism and inhumanity of the machine, the totalitarian tendency of which is symbolized by its all-seeing red "eye." The real challenge lies beyond this latter day "Big Brother," at the frontiers of time and space. It can only be attempted once mankind ceases to devote its ingenuity to conflict. The function of chess in 2001 is analogous to its function in the Cold War: as a harmless surrogate for real war. The film also highlights the distinction between intelligence and sanity. Although a computer may seem to be intelligent, there is something diabolical about this simulated intelligence—a form of moral insanity.

Artificial intelligence has many benign uses, but it also reproduces the distinctively totalitarian combination of impersonality and amorality. Just as an individual who cannot recognize another human as a being like himself is a potential psychopath, so an entire society can refuse to recognize the humanity of a dissident minority, and so fall victim to collective moral insanity.

It is this moral insanity that makes HAL inconceivable without the communist system. The same kind of pitiless instrumentalism that drives HAL to switch off the life-support machines governed ethics behind the Iron Curtain. From the genocidal extermination campaigns of Lenin, Stalin, and Mao to North Korea's artificial famines under Kim Il-Sung and his son Kim Jong-Il, or the more discreet crimes of Deng Xiaoping (who approved the nationwide repression that followed the Tiananmen Square massacre in 1989), human life under communism had no value in and of itself. The end justified literally any means, not least because the inevitable demise of capitalism meant that communists would write the history books, from which dissenters and victims could be excised.

In 1975, some five years before he became president, Ronald Reagan gave a radio broadcast in which he described an incident that had taken place on May 11 that year at the Berlin Wall. A five-year-old child had fallen into the River Spree, which had carried him on to the wrong side of the border. When firemen from the West tried to rescue the boy, an East German patrol prevented them from doing so. Only three hours after the child had drowned did their frogmen recover the body. The mayor of West Berlin would describe it as "an incomprehensible and frightful act." "Communism is neither an economic nor a political system," commented Reagan. "It is a form of insanity—a temporary aberration which will one day disappear from the earth because it is contrary to human nature. I wonder how much more misery it will cause before it disappears." Reagan's view of communism was seen as simplistic at the time, but proved to be more accurate than the equivocations of the Sovietologists.

The demise of Soviet communism could not have happened without the Western ascendancy in technology—specifically in computers. As so often in the history of the West, civilization was saved by innovation. Computers may have the potential to enslave their creators, but so far they have beaten them only at chess. The dark side of artificial intelligence has yet to manifest itself except in science fiction.

Chess played a crucial part in stimulating the development of intelligent machines. Soviet domination of chess throughout the years when the new science of computers was in its embryonic stages might have given them a head start. The Russians did indeed keep pace in the early phase, but even before the microcomputer revolution of the 1980s they had fallen behind in the one field where direct comparisons were possible: cybernetic chess.

The deeper significance of America's double chess victory over the Soviet Union during the 1970s—in both the human game and the computer one—was that it demonstrated the superiority of a society in which information could circulate freely. Back in the 1940s, when power was measured in military firepower, this was not yet so obvious. A generation later, Western information technology was already in a different league from its Soviet counterpart. Although there was no shortage of talent in the Soviet scientific community, those working on computers simply could not compete with societies in which the market, not the state, was the driving force behind innovation. If the Soviet boffins could not compete with the West at chess, the game that they had elevated above all others, what could they compete at? The failure to keep up in the race for information technology ultimately cost the Soviet Union the Cold War. But this was the inevitable consequence of a totalitarian system that had no interest in the dissemination of information—which in fact went to extraordinary lengths to suppress information. A closed society may win wars that depend on brute force, but it has no chance in one that is fought on the chessboard and decided by intelligence—especially artificial intelligence.

13

DEFYING THE
EVIL EMPIRE

BY THE 1970S, THE CRACKS in the colossal edifice of Soviet communism were clearly visible to anyone who cared to look. One of the most obvious manifestations of decay was the defection to the West of many distinguished ornaments of Soviet culture. The first and most spectacular case, in 1961, was that of the Kirov Ballet's rising star, Rudolf Nureyev, who managed to escape his minders in Le Bourget airport near Paris. A pair of French plainclothes policemen drinking coffee found themselves confronted by the exotic young dancer pleading: "I want to stay!" When his KGB minder caught up with Nureyev and tried to drag him away, one of these gendarmes addressed him in a manner slightly reminiscent of Inspector Clouseau: *"On est en France ici!"*

Overnight, Nureyev was transformed from a local hero to a global sensation. Undeterred by the pepper bombs with which French communists tried to disrupt his performances, Nureyev insisted that his defection was "purely artistic and not political"—but its impact was greater than any number of Five Year

Plans. When, the following year, he danced with Margot Fonteyn at Covent Garden, they became the most celebrated duo in the history of ballet. If the "anarchic, hyper-individualistic" Nureyev was "fascinated by the West," as the Ministry of Culture disdainfully complained, that was partly because in the West he could be—and did indeed become—much more than a mere ballet dancer. No amount of pampering by the Soviet state could compare to the celebrity that beckoned in the West. Nureyev was joined by other dancers, such as Mikhail Baryshnikov, musicians such as Mstislav Rostropovich and Vladimir Ashkenazy, writers such as Joseph Brodsky and Alexander Solzhenitsyn, film directors, scientists, and many others. The actions of these "hyper-individualists" spoke more loudly than the words of disinformation campaigns mounted by communist governments and their front organizations in the West.

During the early phases of the Cold War, chess masters rarely figured among the defectors. If they chose to avert their eyes from the police state in which they lived, grandmasters could usually steer clear of politics without compromising their integrity. The Soviet propaganda machine even produced a movie, *Grandmaster* (starring, among others, Viktor Korchnoi), to cash in on the loyalty of these paragons of patriotic virtue: a grandmaster of chess was as Russian as a Volga boatman. But some masters were sensitive to the suggestion that they were merely providing a kind of highbrow entertainment to distract an increasingly critical and restive population. A comment that was made to Viktor Korchnoi in 1974 summed up the attitude of some cynical observers: "You chess players have a special mission. Football and ice hockey players are needed to make people drink less vodka, but they show you to the public so that they read less Solzhenitsyn." If chess was the vodka of the intelligentsia, then the sight of Russian grandmasters playing under the Stars and Stripes was as unthinkable as Muscovites exchanging their Stolichnaya for bourbon. Yet that is exactly what happened.

During the 1970s and 1980s, several Soviet grandmasters defected or were allowed to emigrate. A typical case was Lev Alburt, a Ukrainian grandmaster who defected to the United States in 1979 and later won the U.S. championship in 1984 and 1985. The book of Kiev 1978, a tournament in which he played shortly before his flight, was edited in order to omit all mention of the defector or his games, yet his ghostly presence may be deduced from the scores of the remaining participants. Alburt later wrote a primer, *Secrets of the Russian Chess Masters* — but the best-kept secrets of the Soviet era were defectors like himself.

Another, more poignant case was that of the youngest defector, Gata Kamsky. This prodigy was a Crimean Tartar — a nation uprooted by Stalin and forced to survive in Siberia. Gata was brought up alone by his devoted but pugnacious father, Rustam, a former boxer who has been accused of physically intimidating his son's opponents. The Kamskys defected during a visit to the United States in 1989. Although granted asylum on the grounds of ethnic discrimination, Gata Kamsky refused to play for his adoptive country at board three in the 1990 Olympiad, declaring that he would play "first board or not at all." Not unlike the father of the Hungarian Polgar sisters, all three of whom became chess champions, Kamsky senior was determined to prove that any child is capable of becoming a world champion at something. In Gata's case his myopia made the chessboard a more suitable arena than the boxing ring. Rustam Kamsky took his son out of school aged thirteen and subjected him to a Stakhanovite regime: fourteen hours a day studying chess, no friends, and no other interests.

Kamsky is undoubtedly of world championship caliber, but he never won the right to play a match with Kasparov. After failing to defeat Karpov in a twenty-game match for the FIDE title in 1996, Kamsky temporarily retired from chess, returning to college to study first medicine, then law. After a youth devoted to an experiment and spent under his father's thumb, Kamsky could have been forgiven for abandoning chess for good. Nevertheless, after five years without a single game, he made a comeback and has since embarked on a second chess career.

The most prominent of all the Soviet chess masters to defect to the West was, however, Viktor Korchnoi, a child of the most terrible siege of the Second World War, Leningrad. He was ten when it began in November 1941. Over the next three years, until the siege was lifted, three-quarters of a million people died in Leningrad. He survived only because he was able to use the ration cards of his father, grandmother, uncle, and great-uncle, after they were killed at the front, starved, or froze to death.

Although desperately poor, the Korchnoi family was highly educated—his Jewish mother was a pianist; his father hailed from the Polish nobility—and they ensured that Viktor continued to go to school. In 1943, when the blockade was broken and conditions eased a little, he joined the chess club at the Pioneers' Palace. There he discovered his vocation for chess. The emaciated boy grew into a "frail young man" and Korchnoi recalls a warning from one of his trainers: "Chess requires a great deal of physical and nervous energy. You have to be strong to play well. I advise you to eat oatmeal porridge every morning." So his mother cooked him a pan of porridge for the whole day, every day, and Viktor's results kept pace with his waistline.

Korchnoi may have been a thoroughbred of the Soviet stable, but he never felt wholly comfortable with his situation. Having neglected his history studies for the sake of chess, he was told by the communist students in the Komsomol office, who decided whether their colleagues could resit examinations, that he had no need to pursue an academic career. They assumed that he was already sufficiently privileged: "After all, you're a chess player!" In fact, he very much needed to resit the examination in order to receive the stipend that went with it, and this experience offended Korchnoi's sense of justice. So did the conduct of the organizers of one of his first master tournaments in 1951, when they blackmailed an older opponent into losing a drawn position to enable the promising junior to gain the master title. Even though he benefited from their patronage, Korchnoi already loathed the *nomenklatura*.

Despite his talent, success did not come easily for Korchnoi. He was always stubborn, independent, even a rebel, but he did not become a political dissident until much later. Initially, he strove hard to work the Soviet system, although he found this impossible to do without compromising his integrity. At Hastings 1955–6, one of the first foreign tournaments that Korchnoi won, his fellow Russian, Mark Taimanov—who was celebrated as a pianist no less than as a grandmaster—persuaded him to "compose" their individual game in advance. In his memoirs, Taimanov later boasted about its brilliancy, but the game was of course a fraud.

Later in 1956, Korchnoi was awarded the grandmaster title. He now enjoyed the privilege of foreign travel, a regular monthly stipend of up to 300 rubles (twice the average wages of a worker), and the possibility of earning hard currency. He was now prosperous enough to marry and raise a family, but as one of many Soviet grandmasters he, his wife, and baby had to content themselves with two small rooms in a communal apartment in Leningrad, sharing facilities with several other families.

It was at the Soviet championship in 1960 that Korchnoi surfaced from the pack. From the early rounds he led the tournament, which was played in his hometown. A thousand fans filled the Palace of Culture, built to commemorate Stalin's first Five Year Plan, with hundreds more waiting outside in the freezing midwinter. Then, four rounds from the finish, disaster struck. Against a lesser master, Vladimir Bagirov, Korchnoi—exhausted by a sleepless night helping his wife with their young son—blundered in a winning position by picking up the wrong bishop to recapture a rook. Under the rules of chess, a piece touched must be moved, so Korchnoi had no choice but to resign.

Despondent and humiliated, he had to watch as his main rival, Yefim Geller, won a game against Eduard Gufeld that had clearly been cooked up beforehand. "Gufeld was quite shamelessly throwing the game," Korchnoi later commented. "This can perhaps be explained, but certainly not forgiven." Korchnoi was riled and, in a magnificent game, he defeated Geller to regain the lead, going into the last round. His opponent, Alexei Suetin, refused an offer of a draw from Korchnoi and promptly consulted Geller and Petrosian, who were just behind Korchnoi in joint second place, about what he should do. Suetin ignored Petrosian's advice to agree the draw, and lost. Although both Geller and Petrosian won too, Korchnoi nevertheless finished half a point ahead.

It was only fourteen years later that he discovered his rivals' unsavory last-round machinations, which had become normal among the Soviet chess elite, but of which he had been oblivious at the time. David Bronstein admitted that thinking Korchnoi was "in a bad way" and observing that Petrosian's opponent, Nikolai Krogius, was "unscrupulously and crudely" throwing his game, he had deliberately lost his last-round game against Geller in order to ensure that Petrosian did not win the tournament outright. Korchnoi was shocked by this revelation, since he admired Bronstein as a friend and role model. He realized that "in the professional chess world inside the Soviet Union, the top places lead to colossal privileges, and the battle for these places is bound to involve means not associated purely with chess. Petrosian may have realized this ahead of anyone else."

Until the rise of Karpov in the early 1970s, Tigran Petrosian would be Korchnoi's archenemy. There may have been an element of ethnic rivalry involved too. According to Korchnoi, a common remark heard after Petrosian's first triumph in the Soviet championship was "A cunning Armenian has swindled a dozen Jews." This cynical response reflected the predominance of Soviet Jews in chess, but Petrosian soon found accomplices for his "swindling" among other Jewish grandmasters, such as Geller and Tal. Nor was the clash between Korchnoi and Petrosian merely a matter of ego—it went beyond normal competitive rivalry. Their mutual antipathy was more about politics than personality or prejudice.

Although he was an ethnic Armenian, Petrosian emerged from the Republic of Georgia. In this compatriot of Stalin—whose cult was very much alive in Georgia during the Brezhnev era—Korchnoi saw the corruption of the Soviet system personified. Their rivalry first manifested itself at the 1962 candidates' tournament in Curaçao, where three of the Soviet grandmasters conspired against Fischer, agreeing to draw their games with one another. Korchnoi, who was not among them, was irritated by Fischer's aspersion that he had been designated as a "sacrifice." Korchnoi saw Petrosian, ably seconded by his wife, Rona, as the mastermind of this conspiracy and believed that the real victim was not himself but Paul Keres, who had allowed himself to be drawn into the plot. In the last round, Keres faced Pal Benkö, whom he had always defeated hitherto. But this time, when the game was adjourned overnight, Benkö held a slight advantage, although Keres ought to have drawn. According to Korchnoi, "on the initiative of Petrosian's wife, a painstaking night of analysis was arranged" to help Benkö (a Hungarian-born American) against Keres. The result: Benkö gained his one and only victory over Keres, and Petrosian won the grueling twenty-eight-round tournament. Half a point behind was Keres, who had set the pace until the final stages.

In 1963 Petrosian went on to beat the aging world champion, Botvinnik, and established an ascendancy over Soviet chess that lasted until his defeat by Boris Spassky in 1969. His contemporaries, including Korchnoi, were eclipsed, and Petrosian used his influence in the Politburo to keep it that way. For instance, in 1963 Korchnoi was invited with Keres to the prestigious Piatigorsky Gold Cup tournament at Santa Monica in California. Petrosian intervened with the Soviet authorities to have Korchnoi's name replaced by his own. The Americans would gladly have invited all three Soviet grandmasters and even sent three round-trip air tickets. The third seat, however, was taken not by Korchnoi but by Rona Petrosian.

Gradually, Korchnoi became aware of official disapproval. He was reported by KGB officers (who invariably accompanied Soviet delegations to foreign events) for such things as unauthorized contacts with Westerners, visits to the casino, and his refusal to play at a tournament in Budapest at the express wish of Janos Kádár, the communist Hungarian leader. On the latter occasion, in 1965, the deputy chairman of the USSR Sports Committee summoned Korchnoi and informed him: "You know that in 1956 Soviet tanks smashed holes in the houses of Budapest. You have been selected to, as it were, plug up these holes—by your cultural cooperation!" But Korchnoi defied the request, was reprimanded and, later that year, sent to another tournament in Hungary anyway.

Temporarily banned from travel in the West, Korchnoi made one big concession: in 1965 he joined the Communist Party. "I was under the naive impression that, by my participation in party work, I could correct much that I did not like. I also realized that it would make it easier for me to travel abroad."

Unfortunately, Korchnoi continued to get into trouble. A year later, at a tournament in Havana, he went out to a bar with Tal. Having downed a good deal of rum, Tal was dancing with a young woman when he was set upon by her jealous boyfriend wielding a Coca-Cola bottle. Tal was knocked unconscious and the incident hushed up. Both grandmasters were grounded after this, and Korchnoi did not travel to the West again until 1968.

That year Korchnoi played better than ever before and advanced to within striking distance of the world title. He defeated first Reshevsky, then Tal, and reached the candidates' final for the first time to face Boris Spassky. At this point, Korchnoi became aware of Petrosian's malign influence behind the scenes. Through his Armenian friend Marshal Bagramian, Petrosian deprived Korchnoi of the services of his trainer, Semyen Furman, during his matches against Tal and Spassky. Furman was employed by the Central Army Sports Club, which—under orders from Marshal Bagramian —refused to release him to assist Korchnoi. Having worked with Korchnoi since 1946, Furman had become like a father to him. His absence left Korchnoi depressed and angry with Spassky, whom he wrongly suspected of intriguing against him. Spassky, who was then approaching the best form of his life, would probably have won the match anyway, but Korchnoi did not do himself justice and lost easily. He redeemed himself by winning a strong tournament in Majorca, ahead of Spassky and Petrosian, who had arranged for Korchnoi to be invited in the hope of obtaining his help in the forthcoming world championship match with Spassky.

That was, of course, a vain hope. While Petrosian was enjoying the spectacle of Spassky going down to defeat in his game against Korchnoi, the latter's smoldering resentment burst into flame.

"There's nothing you can do about it, Spassky will be world champion," Korchnoi informed the then title holder.

"Why, what do you mean?" asked a disconcerted Petrosian.

"Well, I'm beating him!" replied Korchnoi, who had a notorious habit of winning games against future world champions. Petrosian did indeed lose to Spassky, and he never forgave Korchnoi for not only refusing to help him but even prophesying his defeat. For all their scientific pretensions, Soviet grandmasters were as superstitious as anybody else.

By the late 1960s, Korchnoi had established himself as the third best player in the USSR, after Spassky and Petrosian, but whereas his two rivals were crushed by Fischer and thereafter rapidly declined, Korchnoi continued to improve. During the years of Soviet hegemony, Korchnoi remained in the shadow of his contemporaries. Yet after Fischer won the world championship, it was Korchnoi who emerged as the leading active player of his generation. His own assertion—that "the generation defeated by Fischer is no longer able to successfully compete with him"—would never be tested, since Fischer retired from active play and refused to defend his title. Nonetheless, Korchnoi achieved his best results during the decade after Fischer demolished Soviet superiority. This was partly a triumph of mind over body. Alone in the ultracompetitive world of late-twentieth-century chess, he maintained his creativity and stamina throughout his fifties, and even beyond. However, the catalyst for this unique phenomenon was Korchnoi's decision to make a bid for freedom from the Soviet Union—the first leading Russian grandmaster to do so.

In 1969 a new chess genius settled in Leningrad: Anatoly Karpov. It was not long before Korchnoi encountered the young man who would not only deny him the crown to which he aspired, but would bring his frustration with the communist system to boiling point. Born in 1951, Karpov had just become world junior champion, although he had yet to distinguish himself clearly from the new wave of young masters who emerged at the end of the 1960s, a decade for Soviet chess during which there had been a dearth of new talent.

Korchnoi was old enough to be Karpov's father, and he made short work of the nineteen-year-old when they met at the 1970 Soviet championship, which Korchnoi won. The two men were still sharing Semyen Furman as their trainer, but after his defeat Karpov decided that when playing Korchnoi, he must avoid playing any opening ideas originating with Furman; Korchnoi could read his old friend's mind too well, even at one remove. Soon, however, Furman hitched his fortunes to the new star; Karpov's gain was Korchnoi's loss. Karpov later declared: "Many times I've thanked my lucky stars that I had the good fortune to meet him and work with him."

Thereafter Korchnoi did not have it so easy with the rapidly improving Karpov. They played a secret training match in 1971, in which Korchnoi gave the younger man the advantage of the White pieces in five out of six games. He could only tie the match. Karpov won their next game en route to his first big tournament victory at the Alekhine Memorial in Moscow.

At Hastings 1971–2, Karpov again raced ahead of the field, while Korchnoi took time to warm up. It was common at Hastings for the Soviet representatives to agree to short draws with each other, but this time it was clear that Korchnoi needed to beat his young rival to have a chance of first prize. This early Korchnoi–Karpov clash at Hastings made an impression on the British spectators. The stocky, balding veteran, now almost fifty, faced a slight, rather unprepossessing youth. A lock of greasy hair fell across Karpov's face, with its pallid complexion and impassive expression. Few outside the Soviet Union had ever set eyes on Karpov before, and of the Western masters only the young Swede Ulf Andersson had played him. He was under no illusions about Karpov's strength, having been one of Karpov's chief rivals at the world junior championship, until he lost their grueling struggle. Andersson saw "Tolya" as a future world champion—and not so far in the future, either. Karpov was already a human calculating machine, with an icy temperament and an unerring strategic instinct, but he had not yet developed the sense of danger that would later become his greatest asset. In their game at Hastings, Korchnoi punished Karpov for his routine play by sacrificing a pawn, evidently catching him off balance. The older man won easily, enabling him to overtake Karpov.

The Russians shared first prize. Thereafter they embarked on a series of simultaneous exhibitions around England. When they met at the airport, Karpov was astonished to see that Korchnoi had five times as much to take home. "Remember this," Karpov recalled his rival telling him. "The level of a grandmaster is determined by his luggage." In his memoirs, Karpov depicts Korchnoi as "driven by two things: 'people are out to get me' and 'where can I scrape up some extra cash?' . . . Yet he could afford just about anything he wanted, and he created his own enemies. That was something he really had a knack for."

This was the era of Fischer, and Karpov's rise was eclipsed by the American. After Spassky's defeat, however, the Soviet authorities were eager for a new Soviet hero to regain the world championship and repair their damaged prestige. Just as Stalin's minions had built up Botvinnik in the early 1930s, so Brezhnev's bureaucrats latched on to Karpov as the man to beat Fischer. The young man was given every privilege, but the main obstacles to his rise were other Soviet grandmasters—chief among them Spassky and Korchnoi. Gradually, therefore, the system turned against these two warhorses, despite their carefully nurtured celebrity status. In order to beat Fischer, the older generation would have to be sacrificed. It is no accident that, in the wake of Karpov's ascent to the chess summit, Spassky and Korchnoi both left the Soviet Union (albeit in very different circumstances).

By 1973, aged just twenty-two, Karpov was already the highest-rated grandmaster in the world after Fischer. He was a generation younger than the Soviet elite, but he was at least as strong as them: a D'Artagnan to the three musketeers, Spassky, Petrosian, and Korchnoi. In the 1973 Leningrad Interzonal, the two home players, Karpov and Korchnoi, vied for supremacy throughout and were level as they reached the last round. According to Karpov, Korchnoi proposed that they should both draw their games and share first prize. Karpov, who was confident of beating his opponent, Torre, refused. He later claimed that this was a sign of Korchnoi's anti-Soviet conduct, insisting: "In our country such 'tricks' are vigorously condemned."

Whether or not this actually happened, Karpov's attempt to throw Korchnoi's allegations of match-fixing back in his face is risible. Not only were such tricks rife among the Soviet elite, they were sometimes ordered by the Soviet authorities. Karpov himself claimed that Korchnoi had deliberately lost his candidates' semifinal match against Petrosian in 1971, on the orders of the USSR Sports Committee, because he was not confident that he could halt Fischer's progress toward the world championship. Korchnoi absolutely denies this story, offering an innocent account of his inexplicable loss in the final game of the match. Karpov admits that "of course, there are no documents confirming this pact, but there is the quality of Korchnoi's play and, most important, a staggering fact, given his nature: after losing to Petrosian, [Korchnoi] remained on good terms with him. This suggests that Korchnoi did not fight, but simply moved to one side." As we have seen, there was bad blood between Korchnoi and Petrosian long before their match, and after it, too. The fact that Petrosian could triumph only after drawing eight mostly hard-fought games against Korchnoi suggests that the match was anything but a walkover. It is, however, entirely plausible that Korchnoi came under pressure to lose.

What is not disputed is that after Petrosian's 1971 victory, both men were summoned to see Sergei Pavlov, the chairman of the Sports Committee. A typical Soviet bureaucrat, who took no account of the two grandmasters' mutual loathing, he ordered Korchnoi to act as Petrosian's second in his forthcoming match with Fischer. Spassky, who heard about it from Petrosian, and Karpov, who heard it from Korchnoi, more or less agree that Korchnoi's reaction was one of utter contempt: "Comrade Pavlov, when I see what disgusting, vile moves Petrosian makes, I do not want to be his second!" This incident had serious consequences for Korchnoi. He had been obstinate and disrespectful toward Pavlov, an important figure in the Soviet hierarchy with the power to damage his career, and he had insulted Petrosian in front of an official. Karpov relates: "This wasn't just an explosion, but a challenge, and Petrosian vowed to annihilate Korchnoi." When Korchnoi fell into disfavor, Petrosian was not slow to seek revenge.

After Spassky's defeat at the hands of Fischer, Korchnoi saw his chance: he was one of the few Russians who had a good record against the American. In the next world championship cycle Korchnoi played better than ever before. The semifinal matches in 1973 pitted Spassky against Karpov and Korchnoi against Petrosian. The Korchnoi–Petrosian match took place in Odessa, because Korchnoi refused to play in Moscow, as in their previous encounter of 1971. "In his estate on the outskirts of Moscow, Petrosian lives like a prince, with all conceivable comforts," Korchnoi later recalled, "whereas I would have had to take refuge in a hotel, with the usual poor Soviet service."

The match began badly for Petrosian, who suffered the humiliation for a former world champion of being checkmated in the first game. A dispute arose over Petrosian's nervous habit of shaking the table by twitching his leg whenever his opponent ran short of time. Whether this was involuntary or deliberate gamesmanship, in the fifth game it led to a public row at the board. Petrosian admonished Korchnoi—"We're not in a bazaar!"—but refused to stop shaking the table. Korchnoi then issued a warning that was audible even to the spectators: "This is your last chance!" The game was adjourned with Korchnoi in a winning position, but Petrosian did not turn up for the resumption. He protested both to the president of FIDE, Max Euwe, and to the Central Committee of the Communist Party, demanding that the match be awarded to him, even though he was losing 3–1. An arbitration committee of Soviet officials, chaired by the mayor of Odessa, met to resolve the dispute. Although he felt himself to be the aggrieved party, Korchnoi agreed to apologize for speaking to his opponent during a game, thereby infringing the rules, which require all complaints to be addressed through the arbitrator. But Korchnoi also drew attention to the Armenians who demonstrated on Petrosian's behalf, asking about his part "in the organization of these mobs." Petrosian then broke off negotiations, declaring: "He has insulted me, he has insulted my people. I won't play against him any more."

It is not unusual for the underdog in a long chess match to create a distraction. On this occasion Korchnoi was confident enough to ignore the transparent attempt to mix chess and politics. Once Petrosian, who had retired to a hospital, was told that his demands had been rejected, he resigned prematurely on the dubious grounds of ill-health. By then, however, the Soviet authorities had already decided that they wanted Karpov, not Korchnoi, to challenge Fischer. First, Karpov had to beat Spassky in the other semifinal. Their match has been identified by Kasparov as a key moment in the history of chess. Spassky still believed himself, with some justice, to be the second-best player in the world, having won the Soviet championship in 1973 ahead of all his rivals. Not only was Karpov–Spassky a clash of generations, it also marked the triumph of a new, more professional approach to opening theory, which involved analyzing ideas right through to the middle- and even the endgame. Karpov had been the star pupil of Botvinnik, who was his role model both ideologically and intellectually. "Karpov worked for 10–12 hours a day!" Kasparov wrote. "Spassky had no conception of the strength of the grandmaster against whom he had been drawn." The ex-world champion won the first game—but that proved to be the only time he beat Karpov in his entire career. Karpov equalized in the third game, took the lead in the fifth, and thereafter never looked back. The final score was 4–1 with six draws. This match broke Spassky, who gave up serious hopes of a comeback and set his sights instead on emigration to the West.

Korchnoi's habitual overconfidence caused him to misunderstand the reasons for Karpov's crushing victory over Spassky. He still thought that he had at least equal chances, but he already sensed the chill of official disapproval. As both players had lived in Leningrad, Korchnoi expected half the match to be played there. Having refused to play the whole match in Moscow, as Karpov wanted, he found that the USSR chess supremo, Baturinsky, had simply added a clause to a document that Korchnoi had already signed, stipulating that Moscow alone would stage the event. When Korchnoi was obliged to play at a later time than he wanted to suit the nocturnal habits of his opponent, he vented his fury by sending an open postcard to Yuri Averbakh, the president of the USSR Chess Federation—a former friend who had opportunistically sided against him. Arriving at the Central Chess Club, it was bound to be seen by others first, and read: "From cowardice to treachery is but one step, but with your attributes you will easily accomplish it." Korchnoi commented: "I had acquired another enemy, but no longer cared. From this point I was playing for a breakout." This fall into disfavor had practical effects. After Korchnoi's friend David Bronstein spent a week helping him to prepare for the match, *Izvestia* (the newspaper for which Bronstein was the chess correspondent) ensured that he was not allowed to report the match. Korchnoi afterwards complained that he had been exhausted by analysis during the match: "I had been unable to persuade a single grandmaster to act as my second."

The stage was set for a contest of two political as well as chess cultures: Karpov, the member of the Central Committee of the USSR Communist Youth, versus Korchnoi, the bourgeois individualist. The odds were against Korchnoi. His enemies Petrosian and Averbakh were helping Karpov, alongside Geller, Tal, and Botvinnik himself. Even Korchnoi's own former trainer, Furman, had switched sides to Karpov, making it even harder for

Korchnoi to anticipate his opponent's traps. Korchnoi claimed that even the neutral chief controller, a Belgian with the exotic name of Alberic O'Kelly de Galway, was biased against him. Among the Soviet public, the match pitted the Stakhanovites against the intelligentsia—and the anti-Semites against the Jews. The Communist Youth sent thugs to support Karpov and intimidate his Jewish opponent. After one game, Korchnoi recalled, "the stage was surrounded by a group of Fascist-like toughs, shouting: 'That's it, that's it, smash him, Tolya!'" Korchnoi also received hate mail and feared that "something might happen to [him] in the street."

The 1974 candidates' final turned out to be one of the most grueling matches ever played and would decide the world championship itself. Karpov won by the narrowest of margins, 12.5 to 11.5. His share of the prize fund was 1,800 rubles—much more than in previous Soviet matches, while still a tiny fraction of the sums that Fischer had earned in the West. Of the twenty-four games, only five had been decisive, but every game was hard fought. If Fischer's victories had been won by blitzkrieg, Karpov's were achieved by attrition. This was chess as trench warfare. Yet the older man stood up to the physical strain better than the younger. It was Karpov who took the first time-out, who lost weight and was visibly exhausted by the end. He lost two of the last five games, one of them in just nineteen moves. Korchnoi's comeback occurred just too late to make up his 3–0 deficit during the first seventeen games.

However, this was also a battle of nerves—and of mind games. At this early stage of the Korchnoi–Karpov duel, their tactics mirrored Fischer's: turning up late or bombarding the officials with complaints. Korchnoi even wrote a formal protest, not to the controller ("How could I, a Soviet man, complain to a foreigner?") but to the organizing committee, about Karpov's discourteous behavior. This protest would later be used by the Soviet authorities against Korchnoi. Criticism of the man who was being groomed to regain the world championship from Fischer was unacceptable.

Karpov had no sooner defeated Korchnoi in their first match

than the Sports Committee began a propaganda campaign to create a united front behind Karpov and against Fischer. Korchnoi refused to join in this agitation. In an interview for the Yugoslav news agency Tanjug, which was printed in the newspaper *Politika*, he vented his frustration. Karpov, he declared, was no more talented than several of his rivals, as was demonstrated by the fact that he took a month and a half to wear down Korchnoi's resistance. "Although I still consider myself superior in the creative sense, as regards willpower he is clearly my superior."

Korchnoi made matters worse by supporting Fischer's demand that the next world championship match should not be the best of twenty-four games, but an open-ended contest in which draws would not count and the winner would be the first to win six games. "My criticism of Karpov was, of course, a crime, but was nevertheless an internal matter," Korchnoi wrote, "whereas my support for Fischer was considered to be an act of treachery."

This was the moment for Petrosian to gain revenge for his humiliation in the semifinal. In the leading Soviet sports magazine, *Sovietsky Sport*, the former world champion denounced Korchnoi's "unsporting" behavior. This was the first salvo of a campaign. "Workers' letters," which demanded that the "unsporting grandmaster" be severely punished, were published in *Sovietsky Sport*. One letter to the editor compared this campaign to the anti-Semitic "Doctors' Plot" during the last days of Stalin, although no such pro-Korchnoi protests were published. Privately, Korchnoi received some support; one writer compared Petrosian to Lysenko, Stalin's favorite geneticist.

Initially, the aim was to humiliate the dissident. To defuse the situation, Korchnoi wrote a brief apology for the interview, which he put down to postmatch blues, but the blatant insincerity of this statement merely compounded his offense, and the editor of the magazine was reprimanded for publishing it. Korchnoi was first ordered to write an explanation for his conduct to the Sports Committee, then—when this was deemed unsatisfactory—was summoned to appear before the committee in Moscow. There he was informed of his punishment: he would be banned from foreign travel for a year and his salary would be cut. This relatively light official penalty was, however, made more onerous by many unofficial ones. Korchnoi found himself at the mercy of the vindictive Leningrad KGB: his home was bugged; mail from abroad was interdicted, including copies of the English-language edition of his own most recent book, his son was victimized by teachers at school, although the boy defiantly wore a badge of his father's from the 1970 Olympiad bearing the name "Korchnoi." False rumors were spread that Korchnoi had applied to emigrate to Israel, which led to hostility towards his family. His income was severely reduced not only by the loss of foreign earnings but by his exclusion from the Soviet media; he had been a familiar face on television. He began to receive threatening letters, sometimes anti-Semitic in character. Fellow chess masters shunned him, and he ceased contact with people he no longer trusted. Korchnoi became so desperate that he even wrote a letter to Marshal Tito, asking for asylum in Yugoslavia, where he still had many admirers. Wisely, he never sent it.

Alongside this persecution of Korchnoi, a parallel propaganda campaign was under way against Fischer. The Leningrad Sports Committee told Korchnoi that it would be in his interests to support the Soviet line. Korchnoi wrote an article that argued that Karpov really wanted to play the match against Fischer and was not being deliberately obstructive, as some Western critics claimed. Karpov was pleased with this olive branch and urged the Soviet authorities to publish it, but this gesture fell far short of their expectations and it never appeared. For the Kremlin, nothing short of vilification of Fischer by Korchnoi would do. The official line, however, contradicted the professional interests of the Soviet chess elite, who had benefited from Fischer's efforts—not to mention their genuine respect for the man who was, on paper at least, the strongest chess player of all time.

Even Karpov shared these misgivings, knowing that he would not be accepted as a true world champion if he won only by default. After the FIDE congress at Nice in 1974 had failed to agree to all of Fischer's conditions for the 1975 world championship match, a second congress was held at Bergen aan Zee in the Netherlands in March 1975. This accepted all but one of Fischer's conditions, but that was not enough to satisfy him and he resigned the FIDE title—while continuing to style himself world champion. A month later in Moscow, Karpov was awarded a gold medal and the title of world champion. Efforts to bring about an unofficial match continued, however. Back channels between Karpov and Fischer were opened courtesy of the Filipinos and Japanese, but when the Central Committee heard about a secret meeting between the two champions in Tokyo in 1976 to discuss a match, it stopped the negotiations.

While the world championship was resolved, the campaign against Korchnoi continued. As Karpov later put it, "Petrosian thirsted for Korchnoi's blood and pursued him everywhere." He wanted Korchnoi to be stripped of his Soviet grandmaster title, thereby effectively ending his career. Karpov claims that he tried to persuade the head of the USSR Chess Federation to halt the anti-Korchnoi campaign, on the grounds that it was being driven by personal grudges. Viktor Baturinsky was astonished: "Don't you know what will happen if we allow Korchnoi to lift his head?" In September 1975, Korchnoi was told that his travel ban had been lifted, but in practice he could not go abroad until the Hastings tournament in December. By then he had settled accounts with Petrosian by defeating him in a big event at Moscow. Ironically, it was Karpov who provided the necessary guarantee of his good conduct that enabled him to travel.

By the time he set off for Hastings, Korchnoi was already preparing to defect. While in England, he sent books, photo albums, and other precious items for safekeeping to an ex-Soviet friend, Gennady Sosonko, in Amsterdam. That same city was Korchnoi's destination for his next trip abroad, in July 1976. Again he brought out valuables, including his archive of documents, letters, etc., but he did not intend to defect yet. During the tournament, however, the opportunity to let off steam in an interview for a French news agency proved irresistible. Smarting under the anti-Semitic attacks that he had endured for the past two years, Korchnoi denounced the Soviet Union's refusal to participate in that year's Olympiad in Israel. He also showed solidarity with Spassky, who had suffered similar chicanery at Soviet hands. "In giving this interview, I had used my right of being a free man; from this time, although I had never essentially bothered with politics, I had become a 'dissident,' and an open one," he later wrote.

The Soviet reaction was instant: an official located the errant grandmaster at his hotel and threatened him: "Haven't you had enough unpleasantness already? Did you really think this would just be ignored?" On the last day of the tournament, Korchnoi was due to report to the Soviet embassy in The Hague. Instead, he went to a police station and requested asylum. It took Tass, the Soviet news agency, several days to report the news. Information about defections was often suppressed altogether, but Korchnoi was too well-known to be ignored: "In the Soviet Union I enjoyed a degree of perfectly official popularity that neither Solzhenitsyn nor Sakharov could boast of, nor even Rostropovich or Barshai, public figures who are much better known in the West than I am."

The witch-hunt against Korchnoi and his family began immediately. The USSR Chess Federation deprived him of all his Soviet titles. Then a letter was published in *Sovietsky Sport*, supposedly signed by over thirty Soviet grandmasters, accusing Korchnoi of "morbid vanity" and demanding that the defector be excluded from the next candidates' tournament to decide a challenger for Karpov. The world champion's name was noticeable by its absence. Karpov published a separate statement, supporting the decision to deprive Korchnoi "of the right to represent the Soviet Chess School in the world arena" and accusing him of "dishonest and dishonorable" conduct, but he was not prepared to argue for exclusion. His victory over Korchnoi in 1974 would be only the first of three "grandiose matches . . . which became the main contest in both of our lives for ten years." Having acquired his title from Fischer by default, Karpov needed to prove his legitimacy by defeating the strongest challenger who was prepared to play, even if that person proved to be Korchnoi. There was also an element of self-interest: Karpov stood to benefit if the next world championship match were to have a political as well as a sporting dimension. Karpov later admitted that "chess players are forever indebted to Fischer for improving the status and rewards of chess" and he even acknowledged that Fischer–Spassky had "heated up interest to such a degree that for a time chess became the number one sport in the world."

But from the Soviet point of view, the prospect of the defector Korchnoi challenging Karpov for the world championship was a nightmare. No sooner had they regained the title for the Soviet Union, albeit by diplomacy rather than over the chessboard, than a far more embarrassing and unprecedented threat had emerged. How could the Soviet media explain the fact that one of the country's most popular grandmasters was now on the other side of the Cold War? Nor was there the slightest doubt that Korchnoi was out for revenge. He had left behind his wife and son when he defected. Their requests for exit visas to Israel were refused, but his campaign to force the Kremlin to let them join him in the West provided an additional motivation to rout his former compatriots at chess. Indeed, it soon became clear that Korchnoi's defection had energized him and that he was playing better than ever before.

In exile Korchnoi had also met Petra Leeuwerik, an Austrian divorcée in her fifties who was then living in Holland. She became his secretary, and their relationship soon became close. Leeuwerik was a passionate anti-communist who had suffered far more than Korchnoi at the hands of the Soviet regime. According to her own account, in 1948 at the age of nineteen she had been kidnapped in the Soviet Zone of Vienna by the KGB, accused of spying for the CIA, and had served eight or nine years in Arctic conditions at a labor camp at Vorkuta. She insisted on her innocence; Colonel Baturinsky was adamant that she had "spied for America." Leeuwerik believed in Korchnoi's destiny and exercised great influence over him, but she was not universally popular with his Western friends and colleagues. Korchnoi's marriage did not survive his defection, even though his wife, Bella, and his son, Igor, refused to disown him or to change their name, and Igor was later imprisoned for refusing to be conscripted. After their emigration, the marriage ended and Petra Leeuwerik eventually married Korchnoi.

Soviet grandmasters, under orders from the Kremlin, boycotted events at which Korchnoi was playing. As he put it, "The Soviets give the organizers . . . a choice: the Russians or Korchnoi. So no Korchnoi!" Yet the Soviet officials failed in their attempt to have the defector excluded from the world championship on the spurious grounds that he was stateless. (In fact, many of the greatest masters of the past, from Alekhine to Lasker, had been deprived of their citizenship and it was part of FIDE's purpose to protect such stateless exiles.) In 1977 Korchnoi defeated Petrosian again in a bad-tempered match during which they never exchanged a word. Then, with the help of two British seconds (Raymond Keene and Michael Stean), he crushed another Soviet grandmaster, Polugayevsky, by the overwhelming score of 5–1 with seven draws. "It is obvious that this is now my fate to struggle with the USSR, making things for them as unpleasant as I can," he wrote in his autobiography, *Chess Is My Life,* published in 1978.

Korchnoi's last hurdle before meeting Karpov again in 1978 was a more complex psychological challenge: he had to defeat Boris Spassky in Belgrade. Not only were the two men friends, but Spassky was also living in France and no longer represented the Soviet Union. However, there was a crucial difference: Spassky had not defected. "Alone amongst millions of émigrés, he holds dual nationality and lives in Paris on a Soviet passport!" Korchnoi later wrote bitterly. "Spassky had been fighting for his political independence for several years. He received permission to leave the USSR only 'by chance,' exactly a month after my own departure. Who knows what price he had to pay for an exit visa?" But if Korchnoi felt any qualms, Spassky was ambivalent about his situation. He no longer had any desire to exert himself for a political system he despised, but neither was he driven by personal ambition, let alone the thirst for vengeance that motivated Korchnoi.

And so the match began badly for Spassky. After eight games, the score was 4–0 to Korchnoi, with four draws. In the West, the press celebrated "Viktor the Terrible"; in Moscow, there was dismay. Then, at this halfway point, something extraordinary happened. Spassky suddenly changed his entire demeanor. Complaining about light reflecting from the board into his eyes, he demanded that he be given a box on stage where he could sit throughout the game out of sight of both the audience and his opponent. He watched it entirely on a demonstration board and would return to the stage only to make his move and then retreat again. Korchnoi protested that this cloak of invisibility was upsetting his own play. Later he commented that Spassky had been hypnotized: "He did not look normal . . . he was swaying, with half-closed eyes, like a medium." For his part, Spassky claimed that the first five rows of spectators were all "Korchnoi's people," whose hostile stare was disturbing his concentration during the third hour of play. Korchnoi countered that "some kind of weapon was being employed against me."

It is still not clear what had really happened. In Moscow there was a strong feeling that Korchnoi must not be allowed to walk away with the match. The Soviet Sports Committee made a final attempt to shield Karpov from the need to defend his title against the "traitor" Korchnoi. Viktor Ivonin, deputy chairman of the Soviet Sports Committee, arrived in Belgrade, along with numerous other officials and grandmaster assistants to help Spassky. It seems that an attempt was made to exploit Korchnoi's superstitious belief in parapsychology. Garry Kasparov has speculated that the mysterious spectators were not fans of Korchnoi at all, but Soviet stooges working for Karpov. Whatever the truth, the power of suggestion was enough to affect Korchnoi's play and he lost an unprecedented four games in a row. The match was nearly abandoned after Korchnoi protested and Max Euwe, the president of FIDE, had to fly in to persuade both players to continue.

At this point, Korchnoi pulled himself together. Believing that a group of Swiss parapsychologists was helping him, albeit at a distance, he managed to halt his "fatal dive." He drew the next two games, then won two more to take the match to 7–4 with seven draws. It was not the result itself that destroyed their friendship—that had survived their previous match in 1968, which Spassky won—but the manner in which it had been achieved. Spassky was dismissive about his rival's performance: "It is not true that Korchnoi has improved; it is just that Petrosian and I are playing much worse than in 1968." Korchnoi retorted: "The only thing I cannot forgive [in] a man with anti-totalitarian views is that he allowed the Soviets to turn the field of battle into a testing ground against me."

Meanwhile Anatoly Karpov, deprived of the chance to play Fischer, was developing a style that would dominate the chess world for over a decade. Having won more tournaments than anyone in history, playing cautious, cold-blooded, strategic chess, he probably came closest to fulfilling the Stakhanovite ideal of Soviet man. For that reason alone he was the least popular of the world champions outside the USSR. As one of the few champions who actually was wholly Russian, however, Karpov was (and remains) much loved in his motherland. And his genius was undeniable; although unexciting, his unspectacular style had no weaknesses, and his intuitive knowledge of where to place his pieces combined well with a cool temperament and painstaking preparation to create an illusion of invulnerability that intimidated all but Korchnoi and, later, Kasparov.

During the 1970s, however, Karpov was built up into a demigod, under the auspices of Vitaly Sevastianov, chairman of the Soviet Chess Federation. Sevastianov was a former cosmonaut who had participated in the 1970 "Cosmos–Earth" chess match, a consultation game played while orbiting aboard *Soyuz-9*. This party stalwart, twice a Hero of the Soviet Union, once asked in *Izvestia*: "Doesn't Karpov have any failings? Probably, like any normal person. But for some reason I haven't tried to find them."

14

THE YOGI VERSUS
THE COMMISSAR

F ROM JULY TO OCTOBER 1978, Viktor Korchnoi played
Anatoly Karpov for the world chess championship at the
holiday resort of Baguio in the Philippines. It proved to
be probably the most ideologically charged—and certainly the
most vituperative—chess match of the entire Cold War. Adding to
the personal and political animosity between the Soviet champion
and the dissident challenger were the bizarre machinations of the
two teams. The Soviet side was led by the KGB commissar, Viktor
Baturinsky, whose official rank was Colonel of Justice. Korchnoi's
awkward squad of Cold Warriors included not only his right-hand
woman, Petra Leeuwerik, but a pair of yogis. At one point, Baturinsky issued a protest headed "Chess match in the Philippines
is not a training ground for Cold War"—but that is precisely what
it was.

Baguio was, as the British expert William Hartston remarked
many years later, "the high point in the history of chess as theater, though it was never clear whether the production was melodrama or farce." The melodrama derived from the fact that Korch-

noi stood alone against the might of what Ronald Reagan would later call the evil empire. A refugee, he was not allowed to play under the flag of his new domicile, Switzerland, and for the purposes of the match was effectively stateless. (On this, as over many other issues, FIDE caved in to Soviet pressure; Korchnoi could only respond with gestures, such as refusing to stand when the Internationale was played at the opening ceremony.) The farce element at Baguio stemmed from the pseudoscience of parapsychology, which seemed to exert a baleful influence on Korchnoi. He believed, for example, that Sharansky's thirteen-year prison sentence was imposed for passing on secrets about parapsychology and that Karpov had "electrodes plugged into his brain to reinforce the link" with his parapsychologists. The Soviet team played on this weakness. It proved just enough to tip the balance.

Just as chess was a surrogate for war, so mind games were a surrogate for chess. The Soviet chess establishment had always taken psychology seriously, and for his match against Fischer, Spassky had been assigned the leading figure in the field, Nikolai Krogius. Spassky's defeat had persuaded Krogius and others that a conventional approach, based on a detailed assessment of the opponent's weaknesses, was insufficient to guarantee victory. Irrational, unbalanced individuals, as Fischer and Korchnoi were seen by Krogius, might be vulnerable to psychological pressure. The psych-ops employed at Baguio marked a descent from gamesmanship into skulduggery. First, there was the disinformation: typical was Karpov's reference to Korchnoi's "strange habit of attaching himself at night to a heating battery. Someone once told him that his abnormal malice could be explained by his whole body being overcharged with static electricity." Furthermore, Karpov's chief parapsychologist was Dr. Vladimir Zukhar, director of the Central Laboratory for Psychology in Moscow, who was reputed to maintain telepathic links with cosmonauts in space.

The 1970s saw a boom in public fascination with the paranormal that alarmed empirical scientists. In 1976 a Committee for the

Scientific Investigation of Claims of the Paranormal was founded in the United States to debunk the burgeoning industry of astrology, UFOs, and psychic phenomena. In the Soviet Union, parapsychology was taken more seriously. Spassky, Karpov, and Korchnoi were not the only grandmasters who believed that they could be hypnotized by the stare of an opponent or a spectator. Their faith in parapsychology was all the stronger because the official ideology was itself a kind of superstition. The new mind-altering drugs that had such a spectacular impact on popular culture in the West were used for more sinister purposes by the KGB. During the Brezhnev era, the authorities conducted a vicious campaign against the very limited freedom that had begun to emerge in the post-Stalin thaw. At the heart of this reaction was the *psikushka* or psychiatric prison, where mind-altering drugs were administered as a punishment for "anti-Soviet" views. This abuse of medical ethics justified itself ultimately by Lenin's notion that anybody who doubted the truth of dialectical materialism must be either mad or bad —probably both.

Hypnosis and parapsychology more generally were part of this continuum. According to Lesley Chamberlain, the dissident writer Leonid Plyusch, who was arrested in 1972 and subjected to "treatment" in a *psikushka,* described how as a young lecturer he and his academic colleagues were bored stiff by the official ideology, preferring to discuss pseudoscientific experiments in hypnosis. During the last decades of communism, a decadent, disoriented culture emerged, shot through with superstition. Masha Gessen, author of *Dead Again: The Russian Intelligentsia after Communism,* quotes a survey of the early 1990s that painted an alarming picture of intellectuals living in "ugly, frightening . . . and hopeless" private worlds, in which a belief in conspiracies and the paranormal figured prominently. These attitudes fed mass delusions from which dissidents were not immune, but in their case the fear of persecution and of psychiatric torture helps to explain their apparent gullibility and paranoia. It is impossible to understand what happened during the Korchnoi–Karpov battles without being aware of the psychopathology of everyday life in the last days of the Soviet empire.

The ghost at the Baguio feast was Bobby Fischer, who had been such a successful exponent of psychological chess warfare. Although he was out of sight but by no means out of mind, it was thanks to him that the rules for the world championship had been changed since 1972, with the winner now being the first to win six games, draws not counting. Korchnoi–Karpov 1978 was the first match for half a century to be of unlimited duration; the last, Alekhine–Capablanca 1927, had gone to thirty-four games over three months. So it was always likely that, despite the twenty-year disparity in age, this match would be a marathon—a grueling test of mental and physical endurance. Fischer's presence could be felt in other ways, too. Korchnoi claimed during the match that the Karpov camp's mind games, including the plan of using Zukhar to disturb his peace of mind, had been prepared for the abortive 1975 match with Fischer. It is unlikely that the American (who, despite his other eccentricities, had no known interest in the paranormal) would have been as susceptible as Korchnoi was to the notion that Zukhar could be linked to Karpov by telepathy, although Fischer would surely not have tolerated Zukhar's intrusive presence either.

The first three games were uneventful draws, but already both sides were testing the boundaries. In the second game, Karpov's assistants handed him yogurt during play—a technical breach of the rules, which prohibited contact between players and those in the auditorium. Korchnoi's head of delegation, Petra Leeuwerik, mounted a protest on the grounds that the yogurt might function as a secret code, enabling the sixteen-strong Soviet team to pass messages to Karpov during the game: "Thus a yogurt after move 20 could signify 'we instruct you to offer a draw'; or a sliced mango could mean 'we order you to decline a draw.' A dish of marinated quails' eggs could mean 'play Ng4 at once' and so on." This bizarre suggestion, which elicited a ferocious response from Colonel

Baturinsky, presented the chief arbiter, Lothar Schmid, with a dilemma. Given the dull progress of the match, the "Great Yogurt
Controversy" was the only thing that interested the press, confirming their assumption that all chess masters were mad, and
Russian chess masters were paranoid to boot. If, however, Schmid
failed to take this storm in a yogurt pot seriously, he would confirm Korchnoi's suspicions that the organizers were inclined to defer to Karpov's big battalions.

Schmid was a respected German grandmaster; patrician and er-
udite, he was the proud owner of the world's largest library of chess
books. He proposed a compromise, whereby only one color of yogurt (violet) could be served at a fixed time by a designated waiter,
but this meant that Karpov had won. While Korchnoi was genuinely suspicious of the yogurt ("It wouldn't have been a bad thing
to take away this 'yogurt' for chemical analysis," he commented),
its real importance was that the incident revealed that Schmid and
the jury were not ready to stand up to Soviet bullying. Nor, even
more seriously, was FIDE President Max Euwe. Although he had
worked miracles to make Fischer play Spassky, he did not seem
to give the emigré Korchnoi the same priority. Despite his efforts,
Euwe had failed to prevent the USSR and its allies from dominat-
ing world chess. Worse still, Euwe handed over to his Filipino representative Florencio Campomanes—who was inclined to defer to
the Russians—before the fourth game. That was the signal for the
mind games to begin in earnest.

Beginning with game four, Zukhar positioned himself in the
fourth row from the front and directed his menacing glare at the
challenger. Korchnoi immediately asked for him to be moved. The
colonel defended "Professor" Zukhar as "a specialist in neurology
and psychology with an unblemished reputation" who was "studying the general psychological state of the World Champion, including during play, and at the same time the behavior of his opponent." Karpov insisted that he needed Zukhar to help him with his
sleep problems, which tended to become serious when he was
tired. Zukhar may well have been trained in hypnotherapy, which

helps patients to relax, but his behavior toward Korchnoi had less to do with hypnosis than intimidation. Baturinsky cunningly insisted that Zukhar was not an "official" member of the Karpov delegation, and so was under no obligation to sit with his colleagues, well away from the stage. The appeals jury ruled that Zukhar could stay.

Korchnoi was sure that his real function was more sinister. "He stared hard at me," wrote Korchnoi afterwards, "trying to attract my attention. . . He sat without moving for the entire five hours—even a robot would have envied his powers of concentration. But whenever it was Karpov's turn to move he simply froze. You could actually feel the colossal thought-work going on inside this man!"

Korchnoi's response was to fire off a series of protests. He also took to wearing reflecting sunglasses and allowed his entourage to harass Dr. Zukhar. Petra Leeuwerik's eighteen-year-old daughter and her boyfriend sat on either side of him for some games. At one point Petra Leeuwerik presented him with a copy of *The Gulag Archipelago,* about which he complained bitterly. In another game she allegedly tickled and kicked him, whereupon Valery Krylov, Karpov's physical trainer, sat on her lap. The absurdity of these antics distracted journalists from the trial of strength at the board.

In the fifth game, Korchnoi built up a big advantage, but fell into time trouble and missed a forced checkmate on the fifty-fifth move. The endgame was defended stubbornly by Karpov; only after 124 moves did Korchnoi allow himself "the pleasure of stalemating the world champion. Firstly, in this way I did not need to offer him a draw. And secondly, however natural stalemate is in a chess game, to be stalemated is slightly humiliating."

In the eighth game, Karpov varied his gamesmanship. Without warning, he abruptly refused the traditional handshake at the commencement of the game, breaking a prematch agreement. Korchnoi was disconcerted by this shock tactic and lost the game. Enraged, he appealed to the chief arbiter to have Zukhar moved out of his line of vision. Belatedly, Schmid made a stand against the Soviets. For the ninth game, Zukhar was moved to a seat farther away from the stage. Korchnoi's confidence instantly improved and he was unlucky not to win. This provoked a protest from the Karpov camp, which succeeded in having Schmid disqualified from ruling on where delegation members could sit in the auditorium. Korchnoi had to be satisfied with a "gentleman's agreement": Zukhar would sit in the seventh row for the duration of the tenth game.

It was this particular game that witnessed a theoretical duel, in which Karpov unleashed a powerful new weapon in the opening, while Korchnoi rose to the challenge and defended brilliantly. Karpov's second, Alexander Zaitsev, who was impressed by the thoroughness of Korchnoi's preparation, confessed himself awestruck: "We had seen Korchnoi's enormous chess potential with our own eyes." Meanwhile, Korchnoi had invited to the match his own parapsychologist from Israel, Dr. Berginer, whose role was to neutralize Zukhar's malign influence. Berginer sat anonymously in the fifth row for the eleventh game, which Korchnoi won, thereby leveling the score. The Soviet side wasted no time in retaliating: "Breaking the verbal gentleman's agreement, from the next game Zukhar again sat in the 4th row," wrote Korchnoi. Berginer was identified and "smothered" by the numerous Soviet team. "It became clear to me that in this situation Berginer was powerless, and he departed after the 14th game."

The match then took what seemed a decisive turn in favor of Karpov. He won both the thirteenth and fourteenth games, one after the other. The thirteenth had been adjourned in Korchnoi's favor, but in the resumption he got into time trouble, spoiled a difficult endgame, and lost. In the fourteenth, the Karpov team had spotted a variation that Korchnoi had rejected as unsatisfactory in the *Encyclopedia of Chess Openings* and found an improvement for White. Korchnoi mounted a heroic if ultimately unsuccessful defense. The match seemed to be slipping away from him.

Friction between the two camps was exacerbated by various incidents, including a remark that Petra Leeuwerik overheard Dr. Zukhar make to another Russian: "Volodya, do you remember, I read in our files that Korchnoi has chronic gonorrhoea." For the fifteenth game, Karpov began rocking his chair, ignoring requests to desist by Schmid. The most influential of the Soviet journalists, Alexander Roshal, who kept up a steady flow of propaganda, blamed Korchnoi for taking "the liberty of insulting the Champion and members of his delegation" (a reference to Korchnoi's remarks about Baturinsky) and for pretending that Karpov was universally admired for his sporting conduct. Korchnoi attributed Roshal's animus to the fact that his father "was eliminated along with millions of other thinking people in a Stalinist torture chamber. The son does not intend to repeat the mistakes of the father. He won't be forced into becoming an individual."

The next crisis came in the seventeenth game. Korchnoi demanded that Campomanes move Zukhar back to the seventh row. Campomanes protested, but Korchnoi shook his fist: "Move him within ten minutes, or I'll deal with him myself." Although the front six rows were cleared of all spectators, Korchnoi had wasted eleven minutes on his clock. "Is it possible to play a serious, intense game after expending so much nervous energy?" he asked rhetorically. Having held the advantage throughout, he blundered in time trouble and "contrived to fall into a ridiculous mate in a drawn position." Even years later, in his memoirs Karpov could not disguise his glee: "I slapped him with a beautiful checkmate using the two knights. One blocked the king while the other delivered the blow. So many chess players dream of realizing something like this on the board once in their lives, but to do it in a match for the World Championship . . ."

With the score now at 4–1, almost everybody expected Karpov to wrap up the match quickly. Korchnoi was close to losing faith in himself: "I was in a terrible state. I claimed my last two time-outs and together with Frau Leeuwerik I went to Manila, to at least relax a little and come to." While there, he consulted a priest psychologist, Father Bulatao. Then he let off steam at an impromptu press conference. Denouncing "the pact of the Soviets with Campomanes," he threatened to abandon the match unless players and

Fidel Castro (right) and Che Guevara (left) take part in a record-breaking simultaneous exhibition at the Havana Chess Olympiad in 1966, with 380 masters playing 6,840 amateurs in Havana's floodlit Plaza de la Revolución. For the Olympiad, Castro tried to impress the Americans and outdo his Soviet patrons by staging the biggest chess extravaganza of the Cold War.

Chess as a substitute for war. The American grandmaster Reshevsky (left) plays the Soviet world champion Botvinnik in a team match in Moscow between the two superpowers in 1955. The Russians won 25–7.

Karpov (left) versus Korchnoi. The Soviet world champion is challenged by the "traitor" at Baguio in the Philippines in 1978. Korchnoi's wife and son were held hostage, while parapsychologists were used on both sides.

Kasparov (left) defeats Karpov to become world champion in November 1985, after their first match was halted earlier that year. These two contested five championship matches between 1984 and 1990.

"The Match of the Century": one of only 500 postcards printed in Iceland to promote the 1972 match between Fischer and Spassky.

Bobby Fischer plays Boris Spassky in the US–USSR match at the Havana Olympiad, 1966. This game was drawn, but as usual the Americans lost overall. Fischer had by far the best score against the Russians of any Western player, but he had never beaten Spassky before they played for the world championship in 1972.

Mind games: Fischer "hypnotizing" Spassky during their match at Reykjavik in 1972, by the Icelandic cartoonist Halldor Petursson. Politics, psychology, and chess combined to make this contest the one true epic of the Cold War.

Avital Sharansky celebrating her refusenik husband's thirty-sixth birthday in a wooden cage outside the old Parliament building in Stockholm, 1984. Natan Sharansky later said that chess saved his sanity in the gulag.

Garry Kasparov plays Natan Sharansky at the latter's home in Israel, ca.1999. Since Vladimir Putin came to power in Russia, Kasparov has adopted the role played by dissidents such as Sharansky under communism.

spectators were separated by a one-way mirrorglass partition, which meant that the players could not see the audience: "The centaur with the head of Zukhar and the body of Karpov must be split in two, otherwise the match is impossible." Another "gentleman's agreement" was proposed by Colonel Baturinsky: Korchnoi must give up his glass screen and his reflecting sunglasses, while Zukhar would sit with the rest of the Soviet delegation.

This deal seemed to satisfy both players; however, it did not take long before a new *casus belli* emerged. The eighteenth game was drawn, but this time it was Korchnoi who had a surprise for the nineteenth game. According to Raymond Keene, "Ms. Leeuwerik flooded the audience with parapsychologists and gurus . . . One group consisted of girl parapsychology students of Father Jaime Bulatao, the Jesuit priest from Ateneo de Manila University . . . This nubile bunch was busy conjuring up good vibrations for Korchnoi, though it later transpired that none of them could play chess." Yet another group proved far more controversial. Two yogis in flowing saffron robes and turbans appeared in the hall. Having sat down, they adopted the lotus position. The Soviet camp reacted immediately. According to Korchnoi, Dr. Zukhar "covered his face with a handkerchief, and within a short time he left the hall — for good, until the end of the game."

The Soviet camp at first tolerated the yogis, while insisting that they wear normal clothes. However, after Korchnoi narrowly escaped with a draw in the twentieth game — prompting the British master Harry Golombek to comment that now he believed in life after death — the Russians held a meeting with Campomanes. Without the slightest trace of irony, Baturinsky, the KGB commissar, denounced the yogis as "terrorists" and demanded that they be excluded from all contact with the Soviet delegation. The Soviet complaint was upheld by Campomanes and the yogis were not only excluded from the playing hall, but also from the hotel and Korchnoi's official car. Confined to the country villa assigned to him, they continued to train him there in meditative arts. Not all the Korchnoi camp approved of this exotic addition to the team.

Karpov quotes the Swiss lawyer Alban Brodbek, who led Korchnoi's delegation in the Merano match three years later, claiming that the yogis engaged in weird rituals, obliging Korchnoi to spear an orange that symbolized Karpov's head. Keene also felt uncomfortable in their presence, yet a photograph of a cheerful Korchnoi standing on his head shows that they undoubtedly boosted his morale.

Known as "Didi" and "Dada," the yogis' real names were Stephen Dwyer and Victoria Shepherd and they belonged to Ananda Marga, an Indian sect whose guru, Sri Sri Anandamurti, was a prisoner of conscience. He had been kept behind bars for seven years without trial, until his release after a campaign by Amnesty International. It emerged that Dwyer and Shepherd, both Harvard graduates, had been on bail for the previous six months, having been convicted on scanty evidence of the attempted murder of an Indian diplomat, Jyoti Suarap Vaid, the previous February. The Marcos government did indeed regard them as terrorists, accusing the Ananda Marga of being a threat to national security. Whether they had had a fair trial was, however, questionable. According to Keene, their trial papers were "full of inconsistencies and even [accuse] Ananda Marga of being Communist-inspired." The yogis were, of course, anti-communist.

However dubious the provenance of the "Margi," they acted on Korchnoi like a tonic. When he arrived for the twenty-first game, Zukhar was sitting in a car waiting for him. The parapsychologist got out and approached Korchnoi, apparently intending to shake his hand. Korchnoi looked Zukhar in the eye and uttered the Sanskrit mantra that he had been taught by the Margi. By Korchnoi's account, Zukhar stopped, covered his face with his arms, and fled. Zukhar knew that Korchnoi believed in parapsychology, and his apparent acknowledgment of the power wielded by the Margi reinforced that belief.

Even so, the twenty-first game marked a revival of Korchnoi's fortunes. Karpov tried to ambush him with a ferocious sacrificial attack, but Korchnoi defended with what Kasparov called "staggering composure" and had reached a favorable endgame before it was adjourned overnight. Not even the legendary Soviet overnight analysis could save the champion this time, and Korchnoi won a grandmasterly victory. The score was now 4–2 with fifteen draws. The advantage fluctuated to and fro from the twenty-second to the twenty-sixth games with Korchnoi pressing all the time, but in the twenty-seventh he blundered and lost. Karpov now led 5–2 and needed only one more victory to clinch the match.

Tired of his role as the underdog, determined to vindicate not only his own reputation but also his cause, Korchnoi asked himself why he so despised his opponent. It was, he concluded, partly personal — Karpov's hypocrisy, his cunning, and his condescending superiority — but it was mainly political. He attributed great power and influence to Karpov — including the arrest of his son, Igor, for evading the draft — and he denounced the German and Dutch organizers who so admired the champion: "Do they not realize that . . . by inviting this angel of death, they are expressing their silent approval for the policies of the Soviet government with its aggressive aims?"

Before the twenty-eighth game, the chief arbiter Lothar Schmid left, pleading urgent business; in reality, he had had enough of Baguio, having long been deprived of any real authority by Campomanes. He was replaced by the Czech grandmaster Miroslav Filip, whom Korchnoi regarded as a Soviet "lackey." The game itself was hard-pounding again, but by the adjournment Korchnoi had a small advantage. He sealed his move in an envelope several times and then had second thoughts, leaving himself less than two minutes a move for the next fourteen moves on resumption. Nonetheless, Karpov's attempt to exploit Korchnoi's time trouble backfired, and he lost. Even the colonel paid tribute: "It was Korchnoi's best game of the match."

Both men were suffering from fatigue. Karpov said he felt "like a zombie," and he quoted Zukhar's response to his complaints of insomnia: "Forgive me, but it's beyond my power to be of any use to you. Your nervous system isn't yielding to mine, so if you want

I can teach you my methods. But I can't put you to sleep." The pretentious vacuity of this advice, incidentally, lends credence to the view that Zukhar was, if not genuinely sinister, at any rate a quack. Yet his absence from Korchnoi's vicinity had undoubtedly enabled the challenger to raise his game.

The score was now 5–3. After a week's delay, the match resumed—and Karpov lost another long ending: 5–4. By now he was visibly rattled. The mind games began again. Korchnoi's autobiography, *Chess Is My Life,* was suddenly withdrawn from sale under a law prohibiting anti-Soviet literature in the Philippines, but Korchnoi did not care. Game thirty was drawn, but in the thirty-first Korchnoi again built up a small advantage in what proved to be a fiendishly difficult rook ending. In the denouement, Korchnoi's mating threat outweighed Karpov's passed pawns on the verge of queening. Having played on for a dozen moves in a hopeless position, the world champion finally capitulated.

Karpov's resignation echoed around the world. The defector's fight back from 4–1 and then 5–2 to tie the score at 5–5 secretly thrilled the millions following the match, not least in the communist world. How had Karpov managed to throw away his huge advantage? Korchnoi had no doubt: "The only concession to which the Soviet side agreed—to remove their psychologist out of my field of vision—cost the champion dearly." But Kasparov denies that Zukhar's absence had anything to do with Korchnoi's comeback: "He fought like a lion! Six years later his example inspired me in the even more hopeless situation which arose after the 27th game of my first match against Karpov in 1984–85 [when Kasparov trailed 5–0]." Although Karpov cannot explain his defeats, he remembers how he felt on the eve of the thirty-second game, on which everything would depend: "I was standing on the precipice, but unlike everyone else, I felt Korchnoi's time had passed and mine would soon come again." At Sevastianov's suggestion, Karpov took a time-out and went to Manila to support the USSR against Yugoslavia at basketball. Meanwhile, FIDE President Max Euwe—who had returned from Holland to witness the end of the match—departed. This was the signal for the colonel to resume psychological warfare. Euwe had told Korchnoi's seconds that if the Soviets attacked the yogis, the match would be halted. But his departure left Campomanes in charge again, and the Filipino shared the Soviet hostility to the Ananda Marga. First, Campomanes denounced the "criminals" Dada and Didi for reappearing at Korchnoi's hotel suite and using the official car. Then the Soviet camp issued an ultimatum, demanding that the "criminal terrorists" cease contact with Korchnoi: "The match organizer Mr. F. Campomanes has several times officially demanded the termination of this connection and in his memorandum of September 13 [after the twenty-first game] he warned about the possibility of terminating the match in the aim of ensuring individual and public security." Rumors spread that Campomanes and the Soviet team were considering a premature end to the match, leaving Karpov still champion. This was no idle threat. Six years later, in a comparable situation, Campomanes would indeed terminate the first Karpov–Kasparov match. The mind games of Baguio paved the way for the debacle of Moscow.

Ray Keene, by now head of Korchnoi's delegation, felt he had no choice but to agree to the removal of the yogis from Korchnoi's private villa outside Baguio. This infuriated Korchnoi and led ultimately to a breakdown of relations with Keene, but worse was to come. When Korchnoi arrived for the thirty-second game, he found the hall full of police, evidently at Campomanes's behest. The atmosphere was no longer that of a sporting contest—it felt like a military confrontation. On the previous day Korchnoi had exchanged glances with his former friends in the Soviet camp—Tal, Yuri Balashov, Yevgeny Vasyukov—and noticed the "malicious glee on their faces." Once the game had begun, he found out why. There, in the fourth row, sat Dr. Zukhar. Keene demanded an explanation from Baturinsky. "It was a gentleman's agreement, binding only for gentlemen," said the colonel.

The game itself was an anticlimax. Playing Black, Korchnoi would have been more than satisfied with a draw. He tried to surprise Karpov in the opening, but the champion reacted "calmly, easily, without emotion." Korchnoi felt uneasy and suspected his seconds of treachery but, as Kasparov points out, it was hardly surprising that Karpov was familiar with the position. However, the inauspicious circumstances—especially the necessity of playing under Zukhar's malevolent gaze—combined with Korchnoi's unjustified sense of betrayal to spoil his concentration. He retreated into a siege mentality, and it was only Karpov's caution that saved Korchnoi's bunker from being shattered early in the opening. Keene observed that Korchnoi "was unrecognizable as the lion who had roared in the four previous games." Many years later, this decisive thirty-second game was subjected to a searching analysis by Kasparov, who concluded that Korchnoi had lost his way on the twenty-seventh move; by playing safe, rather than activating his pieces for a counterattack, Korchnoi threw away his last chance of holding Karpov to a draw. The Black position deteriorated further due to time trouble, and by the time the game was adjourned it was hopeless.

At nine the next morning, Keene phoned Filip, the arbiter, to resign the game on Korchnoi's behalf. However, the match was not quite over. At one o'clock, Korchnoi sent a letter to Filip that read as follows:

> I shall not resume the 32nd game. But I am not going to sign the score sheet [the traditional method of confirming resignation] because the game was played under absolutely illegal conditions. I do not consider this game valid. The match is not finished. I reserve the right to complain to Fidé about the intolerable behavior of the Soviets, the hostility of the organizers, and a lack of activity on the part of the arbiters.

Korchnoi proceeded to boycott the closing ceremony, thereby risking losing his portion of the $585,750 prize fund. When he nonetheless received his check, Campomanes had inscribed it: "Subject to payment only if Korchnoi acknowledges the match is finished." He never did.

And so the war of Zukhar's stare ended. It had lasted more than three months, from July to October. Losing by only the narrowest of margins (6–5 with twenty-one draws), Korchnoi had done far better than anybody else expected. In Kasparov's view, "Korchnoi even played the more interesting chess." He lost because his blunders were bigger and more frequent: "Karpov played, perhaps, not so colorfully, but he nevertheless made fewer mistakes." Karpov had thereby fulfilled the solemn injunction that he had received from the Soviet leader Leonid Brezhnev himself: "You've seized the crown, now hang on to it!" Six years after the humiliation of losing the world championship to an American, Anatoly Karpov had restored Soviet dominion over chess by defeating an even more dangerous enemy. Baguio had erased the memory of Reykjavik.

The Soviet chess professionals did not like to think about what would have happened to them if Karpov had lost. A decade later, thanks to the *glasnost* of the Gorbachev era, the former world champion Mikhail Tal could reveal on television that he had agreed to be Karpov's second at Baguio solely for reasons of self-preservation: "We could not imagine the consequences if an anti-Soviet player, not a Soviet, had become world champion. It is possible that chess would then have been declared a pseudoscience." This was said with a grin, but it was only a slight exaggeration. Two years later, at the Novi Sad Olympiad, Tal had a conversation with Korchnoi in which he apologized for his conduct: "There, in Baguio, we were all afraid for you—if you had won the match, you could have been physically eliminated. Everything had been prepared for this." Roshal, a more slavish adherent of the party line, reproached Tal for "joking" with Korchnoi and feeding his "persecution mania, which periodically turns into megalomania and back again." However, he told an anecdote of his own that throws more light on the mood in the Karpov camp:

> Besides, why should we have been afraid for Korchnoi? Rather we should have been afraid for ourselves! When the score became 5–5, I went down with high blood pressure, and Zukhar,

Balashov, and Zaitsev came to my room. The psychologist said: "I am now going to count to seventeen—when you wake up, all will be well." He counted so tediously and unpleasantly that I did indeed become drowsy. Then I asked: "Has Zukhar gone?" The trainers said: "He's gone. But don't worry—we have something prepared." And I replied to them: "With your preparations we'll most likely end up felling trees." I remember how similar black jokes were also cracked by the experienced Baturinsky. But, fortunately, Tolya [Karpov] won.

Three years after Baguio, Korchnoi, and Karpov faced each other for a rematch, held this time in the Italian resort of Merano. Korchnoi's achievement in fighting his way through a third successive cycle of candidates' matches to challenge Karpov again at the age of fifty was unprecedented in the history of the world championship. To do so, he had overcome formidable resistance from his Soviet contemporaries, represented by his old rival Petrosian and an on-form Polugayevsky, defeating the latter only after two extra tiebreaking games. Even more impressive was Korchnoi's victory over Robert Hübner, an eminent papyrologist and the most talented West German grandmaster since the war. Like Karpov, Hübner was twenty years younger than Korchnoi and playing better than ever before. He resigned the match after blundering a rook.

The stakes at Merano were hardly less than at Baguio. The Soviet media saturated the public with pro-Karpov propaganda, while preparations for the match were more elaborate than ever. An advance party (including the champion) arrived weeks in advance to check such things as radiation levels; food, medical, and other supplies required ten huge container lorries; and by the end, Karpov's entourage had swelled to seventy people. This time Dr. Zukhar was absent, replaced by Kabanov, another psychologist, who was critical of his predecessor and did not imitate his tactics. Yet once again Korchnoi complained of "devilry." He accused the Soviet delegation—again led by Colonel Baturinsky—of bringing with them the latest KGB equipment, blaming them for a sudden, unexplained rise in his blood pressure and watering, painful eyes:

"There is no doubt that Karpov's people were sitting in the front row and using instruments to study my condition—pulse and so on. In addition, I was irradiated—either in the auditorium, or at the country house where I was staying."

Whatever the truth of these allegations, Korchnoi began the match disastrously: he lost three of the first four games, almost without a struggle. Only in the sixth game did Korchnoi hit back, winning a fine attacking game to make the score 3–1. This setback prompted the USSR Sports Committee to convene an emergency team of grandmasters at the Olympic training base at Novogorsk to study openings day and night to provide extra support for Karpov. In the event, there was to be no comeback for Korchnoi: he won only one more game. Kasparov, then eighteen and still living in Baku, describes the wave of panic that emanated from Moscow after Korchnoi routed Karpov in the thirteenth game, even though the score was still 4–2 to Karpov. He was phoned by Nikolai Krogius, the psychologist who was by now running the chess section of the Sports Committee, and ordered to come up with new ideas for Karpov: "I was told that it was my patriotic duty: the 'traitor' had to be smashed at any price. Not having any desire to work for Karpov, I replied that I didn't see any particular need for such assistance: as it was, Korchnoi was bound to lose. But they insistently suggested that I should 'think again.'" Kasparov was protected by his teacher, Botvinnik. "As I later found out, Karpov phoned Krogius and asked whether Kasparov had sent anything from Baku: he wanted to know what his potential rival thought."

That thirteenth game proved to be Korchnoi's last stand. Karpov struck back in the very next game, this time crushing his opponent's trademark Open Variation of the Ruy Lopez, or Spanish Opening. This too was a bloody battle, but it marked Karpov's ascendancy in the theoretical as well as the practical duel. It left Karpov needing only one more win to retain his title. In the next game Korchnoi came close to victory once more, but he no longer had the energy to deliver the coup de grâce. Korchnoi's constant time trouble was a fatal handicap against the machinelike precision of his opponent. In the eighteenth game, Karpov wrapped it up with an endgame that was decided long before the adjournment. After sleeping on the hopeless position, Korchnoi finally drew a line under the decade-long duel with the following note to the arbiters: "I hereby give notice that I am resigning without resumption of play in the eighteenth game and the whole match, and I congratulate Karpov and the entire Soviet delegation for their magnificent electronic technology." These words read ironically today. As we have seen, the 1980s was the decade when it dawned on just about everybody that Soviet electronic technology had fallen hopelessly behind that of the West, with fatal consequences for the communist system. Even for the KGB, the game was up.

The consensus about Merano was that the score—6–2 with ten draws—fairly reflected the respective strengths of the two rivals. Karpov wrote a fulsome telegram to Brezhnev and was rewarded with the Order of Lenin. Beaten but not broken, Korchnoi declared that he would never play a match against Karpov again—not a difficult promise to keep, since he knew that he was no longer equal to the task of overcoming the new and even more talented generation just emerging. The siege warfare of the Karpov–Korchnoi matches and the mind games that accompanied them would have left most veterans happy to retire. Not Korchnoi. Now in his late seventies, he is still playing chess with zest and at the highest level, almost the only septuagenarian to have done so.

Korchnoi, one of the greatest products of the Soviet chess machine, could only achieve his full potential once he had utterly rejected it. Although he lost to Karpov in the end, his life encapsulates the story of chess and the Cold War. But by challenging the Soviet system and forcing it to go to extraordinary lengths to preserve its hegemony over chess, Korchnoi had actually revealed hitherto unsuspected weaknesses. It was left to a younger man, however, to test the system to destruction.

15

SOVIET ENDGAME:
KASPAROV VERSUS KARPOV

I N *NINETEEN EIGHTY-FOUR,* George Orwell created an enduring image of a perfected totalitarianism: "The German Nazis and the Russian Communists came very close to us in their methods, but they never had the courage to recognize their own motives . . . The object of persecution is persecution. The object of torture is torture. The object of power is power . . . If you want a picture of the future, imagine a boot stamping on a human face—forever." By the time the year 1984 arrived, the Soviet Union had endured for so long that few could imagine a world without it. Outwardly, at least, the system was intact. There seemed no reason why it should not last forever. The Cold War, too, seemed perpetual. The dualism of East and West, communist and capitalist, Warsaw Pact and NATO would apparently endure, because the Soviet system required an enemy.

In the microcosm of dystopia that was chess, Soviet hegemony also seemed to have been restored. Fischer, the only man to temporarily defeat the Soviet system, had long since disappeared into self-imposed and increasingly paranoid seclusion. Korchnoi, though still defiant, no longer had the strength. "Not wishing to endure again that which happened to me in Merano," he wrote, "from being a professional I have gradually readjusted to becoming an amateur." In reality, the Soviet Union was much weaker than it seemed. So was its stranglehold over chess. Both in politics and in chess, the system was vulnerable to internal attack. Fischer and Korchnoi had attacked it from outside. What was needed was a man with the courage to undermine it from within. Here chess anticipated politics. It was in the Orwellian year of 1984 that Garry Kasparov, the last Soviet and the first post-Soviet world champion, first made his mark by challenging the personification of the Soviet school of chess, Anatoly Karpov, in a match that began in September. Six months later, on March 10, 1985—three weeks after this marathon contest had been sensationally interrupted—a leader emerged who would preside over the dismantling of the Soviet political system. It was Mikhail Gorbachev, the last head of the Communist Party and Soviet head of state. Seven years and four more Karpov–Kasparov matches later, the Soviet Union was history.

Garry Kasparov was the first Soviet world champion who simply refused to obey the officials of the USSR Chess Federation and the Sports Committee—initially by appealing over their heads to his allies in the Kremlin, but later by openly defying the regime itself. Nurtured to be a Hero of the Soviet Union, he instead became one of its gravediggers. After the Cold War symbolism of the Fischer–Spassky match in 1972, when the American genius broke the Soviet monopoly, no chess duel has had the political resonance of the Karpov–Kasparov matches. The ascendancy of the brash, open-minded, pro-Western Kasparov anticipated the collapse of communism.

He was born Garik Kimovich Weinstein in 1963 in Baku, Azerbaijan. His Armenian-Jewish background made it more likely that the boy would grow up to be a champion not only of chess but of dissidents, too. Indeed, he has hovered between insider and outsider throughout his career. While he grew up in Baku, Kasparov later wrote, his parents' circle "largely consisted of Jewish professors and intellectuals who constantly questioned the official view, not only the blatant propaganda of the Soviet government." The young Garry (or Harry) Weinstein (as he then was) listened to Radio Liberty and Voice of America, then argued about politics with his Communist grandfather. "Sometimes we quarreled, but they were great discussions. I felt that some things he said were wrong." He was seven when his father died, and at twelve he adopted a Russified version of the name of his Armenian mother, Klara Kasparyan, in lieu of his Jewish father's. His chess teacher, Mikhail Botvinnik, observed "that it wouldn't hurt my chances of success in the USSR not to be named Weinstein." But the name change did not shield Kasparov from anti-Semitism, and during the dissolution of the Soviet empire Jews were not the only nationality to suffer from pogroms. When Azerbaijan turned on its Armenian minority in the Baku riots of 1990, Kasparov found that his status as a local hero did not save his family from being targeted by mobs.

Despite his oppositional background, Kasparov began life as a privileged product of the Soviet system. His talent was recognized early; he won the USSR junior (under-eighteen) championship at the age of twelve without losing a single game, despite being by far the youngest participant. He was given at first one, then a second trainer, as well as a stipend, and was enrolled in Botvinnik's chess school, conducted largely as a correspondence course. Soon after his father died, his mother gave up her career as an engineer to dedicate her life to raising her son as the genius she believed him to be. She was even paid a salary as a "chess specialist" by the Azerbaijani Sports Committee, prompting an envious Karpov to comment bitterly in his memoirs: "In the West such a thing wouldn't even have occurred to anyone. If a young talent is insufficiently provided for, then those responsible try to raise his stipend, but what do parents have to do with it? With us and our Soviet system, these wonders are all in the normal course of things." In fact,

Garry's mother, Klara, has been his ubiquitous companion throughout his chess career. Even more than Korchnoi, Spassky, and Fischer, Kasparov is his mother's son.

More seriously, Kasparov joined the Communist Party at eighteen and even after he became world champion he served on the Azerbaijan Komsomol Central Committee. Whether he ever believed in communism must be doubted, but he has been accused of sacrificing his principles to his career. As we have seen, however, even Korchnoi himself had joined the party, and Kasparov would not have enjoyed the opportunity to play abroad while still so young if he had not made this compromise. Aged thirteen, he was sent to France to play in the 1976 world junior championship. Once the teenage Garry began to travel to tournaments in the West, he soon noticed the contrast between the culture of life, liberty, and the pursuit of happiness abroad and the culture of death, tyranny, and squalid corruption at home. "It was a shocking revelation," he told the *Sunday Times* in 2005. "By [the age of] 16, I had no illusions."

Nevertheless, Kasparov knew that his career depended on powerful protectors in the Kremlin. Kasparov was initially supported by the Communist Party leader in Azerbaijan, Gaidar Aliyev. Having been appointed as a regional satrap by Brezhnev in 1969, Aliyev became a Soviet deputy prime minister and the first Muslim member of the Politburo in 1982. He combined the worst aspects of Islamic and communist tyranny. A former KGB torturer, Aliyev crushed everybody who got in his way, both during the Soviet Union and later, when he returned to power in 1993, just two years after the Azeris gained their independence. Aliyev ruled Azerbaijan as a corrupt and bloodthirsty dictator for a further decade until his health collapsed in 2003, when he reluctantly resigned, leaving his son as his successor.

This, then, was the young Kasparov's brutish patron. Despite Aliyev's patronage, the young Kasparov suffered many frustrations in his rise to the summit. Just how essential such support still was became clear in 1983, when the nineteen-year-old Kasparov faced the indefatigable Korchnoi, more than thirty years his senior, in the semifinal of the world championship. The match was due to be played at Pasadena, California, which had offered the remarkable prize fund of $50,000 to host it.

The combination of location and players gave the Pasadena match political significance in the newly reignited Cold War. The American boycott of the 1980 Olympic Games in Moscow, in protest against the Soviet invasion of Afghanistan, still rankled in the Kremlin. The Soviets would later revenge themselves by boycotting the Los Angeles Olympics in 1984. More recently, President Reagan had denounced the Soviet Union in a famous speech to the National Association of Evangelicals on March 8, 1983. Reagan warned against the temptation "to label both sides equally at fault, to ignore the facts of history and the aggressive impulses of an evil empire." That phrase, "evil empire," had been removed from drafts of the speech by State Department officials several times, but the president was determined to use the phrase in order to nail the moral relativism that, as he saw it, bedeviled Western attitudes in the Cold War. Sharansky later recalled the electric impact of these two little words on inmates of the Gulag. "Immediately, there was moral clarity."

Reagan's deliberate polarization of the conflict may have encouraged dissidents, but in the short term it hardened the Soviet attitude against cultural contacts with the United States. The upshot was that the Soviets refused to play the match in Pasadena, claiming that Kasparov's security could not be guaranteed. So the world chess federation ruled that it should go ahead without Kasparov—which meant that for the first time in history a Soviet player was forfeited by FIDE, the organization the USSR had dominated. The other Soviet semifinalist, former world champion Smyslov, was also forfeited in his match against the Hungarian Zoltan Ribili. Although Korchnoi's wife and son were finally allowed to join him in exile, the Soviet boycott against him continued.

This fait accompli left Kasparov furious; he was still the official representative of the Soviet state, but he badly wanted to play the match. Summoned before Boris Stukhalin, the Central Committee member responsible for propaganda and sport, Kasparov was told: "You're still young and can afford to wait three years." He attributed Moscow's unprecedented decision to the KGB, whose former chief Yuri Andropov was now the party boss. Behind them Kasparov thought he detected the influence of Karpov's patrons in the Kremlin, who were throwing obstacles in his path to the summit. By this time the Soviet chess establishment already knew about and disapproved of Kasparov's independent cast of mind. Introducing *The Test of Time*, Kasparov's first collection of games, Alexander Chikvaidze, the chairman of the Soviet Chess Federation, wrote: "At times I advised him to be more diplomatic and more placid in his opinions, but can one halt a battering ram which has swung to the limits of its amplitude?" Although he had yet to play Kasparov, Karpov already felt besieged.

The more immediate threat, however, came from Karpov's old enemy, Korchnoi. If the rift between FIDE and the USSR continued, Karpov might forfeit his title, leaving the émigré dissident Korchnoi as world champion by default. The thought of Karpov suffering the same fate as Bobby Fischer was unthinkable—especially to Karpov himself. Kasparov, meanwhile, had knocked on the doors of the Kremlin, demanding a change of policy. Aliyev, then chairman of the council of ministers, promised to back him and, according to Kasparov, even Andropov himself—then almost on his deathbed—let it be known that "chess must be played nevertheless." Meanwhile Kasparov also met Korchnoi and the two signed a joint statement calling for their match to be played. To collaborate with a man still regarded as a renegade and a traitor in order to overturn official policy showed Kasparov's early independence of spirit.

Which factor precipitated the change of policy is disputed, but to draw a line under the affair the Soviet Sports Committee was obliged to pay a fine to FIDE and to end the boycott of Korchnoi. This extraordinary Soviet climbdown made it possible for the two semifinal matches to be rescheduled in a different venue: London, a less sensitive location than Pasadena. Yet it was still the capital of Margaret Thatcher, the British prime minister who had recently been dubbed "the Iron Lady" by the Soviet media. She had also proved her martial credentials just two years earlier by winning the Falklands War and urging her NATO allies not to back down in the face of a new Soviet provocation: the stationing of medium-range nuclear missiles targeted on Western Europe.

The match began badly for Kasparov, who lost the first game. This, however, proved to be not only the first but also the last game he ever lost to Korchnoi. After a couple of draws, Kasparov struck back and eventually won 4–1 with six draws. So the old challenger passed on the baton to the new, although at the time neither man realized that Kasparov would also inherit Korchnoi's role as a dissident.

This match also marked the beginning of the feud between Kasparov and Karpov. The world champion turned up in London at the invitation of the organizers, but by his own account he was immediately told by a Soviet diplomat that his presence was undesirable. According to Karpov, he promised that he would not attend the match, staying on only to attend to his own business, but was told: "No. It is suggested that you leave London and the sooner the better." Karpov obeyed, feeling angry and humiliated, particularly when he had previously interceded with Campomanes on Kasparov's behalf. It seems clear that Kasparov did not want him at the match, and equally clear that Karpov nursed a justified grievance thereafter.

The new challenger was visibly gaining in strength with each new test. A few months later former world champion Smyslov—at sixty-three the oldest player ever to qualify for the candidates' final—could not win a single game against Kasparov, who was only twenty. Despite his youth, Kasparov's rating (2715) had already overtaken Karpov's (2705). Karpov, however, was still the favorite. In his decade as world champion, Karpov had won or shared first prize in all but two major tournaments in which he took part, some twenty-five victories. Even though no previous champion had done as well, or been as eager to prove himself, Karpov was haunted by an awareness that he had inherited his title from Fischer by default. He was still seen by many, especially in the West, as a pretender to the throne. In the absence of Fischer, a world championship match against the rising star of the younger generation was the best possible way for Karpov to reinforce his legitimacy. He was supremely confident, better prepared than ever before, and at the top of his form. Moreover, he had the *nomenklatura* behind him.

The first world championship match between Karpov and Kasparov began on September 19, 1984, in the traditional venue, Moscow's Hall of Columns, amid feverish excitement and publicity. Some 500 journalists from twenty-seven countries were present for the first game; the audience overflowed on to the streets. The match began disastrously for Kasparov, whose unbridled aggression with the White pieces and counterattacks with Black made no impression on Karpov. After a couple of draws, Karpov (playing White) won an easy victory in the third game. Two more draws, and then Karpov won the sixth and seventh games—the first time in his career that Kasparov had lost twice on the trot. Another draw, and Karpov won again. After two weeks, Karpov already led 4–0 with five draws. The match appeared to be almost over. Nothing so one-sided had been seen at this level since Fischer's 6–0 defeats of Taimanov and Larsen en route to his match against Spassky. That superhuman precedent was, indeed, Karpov's aim: to prove once and for all that he was a true champion by repeating Fischer's feat, only at the world championship level.

Having established a colossal lead by exploiting the experience he had gained over the three Korchnoi matches, Karpov decided to play safe. The next sixteen games were drawn, many of them without a fight. By this time, most of the press had gone home, and the organizers were regretting the open-ended format. On November 24, in the twenty-seventh game, the champion finally struck again. It was a classic Karpov win; Kasparov seemed to make no mistakes, yet he was imperceptibly outplayed in what had seemed to be a drawn endgame. The score was now 5–0 and Karpov was on the verge of a third successful defense of his title—a victory that would have made him one of the greatest champions of them all. He only had to win once more.

But it was not to be. Karpov later offered a lame excuse for his failure to clinch the match at this point: the role of the Azerbaijani parapsychologist Tofik Dadashev, who claimed to have helped Kasparov after he went 4–0 down but later turned against him. Karpov says he only became aware of Dadashev's "interference" years later, so this factor may be safely dismissed. However, Karpov was probably right when he blamed his own "fantastic unluckiness and inexplicably sudden blindness" for his failure to win the thirty-first game. When Kasparov had escaped from the very jaws of defeat, his elation enabled him to score his first win in the very next game, the thirty-second, and this gained him the respite he needed to begin the fight back. There then began a second marathon sequence of fourteen draws. By now, Karpov's lack of stamina, which had led to a sudden collapse toward the end of two of the Korchnoi matches, began to tell against him. "If at this time I had gone over to a sharp game," Karpov recalled, "I could have lost a game, maybe two, but without a doubt I could have won a sixth, and with it the match. I understood this, too, but I can't explain why I rejected any thoughts of such playing in the second half of the match."

The answer is not parapsychology, but character. Elsewhere Karpov writes: "Let us say that a game may be conducted in two ways: one of them is a beautiful tactical blow that gives rise to variations that don't yield to precise calculations; the other is clear positional pressure that leads to an endgame with microscopic chances of victory . . . I would choose [the latter] without thinking twice." He was temperamentally incapable of delivering a knockout.

The war of attrition suited Kasparov, who was gaining experience all the time and began to enjoy the adrenaline-inducing feeling of living on a precipice for months on end. More remarkably, however, he forced himself to imitate his opponent's pythonlike style. It was this flexibility that in the end gave him the upper hand. Fifty days passed without a single decisive game, and both the Soviet and the FIDE authorities were getting desperate. New Year 1985 came and went, yet still the deadlock continued. In the fortieth game, Kasparov almost won again, but the forty-first was one of the greatest missed opportunities of Karpov's career when, having played a brilliant combination, he then lost his nerve and missed a forced win. The game petered out into yet another draw.

Behind the scenes, FIDE president Florencio Campomanes was now trying to broker an end to a match that had become an embarrassment. The match was moved from the Hall of Columns to a less prestigious venue, the Hotel Sport. Kasparov was still 5–1 down, with every game the equivalent of "match point" in tennis, but Karpov's doctors were telling him that his health would not stand any more; he looked like a ghost. Finally, after five months, in the freezing February of 1985, Kasparov achieved the breakthrough for which he had waited so patiently. First, he won the forty-seventh game, his first victory with Black. Then, in the forty-eighth, he beat Karpov again. It was a massacre that left the champion visibly demoralized. Karpov had not won a game for more than two months, while Kasparov had come back from the dead. At the age of twenty-one, he had already made history. Even years later, after scaling unprecedented heights, he would continue to describe this comeback as "my greatest achievement." Although Karpov still led by 5–3, the odds now favored Kasparov. This forty-eighth game was decisive, not only for the two rivals, but for the future of chess.

What happened next was so extraordinary that, twenty-two years later, even the facts remain controversial. After the forty-eighth game, by agreement with the Soviet officials, Campomanes halted play yet again. Only one game had been played in two weeks. The match had now continued for 159 days, only fifty-eight of which had seen any chess. After six days of frenzied negotiations, on February 15 Campomanes summoned a press conference, attended by Kasparov and about 300 journalists, at which he announced that "the match is ended without decision." A new match would begin in September with the score o–o. The FIDE president insisted that he had both players' consent, having spoken to Karpov only twenty-five minutes before, but he also admitted that both wanted to continue. The match was, he declared, becoming a test of physical endurance, so he had decided to end it in the interests of chess as a sport. Richard Owen, the *Times* Moscow correspondent, pointed out that "Mr. Kasparov doesn't look like a man who is psychologically or physically shattered." A few minutes later, Karpov walked into the hall and ascended the stage. Cozily seated next to his old friend Campomanes (who addressed him as "Anatoly") and the Soviet Foreign Ministry representative, the world champion insisted that he was quite happy to resume the match. The Soviet official interjected: "But the decision is taken." Campomanes then invited Kasparov ("Garry") to "come and say your piece." As the challenger moved towards the podium, Campomanes could be heard to say to Karpov and the official: "I told them exactly what you told me to tell them." Karpov replied: "We . . . we, but I don't accept this."

Then Kasparov grabbed the microphone. Addressing Campomanes formally as "Mr. President," he was evidently boiling with rage. Why, if both players were ready to continue, was the match being ended prematurely and inconclusively? Fearing a scene, Campomanes now tried to end the public proceedings. He replied that he had been unable to have a conversation with both players together. "Now I want to talk with both of you," he said. "Let's have ten minutes aside." Both Karpov and Campomanes stood up, as if to leave, but Kasparov was having none of it. Holding up his hand to stop them leaving, he demanded the floor. "The President's profession is to speak. My trade is to play chess. That is why I am not going to compete with him on the podium." Then, "speaking very quickly and angrily," Kasparov continued:

I want to say what I think. I don't intend to demand a continuation because I'm convinced I shall win very easily because the champion feels unwell. He's here, he can proceed, we can see it. But for the first time in five months I have certain chances, let's say about 25% or 30%, and now they are trying to deprive me of those chances by the numerous delays . . . The match should continue . . . without time-outs, without intervals, but it is being prolonged. With each delay his chances are growing while mine are diminishing.

The meeting then adjourned for an hour. Campomanes emerged alone to announce that the match was over. A subtle semantic distinction was apparent in his reference to the two contestants: "The World Champion accepts the decision of the President and the Challenger abides by the decision of the President." This was the result that the Kremlin wanted. Kasparov, as his ominously defiant remarks at the press conference in the Hotel Sport indicated, was out for revenge. He set out, not merely to crush Karpov, but to break open a closed world that he had decided was irredeemably corrupt. He had enjoyed a five-month master class at the champion's expense—"I gave him forty-eight free chess lessons," Karpov said ruefully. Even more important, Kasparov had learned the hard way how to play the Soviet system.

By the time the return match took place in September 1985, the new men in the Kremlin had concluded that the game was up. Neither the West nor the dissidents could be defeated. The Soviet system must adapt or die. The man chosen to succeed the geriatric triumvirate of Brezhnev, Andropov, and Chernyenko in March 1985 was Mikhail Gorbachev. A protégé of the KGB chief Andropov, he was a good communist who had grown up in the shadow of Stalin and Khrushchev, and loyally supported every twist and turn of Soviet policy throughout what later became known as the "years of stagnation." He had been a member of the Politburo when (according to the Italian government's exhaustive inquiry) it approved the attempt on the life of Pope John Paul II by a Turkish assassin working for Bulgarian intelligence. He participated in many other such decisions before becoming party leader. However, Gorbachev was also a pragmatist, and his slogans of *perestroika* ("reconstruction") and *glasnost* ("openness") legitimized a spontaneous wave of democratization which, once started, gained momentum until it became unstoppable.

Kasparov quickly established good relations with the new people around Gorbachev. One of these was the general secretary's chief adviser and ideologist, Alexander Yakovlev, who was now the Politburo member in charge of propaganda — the portfolio that included chess. Yakovlev, who had loyally supported the party line during the Brezhnev era, now intervened on Kasparov's behalf to insist that the rematch should go ahead as promised, against the wishes of the Soviet Chess Federation. The changing of the guard in the Kremlin was symbolized at the second Karpov–Kasparov match by the appearance at the opening ceremony, again in Moscow's Hall of Columns, of the new foreign minister, Eduard Shevardnadze. He made a point of greeting Kasparov warmly, while ignoring Karpov.

This time the duration of the match was limited to twenty-four games; the winner would no longer be the first to win six games, draws not counting. This favored Karpov, who tended to run out of steam sooner than his opponents. However, Karpov began this match at a psychological disadvantage, having failed to clinch the first one despite being 5–0 ahead. Expert opinion now made Kasparov the favorite. The match began with a sensation: Kasparov won the first game. This time Karpov could not blame his loss on fatigue or any other excuse; he had been beaten fair and square. But Karpov had not been champion for ten years for nothing. His self-confidence remained intact and he was still strong enough to stifle Kasparov's initial euphoria. Raymond Keene, the British grandmaster, rightly described Karpov as "essentially repressive" and Kasparov as "basically revolutionary" on, as well as off, the chessboard. After a couple of draws, Karpov struck back, winning the fourth and fifth games to take the lead. A run of five draws followed, in which Kasparov probed for weaknesses. As he later recalled, it was only after he had played Karpov more than sixty times—forty-eight in the first match, fifteen in the second—that he figured out not only how to defend himself, but also how to beat Karpov in the aggressive style that came naturally to him. Just as Bobby Fischer, when only in his teens, had devoured the accumulated knowledge of the Soviet school in order to overthrow its hegemony, so, when he was just in his early twenties, Kasparov's formidably quick and capacious intellect was flexible enough to master the technique that had made Karpov almost unbeatable. Having equalized the score in the eleventh game, Kasparov regained the lead in a brilliant sixteenth game. By now he had got into his stride, making dazzling sacrifices and daring moves to create the most thrilling chess since Fischer–Spassky. When Kasparov won yet again in the nineteenth game, to take a 4–2 lead with only five games left, it looked as if the match was over.

Karpov, though, was not beaten yet. After two more draws, he summoned all his strength to win the twenty-second game: 4–3. Try as he might, Kasparov could not win the twenty-third. So everything hung on the last game. If Karpov—who had the advantage of the White pieces—could win, the match would be drawn and he would retain his title. Kasparov only had to draw the game to win the match. To play for a draw under such tense circumstances would, however, have been out of character for Kasparov. He came out, all guns blazing, with the Sicilian Defense, and Karpov responded with an aggressive pawn thrust, preparing a direct assault on the Black king. In a sharp skirmish, Kasparov's counterattack turned the tables. In desperate time trouble, Karpov passed up a last chance to draw—which would have been tantamount to renouncing his title—and went down to defeat: 5–3, with sixteen draws. Kasparov had become the thirteenth world champion at the age of twenty-two—the youngest in history, beating Mikhail Tal's record by a year. Only Paul Morphy, who lived before the official title was created, was even younger when he beat Adolf Anderssen in 1858. But Kasparov's real achievement was not just to have eclipsed his predecessors; it was to have taken on the Soviet chess establishment and won. Although not yet a dissident, Kasparov had aligned himself with the critics and radicals. Even in the labor camps and prisons, according to Natan Sharansky, the match had been eagerly followed and news of Kasparov's victory was greeted with cheers as a blow for freedom.

However, Karpov had put up much stiffer resistance to Kasparov than Spassky against Fischer eighteen years earlier—and, unlike Spassky, he had been promised a return match by Campomanes. "Karpov is a whole epoch of chess," said Kasparov—but it took another five years for Karpov to accept that his epoch was over. After seventy-two games in two matches, the score between them was tied: 8–8, with fifty-six draws. The return match was due to start as soon as February 1986 and opened up the possibility that Kasparov's reign might last less than six months. The new world champion felt that he should be given a year's grace and denounced the FIDE diktat at a press conference in Amsterdam on December 23, 1985. A week later, in an interview for Associated Press, Campomanes again demonstrated his partisanship for Karpov by threatening to strip Kasparov of his title unless he agreed to play by January 7. Since no venue had yet been agreed, Campomanes was actually flouting his own rules—and by imagining that he could bully Kasparov, the FIDE president had mistaken his man. Kasparov and Karpov both wanted to postpone the match until the summer, so they issued a joint statement to that effect on January 22, 1986. Crucially, the statement was endorsed by the president of the USSR Federation, so Campomanes had no choice but to agree. Kasparov had succeeded in breaking the united front of FIDE and the Soviet machine. On a visit to London in April, Kasparov appeared on the BBC chat show *Wogan* and announced that he was fighting for the future of world chess against an "international mafia." Such public outspokenness on such a platform in a capitalist country would have been inconceivable before, but *glasnost* had given him considerable latitude and he intended to test its limits.

Kasparov was one of the first Soviet celebrities to use the Western media to fight his battles—a strategy he had learned from the dissidents.

An equally important sign that times were changing was the fact that the third match opened on July 28, not in Moscow's Hall of Columns, but in the Park Lane Hotel in London. This was the first time that two Soviet world champions had contested the title outside their own country. Having easily outbid Leningrad, the London organizers had generously agreed to share the match, with twelve games to be played in each city. The contrast in technology between London and Leningrad was illustrated by the giant demonstration boards on which the audience watched the games. In London, electronic monitors registered the moves instantaneously; in Leningrad, "board boys" still moved the pieces manually, just as they had at the first Moscow tournament in 1925. Another contrast was between the entertainments: in Leningrad the Kirov Ballet performed a living chess game, while in London Tim Rice's new hit musical *Chess* dramatized the Cold War clashes of Fischer, Korchnoi, Karpov, and Kasparov. In one respect the British followed the Soviet example: both the BBC and ITV networks televised chess for the first time since Fischer–Spassky. Kasparov left no doubt that he preferred London, where he was invited back to judge the Miss World contest. The opening ceremony was dominated by Margaret Thatcher. The British prime minister had been the first Western leader to establish a close relationship with Gorbachev and his foreign minister, Eduard Shevardnadze, who had given her a blue and white chess set on his last visit: "I give him full marks for diplomacy," she had said. Back in the USSR, the television images of Mrs. Thatcher presiding over a world chess championship match between two Soviet players delighted dissidents and appalled the apparatchiks. Together with Pope John Paul II and President Reagan, she was one of the three conservative revolutionaries who would lead the West to its bloodless victory over communism. Once again, chess provided the perfect symbol.

The third match began with three draws, but with Kasparov

pressing hard, Karpov's resistance crumbled in the fourth game and it turned into a rout. However, Karpov struck back immediately, winning the fifth game convincingly, drawing the next one, and in the seventh he missed a clear win. Thus far the match had been evenly balanced, but in the eighth game Kasparov outplayed Karpov in the most devilish manner. As the game became ever more complex, Karpov lost on time forfeit with ten moves still to make. He later admitted that his mind had felt "paralyzed," and it took him a time-out and two quiet draws to recover. In the eleventh game both players launched ferocious attacks on each other's king until they shared the point, for which they shared a £10,000 brilliancy prize, paid in Victorian gold sovereigns. The twelfth game was also drawn, leaving Kasparov a point ahead as the caravan moved to Leningrad for the second leg. Both players agreed to donate their prize money, some £300,000, to the fund for the recent nuclear disaster at Chernobyl, which had such a profound impact on the Soviet system that Gorbachev later saw it as the single biggest cause of communism's demise.

Back on home ground, the struggle became even more intense. Kasparov won both the fourteenth and the sixteenth games with the Ruy Lopez—the venerable opening in which Fischer had excelled. Botvinnik commented: "Kasparov played perfectly." As in the eighth game, Karpov almost lost on time in the sixteenth and seemed dejected. With Kasparov now three points ahead, it looked as if the match was over. Yet again, however, Karpov bounced back. A smashing victory in the seventeenth game was followed by another in the eighteenth. This was the most dramatic game in the match, in which Kasparov came close to checkmating Karpov's exposed king, but overreached when he had only three minutes left on the clock. Having twice missed the winning move, Kasparov allowed himself to be outplayed in a fiendishly complex endgame. Karpov then crushed Kasparov again in the nineteenth game to level the score—the first time in his career that Kasparov had lost three games in succession.

The match threatened to become a rout, but Kasparov showed

his class by stabilizing the situation with two draws, before rousing himself for one last supreme effort in the twenty-second game. The denouement has become a classic, reproduced countless times: Karpov avoided a complex ending in which he would have had practical chances, in favor of a continuation that allowed Kasparov to win with an elegant combination. With two games left, Kasparov was a point ahead, and this time Karpov had shot his bolt. The last two were quiet draws. Although Kasparov had retained his title by the narrowest of margins, 12.5–11.5, he had little time to prepare before Round IV, which began only a year later, this time in Seville. Karpov defeated the winner of the candidates' tournament, Andrei Sokolov, to earn the right to yet another bout with Kasparov.

The aftermath of the London–Leningrad match was, however, an ugly one. Kasparov attributed his unprecedented collapse in three successive games to the treachery of a second, Evgeny Vladimirov, whom he accused of passing his opening analysis to Karpov. This charge was simply left hanging for lack of evidence, but rumors continued that the Kasparov camp had been infiltrated. Then the magazine *Ogonyok* interviewed a KGB colonel, Viktor Litvinov, who claimed that Kasparov's doctor had spied on him for the KGB. Litvinov, an acquaintance of the Kasparov family, claimed that the KGB regarded the world champion as a political figure, and saw Kasparov as unworthy of the title. Another of Kasparov's seconds, Josip Dorfman, was accused of selling information to the Karpov camp through an intermediary, Alexander Feldman. Karpov vehemently denied the claims, as did Dorfman; Kasparov was skeptical. The mere fact that such allegations could be aired in the Soviet press was proof that *glasnost* was real, but nothing was ever proved. Another of Kasparov's trainers, Mikhail Gurevich, claimed that he had been offered a $30,000 bribe before the 1987 Seville match—a fortune to a Russian in those days.

During the final years of the Soviet Union, when the KGB's power grew apace, such skulduggery was all too credible. At the Dubai Olympiad of 1986, despite Kasparov's magnificent performance for what was still—just about—his country, the Soviet Union entered the last round trailing the United States. Kasparov feared that letting the Americans beat the Russians into second place "would bring recriminations to me for being too busy dabbling in politics to uphold the honor of Soviet sport." When the Soviet team beat Poland, a strong side, by 4–0 in the last round to take the gold medals, everyone suspected foul play. England, which also won 4–0 against a weaker side, nosed ahead of the United States to take silver. Afterwards Soviet Chess Federation president Alexander Chikvaidze, who was also a member of the Central Committee of the Communist Party, sidled up to the English grandmaster Raymond Keene, winked, and asked: "How much did you pay them?" Chikvaidze refused to believe Keene's denials: bribery and "arranged" matches were now routine in the USSR.

By the time the fourth Karpov–Kasparov match began in Seville in October 1987, however, the champion's promise to smash the "international chess mafia" had been partly fulfilled. At a meeting in Brussels the previous February, the Grandmasters Association (GMA) was formed, with Kasparov as president and—more surprisingly—Karpov as vice-president, to defend the interests of the players against the bureaucrats. Within two years, almost every Soviet grandmaster had joined the GMA, despite the disapproval of the old guard, led by Nikolai Krogius. Yet Kasparov was not content with an international trade union: he set up the Union of Soviet Chess Players too—thereby challenging the Soviet Chess Federation's monopoly of power, which it had enjoyed since Krylenko's day. Gorbachev's *perestroika*, or reconstruction, was beginning to transform chess, too, as even Botvinnik acknowledged.

The Seville world championship match was expected to be an easy victory for Kasparov, whose tournament results were now consistently better than Karpov's, but it proved to be the narrowest squeak of all. Kasparov was sick of the sight of Karpov and made no secret of the fact that he did not want to play the match. The first five games were a shock for the overconfident champion. Karpov won the second, and though Kasparov struck back in the fourth, Karpov regained the lead in the fifth game. It was not until the eleventh game that Kasparov took a precarious lead, only to lose it again in the sixteenth game. Once again the outcome was unclear until the end. In the penultimate, twenty-third game, Kasparov fell into a trap in a drawn position, leaving himself a daunting task: he had to win the twenty-fourth and final game to save his title.

Kasparov chose to adopt his opponent's trademark strategy of slow constriction, squeezing Karpov until he cracked. He had judged the psychology exactly right. Afterwards Karpov was contemptuous of this game ("poor in ideas and rich in mistakes") and blamed his defeat on time pressure: "I was presented with a beautiful chance to seize the initiative. Just one accurate move, which I could see, but for some reason considered impossible . . . But I didn't have time; I miscalculated, chose an unsure plan, and lost." Kasparov's interpretation was similar: "I remember the moment when he could play a move fighting for initiative . . . He felt it was the best move, but he couldn't, you know. It was against the logic of the game." On the thirty-third move, Karpov chose a passive rather than an active defense, and found himself a pawn down in the endgame. A draw was still the most likely outcome. Superb analysis by Kasparov and his team during the overnight adjournment enabled him to create chances next day. "I looked into his eyes and I knew that he would lose," said Kasparov. "I could see that he didn't believe that he could save the game. In three moves he made the decisive mistake, a horrible positional mistake. Incredible. He couldn't sustain the tension. In this game he was defeated by psychology more than chess moves."

So the match was drawn, leaving Kasparov in possession of his title. If he had lost, he told the American Fred Waitzkin, "they would have made my life a misery. I might have been forced to leave the country, and I didn't want to do that." Instead of exile, Kasparov had earned himself a three-year respite—three years during which the communist world was turned upside down.

Karpov took his defeat badly, protesting loudly that it was un-

fair for the champion to retain his title if the match was drawn—
even though he had enjoyed the same privilege (as, indeed, had
Emanuel Lasker, who had clung on in the same way against Carl
Schlechter back in 1910). As Karpov's sour grapes impressed no-
body, he steeled himself for the task of clawing his way back again.
Meanwhile, the Soviet Sports Committee, as usual, helped itself
to the lion's share of the prize fund at Seville, which amounted to
2,280,000 Swiss francs. The two players received a mere 137,000
Swiss francs each, but Kasparov was now earning so much in the
West as a celebrity that he could negotiate terms with the Soviet
authorities—usually a fifty–fifty split. His 1987 autobiography,
Child of Change, was initially published only in English and other
Western languages—which did not prevent Colonel Baturinsky
from attempting to sue the author in Russia. The book was as
much manifesto as memoir, taking direct aim at the entire Soviet chess bureaucracy and indirectly at the communist one-party
state. Even so, Kasparov was awarded the Order of Lenin in 1987.
He was still a Communist Party member, he still paid lip service
to Gorbachev, and he even dedicated the first edition of his book to
the Soviet president, but he was already moving toward total opposition.

On June 12, 1987, President Reagan stood at the Berlin Wall to
make his second great Cold War speech, four years after castigat-
ing the "evil empire." Two decades later, his speechwriter, Peter
Robinson, described on the website Powerline how the American
foreign policy establishment took fright at the key line about the
Wall:

> [They claimed] the draft was naive. It would raise false hopes. It
> was clumsy. It was needlessly provocative. [The] State [Depart-
> ment] and the NSC [National Security Council] submitted their
> own alternate drafts . . . no fewer than seven. In each, the call
> to tear down the wall was missing . . . Yet in the limousine on
> the way to the Berlin Wall, the President told [his chief of staff
> Ken] Duberstein he was determined to deliver the controversial
> line. Reagan smiled. "The boys at State are going to kill me,"

he said, "but it's the right thing to do." Minutes later, Reagan called out to the Soviet leader, "If you seek peace, if you seek prosperity for the Soviet Union and Eastern Europe, if you seek liberalization, come here to this gate. Mr. Gorbachev, open this gate. Mr. Gorbachev, tear down this wall!"

Gorbachev ignored Reagan, but his support in the Soviet Union was crumbling as Russians turned to the more radical Boris Yeltsin and other nationalities also found their own voices. In March 1989, both Yeltsin and the most respected of all dissidents, the Nobel Peace Laureate Andrei Sakharov, were elected to the new Congress of People's Deputies, Gorbachev's attempt to emulate parliamentary democracy within a one-party state. Sakharov, the archenemy of communism, was voted the most popular deputy; Gorbachev was seventeenth. (Another member was Anatoly Karpov, now a staunch supporter of *perestroika*.) In a speech that was shown live on Soviet television, Sakharov called for free elections and the abolition of the "leading role of the party." A furious Gorbachev tried to silence Sakharov by pulling the plug on his microphone, but to no avail. The division between Gorbachev's reform communism and the real democrats had become visible to all. It rapidly widened into an unbridgeable gulf.

By the autumn of 1989, the satellite regimes of what Western Europeans persisted in misnaming Eastern Europe had lost authority and legitimacy. Beginning with Poland, one by one they tottered and fell, in a chain reaction of bloodless revolutions that culminated in the opening of the Berlin Wall on November 9, 1989. This, the most important event since 1945, was in fact an accident. Neither the East German nor the Soviet leadership expected the fall of the Wall, let alone its unintended consequence, the fall of communism. At a momentous press conference that evening, Günter Schabowski, the East Berlin party secretary entrusted with announcing an important but limited change of policy—the granting of visas to East Germans who wished to travel to the West—did not even mention the Wall. When Western journalists elicited a few details, Schabowski told them that the new regulations came into force immediately, although the border guards had not been given instructions. It was left to the present author, then a correspondent for the *Daily Telegraph*, to ask the question to which the millions watching live on television wanted an answer: "What will happen to the Berlin Wall?" Schabowski had no adequate answer, and neither did anybody else in the regime. Instead, the answer was given by their victims, who flocked to the checkpoints and demanded to be let through. Two years earlier, Reagan had issued the challenge: "Mr. Gorbachev, tear down this wall!" But it was not Gorbachev who tore down the Wall—it was the people, who emerged blinking into the daylight like the prisoners in Beethoven's opera *Fidelio*. These images of liberation marked a caesura in European history: not only a revolution but a restoration of Western civilization. Dissidents such as Lech Walesa and Václav Havel, now installed in presidential palaces, were leaders of a new kind, utterly different from the pragmatists who had dominated the Cold War.

Although Gorbachev was still idolized abroad, from Trafalgar Square to Tiananmen Square, at home he had irrevocably lost control of the reform process. "Gorby" was a hero only to those who did not have to live under him. By this time Russians, too, were looking for new leadership, men who were untainted by the crimes and lies of the Communist Party. Only Andrei Sakharov had the moral stature to fulfill that role, but he died on December 14, 1989, vainly demanding that Gorbachev concede real democracy to the last. Meanwhile the turmoil in Eastern Europe was spreading inside the Soviet Union.

During the Gorbachev years, the economic malaise of the Brezhnev era had metastasized into a general process of social dissolution that ultimately manifested itself as a fatal political collapse. The result was that the vast structure of the Soviet Union crumbled before the eyes of an incredulous world, leaving little more as its symbolic legacy than Lenin's mummified corpse as a tourist attraction in a renamed Red Square. Indeed, by the time Boris

Yeltsin, who emerged as the first democratically elected president of Russia in 1991, brought the curtain down on the USSR, the entire country had come to resemble the mausoleum of a dead cult. None of this had been intended. Gorbachev had begun his reforms not in order to undermine communism, but to preserve it. "I never for a minute thought," he later recalled in his *Memoirs*, "that the transformations I had initiated, no matter how far-reaching, would result in the replacement of the rule of the 'reds' by that of the 'whites.'" Note that, more than seventy years after the October revolution, the vocabulary of the *nomenklatura* had hardly altered. Trotsky's prophecy of permanent revolution was finally fulfilled — but it was a revolution to overthrow the heirs of the Bolsheviks.

THE LAST STRAW that turned Kasparov from reformer to revolutionary was the conflict over the disputed province of Nagorno-Karabakh in Azerbaijan, where the mainly Armenian and Christian population demanded to be united with Armenia, but were bitterly opposed by the Moscow-backed government. In 1987 Kasparov had signed a letter in support of the jailed Armenian dissidents of Karabakh Committee. Then, in February 1988, an anti-Armenian pogrom broke out in the town of Sumgait near Baku. Kasparov was convinced that the KGB were behind it, "with the knowledge of Gorbachev." He later told an American journalist, Fred Waitzkin, what happened when he visited his native Baku in March 1989: "A group of local communists came and said that unless I repudiated my support, it might not be safe for my grandmother and cousins, who lived year-round in Baku."

Over the next two years, some 200,000 ethnic Armenians deserted the capital. Then, in January 1990, the pogroms reached Baku itself. Kasparov was preparing for his showdown with Karpov on January 13 when he received desperate phone calls from the city. Murders and rapes were being carried out in full view of the Soviet troops, who did nothing to stop them. Kasparov chartered a plane from Moscow and set up a safe haven in a sanatorium.

Some forty people took refuge there, including his grandmother and aunt. Two allies in the KGB rescued the family of his friend Shakarov by pretending to arrest them as American spies.

On the night of January 15, Kasparov was warned that the mob was approaching his camp, where the terrified refugees sat playing cards, guarded by just two armed policemen. "Some time during the night," Kasparov told Waitzkin,

> I asked the major, "If they break in here, will you shoot?" He didn't answer, and so I dealt the cards to [his assistant] Kadzhar; we played a while longer. Then I asked him again, "If they come, will you shoot?" "You know, I have a family. I have three daughters," he said quietly. He didn't look up at me. After a while, I said, "Will you give me your gun?" He thought for a while, and then he answered, "If they come, you have to hit me on the side of the head. Make it look like you took it from me." It was like a scene in a gangster movie.

In fact, the mob never arrived. Kasparov was told that its way had been barred, not by the army but by the local fish mafia. The racketeers had no liking for Armenians, but they were armed and they guarded their territory jealously.

Next day, Kasparov and his friends drove into Baku. Although their Azeri police escort fled, he was able to rescue a few possessions from his apartment. On January 17, Kasparov organized the airlift of his family and many friends, some sixty people in all, to safety. When his chartered aircraft arrived, the crew refused to fly. Only bribery and a perilous bus ride to the chaotic airport succeeded in getting the party out. There were eight free seats on the plane, and an agonizing choice had to be made from the hundreds of freezing, starving refugees waiting in a hangar. Finally, the plane left, but the refugees had nowhere to go in Moscow. Kasparov organized accommodation for them and put up some of them in his apartment.

After Kasparov returned to Moscow, he obtained an audience with the president. "I described what I had seen, but Gorbachev wasn't listening. It was like shouting in a desert." He was equally frustrated by meetings with Western journalists. However, the pogrom had forced Kasparov to take sides. One of the wealthiest and most privileged private citizens in the Soviet Union, he had lost his home in Baku. He decided to break with Gorbachev and the communist system once and for all: "I saw it with my own eyes—the face of communism is the face of death." He blamed the massacres on the Kremlin, which had incited the unrest in order to destroy anti-communist independence movements, whether in Transcaucasia or the Baltic states. In Vilnius, too, peaceful demonstrations had been suppressed by force.

These events took place, of course, against the background of the overthrow of communism in Eastern Europe. Now Kasparov told Waitzkin that he had a new vocation: "Because of Baku, I decided to start a political life. Maybe it's one drop, but it's something I can do. My priorities changed . . . When I was in Baku and people were dying, chess seemed trivial. Before this, for as long as I could remember, chess had been the center of my life."

Within weeks of the flight from Baku, Kasparov had plunged into the maelstrom of emerging democratic politics in the ruins of the one-party state. By April 1990 he was deputy chairman of Democratic Russia, an opposition group campaigning for the overthrow of the Soviet Union. He began a new career, combining chess with politics, denouncing Gorbachev in speeches, broadcasts, and articles for the *Wall Street Journal*, which made him a contributing editor. He was now at home in Manhattan and Martha's Vineyard—maybe more so, his enemies whispered, than in Moscow. His mission was to destroy the man he saw as the last communist dictator.

Nevertheless, the old enemy was still waiting for him. One by one, Karpov had eliminated his other rivals, the last of them the Dutch grandmaster Jan Timman. And so Kasparov prepared himself for the fifth and—as it turned out—final round of their seven years' war. The match began at the Hudson Theater in New York on October 8, with the second leg in Lyons. This time the prize fund was a cool $3 million, the burden shared equally between the two cities, and there was no pretense that a Soviet venue could compete with the West.

But it was no longer an all-Soviet event. Kasparov made a typically flamboyant and extremely powerful gesture. He had been predicting the imminent collapse of the Soviet Union for months. Now, a year before that collapse occurred, he refused to play the match under the Soviet flag, adopting instead the old tsarist flag of Russia. Rather than be driven into exile, he was in effect declaring himself independent—and staying put. On the eve of this unprecedented act of defiance, according to the American journalist Seth Lipsky, members of Kasparov's entourage warned him not to publish the story beforehand because they feared for his life. It did not leak, and the Soviets were presented with a fait accompli. They were indeed scandalized, but instead of threatening Kasparov they protested to the organizers, threatening to abort the match. Rather than call their bluff, the committee ruled: no flag for *either* player. So for the first time since the war, two Russians played for the world chess championship—but not under the red flag of the Bolshevik revolution. A very different kind of revolution was already sweeping away everything that the hammer and sickle had stood for.

This time it was Kasparov who scored the first palpable hit, in the second game. It was a wild one: a speculative bishop sacrifice exposed Karpov's king and, in the ensuing complications, Karpov was outplayed. He was forced to resign before he was mated. It had gradually become apparent that the ex-champion was imperceptibly weakening, while Kasparov had been growing stronger year by year. "At this point in our careers, I am a much better player than Karpov," Kasparov told Waitzkin. "I think this is obvious." Yet this match, too, proved to be as unpredictable as the rest. After Kasparov had failed to break through several times, despite a queen sacrifice in the third game, he had his chance in the sixth—and he blew it. With Karpov's king caught in a trap, all that Kasparov had to do was adjourn the game overnight. However, he moved impetuously, threw away his advantage, and only drew. The following game was a catastrophe for Kasparov—one of the worst games he had ever played. So the match continued for the rest of the New York series, with Kasparov willing to wound yet seemingly afraid to strike. Only two decisive games out of twelve was not exactly crowd-pleasing, but at least the two old rivals were neck-and-neck when they left Manhattan.

At the Palais de Congrès in Lyons the match resumed with three more draws, and the interest outside the chess fraternity began to evaporate. If anything, Karpov had shown himself superior. Only in the sixteenth game did Kasparov gain a real edge. Although Karpov defended stubbornly and resourcefully, the endgame inexorably slipped away from him. On the 102nd move, faced with mate, Karpov resigned. To lose such a marathon would have floored a lesser player, but Karpov at bay was always dangerous. He fought back to win the seventeenth game in splendid style, again equalizing the score. Nothing daunted, Kasparov returned blow for blow and crushed Karpov in the eighteenth. This time there was no comeback. In game nineteen, Kasparov offered a draw in a position that looked overwhelming. The former world champion Boris Spassky suspected a fix, but Kasparov was contemptuous when he heard this. Karpov "is the man who understands chess at the same level as I do," he said. "Who else can I really talk with about these games? Spassky?" If that game could not be won, the next one could. Game twenty was the killer: a queen sacrifice, leading to checkmate. In tones of awe, his fellow grandmaster Mikhail Gurevich revealed that the champion had foreseen the final combination early in the middle-game: "He saw twenty moves ahead calculating deep and complicated variations. It was absolutely incredible."

Karpov did not despair, even though he was now two games down with only four to play. He came close to retrieving one of them in the twenty-first game, but Kasparov made no mistake. He now needed only to draw the twenty-second game to retain his title—and draw it he did. Morally, however, it was important for

Kasparov to win. If he had drawn a second match, then Karpov could justifiably have claimed to have proved himself Kasparov's equal. So the last two games at Lyons mattered to both men. Karpov won the twenty-third, setting up a grand finale in the last game. Although the title did not depend on it, both money and reputation did. Kasparov played to win. His pieces dominated the board. Just as he seemed poised for the coup de grâce, however, the champion offered a draw, which Karpov gratefully accepted. He had lost by the narrowest of margins: 12.5–11.5. Why had Kasparov shown such unaccustomed magnanimity in victory? "It showed strength and fair play," Kasparov said afterward. It also showed something else. Both men knew that they would never play again for the world championship—and that with them the Soviet era in chess had passed into history.

THE KASPAROV–KARPOV DUEL was the climax of the story of chess and the Cold War. That story is also a hitherto untold chapter in the history of liberty. Following Fischer–Spassky and Karpov–Korchnoi, this was the third time that a rivalry over the chessboard assumed a wider geopolitical and philosophical significance. For the duration of Fischer's match with Spassky, Reykjavik became the nodal point of the conflict between communism and capitalism. Korchnoi's valiant attempts to unseat the seemingly invincible Karpov at Baguio and Merano encapsulated the challenge posed to the Soviet system by the dissident movement. It was a trial of strength with the leviathan, which strained every sinew to crush dissidents who deliberately placed themselves outside its jurisdiction and refused to recognize its legitimacy. However, Kasparov's confrontation with Karpov was different. By the mid-1980s the battle between East and West, between two mutually incompatible political systems—"fire and ice," as the East German leader Erich Honecker called them—had become internalized by the USSR. Significantly, Kasparov used the same metaphor about himself and Karpov: "Our contrasting fire and ice chess styles also reflected our 'collaborator versus rebel' reputations away from the board."

The power struggle between East and West had also been a battle between ideology and truth. Karpov versus Kasparov gave dramatic form to this power struggle within the Soviet system during its last decade, as its people finally awoke from their long trance and came to terms with the truth. Kasparov was a quick learner. He was among the first to realize that the system could survive only if it adapted. But he was also among the first to grasp that the system was too sclerotic to adapt—that it was incapable of reform. And he was among the first to comprehend that only revolution—the peaceful overthrow of communism—would suffice. He broke with the Gorbachev regime in 1989, before Boris Yeltsin had severed his ties. Once his own family in Baku had to be rescued from the violence generated by the impending disintegration of the Soviet empire, Kasparov needed no further persuasion. He came to the same conclusion that the dissidents and refuseniks had reached years before. So he joined their ranks.

The prominent dissident Vladimir Bukovsky, who settled in Britain after his release from the Gulag in 1976, became a friend even before Kasparov left the party. At Lyons, during the last match with Karpov, Bukovsky told Fred Waitzkin:

> Garry is very quick . . . And because he is a chess player, you don't have to tell him much. You tell him two moves and he tells you the rest . . . But in truth, though he was a member of the party when we started exchanging views, he had already arrived at similar conclusions about the system. Two years ago [in 1988] we would meet and Garry would say, yes, yes, we have to do something. But our discussions were theoretical. I didn't feel that he was someone who would pull off his jacket and start working. But after the massacre in Baku, he was completely changed. It shocked him. It traumatized him. This spring [1990] he was speaking a new language. "The main enemy is Gorbachev," he told me. "We have to finish off Gorbachev."

Years later, when Vladimir Putin restored Gorbachev to favor as an elder statesman, it was Bukovsky who led a lonely protest when the former Soviet leader visited Cambridge.

In chess, the Gorbachev years coincided with the epic seven years' war between Karpov and Kasparov. Between 1984 and 1990, they played an unprecedented five world championship matches: a grand total of 144 games. Although Kasparov won four of the five matches, in the end his score was only just ahead of Karpov's. Overall, Kasparov won twenty-two of these games to Karpov's twenty; the rest were drawn. In tournaments, the record is much more one-sided: Kasparov won six games, while Karpov won only one. From about 1990, Karpov's strength began to decline. In part, this was a question of stamina, but Karpov was still capable of winning short matches against the much younger grandmasters, Gata Kamsky and Vishy Anand, in 1996 and 1998 respectively. Indeed, his chess career lasted longer than Kasparov's: Karpov was still playing in tournaments in 2007, at the age of fifty-four.

During the second half of the 1980s, the two titans were as evenly matched as any in history. Their struggle for supremacy placed every aspect of modern chess under the microscope, immeasurably enriching the game in the process. Some have compared their rivalry to that of Alekhine and Capablanca, the two greatest players between the world wars. It is true that Karpov modeled himself on the classical, positional style of Capablanca, while Kasparov was drawn rather to the romantic, sacrificial attacks of Alekhine. But Capablanca played Alekhine fewer than fifty times altogether, including a nine-year period after their only title match in 1927 when they did not play at all. If the criterion is the mutual loathing in each case, then the comparison is apt. Kasparov and Karpov, however vicious their verbal guerrilla warfare, have never allowed it to become a substitute for chess. Even so, both men knew from the outset that their struggle for supremacy was much more than a game.

To find a proper comparison for the Karpov–Kasparov matches,

we must look back a century and a half, to the very first series
of games that could be described as a world championship match.
This took place in London in the summer of 1834: a marathon series of six short matches between the French champion, Louis
Charles de la Bourdonnais, and the leading British player, Alexander McDonnell. A total of eighty-five official games were played;
although de la Bourdonnais won forty-five and McDonnell twenty-
seven, with thirteen draws, the less experienced McDonnell was
improving all the time and he even won the last match. There
was no return match because McDonnell died the following year
and de la Bourdonnais followed him in 1840, but their successors,
Pierre Charles Fournier de Saint Amant and Howard Staunton,
played two matches in London and Paris in 1843, in which Staunton avenged McDonnell's defeat and established himself as the
leading chess player and writer. The British and French empires
were the two superpowers of the day and, as in the Cold War, their
rivalry was reflected on the chessboard.

Between the gentlemanly duel at the Westminster Chess Club
in 1834 and the brutal machinations at the Moscow Hall of Columns 150 years later, chess had been transformed. Kasparov (unlike Fischer) might sneer at his nineteenth-century precursors as
amateurs, whom any modern master would have defeated with
ease, but chess belonged to neither time nor place. Politics had
made less progress than chess, which almost uniquely had resisted
the totalitarian takeover of every aspect of culture. However much
the ideologues and gangsters in the Kremlin might try to politicize
the game, they could not control the moves on the board. Chess
has its own logic, its own rule of law, and its own truth. The supreme intellectual product of the Soviet system turned against his
masters, in the process exposing their claims as hollow and mendacious.

16

AFTER THE
COLD WAR

T HE MOST VISIBLE LEGACY of the Cold War on the chessboard is the fact that ever since it ended Garry Kasparov has made his presence felt on the political stage. Kasparov is not only the greatest chess player the world has ever seen, he is also the unofficial leader of the opposition and one of the last hopes of democracy in Russia. He has found a way to defy President Putin—the man he refers to contemptuously as "a mere lieutenant-colonel in the KGB"—with nothing more than his wits to live by. To do this, he has made use of his experience of taking on the Soviet chess establishment, but he has also sacrificed the one art in which he achieved more than anybody before him. After two decades as the highest-rated chess player in the world, Kasparov gave up the game in 2005. He was still only forty-two.

It is hard for a non-chess player to conceive what this must have meant. Mstislav Rostropovich, the greatest Russian cellist, sacrificed his country rather than compromise his principles, preferring to leave Russia in 1974 to begin a new life and career in exile. For Kasparov to give up chess was like Rostropovich giving up the cello. Another comparable case is that of Sakharov. This great physicist was responsible for the Soviet hydrogen bomb and was elected as the youngest-ever Soviet academician in 1953, yet in his forties he gave up his glittering scientific career, choosing not to go into exile but to become the founder and leader of the Soviet dissident movement. Just as the cases of Rostropovich and Sakharov illuminate the existential choices forced upon intellectuals by the Cold War, so the case of Kasparov illuminates the toxic legacy it left behind.

After the formal dissolution of the Soviet Union in December 1991, Kasparov was able to combine chess and politics in the new Russian Federation for another decade. In the 1996 election he threw his weight, and that of his Democratic Russia movement, behind Boris Yeltsin against the communist reactionaries. However, he later regretted his support for the increasingly erratic president, whom he saw as Janus-faced. When Yeltsin died in April 2007, Kasparov pointed out that, after Yeltsin defeated the coup in August 1991 and subsequently presided over the peaceful dismantling of the Soviet Union, "for the first time in Russian history the new ruler did not eliminate the losers to consolidate power. What's more, they were free to participate in political life." While this was a step toward the rule of law and liberal democracy, it also left the "KGB clan" able to make a comeback under different auspices. In 1999 Yeltsin handed over power to Vladimir Putin, who was subsequently confirmed in office by two elections, in neither of which were the opposition parties given fair access to the media. The new *nomenklatura* that seized power under Putin shared his background and outlook. The American magazine *Harper's* reported in May 2007 that, under Gorbachev, 5 percent of senior Soviet officials had a background in the armed forces or security services. Under Putin, the figure rose to 78 percent.

Kasparov's response was to found the United Civil Front, a loose-knit group of human-rights activists and pro-Western opponents of the Putin regime. In his book, *How Life Imitates Chess,*

Kasparov explains that the regime imposed by Putin is "not martial law exactly, call it 'martial law lite.'" The lack of transparency and accountability allows the state to grow indefinitely: "Any criticism of state officials can be termed 'extremism.' a term separated from terrorism by only a comma in Putin's law book."

In the summer of 2006, Kasparov helped to stage the Drugaya Rossiya ("The Other Russia") forum in Moscow to coincide with the G8 summit in St. Petersburg. The Other Russia has since developed into an umbrella organization, representing a broad spectrum of opposition groups, ranging from the National Bolsheviks on the Right to free-market liberals and Leftists. So what does Kasparov himself stand for? "There are millions like me in Russia who want a free press, the rule of law, social justice, and free and fair elections," he wrote. "To achieve these ends my colleagues and I have formed a broad nonideological coalition of true opposition groups and activists. I am working inside Russia and abroad to bring attention to the decimation of Russia's democratic institutions."

It was gratifying for the opposition groups that Putin's chief adviser, Igor Shuvalov, warned Western governments that attendance at the Other Russia forum would be seen as an unfriendly act, and he implicitly threatened reprisals against participants. A number of opposition activists involved with the event were arrested and beaten up by the FSB, as the KGB now called itself. The leading Russians present were the former prime minister Mikhail Kasyanov, and Putin's former economic adviser Andrei Illarionov, who had resigned in protest at the Kremlin's authoritarian "corporate state." Although the meeting was attended by two U.S. Assistant Secretaries of State, the only senior Western diplomat who spoke at the Other Russia was the British ambassador, Sir Anthony Brenton, who wanted to show solidarity with Russians campaigning for a stronger civil society. His speech was interrupted by hecklers, and later Kasparov himself informed delegates from the podium that FSB agents were bundling four participants into vans outside the hotel; they were eventually charged with "hooliganism." The conference was surrounded throughout by aggressive pickets from Putin's youth organization, Nashi ("Ours"). At Nashi training camps, young Russians were taught to hate Kasparov as a traitor, marching past huge photomontage images of him as a prostitute.

Sir Anthony and his family then endured months of constant harassment and intimidation from members of Nashi. Their campaign was stepped up after the murder in November 2006 of Alexander Litvinenko, the exiled former FSB operative and dissident who died in London of radioactive poisoning. The dramatic circumstances surrounding Litvinenko's death, and the fact that on his deathbed he accused Putin of ordering his murder, reminded many people of similar incidents during the Cold War. Broadcasts of the BBC's Russian Service were jammed. Previous unsolved murders, such as that of the leading journalist Anna Politkovskaya or the vice-chairman of the Central Bank, Andrei Kozlov, had been played down by the West. However, Litvinenko's murder in a Western capital could not be ignored—especially as the assassin left a trail of the radioactive toxin Polonium-210. British attempts to extradite the former FSB officer Andrei Lugovoi were rebuffed by the Kremlin, leading to a diplomatic stand-off between the two governments in July 2007.

Kasparov, meanwhile, had his offices raided by the secret police shortly after the Litvinenko affair. Then, in April 2007, the confrontation between Kasparov and the Kremlin escalated dramatically. The Other Russia held rallies in Moscow and St. Petersburg; on April 13 Kasparov was arrested, held overnight, and then released. He insisted that he would not be intimidated, despite the fact that some two hundred journalists have died violently in Russia since 1991. The impression that Russian dissidents could now be murdered with impunity anywhere in the world did not deter Vladimir Putin's leading critics.

Kasparov could not have financed his political ambitions without having made a fortune out of chess, but he is a philanthropist who has promoted the game as an educational tool around the world. Kasparov is not just a chess genius. He is also an individualist, an entrepreneur, and something of a buccaneer. His ambition having propelled him to the top of his cerebral profession, he set about remaking the chess world in his own image. He has, it must be said, enjoyed only limited success. His attempts to take over or replace FIDE ultimately failed. The world chess federation instead fell under the influence of a post-Soviet oligarch: Kirsan Ilyumzhinov, president of Kalmykia, the only Buddhist Asian republic within the Russian Federation.

Ilyumzhinov treats the world chess federation rather as his fellow oligarch Roman Abramovich treats Chelsea Football Club. (Both are cronies of Putin, and Abramovich is also governor of Chukotka province.) Ilyumzhinov has spent much of the minuscule GDP of his remote fiefdom on his extravagant hobby, including the construction of a "Chess City" near the capital, Elista. At Kalmykian schools, chess is compulsory. When it comes to dealing with opposition, Ilyumzhinov is a miniature version of Putin. In 1998 Larisa Yudina, the most prominent journalist in the country, was murdered after accusing Ilyumzhinov of corruption. Three men were convicted, one of them an adviser to Ilyumzhinov, but the latter denied any involvement. Ilyumzhinov, also an ally of Saddam Hussein, was one of the last people to leave Baghdad, just a matter of days before the American-led coalition invaded in 2003.

It is extraordinary that such a disreputable figure should have such a stranglehold over the most venerable and popular game on the planet, but his Chess City at Elista is now the capital of world chess. Ilyumzhinov is wealthy enough to subsidize the poorer members of FIDE, thereby securing their support. He also has his favorites among the grandmasters. In the 2006 world championship match at Elista between the Russian Vladimir Kramnik and the Bulgarian Veselin Topalov, the latter was known to be an ally of Ilyumzhinov. A grotesque scandal, known as "Toiletgate," blew up when Topalov accused Kramnik of secretly consulting a computer during frequent visits to the bathroom, necessitated by a medical condition. Although this allegation was baseless, it was

Kramnik who was eventually forfeited a game—a blatantly unfair decision widely blamed on Ilyumzhinov's influence. The corruption of FIDE is typical of such international organizations, but it is both a cause and a symptom of the diminishing status of chess since the Cold War ended. The popularity of chess has grown but its prestige has declined.

In 1957 Botvinnik and his successor Smyslov became the first Soviet sportsmen to be awarded the Order of Lenin, the highest Soviet civilian honor. Subsequent Soviet world champions also received the same honor. By contrast, after Bobby Fischer won the world championship in 1972, he received no honor, let alone the highest one, the Presidential Medal of Freedom. The British establishment has been even more indifferent to chess. In his essay for the *Sunday Times* about the Fischer–Spassky match in 1972, "The Glorious and Bloody Game," the writer Arthur Koestler praised the Russians for including chess in the school curriculum and "treating their champions as favorite pets." He wondered "how much longer we shall have to wait until the first British master of the royal game will join the ranks of eminent footballers, racing jockeys and cricketers by having a knighthood graciously bestowed on him." Thirty-five years later, Britain has some twenty-five grandmasters, but none has been knighted.

This disparity in the official status accorded to chess in the East and the West lasted throughout the Cold War. Attitudes on both sides were reinforced by the staggering success of Soviet chess in the decades after 1945, and the correspondingly low status of the game in Western countries. However, the resurgence of interest triggered by the Fischer–Spassky encounter whetted the appetites of patrons in the capitalist world. From the early 1970s onwards, chess enjoyed an unprecedented bonanza, as sponsorship and remuneration belatedly caught up with other professional sports.

Long before the Communist Party of the Soviet Union lost its monopoly of power in politics, it had been forced to give up its monopoly over chess, as prestige, publicity, and players followed the money to the West. Capitalists and chess fans both like charisma, and both groups felt a natural affinity with Kasparov. And it was to the West that the Soviet grandmasters gravitated, readily embracing the precarious existence of a self-employed chess professional living by his wits. For many chess masters living under communism, the pressure to conform had been intolerable. The exodus of chess masters who moved to the West after the Berlin Wall fell and travel restrictions were eased was living proof that the Soviet experiment in using chess as an instrument of social engineering and ideological warfare had failed. On the chessboard, as in the marketplace, Adam Smith's invisible hand triumphed over the dead hand of the state.

Hence it was no accident that the capital of international chess during the last quarter of the twentieth century was not Moscow, but London. Thanks to a sustained economic boom throughout this period, the City of London survived the worst that Irish terrorism and municipal socialism could throw at it. One of the beneficiaries was chess. London's financial institutions drew the elite of the communist bloc to participate in a series of events that inspired the British chess renaissance. In the early 1970s there were no British grandmasters; by the end of the century there were dozens, including two serious world championship candidates, Nigel Short and Michael Adams. The two London tournaments of 1982 and 1984—both won by Karpov—had a stronger list of participants than anything seen in Britain since Nottingham 1936. In 1983 London staged the candidates' semifinals, won by Kasparov and Smyslov. The second match between the USSR and the Rest of the World, held in London in June 1984, revealed how far the Soviet grip on world chess had slipped since the first such match in 1970. Apart from the two paladins Karpov and Kasparov, who outclassed their opponents, the Soviet team struggled and won only by a whisker. Most remarkable of all, between 1986 and 2000, London was the scene for three of Kasparov's world championship matches.

Almost as soon as the Cold War had ended, however, the booming market for chess evaporated. The frisson of a proxy war be-

tween superpowers vanished. Chess since the Cold War has enjoyed greater freedom but an ever-lower profile. This has made
it harder to raise money, even for world championship matches.
The present world champion, Vladimir Kramnik, is relatively unknown even in his native Russia. Nevertheless, the chess heroes of
the Cold War can still make headlines. The irony is that while the
last Soviet world champion became passionately anti-communist,
the last American champion became virulently anti-American.
Moreover, it was the Russian who harnessed capitalism for his career, while the American fell back on a communist dictatorship.
Ostentatiously ignoring warnings from the U.S. State Department,
Bobby Fischer accepted some $3 million from the Serbs at a time
when Milosević's Yugoslavia was prosecuting its genocidal war
against Bosnia and was under UN sanctions. Fischer has been a fugitive ever since. Kasparov, on the other hand, succeeded in enlist-
ing one of the greatest entrepreneurs in the West, Rupert Murdoch,
to support chess.

In 1992, for the first time in two decades, Karpov was defeated
in a candidates' match by someone other than Kasparov — the British grandmaster Nigel Short. Hopes rose of a post-Cold War contest to rival Fischer–Spassky, and the *Times* (owned by Murdoch)
was persuaded by, among others, the present author, at the time
the paper's literary editor, to sponsor the match to the tune of £3
million. In 1993 Kasparov and his British challenger, Nigel Short,
broke away from FIDE to form the Professional Chess Association,
a kind of successor to the by now moribund Grandmasters Association. Before the match, Kasparov and Short announced that they
would not play under the auspices of FIDE, which promptly refused to recognize it as a legitimate title contest. In the event,
Kasparov won rather too easily, losing only one game. Two years
later, in 1995, he again defended his title against the much younger
Indian, Viswanathan Anand, this time in New York. Again he won
far more easily than in his matches with Karpov, but thereafter he
was left without a challenger. FIDE ignored him and organized rival world championship events of its own.

In the absence of human challengers, Kasparov played two exhibition matches against the Deep Blue IBM supercomputer in 1996 and 1997. The prize funds were $500,000 and $1.1 million respectively—unprecedented sums for computer chess. Deep Blue's predecessor, Deep Thought, had already drawn a game with Karpov as early as 1990. Although Kasparov's title was not at stake, his self-confidence was. He won the first match in 1996, but only 4–2. After sensationally losing the first game, Kasparov won three, while two were drawn.

By 1997 Deep Blue was much more powerful: it could calculate 200,000,000 positions per second. Even this incredible speed did not, however, enable the computer to exhaust the game's possibilities. According to Raymond Keene, "The total of possible moves in all short games of chess (up to twenty-fiv moves) displayed in the same format as the London telephone directory, would fill all space between earth and the furthest known galaxy, not ten times but ten to the power of twenty times." But Deep Blue was reprogrammed after each game by a powerful team that included chess grandmasters. In effect, Kasparov was playing a new and unknown opponent in each game—one, moreover, that had memorized not only every recorded game that he had ever played, but everybody else's, too. The psychological factor, so important in world championship matches between humans, was entirely one-sided. Kasparov's carbon brain might tire, lose concentration, be discouraged; Deep Blue's silicon brain never would. Moreover, long after the match, the website reporter Jeff Kisselhof accused IBM, which had employed him at the time, of dirty tricks. According to his testimony in the film *Game Over: Kasparov and the Machine*, directed by Vikram Jayanti for Momentum Pictures and shown on the British TV station Channel 4 in 2005, IBM had developed a deliberate strategy of inducing Kasparov's paranoia. Mysterious incidents were compounded by IBM's secretiveness.

And so, despite a good start, Kasparov lost the match: 3.5–2.5. The last game, which was easily the worst of his career, was followed by so many millions of computer buffs and chess fans on the Internet that the World Wide Web came close to overload. An overconfident Kasparov had foolishly signed a contract with no rematch clause. The champion's accusations of cheating were dismissed as sour grapes, while IBM merely refused his demands for a return match or even for a postmortem, and promptly dismantled Deep Blue. It was the best publicity stunt in IBM's history; that was all that mattered to the corporation

Kasparov was so frustrated by his inability to take revenge for this defeat that he did not play against a computer again for six years. In 2003, however, he drew two short matches against the two best chess computer programs in the world, the German Deep Fritz and the Israeli Deep Junior. Both were commercial programs, with a theoretical strength in excess of any human being. It was quite an achievement for Kasparov to show that he could still win games against computers of such mind-boggling power. However, another supercomputer was lurking in Abu Dhabi. Hydra was similar to Deep Blue, but even more powerful. It could analyze to a depth of between eighteen and forty moves ahead, six more than Deep Blue. In 2005 a six-game match was played between Hydra and the leading British grandmaster, Michael Adams. It was a rout: Adams lost five games and drew only one. Hydra has never lost a game to a human. By this time Kasparov had anticipated the ascendancy of machine over man by abandoning chess altogether. The willpower that had crushed so many egos had no impact on microchips.

After five years during which Kasparov had no human challenger, the dot-com boom made it viable for a London consortium, Braingames Network, to organize a championship match in the year 2000. The champion had predicted that his successor would be his protégé and former assistant, Vladimir Kramnik, and so it proved. Kasparov never worked out how to penetrate Kramnik's Berlin Defense, an old variation of the opening invented by Ruy Lopez in the sixteenth century. Lasker had used the Berlin successfully to defeat Tarrasch in 1908, and it had reappeared intermittently since, but it had been out of fashion throughout the Soviet era. Even more successfully than Karpov, the "Berlin Wall," as it was immediately dubbed, enabled Kramnik to neutralize Kasparov's aggression with the White pieces. Kramnik won the match without losing a single game. Kasparov took his defeat with an uncharacteristically good grace. He knew that he was beaten by advancing age as much as by a superior opponent. Coming after the Deep Blue debacle, losing the world championship title that he had held for fifteen years was a huge blow to Kasparov's pride. Once again, he had omitted to demand a rematch clause in the contract and he was punished for his overconfidence. The dot-com bubble burst, draining the pot of money for a return match. Kasparov was left marooned by his own eminence. He was still the greatest player alive, at least according to his rating, but he was no longer world champion and had no means of regaining the title. His chess career had lost its raison d'être.

The end of the Kasparov era in chess in 2000 made much less impression on the public than his defeat by a computer had done three years previously. A man versus machine contest apparently aroused more human interest than a human contest ever would again. Nigel Short contemptuously compared matches such as Kasparov–Deep Blue or Adams–Hydra to a weightlifting contest between a man and a forklift truck. In part, the public was merely exhibiting the perennial fascination for the automaton—from Baron von Kempelen's mechanical Turk to *The Tales of Hoffmann*. But there was another reason why people in the 1990s wanted to pit the greatest genius in chess history against these glorified gadgets. The fact was that more chess was now being played online than over the board. Opponents from anywhere on earth could play one another without meeting, indeed usually without even knowing one another's real names. Internet chess was the biggest single change in the way that chess was played since the nineteenth century. The instant availability of opponents created a vast new demand for chess, while simultaneously threatening the long-term future of traditional chess tournaments, teams, and clubs. Whereas the professionalization of chess by communist ideology was good for the grandmaster, the democratization of chess by capitalist technology was good for the amateur.

Meanwhile, Kasparov was still the highest rated player in the world, with consistently better results than his successor, Kramnik, or indeed anybody else. For five more years he defied the march of time, holding his own against ever younger rivals, keeping up with the latest opening theory and winning almost every tournament in which he played. He even took a kind of revenge by smashing Kramnik's Berlin Defense in a brilliant game at New York. By 2005, however, he had nothing left to prove. At the climax of Nabokov's *The Luzhin Defense*, the eponymous grandmaster hero tells his wife: "I have to drop out of the game." Nabokov had in mind the kind of chess problem that is solved only by self-mate. Luzhin solves his problem by suicide. Kasparov dropped out of the game on the sixty-four squares, but only in order to resume an even more complex game on an altogether grander scale, a game in which the stakes were the future of Russia—and his own survival.

DESPITE THE UNEQUAL struggle, Kasparov and his adversaries in the Kremlin both know that dissidents have an excellent chance of toppling unpopular authoritarian regimes, provided that they enjoy Western support and can mobilize "people power." Putin has reason to fear that Russians could follow the examples of Ukraine and Georgia by overthrowing the regime, if the next Russian elections, due in 2008, were to be rigged. So he is working hard to eliminate any possible threat from intellectuals to the ruling class of former KGB men like himself. Just as in the latter stages of the Soviet Union, there is both a power struggle and a parallel battle of ideas between the intelligentsia and intelligence. Communism lost the battle of ideas to the dissidents, yet the former secret police have never relinquished the levers of power. Russia is still a one-party state; its power and prestige, though, depend on its control of oil and gas rather than the old combination of industry and ideology. The militarism and militancy of the Soviet Union made it a model for Arab nationalists. Now it is Russia that increasingly resembles the petro-despotisms of the Middle East. The concentration of wealth and power in the hands of the state—so characteristic of such energy-dependent economies—is dangerous to democracy and fatal to freedom.

The novel that Kasparov considers the most important work in Russian literature is Mikhail Bulgakov's *The Master and Margarita*. He has read it many times. For him, as for many other Russian intellectuals, this novel—written at the height of the Terror, but only published in 1966–7—captures like no other the nightmarish experience of living in a world beyond good and evil—a world in which people disappear without trace, nobody is safe, nobody can be trusted, and the devil himself has taken up residence in Moscow. "Well, but with sorcery, as everyone knows, once it starts, there's no stopping it," Bulgakov writes.

To be precise, it took a lifetime to stop it: from the successful Bolshevik coup in October 1917 to the failed KGB coup in 1991. After the collapse of the Soviet Union, the Russians awoke from their nightmare. That awakening, too, was a traumatic experience. The truth of what had happened in those seventy-four years was painful—indeed, for most it was too painful to bear. They preferred the dream to the reality, the disease to the cure. At the end of the novel, the master tells Margarita: "They tried too hard to frighten me, and cannot frighten me with anything any more." She replies: "They've devastated your soul!" Russia today is a land of dead souls. One of those souls turned out to be the man whom many Russians had greeted as a savior when he spoke to them on top of a tank in August 1991: Boris Yeltsin.

Eight years after Yeltsin defeated the KGB coup, he was handing over power to Vladimir Putin, a representative of the same sinister fraternity. It was soon apparent that the devil was back in Moscow, alive and well and living in the Kremlin. The black magic was also back, if not on the genocidal scale of the 1930s. The phantasmagorical, theatrical quality of Soviet communism, evoked so well by

Bulgakov, could be glimpsed in Putin's revival of show trials, patriotic parades, and propaganda. And the fear that had pervaded the Soviet Union throughout its history was back, too. Unable to depict the sheer totalitarian horror of his own time, Bulgakov disguises it in a retelling of the confrontation between Jesus (Yeshua) and Pontius Pilate, who echoes men such as Krylenko as he tells his prisoner: "There never has been, is not, and never will be any authority in this world greater or better for people than the authority of the emperor Tiberius!" The exchange culminates in the Roman procurator's anguished question: "'And the kingdom of truth will come?' 'It will, Hegemon,' Yeshua answered with conviction. 'It will never come!' Pilate suddenly cried out in such a terrible voice that Yeshua drew back . . . 'Criminal! Criminal! Criminal!'" The kingdom of truth may not have come to Russia yet, but it is no longer possible to silence those who believe in it.

Kasparov's task is not a straightforward one. It is a battle with ghosts, with a nation that is still so deeply in denial about its totalitarian past that it deludes itself about the authoritarian present, too. At the end of *The Master and Margarita*, Bulgakov depicts Soviet self-deception with delicate irony: "The most developed and cultured people, to be sure, took no part in this tale-telling about the unclean powers that had visited Moscow, even laughed at them and tried to bring the tellers to reason . . . Cultured people adopted the view of the investigation: it had been the work of a gang of hypnotists and ventriloquists with a superb command of their art."

It is in correcting the Putin regime's narrative of the long night of the Russian soul that chess assumes a special importance. In the person of Garry Kasparov, chess connects the Russia of Putin with that of Stalin. The rise and fall of chess as a political metaphor and as an ideological weapon coincided with one of the darkest chapters in the history of mankind. Communism sought to corrupt chess, one of mankind's oldest and most innocent occupations, just as it corrupted everything else that it touched. Here, as in other spheres, it harnessed the idealism of millions, exploiting chess as a means to further its totalitarian ends. The attempt to create a race of supermen by training them to play chess was destined to fail because the system that they were meant to serve was irredeemably mendacious. Lasker's words in his *Manual of Chess* are apt: "On the chess-board lies and hypocrisy do not survive long. The creative combination lays bare the presumption of a lie; the merciless fact, culminating in a checkmate, contradicts the hypocrite."

On a television program in 1995, Henry Kissinger recalled how during the 1970s the Soviet ambassador in Washington, Anatoly Dobrynin, had challenged him to a game of chess. The then Secretary of State explained why he had refused: "The KGB doubtless thought that they could deduce from my play the characteristics of my personality. The collection of games of a chess player is a powerful indication of his character." The Americans were wary of the Soviet habit of treating chess as the logical expression of an entire political or cultural system, preferring to see it as an individual accomplishment. Both sides projected their hopes and fears on to the game.

The Russians won countless battles over the board, but their bid to make chess an extension of the Cold War by other means ended in defeat. Having lost its political resonance when the attempt to use it as a tool of totalitarian transformation was abandoned, chess temporarily reverted to relative obscurity. Even Kasparov himself now sometimes seems exasperated with the game that made his name. Angry with his countrymen for denying him his due, he insists that chess no longer counts for anything in Russia. However, the truth is that no other field of mental strife exhibits so vividly the true significance of the endeavor to abolish human freedom once and for all.

For communism, chess proved recalcitrant. This ancient game—originally conceived as a method of divining the future, later as the realm of *Homo ludens*—functioned in the Cold War as a lie detector. In the most successful of all efforts to expose the monstrosity of the Soviet system, *The Gulag Archipelago*, Alexander Solzhenitsyn chose as his opening epigraph a quotation by Nikolai Krylenko, while presiding as state prosecutor over the Prom party trial in 1930, at which the defendants were convicted of belonging to a nonexistent secret organization. "In the period of dictatorship, surrounded on all sides by enemies," declared Krylenko, "we sometimes manifested unnecessary leniency and unnecessary softheartedness."

In 1917 the population of Russia was 169 million; that of the United States was 103 million. Ninety years later, the United States has almost tripled its population, while Russia's has stagnated. There are many reasons for this contrast, but the most important can be summed up in one word: communism. The true human cost to the Soviet Union is almost impossible to calculate, because its victims are still suffering and dying every day. Seventy years of communism have transformed Russia into a land of demographic and environmental catastrophe, crippled by a moral amnesia that hinders any proper reckoning with the crimes and injustices of the recent past.

The attempt by Krylenko, Lenin's and Stalin's prosecutor, to make chess serve the purposes of the totalitarian state came close to success, but in the end it was chess that heralded the impending collapse of communism. The West, for all its inequalities and insecurities, proved to be more resourceful because it fought for freedom and lived in truth.

EPILOGUE

O N MAY 18, 2007, Garry Kasparov tried to fly to Samara on the Volga to lead a demonstration there for his opposition group, the Other Russia, outside the European Union–Russia summit. Although the demonstration was legal—the Other Russia had been granted permission by the mayor of Samara—Kasparov was nonetheless arrested with twenty-seven journalists and others at Sheremetyevo airport in Moscow, all of whom were prevented from traveling and their passports were confiscated. Later that day Angela Merkel, the German chancellor, gave a press conference with the Russian president. Standing beside Vladimir Putin before the cameras, she said: "I hope that those who this afternoon want to express their opinion will be able to do so. I am somewhat concerned that people had difficulties getting here, but perhaps a possible demonstration can still take place."

These words were heard by millions of Russians. President Putin, impassive as ever but clearly irritated by this very public embarrassment, retorted that the Germans, too, had not ruled out using preventive detention in the run-up to the Heiligendamm G8 summit. "We will not however point the finger at others," he remarked with heavy sarcasm. Mrs. Merkel's response to this, in which she explained the difference between the potentially violent extremism of those detained in Germany and the legitimate democratic opposition of the peaceful protesters in Russia, was censored on Russian TV. Putin dismissed Kasparov, whom he refused to dignify by naming him: "These are political fringe groups. They won't disturb me any further." Yet at Samara he had no choice but to make a public promise that demonstrations by the opposition would be permitted in future and to admit that the actions of the security forces—such as the crushing of the Moscow and St. Petersburg demonstrations in April—"had not always been justified."

Angela Merkel, who had grown up under the meticulous surveillance of the Stasi in East Germany, could not help seeing in Vladimir Putin not only Russia's elected head of state, but also the German-speaking KGB officer who had spied on her compatriots and collaborated with her country's dictatorship. During the mass demonstrations by East Germans in October and November 1989, Putin was a KGB lieutenant-colonel based in Dresden, one of the centers of protest. After the Berlin Wall was opened, Lieutenant-Colonel Putin removed sensitive Stasi files to prevent them falling into the hands of the West. By publicly humiliating the Russian president, Mrs. Merkel was taking a risk, because German public opinion has always been nervous of any diplomatic dispute with Russia. Nonetheless, she knew that her intervention would put pressure on Putin to grant Kasparov and other opponents more latitude. Sure enough, the Other Russia's next protests in Moscow and St. Petersburg passed off without incident.

A few weeks after the Samara incident, on June 5, the Democracy and Security Conference gathered in Prague. Organized by Natan Sharansky, Václav Havel, and the former Spanish prime minister José Maria Aznar López, the event brought together an unprecedented confraternity of dissidents from all over the world. That same day, Putin threatened to target Western Europe with

Russia's nuclear arsenal unless the Americans abandoned plans to station new missile defenses in central Europe. His threats to pull out of existing agreements and begin a new arms race were not idle ones: in July 2007, Russia did indeed abrogate its conventional arms treaty with NATO. A few days earlier, Putin had compared the foreign policy of the Bush administration to that of Nazi Germany. Talk of a "new Cold War" was in the air. In this atmosphere of heightened tension, the Prague meeting took place in the Czernin Palace, home of the Czech Foreign Ministry. Its baroque splendor is haunted by Cold War memories—above all the suspicious death in March 1948 of Jan Masaryk, the Foreign Minister, whose corpse was found in the palace courtyard beneath his open office window. Whether he jumped or whether he was pushed, the Czechoslovak republic founded by his father, Thomas Masaryk, died soon afterward in a communist coup d'état. Now the man who had resurrected Czech liberty and independence, Václav Havel, presided with Natan Sharansky over a unique group of people who aspired to do the same for their own nations.

Among them was Garry Kasparov. As he arrived, Sharansky was giving a press conference with the American senator Joe Lieberman, at which they declared that democracy should be a precondition for membership of the G8, thereby excluding the Putin regime. As Kasparov entered the room, however, the two dissidents embraced warmly. Someone asked whether they ever played chess. Kasparov grinned his wolfish grin, and Sharansky patiently explained: "We are not in the same, er, category. Garry is a genius, but I am just a *patzer* [Yiddish for duffer] nowadays." Nonetheless, at a simultaneous display in Israel, when Kasparov took on numerous opponents, the *patzer* was still good enough to beat the genius.

At Prague, Kasparov developed his response to Putin's provocations in various impromptu remarks to journalists. He declared that, despite the return of the "KGB clan" to power, there was a "huge difference" between the Putin regime and the Soviet one. For one thing, "the Cold War was about ideas. This regime has no

ideology—just stealing." For another, the ruling Russian elite—
not only the oligarchs but a new, much larger class that had pros-
pered under capitalism—had a big stake in the West, where they
did business, owned property, and spent much of their leisure
time. "The ruling class can't afford a new Cold War." Ordinary
Russians did not care about the NATO missiles. "I don't think the
Iron Curtain can be restored," Kasparov said. What about assassi-
nations of dissidents? "Nobody's safe." Even him? "Yeah, me too.
Everyone's in danger." Kasparov predicted a "full-blown crisis" by
the end of 2007, because the question of Putin's successor was still
"a big mystery." He dismissed talk of his own candidature in the
presidential elections due in 2008, saying his task was "to coordi-
nate a broad coalition, not to promote my own ambitions." He was
careful, however, not to rule himself out. "Putin knows he is not
accepted," Kasparov insisted. Then, suddenly, there was a flash of
fire from the old champion: "We are now in the middle-game. For
us, it is the end of the beginning, but for Putin it is the beginning
of the end." Chess and Churchill: a typically Kasparovian combination.

The formal speech that Kasparov gave at the Prague conference
was more polished. His thesis—straight out of Bulgakov—was
that Russia is a theater, Putin is its consummate impresario, and
the West is the audience. The "superficial display of democratic
institutions" should deceive nobody. "Russia is a police state masquerading as a democracy," he explained. "Putin needs help to keep
up this pretense." The West, he said, was too easily impressed by
this "staged democracy," which had already begun with Yeltsin's
second election victory in 1996. The fear of a return to communism had blinded the West to the new danger: "More important
than strong leaders are strong laws and institutions." The Russian
people, he said, had seen no benefit from democracy and the free
market, and over the past seven years Putin had done grave damage to democracy, not only in Russia but abroad, too. Again and
again, Kasparov's plea is for the West to pay proper attention and
oblige the Russians to play by the rules. The British had opened

doors for Russian oligarchs to export their "questionable assets," whereas the Americans had been more circumspect. "We do not ask for help," he said proudly. Instead, he implored "the free world to stop providing Putin with democratic credentials" that secure his legitimacy.

Every time Kasparov walked into the room, the atmosphere crackled with electricity, photographers appeared, and reporters recorded his every word. Despite Kasparov's protestations, he looked every inch a president-in-waiting. Yet though he was one of the best-known Russians in the world, it was unclear how many Russians wanted to be identified with Kasparov. With anti-Semitism and xenophobia once again being exploited by the Putin regime, Kasparov's Western connections—he divided his time between Moscow and New York, where his family was domiciled—and of course his Armenian-Jewish background were once more in the foreground. This explained the need to prove his patriotic credentials. In his book, *How Life Imitates Chess,* he wrote: "I spent twenty-five years representing the colors of my country and I believe I am continuing to do so."

Given the state's control of resources—oil economies tend to favor authoritarian politics—and Russia's alarming demographic structure, the outlook is grim. While President Putin promised a restoration of Russia to the status of a great power, he said nothing about the extent to which the legacy of the Soviet Union promises to blight Russian prospects far into the future. Russia has one of the lowest fertility rates (1.2 children per woman), one of the highest abortion rates (70 percent of pregnancies are terminated), one of the lowest life expectancies (58.9 years for males born in 2000), and one of the worst health profiles (HIV, viral hepatitis, and tuberculosis are endemic) in the Western world. Consequently, Russia's population is predicted to decline from 148 million at the end of the Soviet Union to below 130 million by 2015. By the end of the twenty-first century there are likely to be fewer Russians than Britons.

To depose Putin, Kasparov will have to create a highly disci-

plined political movement, able to draw on deep reserves of patriotic sentiment. Kasparov will not find it easy to simultaneously
woo the electorate, tell them the truth about themselves, and stay
alive. It would be so much easier for him to settle down in comfortable self-imposed exile, following in the well-trodden path of those
chess-obsessed émigrés Prokofiev and Nabokov. Yet he views that
as a betrayal. As Kasparov saw it, by 2005 he had a choice: give up
Russia, or give up chess. And he chose to give up chess.

He explains that his decision to retire from professional chess
was "largely based on what I saw as the need to join the resistance
to the catastrophic expansion of authoritarian state power in my
home country." Why did he make the decision to exchange supremacy in chess for the risk of politics? Kasparov argues that he
was forced to leave his "comfort zone" of chess by the need to "be
where I thought I was most wanted and needed," above all by the
thought of posterity. "I don't want my nine-year-old son to worry
about Russian military service in an illegal war such as Chechnya
or to fear the repression of a dictatorship," he declares, although he
concedes that this decision is seen by many as foolhardy: "After
all, having his father attacked or jailed won't be of much benefit to
my son." But Kasparov merely shrugs off all thoughts of assassination or incarceration: "There are some things that simply must be
done . . . this is a fight that must be fought."

Garry Kasparov's lone battle with the resurgent Russian police
state has now lasted more than two decades, ever since the machinations that prematurely halted his first match with Karpov. He
has grown used to harassment and the sabotaging of his attempts
to organize serious opposition to Vladimir Putin's incipient au-
thoritarianism. But Kasparov knows that the game that he is now
playing with Putin is for his life.

ESSAY ON SOURCES

A NY STUDY OF CHESS and the Cold War must take account of two simultaneous, complementary, but distinct histories, neither of which normally takes much cognizance of the other. The historiography of chess is generally written by the game's more academic enthusiasts, whose interest in politics is likely to be peripheral. Chess has hitherto been even more marginal to the political history of the Cold War. The present volume is therefore an attempt at a concordance of two mutually incompatible branches of scholarship. I do not read Russian, so this book is based largely on secondary sources.

The two books that have informed my work throughout, and to which I should like to pay tribute, coincidentally have almost identical titles: *Soviet Chess* by D. J. Richards (Oxford, 1965) and *Soviet Chess, 1917–1991* by Andrew Soltis (Jefferson, North Carolina, and London, 2000). Although these two authors come at their subject from opposite directions—the former as a political historian of Russia, the latter as a grandmaster and historian of chess—the present book tries to synthesize their research.

A few other general works have also been invaluable across the entire field. *The Oxford Companion to Chess* by David Hooper and Kenneth Whyld (Oxford, 1992) is an essential reference book, especially valuable on the personalities who dominated the history of the game before and during the Cold War. I have also made considerable use of the collection of documents by Dmitry Plisetsky and Sergey Voronkov, published as *Russians versus Fischer* (London, 2005). For the world championship matches themselves, the contemporary accounts by Raymond Keene and various collaborators can now be supplemented by the generally superlative analysis by Garry Kasparov in his series of volumes, *My Great Predecessors*, particularly those on Fischer, Korchnoi, and Karpov. On the political and cultural history of the Soviet Union, the works of Robert Conquest, Richard Pipes, Anne Applebaum, Orlando Figes, Simon Sebag Montefiore, and Robert Service have all been invaluable.

In the introduction, the story about Charles I's chess set at Windsor comes from H. J. R. Murray's *A History of Chess* (Oxford, 1913), which still holds its own nearly a century after it was first published. On Orwell's coinage of the term "Cold War," the authority is the *Oxford English Dictionary*. My source for Sammy Reshevsky as "champion of the free world" and the *New York Times*'s challenge is Andrew Soltis.

In Chapter 1, the adage attributed to Moses Mendelssohn is often quoted, but I have been unable to trace the source. It is not mentioned in Alexander Altmann's definitive biography (London, 1973), which does, however, confirm both Mendelssohn's passion for and skill at chess, and the fact that he and Lessing were first brought together by their mutual interest in the game. However, if Mendelssohn did not say it, the quote is certainly *ben trovato*. On Jacobus de Cessolis and medieval chess neologisms, I have relied on Murray, and Hooper and Whyld. Murray is again my main source for the history of Islamic chess and Horsey's account of the death of Ivan the Terrible. On Eisenstein's film, there is a large literature, but Orlando Figes summarizes it well in *Natasha's Dance*

(New York and London, 2002). The Mendelssohn–Lessing–Lavater chess portrait and its background in *Nathan the Wise* is discussed by Jonathan M. Hess in *Germans, Jews and the Claims of Modernity* (New Haven and London, 2002). On Howard Staunton, the best book is R. D. Keene and R. N. Coles, *Howard Staunton: The English World Chess Champion* (British Chess Magazine, 1975). The accounts of the tsarist St. Petersburg tournaments draw on J. Hannak's *Emanuel Lasker* (London, 1959), Lasker's own book of the 1909 tournament (Dover reprint, 1971), and Tarrasch's book of the 1914 tournament (Caissa Editions, 1993).

Chapter 2 is most indebted to Robert Service's *Lenin: A Biography* (London, 2000) and to Leonard Schapiro's essay on "Lenin's Intellectual Formation" in *Russian Studies* (London, 1986) for its discussion of the influence of Chernyshevsky on both Vladimir and Alexander Ulyanov. It also owes much to the excellent edition of Chernyshevsky's *What Is to Be Done?* translated by Michael Katz (Ithaca and London, 1989). On Soviet Russia's isolation and the visit of American intellectuals in 1927, see in addition to Figes, Pipes, and other historians of Russia, the recent book by Amity Shlaes, *The Forgotten Man: A New History of the Great Depression* (London, 2007), especially Chapter 2, "The Junket." The stories about Rousseau, Marx, and other revolutionaries come from a variety of sources, including Mike Fox and Richard James, *The Even More Complete Chess Addict* (London, 1993), Hooper and Whyld, and Richard Eales's *Chess: The History of a Game* (London, 1985), which is also the source of the *Pravda* description of Botvinnik's triumph at Nottingham in 1936.

My account in Chapter 3 of the emergence of chess as central to the cultural life of Soviet Russia and the impact of Stalin's Red Terror leans heavily on Soltis's *Soviet Chess, 1917–1991*, in particular, his research on the key figures of Ilyin-Genevsky and Nikolai Krylenko—but also on D. J. Richards. I have supplemented the section on Krylenko with material drawn from other historians, including Conquest, Pipes, Figes, Applebaum, and Sebag Montefiore. The anecdote about Krylenko playing chess with Lenin comes from Soltis, while the Gorky quotes on human experiments are found in Courtois *et al., The Black Book of Communism* (Cambridge, Mass., and London, 1999).

The material in Chapter 4 on chess-playing Russian writers, musicians, and other artists has been gleaned from various sources, including Fox and James, Soltis, and Hooper and Whyld, while I owe much of the background to Orlando Figes and Ronald Hingley. On Pasternak, as well as his own *Essay in Autobiography* (London, 1959), I have relied on Simon Sebag Montefiore and Edvard Radzinsky for the incident with Stalin. The quotations from C. H. O'D. Alexander and Marshal Malinovsky, as well as the account of psychology and chess in the Soviet Union, come from D. J. Richards.

The émigré culture depicted in Chapter 5 takes Emanuel Lasker as its starting point. Besides the books by and on Lasker by Hannak and Soltis, I am indebted to the late Heinrich Fraenkel, who wrote the Assiac column in the *New Statesman* for some forty years and who knew Lasker during the last part of his life. I was alerted to his connection with his niece, the cellist and Holocaust survivor Anita Lasker Wallfisch, by her appearance in a BBC television documentary on the sixtieth anniversary of the liberation of Auschwitz in January 2005 and her interview with the *Guardian*, which is quoted. The anecdote about Marcel Duchamp's obsession with chess I owe to Fox and James.

Alekhine still lacks a satisfactory biography, but Pablo Morán's *Agony of a Chess Genius* (Jefferson, NC, 1989) can be supplemented by information from chess websites. I am again indebted to Soltis, and to Hooper and Whyld's *Oxford Companion*, for details of his relationship with the Soviet authorities. On Alekhine's behavior during the match with Euwe, the latter's biographer, Alexander Münninghoff, was most useful.

Nabokov's own introduction to his novel *The Luzhin Defense* is supplemented by the first volume of Brian Boyd's biography, *Vladimir Nabokov: The Russian Years* (London, 1990). Curt von Bardeleben is described by Edward Lasker in his *Chess Secrets* (London, 1952) and in *The Hastings Chess Tournament 1895*, edited by Horace F. Cheshire (New York, 1962). In the section on Luzhin's archetypes, I mention Nimzowitsch only briefly. He was not only a great practical player, but the most important chess theoretician of the early twentieth century. Raymond Keene's *Aron Nimzowitsch: A Reappraisal*, first published in 1974, includes a translation from the Russian of "How I Became a Grandmaster," a booklet he published in 1929. It includes the following revealing passage about the place of chess in his strictly orthodox Jewish family in Riga during the 1890s, while illustrating the magnetic attraction that the game exercised on the generation of Russian Jews who either, like Nimzowitsch himself, went into exile, or who (like Botvinnik) acted as chess missionaries of the revolution:

> My first acquaintance with chess took place under the sign of *solemnity*. In our family chess was regarded with great respect, for our father, himself an ardent devotee of the game, more than once held forth to us on its astonishing beauties. I would often ask him to show me what it was all about, but Father always refused, saying that "it's too soon for a lad like you to be thinking about chess." In the end he consented, however, and this hallowed occasion was arranged for my nameday when I was eight. Yet I remember being a little disappointed, since the moves of rook, bishop, knight etc. seemed to me devoid of all combinative interest. I ought to mention that even before becoming acquainted with chess I had a strong penchant for combination as such, since all the efforts of my teachers, and of my father first and foremost, had been specifically aimed at fostering in me a gift for association and a love for that world of scholastic argument and intricate sophistries which is so well known to anyone who has ever been concerned to study the Talmud. Nevertheless, my disappointment soon gave way to a feeling of keen curiosity. About three weeks after my first lesson, Father showed me some combinations, including a smothered mate . . . and three months later, as a reward for progress at school, he demonstrated to me Anderssen's Immortal Game; I not only understood it, but at once fell passionately in love with it.

Chapter 6 is dominated by the figure of Mikhail Moiseyevich Botvinnik. Despite the fact that he bestrides the whole history of Soviet chess, he too lacks a good biography. Besides Soltis's *Soviet Chess* and the three collections of his games and writings cited in the bibliography, I have gathered information from a wide range of sources. Botvinnik's essay on "The Russian and Soviet School of Chess," found in *One Hundred Selected Games* (New York, 1960), is the single most seminal work on the subject. On the question of whether Keres deliberately lost to Botvinnik at the 1948 match-tournament for the world championship, Soltis summarizes the evidence as well as being indispensable on the Soviet attitude to Reshevsky. On the role of Tchigorin as a precursor to the Soviet school, Kotov and Yudovich's tract *The Soviet School of Chess* (New York, 1961) is the main source; the comment by Gerald Abrahams comes from his *The Chess Mind* (London, 1960). The statistics on Soviet chess in the 1950s and 1960s are from *The Delights of Chess* (New York, 1974) by Assiac (Heinrich Fraenkel), who took them from official sources.

With regard to Chapter 7, the literature on Jews, Bolshevism, and anti-Semitism in Russia is, of course, vast. Leonard Schapiro's essay on "The Role of the Jews in the Russian Revolutionary Movement," in his *Russian Studies* (London, 1986), is a good starting point. On Stalin's anti-Semitism, Sebag Montefiore supersedes earlier historians. I am again indebted to Soltis on David Bronstein, not only for his own autobiographical works but also for the obituaries that appeared in the *Times* and *Daily Telegraph* at the time of his death in 2007.

For the trial and imprisonment of Natan Sharansky (or Anatoly Shcharansky, as he then was), he is himself the most important source. For my account of this period and his more recent career outside Russia, I have relied heavily on his memoirs, *Fear No Evil* (London, 1988), and on private conversations, together with Martin Gilbert's biography (London, 1986). Their accounts are supplemented by other sources, including the autobiographies of Richard Pipes and Markus Wolf. A translation of Stefan Zweig's novella,

The Royal Game (London, 1981), is collected and introduced by John Fowles. Finally, Charles Murray's writings on Jewish intellectual uniqueness and its relationship to chess are controversial but mandatory.

Turning in Chapter 8 to America, the story of Paul Morphy has been told many times, originally by his promoter, Frederick Edge, in *The Exploits and Triumphs in Europe of Paul Morphy the Chess Champion* (New York, 1859), but Hooper and Whyld offer a useful corrective, as does the Staunton biography by Keene and Coles. Quotes from his banquet with Oliver Wendell Holmes come from the well-researched historical novel, *The Chess Players* (London, 1961), by Frances Parkinson Keyes.

Harry Nelson Pillsbury and Frank Marshall are less well served than Morphy with biographers, but on Capablanca there is an abundance of material, notably in Edward Winter's *Capablanca* (Jefferson, NC, 1989). In his own book, Soltis documents his relations with the Soviets. Reuben Fine's *The Psychology of the Chess Player* (New York, 1956) has informed this account; his classic *Basic Chess Endings* (New York, 1941) is dedicated to Emanuel Lasker. For his career and Sammy Reshevsky's, I have relied heavily on Hooper and Whyld, on discussions with Raymond Keene, on Bronstein's book of the 1953 Zurich candidates' tournament and — for the abortive match with Botvinnik — on Soltis.

Bobby Fischer, to whose career Chapters 9–11 are largely devoted, presents particular problems. I am deeply indebted throughout to David Edmonds and John Eidinow, whose book *Bobby Fischer Goes to War* (London, 2004) threw new light on Fischer's family background, his mother's involvement in communist politics, which attracted FBI surveillance, the identity of his biological father, and much else. Dmitry Plisetsky and Sergey Voronkov's volume *Russians versus Fischer* (London, 2005) has added many insights from hitherto unknown Soviet sources. Frank Brady's biography, although last updated in the 1970s, is still essential for its firsthand account of Fischer's chess career — for example, the comical misunderstandings with Mikhail Tal. The 1962 Curaçao candidates' tournament is covered in depth by Jan Timman's study (Alkmaar, Netherlands, 2005), which I have supplemented from other sources. The section on Fischer in Havana is indebted mainly to Brady, but photographs of Fischer playing Castro on chess websites were helpful in working out how the Cubans exploited the propaganda opportunity this presented.

Fischer's checkered encounters with the Russians up to his comeback in 1970 are well documented by Plisetsky and Voronkov. Little was added by the massive coverage that accompanied his reappearances in 2001 and 2005, after the attacks on America on September 11 and later his arrest in Japan, the failed extradition to the United States, and the eventual granting of asylum in Iceland. Edmonds and Eidinow have done more to illuminate this dark corner of Fischer's psyche by their research into his origins than any of the essays in speculative psychology by the press.

Turning to Chapter 10—the run-up to the great match—Garry Kasparov's *My Great Predecessors, Part IV* (London, 2003–6), is invaluable on why Fischer achieved such astonishing ascendancy over the Soviet machine. The account of the 1970 Soviet Union versus Rest of the World match in Belgrade and its aftermath draws mainly on Plisetsky and Voronkov, Soltis, and Brady. The portrait of Boris Spassky relies on material from these authors as well as Edmonds and Eidinow, Cafferty, and other sources. Fischer's defeat of Taimanov and the latter's subsequent fate are described in painstaking and painful detail by both Kasparov and Plisetsky. The Solzhenitsyn quotes come from his volume of speeches and essays, *The Russian Question* (London, 1998), while the translation of Homer's *Iliad* used in this chapter and the next is by E. V. Rieu, revised by Peter Jones with D. C. H. Rieu.

There is a large literature on the Fischer–Spassky match itself, but all previous discussions of the games have been rendered obsolete by Kasparov's analysis. On the politics and psychology, Edmonds and Eidinow have again replaced earlier accounts, while Plisetsky and Voronkov are indispensable on what was happening inside the Soviet camp. Karpov's memoir *Karpov on Karpov* (New York, 1991) adds a (hostile) insight into Spassky's state of mind. Of the accounts by watching journalists gathered in Reykjavik, the best vignettes are Heinrich Fraenkel's piece in *The Delights of Chess* (New York, 1974), Harold C. Schonberg's account in *Grandmasters of Chess* (New York and London, 1974), and Arthur Koestler's *Sunday Times* article, "The Glorious and Bloody Game," while George Steiner's *The Sporting Scene* (London, 1973) is a rich but discursive essay by *The New Yorker*'s correspondent. Edmonds and Eidinow are most reliable on the claims and the reality of dirty tricks by both sides; the memoirs of former KGB colonel Georgy Sannikov are emphatically not to be trusted. On the suppression of dissidents during the match, I relied on Sharansky's *Fear No Evil* and Richard Lourie's biography, *Sakharov* (Hanover, NH, and London, 2002). Spassky's postmatch interrogation is documented by Plisetsky and Voronkov, while his own recollections and the story of Nixon's abortive invitation to Fischer come from Kasparov.

As an authoritative history of chess and the computer has yet to be written, Chapter 12 draws on an eclectic range of printed and electronic sources, the most important being Monty Newborn's *Kasparov versus Deep Blue: Computer Chess Comes of Age* (New York, 1997). The early chess automatons are chronicled in general chess works such as Hooper and Whyld, but on the Turk I also made use of the German novelist Robert Löhr's learned historical novel, *Der Schachautomat* (Munich, 2005). On Leibniz and Euler, I have used scientific reference works, such as *The Fontana History of the Mathematical Sciences*, but for such modern figures as Leonardo Torres y Quevedo, Alan Turing, Claude Shannon, John von Neumann, and Arthur C. Clarke, I have also used web sources as well as their own writings. For example, Turing's biographer, Alan Hodges, maintains an excellent website that includes many of Turing's key works and the first chess game with a computer. On Botvinnik's role in Soviet computer chess, Newborn is again essential. I have also used Karpov's memoirs, Soltis's *Soviet Chess*,

Ronald Reagan's collected talks and articles (edited by Kiron K. Skinner *et al.*), and Raymond Keene's oral testimony on the backwardness of 1980s Soviet technology.

Korchnoi's one-man war against the Soviet system, which forms the core of Chapters 13 and 14, is chiefly indebted to Part V of Kasparov's *My Great Predecessors* for its account of what happened on the chessboard. To the memoirs of Korchnoi and Karpov, I have added my own impressions of Hastings 1972 as a fourteen-year-old observer of their earliest clash outside Russia. On the 1978 match at Baguio, Korchnoi's polemic *Anti-Chess*, later revised as *Persona non Grata* (Davenport, Iowa, 1981), provides useful if not always reliable material to add to Keene's insider commentary. The comments by Russian grandmasters after the match about what would have happened to Korchnoi—and to Soviet chess—if he had won come from Kasparov.

The rivalry of Karpov and Kasparov is recounted in Chapter 15. My narrative owes much to Keene and his various collaborators for the five matches. The autobiographical writings of both players and the interviews in Fred Waitzkin's *Mortal Games* (New York, 1993) help to explain the political background. The quote from Reagan's speechwriter was from the website Power Line.

For Chapter 16, covering the post-Soviet era, Kirsan Ilyumzhinov's takeover of FIDE and Kasparov's role in the opposition to Putin, I have relied largely on news reports by the BBC, the *Times*, *Daily Telegraph*, and other papers, together with Internet chess websites. Kasparov's own articles appear regularly in the *Wall Street Journal* and he gives frequent interviews. On the match between Kasparov and the IBM computer Deep Blue, I have consulted Newborn, books by Keene, print and web sources, plus the film *Game Over*.

More than any other chapter, the epilogue is based on firsthand observation of, and conversations with, Kasparov. The alarming facts and figures about Putin's Russia come from Mark Steyn's *America Alone* (Washington, DC, 2006).

BIBLIOGRAPHY

Abrahams, Gerald. *The Chess Mind*. London: Penguin, 1960.

Albats, Yevgenia. *KGB: State Within a State*. London: I. B. Tauris, 1995.

Alekhine, Alexander. *Alekhine's Greatest Games of Chess*. London: Batsford, 1989.

Alexander, C. H. O'D. *Alekhine's Best Games of Chess, 1938–1945*. London: Bell, 1966.

Altmann, Alexander. *Moses Mendelssohn: A Biographical Study*. London: Routledge, 1973.

Applebaum, Anne. *Gulag: A History of the Soviet Camp*. New York and London: Penguin, 2003.

Assiac [Heinrich Fraenkel]. *The Delights of Chess*. New York: Dover, 1974.

Botvinnik, Mikhail. "The Russian and Soviet School of Chess," in Botvinnik, *One Hundred Selected Games*. New York: Dover, 1960.

Botvinnik, Mikhail. *Mikhail Botvinnik: Master of Strategy*. London: Batsford, 1972.

Botvinnik, Mikhail, translated by E. Strauss, *Half a Century of Chess*. London: Cadogan, 1996.

Boyd, Brian. *Vladimir Nabokov*, vol. I: *The Russian Years*. London: Chatto, 1990.

Brady, Frank. *Bobby Fischer*. London: Batsford, 1974.

British Chess Magazine. *The Grand International Masters' Chess Tournament at St. Petersburg, 1914*. St. Leonards-on-Sea, UK: BCM, 1914.

Bronstein, David. *Zurich International Chess Tournament, 1953.* New York: Dover, 1979.

Bronstein, David. *David against Goliath,* vol. 2: *Secret Notes.* London: Trafalgar Square, 2004 and 2007.

Bronstein, David, and Furstenberg, Tom. *The Sorcerer's Apprentice.* London and New York: Cadogan, 1995.

Bulgakov, Mikhail, translated by Richard Pevear and Larissa Volokhonsky. *The Master and Margarita.* New York and London: Penguin, 1997.

Burleigh, Michael. *Sacred Causes: Religion and Politics from the European Dictators to Al Qaeda.* New York and London: HarperCollins, 2006.

Cafferty, Bernard. *Boris Spassky: Master of Tactics.* London: Batsford, 1972.

Capek, Karel, translated by Paul Selver and Nigel Playfair. *R. U. R. Rossum's Universal Robots: A Fantastic Melodrama in Three Acts.* London and New York: Samuel French, 1923.

Chamberlain, Lesley. *Motherland: A Philosophical History of Russia.* London: Atlantic, 2004.

Chamberlain, Lesley. *The Philosophy Steamer: Lenin and the Exile of the Intelligentsia.* London: Atlantic, 2007.

Chernyshevsky, Nikolai, translated and edited by Michael R. Katz. *What Is to Be Done?* Ithaca and London: Cornell University Press, 1989.

Clarke, P. H. *Mikhail Tal: Master of Sacrifice.* London: Batsford, 1991.

Clarke, P. H. *Tigran Petrosian: Master of Defence.* London: Batsford, 1992.

Conquest, Robert. *The Great Terror: Stalin's Purge of the Thirties,* revised edition. New York and Oxford: Oxford University Press, 1990.

Courtois, Stéphane, Werth, Nicolas, *et al. The Black Book of Communism: Crimes, Terror, Repression.* Cambridge, Mass., and London: Harvard University Press, 1999.

Damsky, Yakov. *The Batsford Book of Chess Records.* London: Batsford, 2005.

Eales, Richard. *Chess: The History of a Game.* London: Batsford, 1985.

Edge, Frederick. *The Exploits and Triumphs in Europe of Paul Morphy the Chess Champion.* New York: D. Appleton, 1859; Dover reprint, 1973.

Edmonds, David, and Eidinow, John. *Bobby Fischer Goes to War: The True Story of How the Soviets Lost the Most Extraordinary Chess Match of All Time.* London: Faber, 2004.

Ferguson, Niall. *The War of the World: Twentieth-Century Conflict and the Descent of the West.* New York and London: Penguin, 2007.

Figes, Orlando. *A People's Tragedy: The Russian Revolution, 1891–1924.* London: Jonathan Cape, 1996.

Figes, Orlando. *Natasha's Dance: A Cultural History of Russia.* New York and London: Penguin, 2002.

Fine, Reuben. *Basic Chess Endings*. New York: David McKay, 1941.

Fine, Reuben. *The Psychology of the Chess Player*. New York: Dover, 1956.

Fischer, Bobby. *My 60 Memorable Games*. London: Faber, 1972.

Fox, Mike, and James, Richard. *The Complete Chess Addict*. London: Faber, 1987.

Fox, Mike, and James, Richard. *The Even More Complete Chess Addict*. London: Faber, 1993.

Gaddis, John Lewis. *The Cold War*. New York and London: Penguin, 2006.

Garton Ash, Timothy. *History of the Present*. New York and London: Penguin, 1999.

Gatrell, Peter. *Russia's First World War: A Social and Economic History*. Harlow, UK: Pearson Longman, 2005.

Gerrard, Jasper. "Arrogant? No, I'm just the best." Interview of Garry Kasparov, *Sunday Times*, March 20, 2005.

Gilbert, Martin. *Shcharansky: Hero of Our Time*. London: Macmillan, 1986.

Golombek, Harry, with J. du Mont. *Capablanca's Hundred Best Games of Chess*. London: Bell, 1959.

Gorbachev, Mikhail. *Memoirs*. New York and London: Doubleday, 1996.

Hannak, J., foreword by Albert Einstein, translated by Heinrich Fraenkel. *Emanuel Lasker: The Life of a Chess Master*. London: André Deutsch, 1959.

Hartston, William. *The Guinness Book of Chess Grandmasters*. London: Guinness, 1996.

Herrnstein, Richard J., and Murray, Charles. *The Bell Curve: Intelligence and Class Structure in American Life*. New York and London: Free Press, 1994.

Hess, Jonathan M. *Germans, Jews and the Claims of Modernity*. New Haven and London: Yale University Press, 2002.

Hingley, Ronald. *The Russian Mind*. London: Bodley Head, 1977.

Hodges, Alan. *Alan Turing: The Enigma*. New York: Simon & Schuster, 1983.

Hooper, David, and Whyld, Kenneth. *The Oxford Companion to Chess*, new edition. Oxford: Oxford University Press, 1992.

Hosking, Geoffrey. *The Awakening of the Soviet Union*. London: William Heinemann, 1990.

Jones, Peter (editor), and E. V. Rieu (translator). *Homer: The Iliad*. Craster and London: Achilles Press, 2003.

Karpov, Anatoly, translated by Todd Bludeau. *Karpov on Karpov: Memoirs of a Chess World Champion*. New York: Macmillan, 1991.

Karpov, Anatoly, and Roshal, Aleksandr, translated by Kenneth P. Neat. *Chess Is My Life*. Oxford: Pergamon, 1980.

Kasparov, Garry. *The Test of Time*. London: Pergamon, 1986.

Kasparov, Garry. *How Life Imitates Chess*. London: William Heinemann, 2007.

Kasparov, Garry, with Donald Trelford. *Unlimited Challenge: An Autobiography*. New York and London: Grove Weidenfeld, 1990.

Kasparov, Garry, with Dmitri Plisetsky. *My Great Predecessors, Parts I–V*. London: Everyman Chess, 2003–6.

Keene, Raymond. *Karpov–Korchnoi, 1978: The Inside Story of the Match*. London: Batsford, 1978.

Keene, Raymond. *Battle of the Titans: Kasparov–Karpov New York–Lyons*. London: Batsford, 1991.

Keene, Raymond. *Fischer–Spassky II: The Return of a Legend*. London: Batsford, 1992.

Keene, Raymond. *Aron Nimzowitsch: A Reappraisal*. London: Batsford, 1999.

Keene, Raymond. *Chess Terminators: The Rise of the Machines from Deep Blue to Hydra*. London: Hardinge Simpole, 2005.

Keene, Raymond, and Coles, R. N. *Howard Staunton: The English World Chess Champion*. St. Leonards-on-Sea, UK: British Chess Magazine, 1975.

Keene, Raymond, with David Goodman and John Groser. *Docklands Encounter: USSR v. The World*. London: Batsford, 1984.

Keene, Raymond, and Jacobs, Byron. *The Moscow Challenge: Karpov–Kasparov, the 1984 World Championship*. London: Batsford, 1985.

Keene, Raymond, and Goodman, David. *Manoeuvres in Moscow: Karpov–Kasparov II*. London: Batsford, 1985.

Keene, Raymond, and Goodman, David. *The Centenary Match: Kasparov–Karpov III*. London: Batsford, 1986.

Keene, Raymond, and Goodman, David. *Showdown in Seville: Kasparov–Karpov IV*. London: Batsford, 1987.

Keene, Raymond, and Divinsky, Nathan. *Warriors of the Mind: A Quest for the Supreme Genius of the Chess Board*. London: Hardinge Simpole, 1989.

Keyes, Frances Parkinson. *The Chess Players*. London: The Book Club, 1961.

Klima, Ivan, introduction to Capek, Karel. *War with the Newts*. London: Penguin, 1998.

Koestler, Arthur. "The Glorious and Bloody Game," first published in the *Sunday Times*, 1972. Collected in *Kaleidoscope: Essays*. London: Hutchinson, 1981.

Korchnoi, Viktor. *Chess Is My Life*. New York: Arco, 1978.

Korchnoi, Viktor, with Lenny Cavallaro. *Persona non Grata* (formerly *Anti-Chess*). Davenport, Iowa: Thinker's Press, 1981.

Kotov, Alexander, and Yudovich, Mikhail. *The Soviet School of Chess.* New York: Dover, 1961.

Krauthammer, Charles. "Just How Dangerous Is Chess?," *Time,* April 26, 2005.

Krogius, Nikolai. *Psychologie im Schach.* East Berlin: Sportverlag, 1983.

Lasker, Edward. *Chess Secrets I Learned from the Masters.* London: Hollis and Carter, 1952.

Lasker, Emanuel. *Lasker's Manual of Chess.* New York: Dover, 1960.

Lasker, Emanuel (ed.). *The International Chess Congress, St. Petersburg, 1909.* New York: Dover, 1971.

Lawson, Dominic. *The Inner Game.* London: Macmillan, 1992.

Löhr, Robert. *Der Schachautomat.* Munich: Piper, 2005.

Lourie, Richard. *Sakharov: A Biography.* Hanover, NH, and London: Brandeis University Press, 2002.

Marozzi, Justin. *Tamerlane: Sword of Islam, Conqueror of the World.* London: HarperCollins, 2005.

Marshall, Frank. *Frank J. Marshall's Best Games of Chess.* New York: Dover, 1960.

Matanovic, Aleksandar (ed.). *Encyclopedia of Chess Openings* (includes Korchnoi's analysis of the Open Defense to the Ruy Lopez). London: Batsford, 1974.

Morán, Pablo, edited and translated by Frank X. Mur. *A. Alekhine: Agony of a Chess Genius.* Jefferson, NC: McFarland, 1989.

Murray, Charles. *Human Accomplishment: The Pursuit of Excellence in the Arts and Sciences, 800 BC to 1950.* New York and London: HarperCollins, 2003.

Murray, Charles. "Jewish Genius," in *Commentary,* April 2007.

Murray, H. J. R. *A History of Chess.* Oxford: Oxford University Press, 1913.

Nabokov, Vladimir, translated by Michael Scammell with the author. *The Luzhin Defense.* New York and London: Penguin, 1994.

Neumann, John von, and Morgenstern, Oskar. *Theory of Games and Economic Behavior.* Princeton: Princeton University Press, 1944.

Newborn, Monty. *Kasparov versus Deep Blue: Computer Chess Comes of Age.* New York: Springer, 1997.

Orwell, George, introduction by Ben Pimlott. *Nineteen Eighty-Four.* New York and London: Penguin, 2000.

Overy, Richard. *Russia's War.* London: Penguin, 1998.

Pasternak, Boris. *An Essay in Autobiography.* London: Collins Harvill, 1959.

Pipes, Richard. *The Russian Revolution, 1899–1919.* London: Collins Harvill, 1990.

Pipes, Richard. *Vixi: Memoirs of a Non-Belonger.* New Haven and London: Yale University Press, 2003.

Plisetsky, Dmitry, and Voronkov, Sergey. *Russians versus Fischer*. London: Everyman Chess, 2005.

Poipe, Jacques. *Harry Nelson Pillsbury: American Chess Champion*. Ann Arbor: Pawn Island Press, 1996.

Radzinsky, Edvard. *Stalin*. New York and London: Doubleday, 1996.

Reinfeld, Fred, and Fine, Reuben. *Lasker's Greatest Chess Games: 1889–1914*. New York: Dover, 1965.

Richards, D. J. *Soviet Chess*. Oxford: Clarendon Press, 1965.

Schapiro, Leonard. "The Role of the Jews in the Russian Revolutionary Movement" and "Lenin's Intellectual Formation," in Schapiro, *Russian Studies*. London: Collins Harvill, 1986.

Schonberg, Harold C. *Grandmasters of Chess*. New York and London: Davis-Poynter, 1974.

Sebag Montefiore, Simon. *Stalin: The Court of the Red Tsar*. London: Weidenfeld & Nicolson, 2003.

Sergeant, P. W., and Watts, W. H. *Pillsbury's Chess Career*. New York: Dover, 1966.

Service, Robert. *Lenin: A Biography*. London: Macmillan, 2000.

Sharansky, Natan, translated by Stefani Hoffman. *Fear No Evil*. London: Weidenfeld & Nicolson, 1988.

Sharansky, Natan, with Ron Dermer. *The Case for Democracy: The Power of Freedom to Overcome Tyranny and Terror*. New York: Public Affairs, 2004.

Shlaes, Amity. *The Forgotten Man: A New History of the Great Depression*. London: Cape, 2007.

Skinner, Kiron K., Anderson, Annelise, and Anderson, Martin. *Reagan in His Own Hand: The Writings of Ronald Reagan That Reveal His Revolutionary Vision for America*. New York: Simon & Schuster, 2002.

Soltis, Andrew. *Soviet Chess, 1917–1991*. Jefferson, NC, and London: McFarland, 2000.

Soltis, Andrew. *Why Lasker Matters*. London: Batsford, 2006.

Solzhenitsyn, Aleksandr I. *The Gulag Archipelago: An Experiment in Literary Investigation*. New York: Harper & Row, 1973.

Solzhenitsyn, Aleksandr. *The Russian Question at the End of the Twentieth Century*. London: Harvill, 1995.

Steiner, George. *The Sporting Scene: White Knights of Reykjavik*. London: Faber, 1972.

Steyn, Mark. *America Alone: The End of the World as We Know It*. Washington, DC: Regnery, 2006.

Tarrasch, Siegbert. *St. Petersburg 1914 International Chess Tournament*. Yorklyn, DE: Caissa Editions, 1993.

Tarrasch, Siegbert. *Die Moderne Schachpartie*. Leipzig: Hans Hedewig's Nachfolger, Curt Ronneger, 1921.

Timman, Jan. *Curaçao 1962: The Battle of Minds That Shook the Chess World*. Alkmaar, Netherlands: New in Chess, 2005.

Wade, Robert G., and O'Connell, Kevin J. (eds). *The Games of Robert J. Fischer*, new edition. London: Batsford, 1972.

Waitzkin, Fred. *Mortal Games: The Turbulent Genius of Garry Kasparov*. New York: Putnam's, 1993.

Winter, Edward. *Capablanca: A Compendium of Games, Notes, Articles, Correspondence, Illustrations, and Other Rare Archival Materials on the Cuban Chess Genius José Raúl Capablanca, 1888–1942*. Jefferson, NC: McFarland, 1989.

Wolf, Markus, with Anne McElvoy. *Man Without a Face: The Memoirs of a Spymaster*. London: Jonathan Cape, 1997.

Zweig, Stefan. *The Royal Game and Other Stories*. London: Jonathan Cape, 1981.

INDEX